Communications
in Computer and Information Science 2091

Rationale

The CCIS series is devoted to the publication of proceedings of computer science conferences. Its aim is to efficiently disseminate original research results in informatics in printed and electronic form. While the focus is on publication of peer-reviewed full papers presenting mature work, inclusion of reviewed short papers reporting on work in progress is welcome, too. Besides globally relevant meetings with internationally representative program committees guaranteeing a strict peer-reviewing and paper selection process, conferences run by societies or of high regional or national relevance are also considered for publication.

Topics

The topical scope of CCIS spans the entire spectrum of informatics ranging from foundational topics in the theory of computing to information and communications science and technology and a broad variety of interdisciplinary application fields.

Information for Volume Editors and Authors

Publication in CCIS is free of charge. No royalties are paid, however, we offer registered conference participants temporary free access to the online version of the conference proceedings on SpringerLink (http://link.springer.com) by means of an http referrer from the conference website and/or a number of complimentary printed copies, as specified in the official acceptance email of the event.

CCIS proceedings can be published in time for distribution at conferences or as post-proceedings, and delivered in the form of printed books and/or electronically as USBs and/or e-content licenses for accessing proceedings at SpringerLink. Furthermore, CCIS proceedings are included in the CCIS electronic book series hosted in the SpringerLink digital library at http://link.springer.com/bookseries/7899. Conferences publishing in CCIS are allowed to use Online Conference Service (OCS) for managing the whole proceedings lifecycle (from submission and reviewing to preparing for publication) free of charge.

Publication process

The language of publication is exclusively English. Authors publishing in CCIS have to sign the Springer CCIS copyright transfer form, however, they are free to use their material published in CCIS for substantially changed, more elaborate subsequent publications elsewhere. For the preparation of the camera-ready papers/files, authors have to strictly adhere to the Springer CCIS Authors' Instructions and are strongly encouraged to use the CCIS LaTeX style files or templates.

Abstracting/Indexing

CCIS is abstracted/indexed in DBLP, Google Scholar, EI-Compendex, Mathematical Reviews, SCImago, Scopus. CCIS volumes are also submitted for the inclusion in ISI Proceedings.

How to start

To start the evaluation of your proposal for inclusion in the CCIS series, please send an e-mail to ccis@springer.com.

Anshul Verma · Pradeepika Verma ·
Kiran Kumar Pattanaik ·
Sanjay Kumar Dhurandher · Isaac Woungang
Editors

Advanced Network Technologies and Intelligent Computing

Third International Conference, ANTIC 2023
Varanasi, India, December 20–22, 2023
Proceedings, Part II

 Springer

Editors
Anshul Verma
Banaras Hindu University
Varanasi, Uttar Pradesh, India

Kiran Kumar Pattanaik
ABV-Indian Institute of Information
Technology and Management
Gwalior, Madhya Pradesh, India

Isaac Woungang
Ryerson University
Toronto, Canada

Pradeepika Verma
Indian Institute of Technology Patna
Patna, India

Sanjay Kumar Dhurandher
Netaji Subhas University of Technology
New Delhi, India

ISSN 1865-0929   ISSN 1865-0937 (electronic)
Communications in Computer and Information Science
ISBN 978-3-031-64063-6   ISBN 978-3-031-64064-3 (eBook)
https://doi.org/10.1007/978-3-031-64064-3

This Springer imprint is published by the registered company Springer Nature Switzerland AG
The registered company address is: Gewerbestrasse 11, 6330 Cham, Switzerland

If disposing of this product, please recycle the paper.

Preface

The 3rd International Conference on Advanced Network Technologies and Intelligent Computing (ANTIC 2023) was organized by the Department of Computer Science, Institute of Science, Banaras Hindu University, Varanasi, India in hybrid mode from 20th to 22nd December 2023. ANTIC 2023 aimed to bring together leading academicians, scientists, research scholars, and UG/PG graduates across the globe to exchange and share their research outcomes. It aimed to provide a state-of-the-art platform to discuss all aspects (current and future) of Advanced Network Technologies and Intelligent Computing. This enabled the participating researchers to exchange their ideas about applying existing methods in these areas to solve real-world problems.

ANTIC 2023 solicited two types of submissions: full research papers (equal to or more than 12 pages) and short research papers (between 8 and 11 pages). These papers identify and justify a principled advance to the theoretical and practical foundations for the construction and analysis of systems, where applicable supported by experimental validation. A total of 487 research papers were received through the EquinOCS portal of Springer and 100 papers (20.53%) were accepted after the rigorous review process (Double Blind). Each paper was reviewed by at least three reviewers. Out of 100 accepted papers, 89 papers (89%) are full papers and 11 papers (11%) are short papers. All 100 accepted papers have been selected for publication in the Communications in Computer and Information Science (CCIS) series of Springer and are grouped into two thematic categories: Advanced Network Technologies and Intelligent Computing.

We would like to thank everyone who helped to make ANTIC 2023 successful. In particular, we would like to thank the authors for submitting their papers to ANTIC 2023. We are thankful to our excellent team of reviewers from all over the globe who deserve full credit for the hard work put in to review the high-quality submissions with rich technical content. We would also like to thank the members of the Advisory Committee and Program Committee for their guidance and suggestions in making ANTIC 2023 a success. We would also like to thank all the Track Chairs, and Organizing Committee and Technical Program Committee members for their support and co-operation.

December 2023

Anshul Verma
Pradeepika Verma
Kiran Kumar Pattanaik
Sanjay Kumar Dhurandher
Isaac Woungang

Organization

Chief Patron

Sudhir K. Jain (Vice-chancellor)   Banaras Hindu University, India

Patron

V. K. Shukla (Rector)   Banaras Hindu University, India

Co-patrons

Anil Kumar Tripathi (Director)   Institute of Science, Banaras Hindu University, India

Sukh Mahendra Singh (Dean)   Faculty of Science, Banaras Hindu University, India

Advisory Board

Anil Kumar Tripathi   Indian Institute of Technology (BHU), Varanasi, India

Anupam Shukla   Sardar Vallabhbhai National Institute of Technology, India

Jagannathan Sarangpani   Missouri University of Science and Technology, USA

M. M. Gore   Motilal Nehru National Institute of Technology, India

Manish Gaur   Institute of Engineering & Technology, Lucknow, India

Rajeev Srivastava   Indian Institute of Technology (BHU), Varanasi, India

Rajkumar Buyya   University of Melbourne, Australia

Sanjay Kumar Madria   Missouri University of Science & Technology, USA

Sanjay Kumar Singh   Indian Institute of Technology (BHU), Varanasi, India

Sundaraja Sitharama Iyengar   Florida International University, USA

Bhartendu K. Singh   Indian Institute of Information Technology,
                                        Design & Manufacturing, Jabalpur, India
G. C. Nandi   Indian Institute of Information Technology,
                                        Allahabad, India
Ashutosh Kumar Singh   Indian Institute of Information Technology,
                                        Bhopal, India
Deepankar Dasgupta   University of Memphis, USA

General Chairs

Isaac Woungang   Ryerson University, Canada
Sanjay Kumar Dhurandher   Netaji Subhas University of Technology, India
K. K. Pattanaik   ABV-Indian Institute of Information Technology
                                        and Management, Gwalior, India

Conference Chair

S. Karthikeyan   Banaras Hindu University, India

Program Chairs

Pramod Kumar Mishra   Banaras Hindu University, India
Vivek Kumar Singh   Banaras Hindu University, India
Anshul Verma   Banaras Hindu University, India

Convener

Anshul Verma   Banaras Hindu University, India

Organizing Secretaries

Gaurav Baranwal   Banaras Hindu University, India
Ankita Vaish   Banaras Hindu University, India
Sachchida Nand Chaurasia   Banaras Hindu University, India
Pradeepika Verma   TIH, Indian Institute of Technology, Patna, India

Track Chairs

Udai Shanker	Madan Mohan Malaviya University of Technology, India
Rama Abirami Karuppaia	Curtin University, Malaysia
Ucuk Darusalam	Universitas Nasional, Indonesia
Ashutosh Singh	United College of Engineering and Research, Allahabad, India
Pramod Kumar Singh	ABV-Indian Institute of Information Technology and Management, Gwalior, India
Michael Baron	Charles Sturt University, Australia
Puneet Misra	University of Lucknow, India
Vijay Bhaskar Semwal	Maulana Azad National Institute of Technology, India
Joseph G. Vella	University of Malta, Msida, Malta
Pravir Singh Gupta	Perceive Inc, USA
Prashant Singh Rana	Thapar Institute of Engg. and Tech., India
Sanjeev Sharma	Indian Institute of Information Technology, Pune, India
Rajiv Ranjan Tewari	University of Allahabad, India
Antriksh Goswami	National Institute of Technology, Patna, India
Pawan Kumar Chaurasia	Babasaheb Bhimrao Ambedkar University, India
Nanhay Singh	Netaji Subhas University of Technology, India
Dharmendra Prasad Mahato	National Institute of Technology, Hamirpur, India
Vaibhav Soni	Maulana Azad National Institute of Technology, India
Fatima Zahra Fagroud	Hassan II University of Casablanca, Morocco
Oluwatobi Noah Akande	Baze University, Nigeria
Jyoti Singh Kirar	Jawaharlal Nehru University, India
Koushlendra Kumar Singh	National Institute of Technology, Jamshedpur, India
Salem Sati	Misurata University, Libya
Rahul Kumar Verma	Indian Institute of Information Technology, Lucknow, India
Mohamed Fazil Mohamed Firdhous	University of Moratuwa, Sri Lanka
Dinesh Kumar	National Institute of Technology, Jamshedpur, India
Shubhra Jain	Indian Institute of Information Technology, Lucknow, India
Shantanu Agnihotri	Bennett University, India
Shivani Sharma	Thapar Institute of Engineering & Technology, India

Vandna Rani Verma	Galgotia College of Engineering and Technology, India
Huy-Trung Nguyen	People's Security Academy, Vietnam Ministry of Public Security, Vietnam
Aymen Salman	Al-Nahrain University, Iraq
Vibhav Prakash Singh	Motilal Nehru National Institute of Technology, India
Prasanalakshmi Balaji	King Khalid University, Saudi Arabia
Gyanendra K. Verma	National Institute of Technology, Raipur, India
Sachi Nandan Mohanty	COEP Technological University, India
Chandrashekhar Azad	National Institute of Technology, Jamshedpur, India
Pragya Dwivedi	Motilal Nehru National Institute of Technology, India
Om Jee Pandey	Indian Institute of Technology (BHU), Varanasi, India
Pradeepika Verma	TIH, Indian Institute of Technology, Patna, India
Naveen Kumar	Chitkara University, India

Organizing Committee

Achintya Singhal	Banaras Hindu University, India
Manoj Kumar Singh	Banaras Hindu University, India
Rakhi Garg	Banaras Hindu University, India
Manjari Gupta	Banaras Hindu University, India
Vandana Kushwaha	Banaras Hindu University, India
Awadhesh Kumar	Banaras Hindu University, India
Manoj Mishra	Banaras Hindu University, India
S. Suresh	Banaras Hindu University, India
Sarvesh Pandey	Banaras Hindu University, India
Vibhor Kant	Banaras Hindu University, India

Technical Program Committee

A. Senthil Thilak	National Institute of Technology, Surathkal, India
Abdus Samad	Aligarh Muslim University, India
Abhay Kumar Rai	Banasthali Vidyapith, India
Abhilasha Sharma	Delhi Technological University, India
Ade Romadhony	Telkom University, Indonesia
Afifa Ghenai	Constantine 2 University, Algeria

Ajay	JECRC University, India
Ajay Kumar	Chandigarh University, India
Ajay Kumar	Central University of Himachal Pradesh, India
Ajay Kumar Gupta	Madan Mohan Malaviya University of Technology, India
Ajay Kumar Yadav	Banasthali Vidyapith, India
Ajay Pratap	Indian Institute of Technology (BHU), Varanasi, India
Akande Noah Oluwatobi	Landmark University, Nigeria
Akash Kumar Bhoi	KIET Group of Institutions & Sikkim Manipal University, India
Alberto Rossi	University of Florence, Italy
Aleena Swetapadma	Kalinga Institute of Industrial Technology, India
Ali El Alami	Moulay Ismail University, Morocco
Amit Kumar	BMS Institute of Technology and Management, India
Amit Kumar	Jaypee University of Engineering and Technology, India
Amit Rathee	Government College Barota, India
Angel D.	Sathyabama Institute of Science and Technology, India
Anil Kumar	London Metropolitan University, UK
Anirban Sengupta	Jadavpur University, India
Anita Chaware	SNDT Women's University, India
Anjali Shrikant Yeole	VES Institute of Technology, India
Anjula Mehto	Thapar Institute of Engineering and Technology, India
Ankur Jain	IGDTUW, India
Ansuman Mahapatra	National Institute of Technology, Puducherry, India
Antriksh Goswami	Indian Institute of Information Technology, Vadodara, India
Anupam Biswas	National Institute of Technology, Silchar, India
Anuradha Yarlagadda	Gayatri Vidhya Parishad College of Engineering, India
Anurag Sewak	Rajkiya Engineering College, Sonbhadra, India
Arun Kumar	ABV-Indian Institute of Information Technology and Management, India
Arun Pandian J.	Vel Tech Rangarajan Dr. Sagunthala R&D Institute of Science and Technology, India
Ashish Kumar Mishra	Rajkiya Engineering College, Ambedkar Nagar, India

Ashutosh Kumar Singh	United College of Engineering and Research, India
Aymen Jaber Salman	Al-Nahrain University, Iraq
B. Surendiran	National Institute of Technology, Puducherry, India
B. Arthi	SRM Institute of Science and Technology, India
B. S. Charulatha	Rajalakshmi Engineering College, India
Balbir Singh Awana	Vanderbilt University, USA
Baranidharan B.	SRM Institute of Science and Technology, India
Benyamin Ahmadnia	Harvard University, USA
Bharat Garg	Thapar Institute of Engineering & Technology, India
Bharti	University of Delhi, India
Bhaskar Mondal	National Institute of Technology, Patna, India
Binod Prasad	ABV-Indian Institute of Information Technology and Management, India
Boddepalli Santhi Bhushan	Indian Institute of Information Technology, Allahabad, India
Brijendra Singh	VIT, India
Chanda Thapliyal Nautiyal	DU Govt. Degree College, Narendranagar, India
Chandrashekhar Azad	National Institute of Technology, Jamshedpur, India
Chetan Vyas	United University, Prayagraj, India
Chittaranjan Pradhan	Kalinga Institute of Industrial Technology, India
D. Senthilkumar	Anna University, India
Dahmouni Abdellatif	Chouaib Doukkali University, Morocco
Darpan Anand	Chandigarh University, India
Deepak Kumar	Banasthali Vidyapith, India
Dharmveer Kumar Yadav	Katihar Engineering College, India
Dhirendra Kumar	Delhi Technological University, India
Dinesh Kumar	Motilal Nehru National Institute of Technology, India
Divya Saxena	Hong Kong Polytechnic University, China
Ezil Sam Leni A.	KCG College of Technology, India
Gargi Srivastava	Rajiv Gandhi Institute of Petroleum Technology, India
Gaurav Gupta	Shoolini University, India
Gyanendra K. Verma	National Institute of Technology, Kurukshetra, India
Hardeo Kumar Thakur	Manav Rachna University, India
Hasmat Malik	Netaji Subhas University of Technology, India
Inder Chaudhary	Delhi Technological University, India
Itu Snigdh	Birla Institute of Technology, India

J. K. Rai	Defence Research and Development Organisation, India
J. Jerald Inico	Loyola College, India
Jagadeeswara Rao Annam	Gudlavalleru Engineering College, India
Jagannath Singh	Kalinga Institute of Industrial Technology, India
Jagdeep Singh	Sant Longowal Institute of Engineering and Technology, India
Jainath Yadav	Central University of South Bihar, India
Jay Prakash	National Institute of Technology, Calicut, India
Jaya Gera	Shyama Prasad Mukherji College for Women, India
Jeevaraj S.	ABV-Indian Institute of Information Technology & Management, India
Jolly Parikh	Bharati Vidyapeeth's College of Engineering, India
Jyoti Singh	Jawaharlal Nehru University, India
K. T. V. Reddy	Pravara Rural Education Society, India
Kanu Goel	Amity University, India
Koushlendra Kumar Singh	National Institute of Technology, Jamshedpur, India
Kunwar Pal	National Institute of Technology, Jalandhar, India
Lakshmi Priya G.	VIT University, India
Lalatendu Behera	National Institute of Technology, Jalandhar, India
Lokesh Chauhan	National Forensic Science University, Goa Campus, India
M. Joseph	Michael Research Foundation, India
M. Nazma B. J. Naskar	Kalinga Institute of Industrial Technology, India
M. Deva Priya	Sri Krishna College of Technology, India
Mahendra Shukla	LNM Institute of Information Technology, India
Mainejar Yadav	Rajkiya Engineering College, Sonbhadra, India
Manish Gupta	Amity University, India
Manish K. Pandey	Birla Institute of Technology, India
Manish Kumar	M S Ramaiah Institute of Technology, India
Manpreet Kaur	Manav Rachna University, India
Mariya Ouaissa	Cadi Ayyad University, Morocco
Mariyam Ouaissa	Moulay Ismail University, Morocco
Meriem Houmer	Ibn Zohr University, Morocco
Minakhi Rout	Kalinga Institute of Industrial Technology, India
Mohd Yaseen Mir	National Central University, Taiwan
Mohit Kumar	National Institute of Technology, Jalandhar, India
Monica Chauhan Bhadoriya	Madhav Institute of Technology & Science, India
Muhammad Abulaish	South Asian University, India

Mukesh Mishra	Indian Institute of Information Technology, Dharwad, India
Mukesh Rawat	Meerut Institute of Engineering and Technology, India
Mukta Sharma	Michigan State University, USA
Nagarajan G.	Sathyabama Institute of Science and Technology, India
Nagendra Pratap Singh	National Institute of Technology, Hamirpur, India
Nandakishor Yadav	Fraunhofer Institute for Photonic Microsystems, Germany
Narendran Rajagopalan	National Institute of Technology, Puducherry, India
Neetesh Kumar	IIT Roorkee, India
Nisha Chaurasia	National Institute of Technology, Jalandhar, India
Nisheeth Joshi	Banasthali Vidyapith, India
Nitesh K. Bharadwaj	O P Jindal University, India
Om Jee Pandey	SRM University, India
P. Manikandaprabhu	Sri Ramakrishna College of Arts and Science, India
Partha Pratim Sarangi	KIIT Deemed to be University, India
Pavithra G.	Dayananda Sagar College of Engg., India
Pinar Kirci	Bursa Uludag University, Turkey
Piyush Kumar Singh	Central University of South Bihar, India
Pooja	University of Allahabad, India
Prabhat Ranjan	Central University of South Bihar, India
Pradeeba Sridar	Sydney Medical School Nepean, Australia
Pradeep Kumar	University of KwaZulu-Natal, South Africa
Prakash Kumar Singh	Rajkiya Engineering College, India
Prakash Srivastava	KIET Group of Institutions, India
Prasenjit Chanak	Indian Institute of Technology (BHU), Varanasi, India
Prateek Agrawal	Lovely Professional University, India
Praveen Pawar	Indian Institute of Information Technology, Bhopal, India
Preeth R.	Indian Institute of Information Technology, Design and Manufacturing, Kurnool, India
Preeti Sharma	Chitkara University Institute of Engineering and Technology, India
Priya Gupta	Jawaharlal Nehru University, India
Priyanka Verma	University of Galway, Ireland
Pushpalatha S. Nikkam	SDM College of Engineering and Technology, India
R. Rathi	VIT, India

Raenu Kolandaisamy   UCSI University, Malaysia
Rahul Kumar Verma   Indian Institute of Information Technology,
                              Lucknow, India
Rahul Kumar Vijay   Banasthali Vidyapith, India
Ramesh Chand Pandey   Rajkiya Engineering College, Ambedkar Nagar,
                              India
Rashmi Chaudhry   Netaji Subhas University of Technology, India
Rashmi Gupta   Atal Bihari Vajpayee University, India
Ravilla Dilli   Manipal Institute of Technology, India
Revathy G.   Sastra University, India
Richa Mishra   University of Allahabad, India
Rohit Kumar Tiwari   Madan Mohan Malaviya University of
                              Technology, India
Rohit Singh   International Management Institute, Kolkata,
                              India
S. Gandhiya Vendhan   Bharathiar University, India
Sadhana Mishra   ITM University, India
Sanjeev Patel   NIT Rourkela, India
Santosh Kumar Satapathy   Pandit Deendayal Energy University, India
Saumya Bhadauria   ABV-Indian Institute of Information Technology
                              and Management, India
Saurabh Bilgaiyan   Kalinga Institute of Industrial Technology, India
Saurabh Kumar   LNM Institute of Information Technology, India
Seera Dileep Raju   Dr. Reddy's Laboratories, India
Shailesh Kumar   Jaypee Institute of Information Technology, India
Shantanu Agnihotri   Bennett University, India
Shiv Prakash   University of Allahabad, India
Shivam Sakshi   Indian Institute of Management, Bangalore, India
Shivani Sharma   Thapar Institute of Engineering & Technology,
                              India
Shubhra Jain   Thapar Institute of Engineering & Technology,
                              India
Shyam Singh Rajput   National Institute of Technology, Patna, India
Siva Shankar Ramasamy   Chiang Mai University, Thailand
Sonali Gupta   J. C. Bose University of Science and Technology,
                              YMCA, India
Sonu Lamba   Thapar Institute of Engineering & Technology,
                              India
Sri Vallabha Deevi   Tiger Analytics, India
Srinidhi N. N.   Sri Krishna Institute of Technology, India
Sudhakar Singh   University of Allahabad, India
Sudhanshu Kumar Jha   University of Allahabad, India

Suneel Yadav	Indian Institute of Information Technology, Allahabad, India
Sunil	Jamia Millia Islamia, India
Sunil Kumar Chawla	Chandigarh University, India
Suparna Biswas	Maulana Abul Kalam Azad University of Technology, India
Suresh Raikwar	Thapar Institute of Engineering & Technology, India
Sushopti Gawade	Vidyalankar Institute of Technology, India
Syed Mutahar Aaqib	Government PG Degree College, Baramulla, India
U. Anitha	Sathyabama Institute of Science and Technology, India
V. D. Ambeth Kumar	Panimalar Engineering College, Anna University, India
Venkanna U.	National Institute of Technology, Trichy, India
Vijay Kumar Dwivedi	United College of Engineering and Research, India
Vikas Mohar	Madhav Institute of Technology & Science, India
Vinay Kumar Jain	SSTC-SSGI, India
Vinay Singh	ABV-Indian Institute of Information Technology and Management, India
Vinita Jindal	University of Delhi, India
Vinod Kumar	University of Allahabad, India
Vishal Pradhan	KIIT University, India
Vishal Shrivastava	Arya College of Engineering and IT, India
Vivek Kumar	PSIT Kanpur, India
Yadunath Pathak	Visvesvaraya National Institute of Technology, Nagpur, India
Yogish H. K.	Ramaiah Institute of Technology, India
Vijay Kumar Sharma	Shri Mata Vaishno Devi University, India
Muhammad Sajjadur Rahim	University of Rajshahi, Bangladesh
Anjana Jain	Shri G. S. Institute of Tech. and Sc., India
K. Ramachandra Rao	Shri Vishnu Engineering College for Women, India
Mamta Dahiya	SGT University, India
Satyadhyan Chickerur	KLE Technological University, India
Amit Kumar Mishra	Jain University, India
P. Shanmugavadivu	Gandhigram Rural Institute (Deemed to be University), India
K. RaviKanth	Aurora University, India
Radhakrishna Bhat	Manipal Institute of Technology, Manipal Academy of Higher Education, India

Prateek Pandey   Jaypee University of Engineering & Technology,
                                       India
Rishi Raj Sharma   Defence Institute of Advanced Technology, India

Contents – Part II

Intelligent Computing

Advanced Network Technologies

An Insider Threat Resilient Framework Based on Honey Traps in a Function-Based Access Control Environment

Kartikey Jangir[✉] and Dharmendra Prasad Mahato

Department of Computer Science and Engineering, National Insitute of Technology,
Hamirpur 177005, India
{195535,dpm}@nith.ac.in

Abstract. Insider threats present a formidable security challenge in corporate environments, distinct from external threats due to insiders' intricate knowledge of an organization's access infrastructure, policies, and scheduling. The complexity, time, and expertise required to detect, model, and timestamp insider threats render them especially challenging to mitigate. While various strategies to counter insider threats have been proposed, our research introduces a novel approach to counter insider threats by combining Function-Based Access Control (FBAC) with honey traps, enhancing our capability to proactively identify and monitor potential insider threats. The incorporation of the Honey Trap Factor (H) allows us to quantify the effectiveness of our honey traps in a novel manner. The rigorous evaluation of our approach demonstrates its ability to detect correlated attributes and adapt policy sets, marking a substantial step forward in proactive insider threat detection and mitigation.

Keywords: Honey Traps · Insider Threats · Function based Access Control

1 Introduction

In today's increasingly connected digital environment, organizations face complex and changing threats. Although external threats often attract attention, the risks posed by an organization (known as internal threats) have a significant but often overlooked impact on information security, intellectual property, and corporate integrity. [1] According to Cyber and Infrastructure Security Agency (CISA), "insider threat is characterized by the misuse of authorized access, whether intentional or unintentional, with the intent to cause harm to the Department's mission, resources, personnel, facilities, information, equipment, networks, or systems."

Insider threats pose a significant challenge, as they originate from individuals with authorized access to an organization's sensitive data and systems. These

A. Verma et al. (Eds.): ANTIC 2023, CCIS 2091, pp. 3–16, 2024.
https://doi.org/10.1007/978-3-031-64064-3_1

threats can be either malicious, intending to cause harm, or unintentional, resulting from negligence or mistakes. To combat insider threats, various detection techniques have emerged, among which honey frameworks stand out as a unique and effective approach. Motivations behind these threats may include financial gain, surveillance, negligence, or indifference. Detecting and mitigating insider threats requires a multifaceted approach that combines technology, strategic planning, and a deep understanding of human behavior. [3] A recent study on insider threats conducted by the Cybersecurity Insiders Research Team unveiled concerning statistics. Their findings indicated that a staggering 98% of organizations are susceptible to insider attacks. Furthermore, within this group, 49% of organizations can only identify insider threats after sensitive data has already been exfiltrated from their systems[2]. This research paper explores new ways to solve and mitigate the problem of insider threats in a security organization using Honey Traps.

Traditionally, detection of insider threats relies on behavioral monitoring, user access logs, and privileged account management. However, the rapid changes used by malicious actors, combined with the lack of visibility into their activities, often make it difficult for organizations to identify and prevent this threat. In 2020, the Securonix Threat Research Team conducted a comprehensive analysis of 300 security incidents spanning various organizations across eight different sectors. The findings revealed that incidents involving the misuse of privileges accounted for the second most common type of security breaches, representing 19% of all cases [4].

While standard security measures have predominantly focused on external threats, insider threats have grown in sophistication and elusiveness. In contrast to external threats, which are frequently expected and proactively defended against, insider threats often remain undetected for extended periods, resulting in substantial security breaches [5]. Furthermore, the intricate nature of identifying insider adversaries significantly compounds the challenges associated with mitigating these threats [6]. In this context, the research paper addresses the imperative for an advanced framework that leverages honeypots and honey files in the context of Function-Based Access Control (FBAC) for enhancing the detection and mitigation of insider threats.

The modern organizational landscape is characterized by the accumulation of vast volumes of data, accessed by a diverse set of users, each with unique roles and responsibilities. While the majority of these individuals act with integrity and in alignment with their prescribed functions, a minority may exploit their legitimate access for illicit purposes. Likewise, in a survey conducted by Cybersecurity Insiders, a community consisting of 400,000 information security professionals [6], the results showed that out of 373 participating organizations, 72% reported witnessing a high frequency of insider attacks in the past 12 months, with 65% confirming instances of malicious insider activities during the same period [7]. Such insider threats manifest in numerous ways, including unauthorized data exfiltration, privilege misuse, and other clandestine activities that can be particularly challenging to detect. Understanding the context, motivations, and behaviors associated with insider threats is imperative for proactive defense.

Function-Based Access Control (FBAC) stands as an innovative paradigm within the domain of access control. It extends beyond the traditional Role-Based Access Control (RBAC) model, aligning access permissions directly with job functions and roles within the organization. FBAC ensures that users have precisely required access to perform their designated functions, enhancing security by minimizing unnecessary access.

Lastly, the deception-based approach employs decoy assets, commonly referred to as honey elements, including honey permissions [12], honeypots [14], honey files [8], honey documents [9], honey tokens [10,15], honey words [13], and honey encryption [11], to entice and monitor potential insider threats. Honey frameworks employ deception tactics to lure potential malicious insiders into revealing their intentions. By creating enticing but fake data or systems, known as honeypots, honey frameworks can identify and track suspicious activities. When an insider accesses or interacts with these honeypots, it triggers an alert, notifying security teams of a potential threat.

Ultimately, this research equips organizations with a powerful strategy to safeguard their data and reputation in an increasingly perilous digital landscape through the use of deception.

The remainder of this paper is structured as follows: Sect. 2 provides the background information. Section 3 summarizes the state of the art and related work. Section 4 describes the Problem statement. In Sect. 5, we discuss the proposed framework. Section 6 describes the experiment and results. In Sect. 7, we conclude and discuss the conclusion and future work.

2   Background

Access control has been a fundamental aspect of security systems throughout the history of computing and information technology. The evolution of access control systems can be delineated through several key phases:

- **Discretionary Access Control (DAC)**: Early access control models, such as the Unix file permissions system, were discretionary, allowing users to determine access to their resources. DAC granted a high degree of autonomy but also posed significant security risks.
- **Mandatory Access Control (MAC)**: Developed by the U.S. Department of Defense, MAC models, like the Bell-LaPadula model, introduced strict, government-defined security policies that assigned labels to subjects and objects, controlling access through predefined rules.
- **Role-Based Access Control (RBAC)**: RBAC emerged in the 1990s as a response to the complexity of DAC and MAC. It introduced roles with specific permissions, simplifying access control management.
- **Attribute-Based Access Control (ABAC)**: ABAC extended access control to include various attributes, such as user characteristics, resource properties, and environmental conditions. This model offered fine-grained control.

- **Function-Based Access Control (FBAC)**: Building upon RBAC and ABAC, FBAC aligns access permissions with job functions, minimizing unnecessary access and providing a robust security foundation.

Function-Based Access Control (FBAC) has emerged as a versatile and robust approach, offering unique advantages in the realm of access control. The core of FBAC lies in its ability to fine-tune the precision and scope of access control. By associating access permissions with individual job functions and roles, FBAC ensures that users are granted access only to the specific resources essential for their designated tasks. This meticulous control minimizes the risk of unauthorized disclosures, reducing the potential for harm or compromise of sensitive information, a vulnerability commonly observed in other access control systems.

However, FBAC's strength goes beyond its precision; it embodies adaptability and flexibility to accommodate changes within organizations. FBAC exhibits a remarkable ability to seamlessly adapt to evolving roles and organizational shifts, thereby reducing the administrative overhead often linked with managing access control systems. This adaptability ensures that access permissions remain aligned with the dynamic nature of modern workplaces.

Moreover, the integration of FBAC not only enhances security but also bolsters the organization's capability to address internal threats effectively. It provides a solid foundation for the implementation of honeypots and honey files, critical components in the detection of unauthorized activities and potential malicious insider threats. This integration enhances an organization's security posture and improves its ability to promptly identify and respond to insider threats.

Streamlining compliance is another appealing facet of FBAC. FBAC simplifies the compliance process by ensuring that access permissions are directly linked to specific roles and responsibilities. This connection streamlines the auditing process and simplifies compliance with labor and data protection regulations.

Ultimately, FBAC simplifies access control by eliminating unnecessary access permissions, enabling administrators to allocate their efforts and resources more effectively in managing specific tasks. The benefits of FBAC extend to not only enhanced security but also improved operational efficiency, making it a sound choice in the ever-evolving field of access control systems.

3   State of the Art and Related Work

3.1   Insider Threat

Insider threats have been a persistent concern in the realm of cybersecurity, prompting extensive research efforts to develop effective detection and mitigation strategies. These strategies encompass a diverse array of approaches, ranging from behavioral analysis to innovative technologies.

Jiang et al. [20] introduced a model that harnesses deep learning and Graph Convolutional Networks (GCN) for insider threat identification. Hashem et al.

[21] introduced a method for detecting potential insiders by analyzing electrical signals generated by human biological activities, including electroencephalography (EEG), electrocardiogram (ECG), and electromyography (EMG). Brown et al. [5] presented an insider threat detection framework that explores the connection between word usage and various risk factors, which can be of a psychological or behavioral nature. Greitzer et al. [22] explored the correlation between employees' behavioral states and the associated risks of insider threats. These states encompass factors such as disgruntlement, anger management issues, performance, stress, and aggressive behavior. More recently, Paxton et al. [9] introduced a framework based on natural language processing that utilizes written and recorded incident notes to model insider attacks.

3.2 Function Based Access Control (FBAC)

Function-Based Access Control (FBAC) [16] is a form of access control that focuses on regulating access to specific functions or operations within a software application or system. [16] In FBAC, access to certain functionalities or features is controlled based on the user's role, privileges, or other attributes. This model is often used to ensure that users are only able to perform actions that are appropriate for their role or authorization level.

Key characteristics of Function-Based Access Control (FBAC) include:

- **Granular Control:** FBAC allows for fine-grained control over the functions or operations within an application. It can specify who can perform a particular function and under what conditions.
- **Role-Based:** Similar to Role-Based Access Control (RBAC), FBAC often involves associating functions with roles, and users are assigned roles based on their job responsibilities or permissions.
- **Dynamic:** FBAC can be flexible and dynamic, allowing for adjustments to access controls as roles or responsibilities change.
- **Conditional Access:** Access to functions may be based on conditions such as time of day, location, or specific attributes.
- **Customization:** FBAC can be tailored to the specific needs and structure of an application, making it adaptable to various use cases.
- **Enhanced Security:** By controlling access to functions, FBAC helps protect sensitive operations and data by ensuring that only authorized users can perform critical actions.

Function-Based Access Control can be used in a variety of applications, including web-based systems, enterprise software, and databases, to manage user privileges and restrict access to critical functions, such as administrative tasks or financial transactions.

3.3 Deceptive Honey Framework System

Honey Framework is a cybersecurity framework that incorporates the use of honey traps as part of its security strategy. This framework involves the deployment of deceptive resources, such as decoy servers, files, or networks, to lure attackers. These honeypots or honey traps are designed to mimic genuine assets or vulnerabilities, making them attractive targets for cybercriminals. When an attacker interacts with these deceptive resources, their activities are closely monitored, and their behavior is analyzed.

Bercovitch and colleagues [17] proposed an innovative "HoneyGen" system designed to mine rules for capturing the characteristics of real data, enabling the generation of synthetic data based on these rules. In a similar vein, Bhagat and team [18] advocated the use of honeypots as a solution for addressing network intrusion detection challenges. Bowen et al. [19] introduced the Decoy Document Distributor (D3) model, which leverages a rule-based approach to automatically create and disseminate decoy documents throughout a file system, enticing potential malicious users. Honey traps are a deceptive technique or method used to detect and thwart potential threats or malicious activities by luring attackers into a controlled and monitored environment. The primary goal of a honey trap is to divert and engage potential attackers or intruders, gather information about their tactics, and protect the real, sensitive assets of an organization from compromise.

Key aspects and goals of a Honey Framework include:

- Detection: Identifying potential threats or attackers by luring them into the honey trap environment.
- Analysis: Monitoring and analyzing the attacker's tactics, techniques, and procedures to understand their methods and intentions.
- Early Warning: Providing early warnings of potential security breaches or attacks.
- Distracting Attackers: Diverting attackers' attention away from real, critical assets, thus safeguarding them.
- Data Collection: Gathering valuable threat intelligence and insights into emerging cyber threats.
- Countermeasures: Developing and implementing appropriate security measures based on the insights gained from attackers' interactions with the honey traps.

The success of a honey framework relies on creating a convincing and enticing environment that attracts attackers while ensuring that the real systems remain secure. It can be a valuable addition to an organization's overall cybersecurity strategy, helping to detect, analyze, and mitigate threats more effectively. Honey frameworks are just one example of deception-based cybersecurity strategies designed to enhance security posture and safeguard critical assets.

4   Problem Statement

In the realm of modern information security, the looming shadow of insider threats continues to cast a daunting challenge for organizations worldwide. This challenge extends beyond mere data breaches, encompassing the jeopardization of sensitive information, disruption of operations, and the compromising of invaluable intellectual property. A startling revelation from recent surveys underscores the severity of this issue: a staggering 60% of businesses have reported grappling with at least one insider breach within the past year. These incidents, often veiled in sophistication and clandestinity, evade detection through the conventional lens of passive monitoring and analysis of employee activities. Consequently, the need for a paradigm shift towards a proactive and adaptable Insider Threat Framework, harnessing the capabilities of cutting-edge honey trap technology, emerges as a dire necessity. Moreover, integrating the invaluable insights derived from Function-Based Access Control (FBAC) stands poised as a critical augmentation to fortify this Framework in its mission to combat insider threats effectively.

Central to this challenge is the realization that a reactive approach, though prevalent, falls short in anticipating and preemptively addressing malicious behaviors brewing within organizational confines. The necessity for a more assertive system that actively seeks out and identifies insider threats becomes glaringly apparent. The inadequacies of existing methods, entangled in their passive nature, must be transcended to proactively counteract the evolving spectrum of insider threats.

While traditional access control mechanisms serve as the bedrock of security frameworks, they often prove inadequate in harmonizing with the dynamic landscape of insider threats. These mechanisms, albeit crucial, inadvertently bestow excessive access upon employees, inadvertently paving the path to potential insider threats. To thwart these lurking dangers, a nuanced, and meticulously detailed access control system emerges as an indispensable necessity, offering granular control over access rights while navigating the delicate balance between access and security.

Critical to this endeavor is the nuanced understanding that insider threats are not monolithic; they manifest along a diverse continuum encompassing unintentional negligence to meticulously orchestrated malevolence. To effectively combat this multifaceted challenge, a comprehensive and holistic approach becomes indispensable, one that is finely attuned to capturing these nuances, thereby enabling the proactive detection and mitigation of insider threats.

5   Proposed Framework

The proposed research aims to develop an innovative Insider Threat Framework that combines Function-Based Access Control with the utilization of honey traps, including honeypots, honey files, and honey tokens. This framework will enable organizations to align access permissions precisely with job functions, proactively lure potential threats, monitor their interactions, and swiftly identify and respond to insider threats. The research will further aim to provide insights into real-world use cases, advanced analytics, user behavior profiling, and threat intelligence integration, culminating in a robust and adaptive solution to address insider threats effectively within dynamic organizational environments.

- **Sensitive File Marker:** The framework incorporates a Sensitive File Marker, which serves as a crucial element in the detection of insider threats. This marker is designed to identify files or resources with sensitive or confidential information. It helps establish a baseline for what data should be considered sensitive within the system.
- **Honey Tokens Generator:** The Honey Tokens Generator assumes a crucial role in generating deceptive tokens for honey traps. These tokens simulate the attributes of real sensitive files, rendering the honey traps indiscernible from genuine data. This element is essential for enticing potential insider threats to engage with the deceptive resources.
- **Honey Trap Factor (H):** The Honey Trap Factor (H) represents a quantifiable metric within the framework. It assesses the effectiveness and attractiveness of the honey traps. A higher H value indicates more convincing honey traps, increasing the likelihood of detecting malicious insider activities.

5.1   Honey Trap Integration in FBAC

The framework seamlessly integrates honey traps with actual code, ensuring that these deceptive resources closely resemble sensitive files. By doing so, it effectively blurs the line between real data and honey traps, making it challenging for potential malicious insiders to distinguish between the two. Access to these honey traps is limited to a select few authorized personnel, thereby minimizing the risk of accidental interactions.

5.2   Honey Trap Activation Function

A critical component of the framework is the Honey Trap Activation Function, which is programmed to execute at regular intervals, typically every minute. Its primary purpose is to actively monitor and detect any unauthorized attempts to edit or duplicate the honey traps. When such unauthorized activities are detected, the activation function triggers alert mechanisms or takes further preventive actions to thwart potential threats.

5.3   Working

The innovative Insider Threat Framework developed in this research paper involves a comprehensive methodology designed to effectively counter insider threats within dynamic organizational environments. The methodology integrates various elements as we have shown in Fig. 1, including user requests, a centralized Honey Trap Activation Function (controller), a control center for quarantining intrusive machines, a database, the Sensitive File Marker, and the Honey Token Generator. Additionally, it connects to an Intrusion Detection System and notifications, an FBAC repository, a policy repository, a context repository, and policy administration. This methodology is vital for proactively identifying and mitigating insider threats.

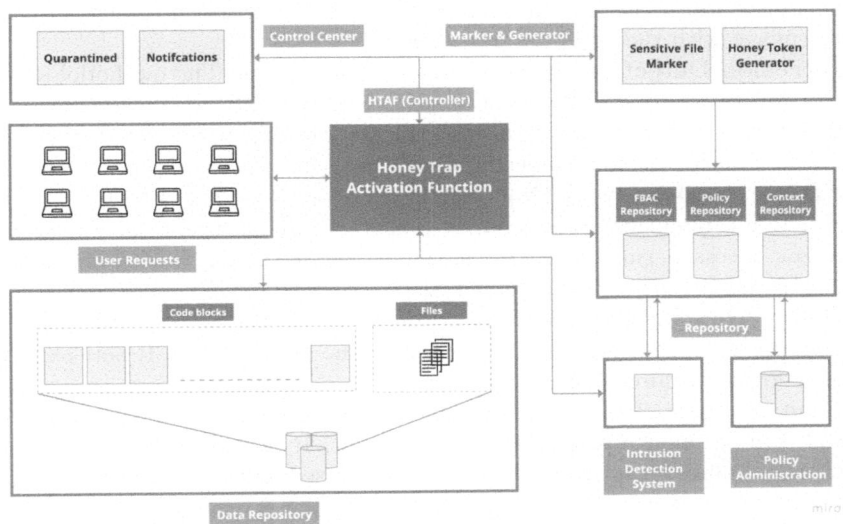

Fig. 1. Architecture

– **User Requests:** The framework incorporates the analysis of user requests, providing insights into interactions with the organization's systems. Understanding user behavior is a crucial aspect of identifying potential insider threats.
– **Centralized Honey Trap Activation Function (Controller):** The core of the methodology is the centralized Honey Trap Activation Function, programmed to execute at regular intervals, typically every minute. Its primary purpose is to actively monitor and detect any unauthorized attempts to edit or duplicate the honey traps. When such unauthorized activities are detected, the activation function triggers alert mechanisms or takes further preventive actions to thwart potential threats.
– **Control Center:** This component serves as a command center for managing the honey traps. It can quarantine intrusive machines and maintain the integrity of the deceptive resources.
– **Database:** The database is crucial for storing information about sensitive files and user interactions. It plays a key role in profiling user behavior and threat intelligence.
– **Sensitive File Marker:** The framework incorporates a Sensitive File Marker, which is instrumental in identifying files or resources with sensitive or confidential information. It helps establish a baseline for what data should be considered sensitive within the system.
– **Honey Token Generator:** The Honey Tokens Generator assumes a crucial role in generating deceptive tokens for honey traps. These tokens simulate the attributes of real sensitive files, rendering the honey traps indiscernible from

genuine data. This element is essential for enticing potential insider threats to engage with the deceptive resources.

- **Intrusion Detection System and Notifications:** The methodology links the framework to an Intrusion Detection System (IDS) that actively scans for malicious activities. When potential insider threats are detected, the system triggers notifications to relevant authorities.
- **FBAC Repository:** A Function-Based Access Control (FBAC) repository stores and manages access control policies based on users' job functions. It aligns access permissions with specific roles, ensuring that users can only access what is required for their tasks.
- **Policy Repository:** The Policy Repository stores access control policies, defining the rules and permissions within the organization. It acts as a reference for the enforcement of access controls.
- **Context Repository:** The Context Repository contains information about the context in which access requests occur. It assists in making real-time decisions about granting or denying access based on the prevailing conditions.
- **Policy Administration:** Policy administration is responsible for overseeing and managing access control policies, ensuring they align with the organization's security requirements.

6   Experiment and Results

In the realm of insider threat detection, where the potential for security breaches originating from within the organization is a persistent concern, the deployment of honey traps has emerged as a proactive and dynamic solution. Honey traps, also known as honeypots, represent a strategic approach to identifying and mitigating insider threats by strategically placing deceptive resources within the network environment. These deceptive elements are designed to entice potential malicious insiders into revealing their intentions, providing valuable insights into their activities.

6.1   Impact of Honey Trap Factor (H) on Intrusion Detection Frequency

The probability of an insider threat successfully accessing honey traps within the realm of actual sensitive data is a critical concern for organizations seeking to bolster their security posture. This probability is inherently tied to the Honey Trap Factor (H), which is a variable that spans the range between 0 and 1. The Honey Trap Factor plays a pivotal role in determining the level of deceptiveness and allure of the honey traps, making it a key parameter in Function-Based Access Control (FBAC) systems.

In Fig. 2 the relationship between the Honey Trap Factor (H) and the frequency of intrusion detection is a subject of paramount importance in the context of security research. The name for this relationship can be aptly termed "H Factor with Respect to Intrusion Detection Frequency." It signifies the extent to

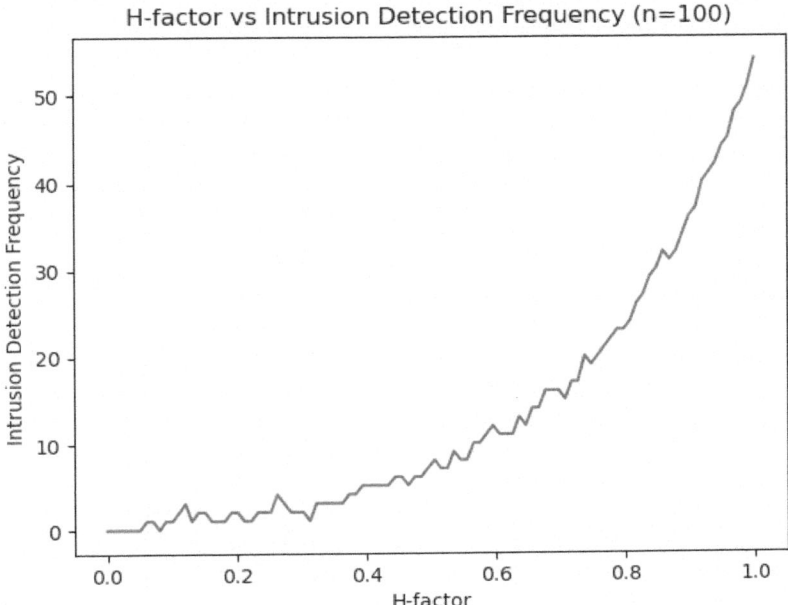

Fig. 2. H factor vs IDF

Table 1. Intrusion Detection Frequency with H Factor

S.No.	H Factor	Intrusion Detection Frequency
1	0	0
2	0.22	1
3	0.23	2
4	0.36	3
5	0.37	4
6	0.39	5
7	0.74	20
8	0.75	19
9	0.76	20
10	0.77	21
11	0.78	22
12	0.79	23
13	0.8	23
14	0.81	24
15	0.82	26
16	0.97	48
17	0.98	49
18	0.99	51
19	1	55

which variations in the Honey Trap Factor influence the ability to detect and thwart potential insider threats effectively.

As the dataset in Table 1 shows that the Honey Trap Factor increases within the defined range, there is a noticeable shift in the dynamics of intrusion detection. The higher the H factor, the more alluring and convincing the honey traps become, thereby enticing malicious insiders toward these deceptive resources. Consequently, with an elevated H factor, the likelihood of an insider threat attempting to interact with these traps also increases.

7   Conclusion and Future Work

In this research, we introduced a novel framework that combines Function-Based Access Control (FBAC) with honey traps to effectively address insider threats. This integration enhances our ability to proactively identify and monitor potential insider threats. We utilized the Honey Trap Factor (H) to quantify the effectiveness of our honey traps.

Our approach was rigorously evaluated and proven effective in identifying correlated attributes and modifying policy sets without affecting access control usability. This represents a significant advancement in proactive insider threat detection and mitigation.

For future work, we plan to explore advanced techniques, potentially including deep learning, to further refine attribute generation. We also aim to conduct a comprehensive user study to assess practical effectiveness and usability.

Our ongoing priorities include integrating threat intelligence and machine learning, optimizing the Honey Trap Factor, and expanding research to address scalability and adaptability for organizations of varying sizes and complexities. Our ultimate goal is to provide a robust solution for safeguarding against insider threats while upholding trust and integrity in digital operations.

References

1. Ponemon Institute is pleased to present the findings of the 2022 Cost of Insider Threats Global Report. https://static.poder360.com.br/2022/01/pfpt-us-tr-the-cost-of-insider-threats-ponemon-report.pdf
2. Deakinand, R.E., Kildea, D.G.: A note on standard deviation and RMS. Austral. Surveyor **44**(1), 74–79 (1999)
3. Kaghazgaran, P., Takabi, H.: Toward an insider threat detection frame- work using honey permissions. J. Internet Serv. Inf. Secur. **5**, 19–36 (2015)
4. Cyber and Infrastructure Security Agency (CISA): Defining Insider Threats (2022). https://www.cisa.gov/topics/physical-security/insider-threat-mitigation/defining-insider-threats, https://www.cisa.gov/defining-insider-threats. Accessed 14 Nov 2022

5. Brown, C.R., Watkins, A., Greitzer, F.L.: Predicting insider threat risks through linguistic analysis of electronic communication. In: 2013 46th Hawaii International Conference on System Sciences, pp. 1849–1858 (2013). https://doi.org/10.1109/HICSS.2013.453
6. Hu, V., et al.: Guide to attribute based access control (ABAC) definition and considerations. National Institute of Standards and Technology Special Publication, January 2014, pp. 162–800 (2014)
7. Ge, M., Cho, J.-H., Kim, D., Dixit, G., Chen, I.-R.: Proactive defense for internet-of-things: moving target defense with cyber deception. ACM Trans. Internet Technol. **22**, 1, Article 24, 31 p. (2021). https://doi.org/10.1145/3467021
8. US Department of Homeland and Security: Moving Target Defense (2018). https://www.dhs.gov/science-and-technology/csd-mtd. Accessed 17 Oct 2022
9. Paxton-Fear, K., Hodges, D., Buckley, O.: Understanding Insider Threat Attacks Using Natural Language Processing: Automatically Mapping Organic Narrative Reports to Existing Insider Threat Frameworks, pp. 619–636 (2020)
10. Pennington, J., Socher, R., Manning, C.D.: Glove: global vectors for word representation. In: Proceedings of the 2014 Conference on Empirical Methods in Natural Language Processing (EMNLP), pp. 1532–1543 (2014)
11. Schneider, T.D.: Information content of individual genetic sequences. J. Theor. Biol. **189**(4), 427–441 (1997)
12. Securonix: 2020 Insider Threat Report (2020). https://www.securonix.com/resources/2020-insider-threat-report/. Accessed 17 Oct 2022
13. SolarWinds: New Market Research - SolarWinds Survey Investigates Insider Threats to Federal Cybersecurity (2015). https://thwack.solarwinds.com/resources/f/federal-government/1461/new-market-research---solarwinds-survey-investigates-insider-threats-to-federal-cybersecurity. Accessed 19 Oct 2022
14. Srinivasa, S., Pedersen, J.M., Vasilomanolakis, E.: Towards systematic honeytoken fingerprinting. In: 13th International Conference on Security of Information and Networks (Merkez, Turkey) (SIN 2020), Article 28, 5 p. Association for Computing Machinery, New York, NY, USA (2020). https://doi.org/10.1145/3433174.3433599
15. Theoharidou, M., Kokolakis, S., Karyda, M., Kioun-touzis, E.: The insider threat to information systems and the effectiveness of ISO17799. Comput. Secur. **24**, 472–484 (2005). https://doi.org/10.1016/j.cose.2005.05.002
16. Desmedt, Y., Shaghaghi, A.: Function-based access control (FBAC): from access control matrix to access control tensor. In: Proceedings of the 8th ACM CCS International Workshop on Managing Insider Security Threats. ACM (2016)
17. Bercovitch, M., Renford, M., Hasson, L., Shabtai, A., Rokach, L., Elovici, Y.: HoneyGen: an automated honeytokens generator. In: Proceedings of 2011 IEEE International Conference on Intelligence and Security Informatics, pp. 131–136 (2011). https://doi.org/10.1109/ISI.2011.5984063
18. Bhagat, N., Arora, B.: Intrusion detection using honeypots. In: 2018 Fifth International Conference on Parallel, Distributed and Grid Computing (PDGC), pp. 412–417 (2018). https://doi.org/10.1109/PDGC.2018.8745761
19. Bowen, B.M., Hershkop, S., Keromytis, A.D., Stolfo, S.: Baiting inside attackers using decoy documents. In: SecureComm (2009)
20. Jiang, J., et al.: Anomaly detection with graph convolutional networks for insider threat and fraud detection. In: MILCOM 2019 - 2019 IEEE Military Communications Conference (MILCOM), pp. 109–114 (2019). https://doi.org/10.1109/MILCOM47813.2019.9020760

21. Hashem, Y., Takabi, H., Gol, M.G., Dantu, R.: Towards insider threat detection using psychophysiological signals. In: Proceedings of the 7th ACM CCS International Workshop on Managing Insider Security Threats (Denver. Colorado, USA) (MIST '15), pp. 71–74. Association for Computing Machinery, New York, NY, USA (2015). https://doi.org/10.1145/2808783.2808792
22. Greitzer, F.L., Kangas, L.J., Noonan, C.F., Dalton, A.C., Hohimer, R.E.: Identifying at-risk employees: modeling psychosocial precursors of potential insider threats. In: Proceedings of the Annual Hawaii International Conference on System Sciences, pp. 2392–2401 (2012). https://doi.org/10.1109/HICSS.2012.309

Performance Comparison of QoS Aware Power Allocation and Optimization Techniques for the Small-Cell 5G Networks

D. Srinivasa Rao[1]([✉]) [iD], Ch. Rajasekhar[2] [iD], and GBSR Naidu[3] [iD]

[1] GMR Institute of Technology, Rajam, India
{srinivasarao.d,naidu.gbsr}@gmrit.edu.in
[2] GITAM School of Technology, GITAM (Deemed to be University),
Visakhapatnam, India
rchukka@gitam.edu
[3] GMR Institute of Technology, Rajam, India

Abstract. The deployment of small cells in highly dense areas or buildings, and offices is a key technique in upcoming 5G networks that enhance the signal coverage and capacity. However, the presence of co-channel cells may result in interference among the user stations and degrade the overall system capacity. Hence, resource optimization techniques are required in these scenarios to improve the system capacity and user quality. In this study, the power allocation problem among the interfering user stations is considered by guaranteeing their Quality of Service (QoS) requirements. To solve the non-convex optimization problem, some of the algorithms like Sequential quadratic programming (SQP), Log-space sequential quadratic programming (LSQP), Interior point Trust Region (IPTR) are discussed. The performance comparison is done with these algorithms to analyse the effect on sum rate, individual rates and computational complexity in small cell network scenarios. The results show that the LSQP technique has improved sum and user rate performance compared to SQP and trust region-based methods.

Keywords: Interference · Power Allocation · Optimization · QoS · SQP · Complexity

1 Introduction

In the current 5G era, many radios are being deployed to enhance the network coverage, capacity, deliver high data rates with low latency [1]. However, the major problem with 5G radios is that the higher frequencies are unable to penetrate through large and tall indoor buildings in urban centres. Macro cells provide good coverage at the outdoor and cell edges. Hence, to extend the coverage to indoor settings small cells like femto, pico, and micro cells have been deployed in 4G and 5G networks. Figure 1 typically presents a heterogeneous

ⓒ The Author(s), under exclusive license to Springer Nature Switzerland AG 2024
A. Verma et al. (Eds.): ANTIC 2023, CCIS 2091, pp. 17–28, 2024.
https://doi.org/10.1007/978-3-031-64064-3_2

network that contains Marco cells and small cells to provide the network coverage over a large metropolitan area. Further, due to their compact size and low cost, they can be easily deployed in outdoor and indoor locations like shopping malls, sports arena, entertainment zones, office buildings, residential complexes, manufacturing plants and enterprise facilities. Although small cell deployment brought several advantages to the cellular networks, vast and unplanned installation of these cells increases expenditure to the operators and produces severe interference among the macro cells and neighbouring small cells [2]. It results in degradation of overall system capacity and provides poor Quality of Service (QoS) to the user stations in the entire network. Effective resource management among the user stations in heterogeneous networks may reduce the interference and improve the service quality, and optimal power allocation is one of the major content of resource allocation.

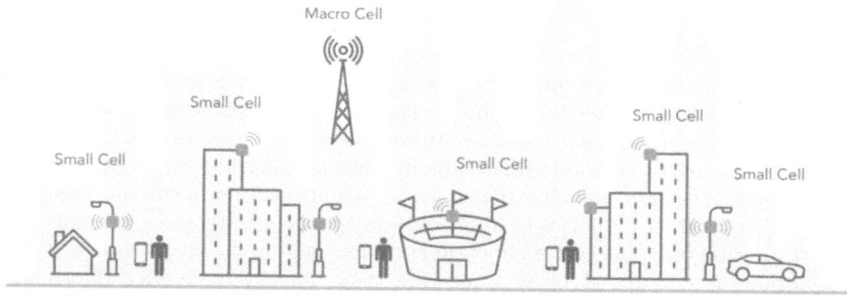

Fig. 1. Heterogeneous network.

The Small Cell Forum (SFC) predicts that around 38.3 million small cells will be installed by 2026, and enterprises contribute a significant share among these deployments, followed by rural and urban' service providers [3]. Due to this reason, there has been an increase in the research on resource management techniques such as inter-cell interference reduction, power optimization, and QoS management in small cell networks [4–12]. Wide deployment of small and low power cells in a macro BS necessitates the need to development efficient resource allocation techniques to effectively manage the interference. The author in [4], proposed two uplink resource allocation algorithms namely optimization and heuristic to reduce the interference caused by macro base station to adjacent femto cells. It was shown that the proposed schemes improved the overall capacity of the femto cells. In [5], the author considered a two-tier network and proposed a cluster algorithm to minimize the interference among the cluster of femto cells. In addition the user mobility was also studied using a dynamic resource allocation algorithm and shown the improvement in terms of capacity and computational time. In [6], the author proposed a two stage resource allocation algorithm to mitigate the interference among the adjacent femto cells. In the first stage the interference levels at each femto cell was identified and in the second stage the power levels were adjusted to mitigate the interference.

The author in [7], presented an energy-efficient power allocation scheme for heterogeneous small cell networks. The studied scheme allocates resources to each small cell based on channel states and power consumption of the circuits. It was different from conventional resource allocation schemes that would focus only on throughput maximization. A joint power allocation and user assignment scheme was proposed in [8] to optimize the power and achieve the fairness among different users in heterogeneous cognitive radio networks. In [9], the author considered the power allocation problem in heterogeneous small cell networks and implemented a numerical method to increase the network capacity. With the wide 5G small cell deployment and the co-channel deployment poses interference problem to the neighbouring user stations. Due to this, the QoS (Quality of Service) of the users operating under low power cells may get degraded resulting in poor performance. In [10], the author studied the problem of power consumption in the small cell networks by taking QoS into account. The power consumption was minimized by optimal precoding and antenna selection while satisfying QoS requirements. The author in [11] proposed an efficient resource allocation approach for 5G Femto cells that guarantee QoS to high priority and best effort users effectively. In [12], the resource allocation problem in complex small cell networks was considered. A machine learning based Q-learning approach was proposed to manage the resources among the Femto cells and provide QoS guarantee to the users in the network. In [13], a reinforcement learning algorithm was implemented in 5G access networks to allocate the transmit power and improve the energy efficiency of users. In addition, the author in [14] presented a reinforcement learning strategy to minimize interference between macro and small cells and increase user service quality. From the above discussion it was clear that resource allocation and power allocation in small cell networks is a non-convex optimization problem, and it is highly needed to develop optimization algorithms to address this issue. Further QoS is also an important aspect to be considered while designing solutions. In this paper, we consider some of the recent optimization algorithms like SQP [15], LSQP [16] and, IPTR [17] to solve the problem with less complexity and enhanced QoS performance. The primary contributions of this study are outlined below:

1. A heterogeneous network that comprise a macro BS and cluster of small cells is considered and studied the QoS aware power allocation problem in co-channel scenario.
2. Some of the recent power allocation and optimization techniques like SQP [15], LSQP [16] and IPTR [17] were analysed and discussed.
3. The evaluation is done using MATLAB and, the performance of these techniques is studied using QoS metrics like sum rate, individual rates, convergence rate.

The remainder of the paper is structured as follows: Sect. 2 explains the system model and problem formulation. The strategies for power allocation and optimization to address the non-convex optimization problem are presented in Sect. 3. Section 4 provides a discussion of simulation findings. Lastly, Sect. 5 concludes the work.

2 System Model and Problem Formulation

2.1 System Model

In this work, a heterogeneous network operating with a single macro-cell and multiple small cells is considered as depicted in Fig. 1. It is assumed that there are 'M' small cells, whereby, each small-cell base station is equipped with 'N' antennas. Consider each small-cell is serving 'K' user stations that are equipped with single antennas. The users will be served by the small cells based on their application demands, received data rates and Quality of Service requirements. The wireless channel is assumed to follow Rayleigh fading with i.i.d (independent and identically distributed) Gaussian random variables. Let χ_{km} be the transmitted signal at the m-th small cell, thereby the received signal at the k-th user station is expressed as,

$$y_{km} = \sum_{m=1}^{L} h_{km}\sqrt{p_{km}}\chi_{km} + \sum_{i\neq m}\sum_{m=1}^{L} h_{km}\sqrt{p_{mi}}\chi_i + n_k \tag{1}$$

where p_{km} represents the transmitted signal power from m-th small cell to k-th user stations and, h_{km} is the corresponding channel gain. The term n_k represents the zero mean and unit variance Gaussian noise. σ^2 represents the noise variance.

Based on Eq. 1, the signal to interference plus noise ratio (SINR) of k-th user station in m-th small cell can be expressed as,

$$SINR_{k,m} = \frac{h_m^H p_k h_m}{\sum_{i\neq m} h_i^H p_k h_i + \sigma^2} \tag{2}$$

2.2 Problem Formulation

To provide satisfied QoS in small cells, one of the primary objectives is to be maximize the data rates at each user station and minimize the interference. This is achieved through the efficient power allocation and resource management. However the power allocation and optimization is subject to various constraints at each user station. The problem formulation is done as follows:

$$C = \max_{P_{k,m} R_{k,m}} \log_2(1 + SINR_{k,m})$$

$$\sum_{m=1}^{L} R_{i,m} \geq R_{\min}, \forall i \in K \tag{3}$$

$$P_{i,m} \geq 0, \forall i \in K \tag{4}$$

$$\sum_{i=1}^{M} I_{k,i\neq m} \leq I_{th} \tag{5}$$

where 'C' is the system capacity and is subject to various constraints. To guarantee the fairness and obtain the minimum data rate, each user station is required to achieve R_{min} represented in Eq. 3. The constraints defined in Eqs. 4 and 5 represent the allowed transmit power, and the interference threshold at each user station.

3   Power Allocation and Optimization Techniques

The transmit power control is a key factor in the 5G small-cell networks to effectively manage the radio resources and enhance the QoS. For these networks, the power allocation method must be considered to ensure that the resource utilization is at the optimal level. Sometimes it is required to evaluate the complex objective functions and constraints in solving the Non-linear problems (NLP). To solve these functions, there exists optimization techniques namely, Sequential Quadratic Programming, Logspace Sequential Quadratic Programming, and Interior point Trust Region considered to be suitable for many applications.

3.1   Sequential Quadratic Programming

SQP is one of the most advanced approaches for performing constrained non-linear optimization issues. The general effectiveness of SQP may be attributed to two fundamental factors. Firstly, the QP sub-problem is simple to build since the sub problem requires only function analyses. Regardless of the complexity of the actual functions, the SQP method is suitable for different problem forms. Secondly, as it is convex and well-established, the QP sub problem is simple to solve. This convexity is critical as, unlike most other NLPs, convex optimization issues can be addressed consistently and efficiently. The QP sub problem form using quadratic estimate of the Lagrangian component is given by,

$$\min_{d} f(x_k) + \nabla f(x_k)^T d + \frac{1}{2}d^T H_k d \tag{6}$$

Hence, the QP sub problem requires only the function evaluation and their gradients. Hk is the Hessian matrix of the Lagrangian function, 'd' represents the direction vector from current point to next point.

3.2   Logspace Sequential Quadratic Programming

The application of log-transformations to conventional SQP is an established approach for increasing the performance of the basic non-linear system; hence, it does not represent a substantial development in the field. However, because of its underlying geometric programming mathematics, LSQP is a generic and systematic method to non-linear optimisation and offers better comprehension.

The log transformation helps in solving the non-linear problems with a series of approximate quadratic sub problems. The QP sub problem of SQP has been replaced with log transformation, and the new problem formulation is given by,

$$\min_d \ \log f(x_k) + \frac{1}{f(x_k)}(x_k \odot \nabla f(x_k))^T d + \frac{1}{2}d^T H_k d \tag{7}$$

3.3   Interior Point Trust Region

Under reasonable assumptions, Newton's technique converges substantially to a stationary point, and the convergence becomes challenging if the initial point is distant from the required solution. Trust-region is an approach that provides convergence from any starting point while also overcoming the drawbacks of traditional approaches. Furthermore, Trust-region approaches may generate substantial global convergence, which is particularly significant in performing smooth non-linear programming and are less susceptible when dealing with error estimation. Also, the objective function of the model does not have to be convex and positive definite. The trust-region form associated with quadratic programming sub problem is expressed as,

$$\min_d \ \log f(x_k) + \frac{1}{f(x_k)}(x_k \odot \nabla f(x_k))^T d + \frac{1}{2}d^T H_k d \tag{8}$$

where $'B_k'$ represents arbitrary symmetric matrix and $'P_k'$ is the diagonal scaling matrix.

4   Simulation Results

In this section, the performance comparison results of the power optimization techniques are presented and discussed. The simulation scenario includes a two-tier small cell network with 'M' small cells equally distributed in the range of a macro station. To assess performance, consider the capacity of small cells situated on the outer portion of a macrocell. Table 1 shows the simulation parameters used in the study. At each time slot, the users are selected randomly in the small cells. For the purpose of simulation, at each time slot, the users are selected randomly in the small cells. The number of small cells is set to 5, minimum rate is 0.2, and the maximum transmitted power is 3W. The system evaluation is done using three techniques namely SQP [15], LSQP [16] and, IPTR [17]. At first, the total achievable rate (or) sum rate is obtained by changing the available user power, and the effect is illustrated in Fig. 2. It can be seen that the overall rate increases with increased per user available power for all the schemes. However, the quadratic programming techniques SQP and LSQP significantly outperforms the trust region technique. Further, the gap between the trust region approach and the quadratic programming techniques increases with higher values of the available user power. This is due to the more efficient allocation of available power using the LSQP approach than the other suboptimal techniques.

Table 1. Simulation setup.

Parameters	Values
User selection	Random
Macro-cell coverage	500 m
Small-cell coverage	200 m
Frequency	2 GHz
Transmit power	3 W
Number of small cells	5
Threshold rate	0.2

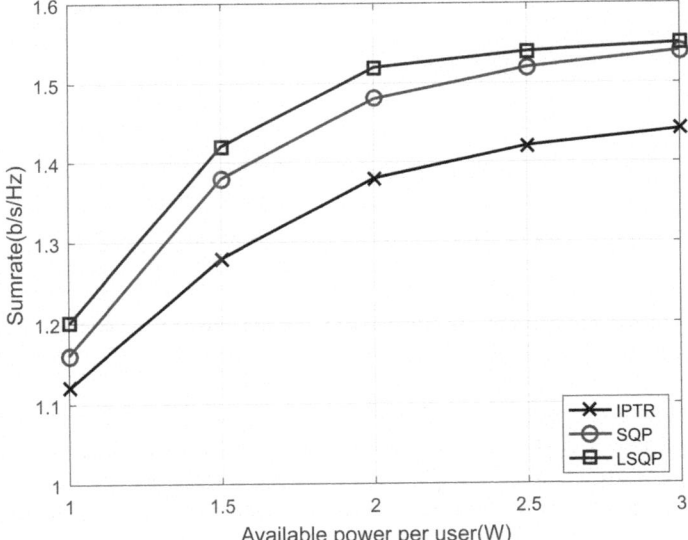

Fig. 2. User power vs sum rate.

Next, the sum rate performance of the three schemes is obtained by varying the required threshold rates of each user, and is depicted in Fig. 3. As perceived, in all the schemes, the sum rate decreases with an increase in required threshold rates. This is because the power consumption of poor (or) low SINR users is increased to achieve higher rates. It resulted in significant increase of the overall interference. Another possible reason is when the transmit power limit of the user with low SINR exceeds its full capacity and fails to attain the necessary service quality. In such cases, the transmit power of users with good (or) high SINR is decreased to mitigate the effect of interference. However, the overall rate of the IPTR approach declines when the threshold rate is higher than 0.15 b/s/Hz and remains nearly constant between 0.05 and 0.15. Although quadratic program-

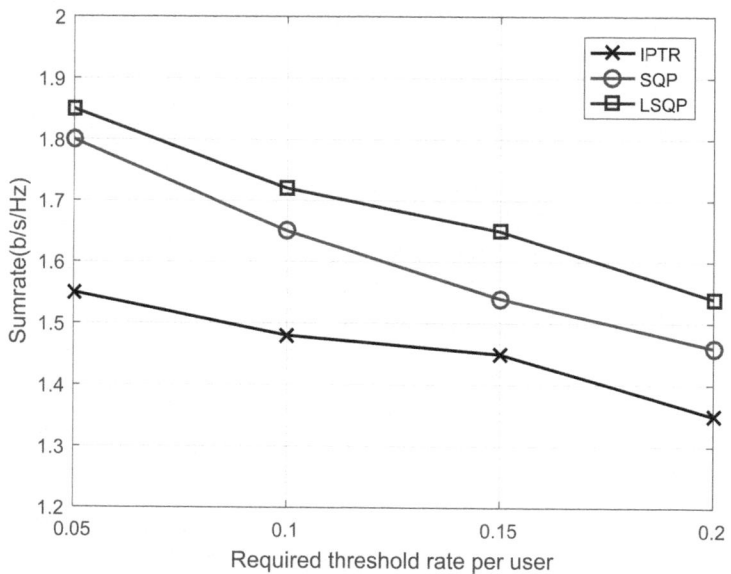

Fig. 3. Threshold rate vs sum rate.

ming techniques perform well by increasing the achieved rate of individual users, this improvement is insufficient to account for the overall decline in network performance.

The impact of varying the available user power on the achievable data rate of each user equipment is shown in Fig. 4. It is observed that each user has achieved minimum QoS requirement. Another key finding is that user 1 and user 2 (high rate users) achievable rates increase with the increase in available user power. However, they do not have an effect on the rate of user 3 and user 4 (low rate users). This is because power is distributed equally to low rate users to satisfy the minimum required rates. At the other side, high rate users are allocated power to enhance the sum rate of the system. Therefore, raising the power allocation merely improves the attainable rate of these users. The user achievable rates by varying the required threshold rate is shown in Fig. 5. It is observed that the data rates of user 3 and user 4 increase until they satisfy the minimum quality requirement. It is notable to observe that the possible rate of user 1 and user 2 falls as QoS requirements increase. The assignment of greater transmit power by high rate users has increased system interference, and as a result, the transmit power of low rate users may be lowered.

Figure 6 depicts the convergence performance of the optimization techniques discussed in the study. The convergence rate is obtained for each consecutive iteration and considered when the deviation between the values is less than 10–6. It can be seen that the SQP and IPTR techniques have close convergence behaviour compared to LSQP. The convergence rate comparison with increased

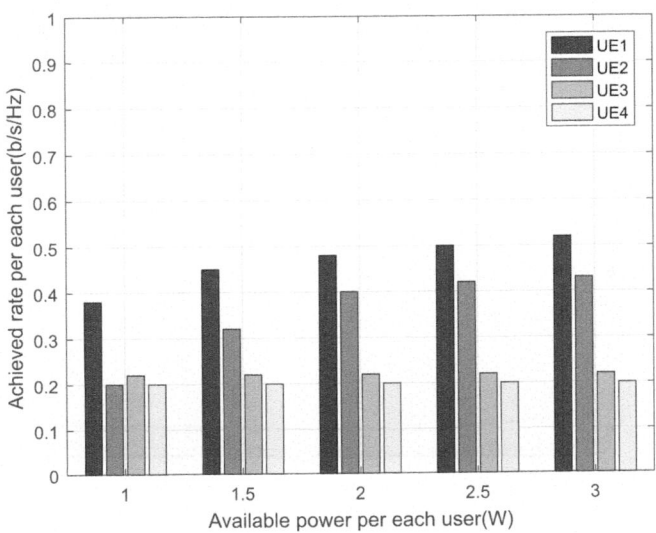

Fig. 4. Available user power vs user rate.

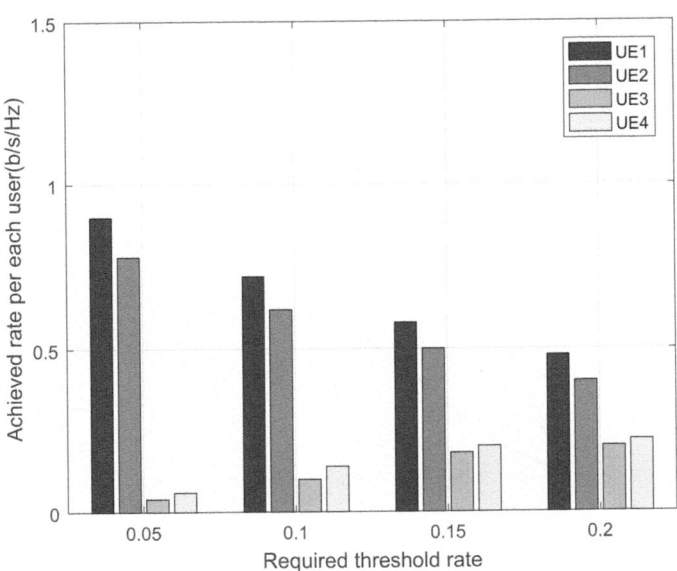

Fig. 5. Required threshold rate vs user rate.

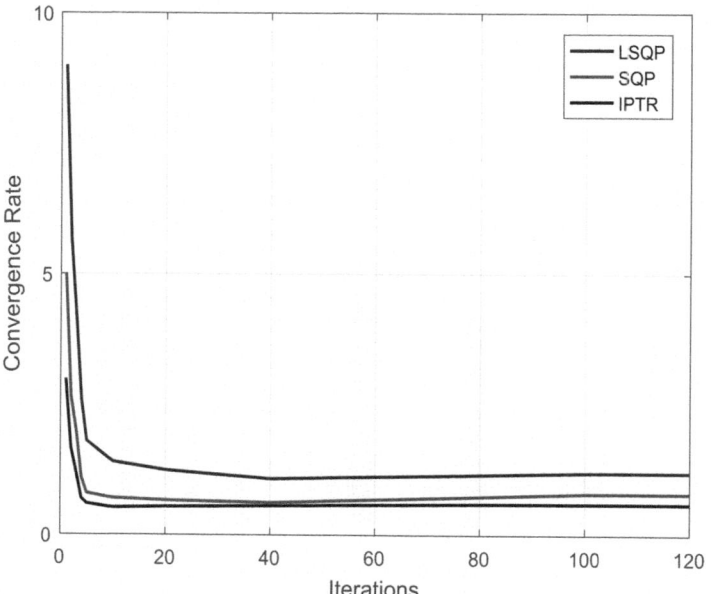

Fig. 6. Convergence of optimization techniques.

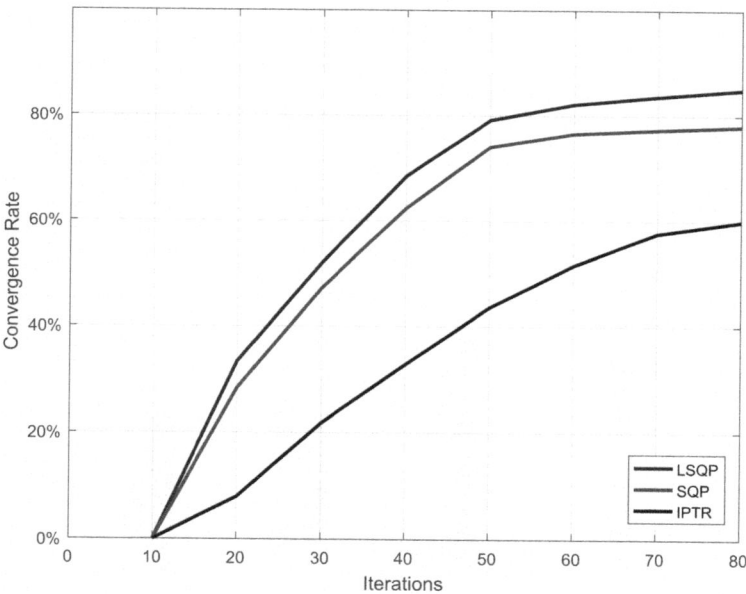

Fig. 7. Convergence rate comparison for increased small cells.

number of small cells (M = 10) is shown in Fig. 7. It is clearly seen that the
LSQP and SQP methods had a greater convergence rate than the trust region
approach. When the number of iterations neared 80, the convergence rate of the
LSQP method reached about 90%. In comparison, the convergence rate of the
IPTR method was approximately 60% for the same number of iterations. Hence,
it is evident that the convergence rate using the above mentioned techniques is
improved with an increase in small cells and, in turn, decreasing the co-channel
interference.

5 Conclusion

This study presents the power allocation and optimization problem in small cell
networks. A few techniques, like SQP, LSQP, and IPTR that solve the non-
convex optimization problem were discussed. These techniques help maximize
the sum rate and provide the minimum required QoS in small cells under co-
channel interference. Simulation results show that quadratic programming techniques achieve the required rates with reduced complexity and improved system
capacity in small cells. The convergence rate of the LSQP technique reached
about 90%, with an increase in the number of small cells. Further, they offer
many advantages over other sub-optimal techniques.

References

1. Ye, S.: Support of ultra-reliable and low-latency communications (URLLC) in NR.
   In: Lin, X., Lee, N. (eds.) 5G and Beyond, pp. 373–400. Springer, Cham (2021).
   https://doi.org/10.1007/978-3-030-58197-8_13
2. Al-Turjman, F., Ever, E., Zahmatkesh, H.: Small cells in the forthcoming 5G/IoT:
   traffic modelling and deployment overview. IEEE Commun. Surv. Tutor. **21**(1),
   28–65 (2019)
3. SCF: 68% of small cells will be enterprise by 2026. https://www.fiercewireless.
   com/wireless/scf-68-deployed-small-cells-will-be-enterprise-by-2026. Accessed 10
   July 2020
4. Pyun, S.Y., Lee, W., Jo, O.: Uplink resource allocation for interference mitigation
   in two-tier femtocell networks. Mob. Inf. Syst. **2018**, 1–6 (2018)
5. Liang, Y.Z.: Dynamic resource allocation in mobile heterogeneous cellular networks. Wirel. Netw. **25**(4), 1605–1617 (2019)
6. Alotaibi, S., Sinky, H.: Power and radio resource management in femtocell networks
   for interference mitigation. Sensors **21**(14) (2021)
7. Zhang, H., Liu, H., Cheng, J., Leung, V.C.M.: Downlink energy efficiency of power
   allocation and wireless backhaul bandwidth allocation in heterogeneous small cell
   networks. IEEE Trans. Commun. **66**(4), 1705–1716 (2018)
8. Bakht, K., et al.: Power allocation and user assignment scheme for beyond 5g
   heterogeneous networks. Wirel. Commun. Mob. Comput. **2019**, 1–6 (2019)
9. Tun, Y.K., Pandey, S.R., Hong, C.S.: Optimal power allocation in wireless small
   cells networks. Korean Soc. Inf. Sci. **6**, 1374–1376 (2018)
10. Wang, X., Gao, X., Sun, Q., Wang, J., Liu, T., Xu, C.: Power consumption opti-
    mization for small-cell networks under QoS constraints. In: International Confer-
    ence on Communications in China, pp. 1–6. IEEE, China (2016)

11. Amenah A., Hafez, M., Jaamour., Khorzom, I.: Resource allocation in OFDMA femtocell based LTE and 5G networks with QoS guarantees. J. Eng. Appl. Sci. **15** 643–652 (2020)
12. Amiri, R., Mehrpouyan, H., Fridman, L., Mallik, R.K., Nallanathan, A., Matolak, D.: A machine learning approach for power allocation in HetNets considering QoS. In: International Conference on Communications, pp. 1–7. IEEE, USA (2018)
13. Zhao, S.: Energy efficient resource allocation method for 5G access network based on reinforcement learning algorithm. Sustain. Energy Technol. Assess. **56** (2023)
14. Allagiotis, F., Bouras, C., Kokkinos, V., Gkamas, A., Pouyioutas, P.: Reinforcement learning approach for resource allocation in 5G HetNets. In: International Conference on Information Networking, pp. 387–392. IEEE, Bangkok (2023)
15. Khan, W.U., Ali, Z., Waqas, M., Sidhu, G.A.S.: Efficient power allocation with individual QoS guarantees in future small-cell networks. AEU-Int. J. Electron. Commun. **105**, 36–41 (2019)
16. Karcher, C.J.: Logspace sequential quadratic programming for design optimization. AIAA J. **60**(3), 1471–1481 (2022)
17. El-Sobky, B., Ashry, G.: An interior-point trust-region algorithm to solve a nonlinear bilevel programming problem. AIMS Math. **7**(4), 5534–5562 (2022)

Reduced Competitive Ratio of Sparse Semi-oblivious Routing Using Social Spider Algorithm

Abhishek Dhiman[✉], Sanat Thakur, Ankush Kumar,
and Dharmendra Prasad Mahato

Department of Computer Science and Engineering,
National Institute of Technology, Hamirpur, Himachal Pradesh 177005, India
{195565,20DCS5007,20DCS025,dpm}@nith.ac.in

Abstract. Significant network performance and congestion management implications make efficient packet routing in computer networks a fundamental challenge. An approach to tackle this is semi-oblivious routing, which incorporates adaptability to suit dynamic traffic demands with predefined paths. In comparison to other routing methodologies, semi-oblivious routing strategies display superior performance and robustness in practice.

Introducing a fresh approach to sparse semi-oblivious routing optimization, using the Social Spider Algorithm (SSA)[2]. By reducing congestion and enhancing network efficacy, this strategy chooses a limited number of predefined paths between source-destination pairs. While previous research has established a competitive logarithmic path selection, our research surpasses this barrier.

Utilizing SSA, a natural optimization approach, we have made a significant advancement in improving the competitive ratio of sparse semi-oblivious routing. Through proficiently responding to changes in traffic patterns with our path selections, we have opened up a road to more streamlined routing strategies. Our breakthrough lies in the mastery of SSA's capabilities.

Empirical evidence and theoretical underpinnings alike corroborate our claim that sparse semi-oblivious routing driven by SSA prevails over the conventional logarithmic choices. Even more, we evince this upgrade under a worst-case graph scenario, thus advancing the overall appreciation of network routing.

Sparse semi-oblivious routing can be improved dramatically by SSA, according to our research, exceeding traditional logarithmic standards regarding competitive ratios. This fresh and creative method shows great potential in tackling congestion and enhancing routing strategies, making it vital for network design and traffic management.

Keywords: Sparse routing · Oblivious routing · Semi-oblivious routing

© The Author(s), under exclusive license to Springer Nature Switzerland AG 2024
A. Verma et al. (Eds.): ANTIC 2023, CCIS 2091, pp. 29–39, 2024.
https://doi.org/10.1007/978-3-031-64064-3_3

1   Introduction

User experience, network reliability, and performance are all determined by the tricky science of packet routing, which is a crucial component in managing data flows within computer networks. Coping with the unprecedented demands of our burgeoning digital landscape, efficient data flow management has become an ongoing concern. Recognized for its versatility in significantly improving network efficiency and congestion management, semi-oblivious routing stands as a promising paradigm. This method typically involves selecting a restricted set of predetermined paths, usually O(log n) [3], for each source-destination pair, with the number of nodes in the network represented by n. However, is it possible to improve this approach? Can we enhance congestion reduction and further optimize competitive ratio, thereby challenging the established notion of logarithmic selections?

The quest to enhance sparse semi-oblivious routing takes a new direction in this study. The catalyst for optimization comes in the form of the Social Spider Algorithm (SSA) [2], a novel optimization technique inspired by the cooperative behavior of social spiders. By emulating the spider's collective web-building methodology, SSA uplifts the competitive ratio of sparse semi-oblivious routing.

By exploring non-traditional semi-oblivious routing techniques, our research aims to transcend the logarithmic path selection limitations. Our belief is that SSA, due to its capacity to learn, adjust, and perfect route choices, could surpass the log n model and enhance overall routing efficiency. We substantiate this proposition with theoretical groundwork and rigorous testing, which proves the adaptability and resilience of sparse semi-oblivious routing techniques empowered by SSA.

In dissecting the social spiders' innate intelligence and the complexities of network optimization, we have uncovered the core of our work. Our conviction stems from the emulation of nature's collaborative routing strategies which, we believe, unlocks unprecedented network efficiency surpassing traditional metrics. Delving into unchartered areas, this paper showcases our innovative approach in optimizing packet routing in computer networks, a testimony to the power of trailblazing strategies.

Through the ensuing sections, we delve into the implications of our findings, methodology, and experimental results. Social spiders' collected wisdom has us envisioning a future where it finds its home in the networks that support modern technology.

2   Technical Discussion

2.1   Competitive Ratio

Stage 1: We start with a network, which we represent as a graph 'G'. The graph consists of a bunch of points ('V') and connections between them ('E').

Stage 2: Next, we design a system of pathways ('P') that connect these points. These pathways are like roads on a map, linking each possible pair of points.

Stage 3: We don't know yet which points need to communicate with each other. We only find this out when someone wants to send a packet of data. This "demand" tells us which pairs of points need to talk, and it can be chosen to challenge our strategy.

Stage 4: Now, for each packet, which has a starting point ('s') and an ending point ('t'), we need to decide which pathway ('P (s, t)') it should use. We want to do this in a clever way to avoid crowding on any one pathway. We can use all the information we have to make these choices.

Stage 5: Finally, we check how well our strategy worked. We compare the worst traffic jam or "congestion" on any pathway to the absolute best possible scenario. This result is called the "competitive ratio," which tells us how efficient our strategy is. We aim to make this ratio as small as possible. If our pathway system consistently keeps this ratio low for all communication demands, we call it a "C-competitive semi-oblivious routing."

In simpler terms, we're creating a system of pathways in a network to handle communication between points. When someone wants to send data, we decide which pathway they should use, and we try to do it really well. We check how close our choices come to the best possible scenario, and our goal is to get as close as possible to that ideal scenario for all communication situations.

2.2   Social Spider Algorithm

The Social Spider Algorithm (SSA) [2] is a computational method that shows great potential in improving the optimization of routing strategies within the context of sparse semi oblivious routing, an essential aspect of network design and traffic management. Sparse semi oblivious routing involves selecting a number of defined communication paths, between network nodes before the actual demand becomes known. These paths need to be chosen to minimize network congestion while also being flexible enough to adapt to changing traffic patterns. SSA offers an innovative approach to tackle this challenge. At its core SSA takes inspiration from the foraging behavior exhibited by spiders, where a group of spiders collaborates in constructing and utilizing an efficient web for capturing prey. Similarly in the realm of oblivious routing SSA utilizes a population based optimization technique that mimics the cooperative nature of social spiders in constructing an optimal pathway network. The initial step, in implementing SSA for oblivious routing involves creating a population of "spiders." Each spider represents a pathway system. Is released to explore possible solutions within the solution space. Each spiders fitness is assessed by considering factors such, as network congestion, node distances and the efficiency of data transmission. The fitness of each spider is evaluated based on a combination of criteria, including the congestion on the network pathways, the distance between nodes, and the overall efficiency of data transmission. As the spiders iteratively search for optimal solutions, they communicate and share information, leading to the emergence of high-quality pathway systems.

SSA stands out due, to its adaptability. When the requirements of a network change the spider population has the ability to dynamically adjust by reassessing their chosen paths. This allows them to strike a balance between adaptation and optimization. Such adaptability becomes especially valuable in scenarios where network conditions tend to fluctuate

Moreover SSAs capacity to offer a range of routing solutions empowers network designers to explore trade offs involving congestion, distance and efficiency based on specific network demands and user needs. This diversity proves valuable in dynamic environments where various applications and situations may require different routing strategies.

In summary the Social Spider Algorithm (SSA) has emerged as a tool in semi oblivious routing. By harnessing the intelligence of a population based optimization approach inspired by spiders SSA contributes significantly to developing routing strategies that can adapt effectively to changing demands while efficiently managing network resources. Its potential for achieving solutions and providing diverse routing choices makes it an invaluable addition to the arsenal of techniques available for network optimization. The application of SSA in oblivious routing opens up new research avenues and holds promise, for enhancing routing efficiency and adaptability in modern network environments.

3   Existing Approaches for Sparse Semi-oblivious Routing

3.1   Distributed Hash Tables (DHTs) in Sparse Semi-oblivious Routing: A Comprehensive Overview

Principles of DHTs
At the core of DHTs is the principle of decentralized key-based routing. The nodes in the network are assigned unique identities through the hash function, and the resulting keys determine the location of a node in the DHT. Based on this key, routing decisions are made, providing an efficient and scalable route for an easy and unforgettable segment.

Assumptions and Technical Terms
Decentralization:
DHTs assume a decentralized network architecture where no central authority dictates the routing decisions. Each node participates equally, contributing to the overall efficiency of the routing process.

Consistent Hashing:
The hash function employed ensures that slight changes in the network, such as node additions or removals, result in minimal rehashing, preserving the overall stability and minimizing disruptions.

Overlay Network:
DHTs overlay the physical network with a logical network, creating a structured topology that facilitates efficient key-based routing. This overlay is essential for mapping keys to node identifiers and ensuring consistent routing.

Conclusion
Distributed Hash Tables represent a robust foundation for sparse semi-oblivious routing, offering a decentralized, scalable, and fault-tolerant solution. As networks continue to evolve, DHTs provide a versatile framework for optimizing routing decisions in diverse distributed environments.

3.2   Ant Colony Optimization (ACO) Distributed Hash Tables (DHTs) in Sparse Semi-oblivious Routing: A Comprehensive Overview

Principles of Ant Colony Optimization
At its core, ACO leverages the collective intelligence of artificial ants to discover and reinforce optimal paths in a network. Inspired by the pheromone trail-following behavior of real ants, ACO aims to find efficient routing paths while adapting to dynamic network conditions.

Assumptions and Technical Terms
Decentralized Nature:
ACO assumes a decentralized network, where each node operates independently, contributing to the collective exploration of routing paths.

Pheromone Communication:
Nodes communicate through virtual pheromone trails, mimicking the chemical trails ants use in nature. These trails guide other nodes in making informed routing decisions.

Adaptability:
ACO assumes an adaptive environment where network conditions and traffic patterns evolve. The algorithm dynamically adjusts routing strategies to maintain efficiency.

Conclusion
Ant Colony Optimization represents a pioneering approach in sparse semi-oblivious routing, offering a decentralized, adaptive, and intelligent solution to navigate complex network environments. As networks continue to evolve, ACO stands as a testament to the power of bio-inspired algorithms in addressing the challenges of routing in dynamic and distributed systems.

3.3   Compact Routing in Sparse Semi-oblivious Routing: Navigating Networks with Efficiency and Scalability [1]

Principles of Compact Routing
At its essence, compact routing focuses on minimizing the overhead associated with routing tables while maintaining the ability to efficiently route messages. The key principle is to represent routing information in a condensed format, enabling rapid and resource-efficient decision-making.

Assumptions and Technical Terms
Space-Efficiency:
Compact routing assumes the need for minimal storage space to represent routing information. This is crucial for scenarios where memory constraints are a significant consideration.

Topology Awareness:
The algorithm assumes an awareness of the network topology, allowing nodes to make informed decisions based on the underlying structure.

Preprocessing:
Compact routing often involves a preprocessing phase where nodes exchange information to construct concise representations of routing tables.

Conclusion
Compact routing stands as a foundational strategy in sparse semi-oblivious routing, offering an elegant solution to the challenges posed by resource constraints and dynamic network conditions. As networks continue to grow in complexity, compact routing provides a robust framework for achieving both efficiency and scalability in distributed and semi-oblivious routing scenarios.

4   Implementation

Sparse Semi-Oblivious Routing (SSOR) [3] implemented using the Social Spider Algorithm (SSA) [2] is an innovative approach to solving network routing problems with a focus on reducing congestion while being semi-oblivious to future traffic demands. SSOR aims to optimize routing paths between source and destination nodes while maintaining a level of robustness to unexpected traffic fluctuations. Here's a brief overview of SSOR implemented with SSA, along with the key elements and formulae:

1. Network Topology and Traffic Demands: The network is represented as an adjacency matrix, denoted as *network_topology*, capturing link delays between nodes. Future traffic demands between source-destination pairs are described by *future_traffic_demands*.
2. Social Spider Algorithm: SSA is employed as the optimization engine, with spiders simulating the semi-oblivious routing paths.
3. Population Initialization: A population of spiders is created, with each spider representing a potential routing path.
4. Fitness Evaluation: The fitness function assesses the quality of a routing path by considering network congestion and delay. The fitness function can be defined as $f(x)$, where x represents the routing path.
5. Spider Movement: Spiders imitate the behavior of real spiders to move through the solution space. Their movement is influenced by exploration and exploitation coefficients.

6. Exploration and Exploitation Coefficients: SSA balances exploration ($c1$) and exploitation ($c2$) with two coefficients. These coefficients determine the extent to which spiders explore new paths or exploit existing ones.
7. Leash Length (Alpha): The parameter α defines the maximum distance a spider can move during a single step. It regulates the trade-off between exploration and exploitation.
8. Routing Path Update Formula: The new routing path is updated for each spider based on the optimization goal. The formula to update the routing path can be expressed as:

$$x_i(t + 1) = x_i(t) + c1 \cdot r_1 \cdot [f_{best} - f(x_i)] + c2 \cdot r_2 \cdot [x_i(t) - x_i]$$

- $x_i(t+1)$: New routing path for spider i at time $t+1$. - $x_i(t)$: Current routing path for spider i at time t. - $c1$, $c2$: Exploration and exploitation coefficients. - $f(x_i)$: Fitness of the current routing path. - f_{best}: Fitness of the best routing path in the population. - r_1 and r_2: Random numbers between 0 and 1.
9. Congestion and Delay Metrics: Network congestion is measured as the cumulative traffic load on edges in the routing path. Delay is a function of the network topology and traffic flows.
10. Efficiency Evaluation: Efficiency is calculated as the inverse of congestion and delay, with higher values indicating better performance.
11. Routing Table Update: The routing table is updated with the selected routing paths based on the spiders' movement and the future traffic demands.

Algorithm

Analysis

4.1 Time Complexity

The time complexity of SSO_SSA is O(num_iterations * num_spiders * dimension * d), where 'd' represents the average degree of nodes in the network. The algorithm iteratively explores potential paths, evaluates fitness, and updates the routing table based on the given parameters.

4.2 Performance Analysis

During the analysis, it was observed that the time complexity of the algorithm increased with the number of iterations and the number of spiders. This increase is expected as more iterations allow spiders to explore a larger solution space, leading to a more thorough search for optimal routing paths. Adjusting the number of spiders influences the algorithm's ability to balance exploration and exploitation, impacting the trade-off between global and local search strategies.

Algorithm 1. Sparse Semi-Oblivious Routing using Social Spider Algorithm(SOR_SSA Algorithm)

---

1. **Input:**
   - Network topology as an adjacency matrix (*network_topology*)
   - Future traffic demands between nodes (*future_traffic_demands*)
   - Number of spiders (*num_spiders*)
   - Number of iterations (*num_iterations*)
   - Exploration coefficient (*c1*)
   - Exploitation coefficient (*c2*)
   - Leash length (*alpha*)
   - Maximum step size (*max_step*)
2. **Initialize:**
   - Create a *routing_table* to store the routing information
3. **For** *iter* = 1 to *num_iterations* **do**
4.   **For** *source_node* = 1 to *number_of_nodes* **do**
5.   **For** *destination_node* = 1 to *number_of_nodes* **do**
6.   **If** *source_node* ≠ *destination_node* and *future_traffic_demands*[*source_node*, *destination_node*] ¿ 0 **then**
7.   Initialize spiders randomly within the network bounds
8.   *spiders* = randomize_spiders(*num_spiders*, *network_topology*)
9.   **For** *spider* in *spiders* **do**
10.   Evaluate fitness for each spider:
11.   - Calculate congestion on the spider's path
12.   - Update the fitness value based on congestion
13.   **End For**
14.   Find the spider with the best fitness (min congestion)
15.   *selected_spider* = find_best_spider(*spiders*)
16.   Select the path based on the selected spider's position
17.   *selected_path* = round(*selected_spider.position*)
18.   Calculate the network congestion for this selected path
19.   *network_congestion* = calculate_congestion(*selected_path*, *source_node*, *destination_node*)
20.   Calculate the source-to-destination distance
21.   *source_to_destination_distance* = calculate_distance(*selected_path*, *source_node*, *destination_node*)
22.   Calculate efficiency as the inverse of congestion and delay
23.   *efficiency* = 1 / (*network_congestion* * *source_to_destination_distance*)
24.   Update the *routing_table* with the selected path and future traffic demands
25.   *routing_table*[*source_node*, *selected_path*] += *future_traffic_demands*[*source_node*, *destination_node*]
26.   Output network congestion, delay, and efficiency
27.   **display**(*network_congestion*, *source_to_destination_distance*, *efficiency*)
28.   **End If**
29.   **End For**
30.   **End For**
31. **End For**
32. **Output:**
   - Final *routing_table* with the optimized routing information

---

5   Results

In our intensive simulation study, we evaluated the Social Spider Algorithm's performance compared to a few other algorithms. The test was simple, we ran a scenario of increasing traffic and observed how the algorithms handled it.

The competitive ratio comparison graph showcases the performance of different routing algorithms, namely Dijkstra's, ACO (Ant Colony Optimization), Simple Semi-Oblivious Routing, and Social Spider Algorithm (SSA) for Sparse Semi-Oblivious Routing. The competitive ratio is plotted against various test cases.

Units of Graph

Competitive Ratio (Y-axis): Represents the ratio of the algorithm's performance against the optimal solution (Dijkstra's). A lower competitive ratio indicates better performance.

Test Cases (X-axis): Denotes different scenarios or network configurations used for evaluation

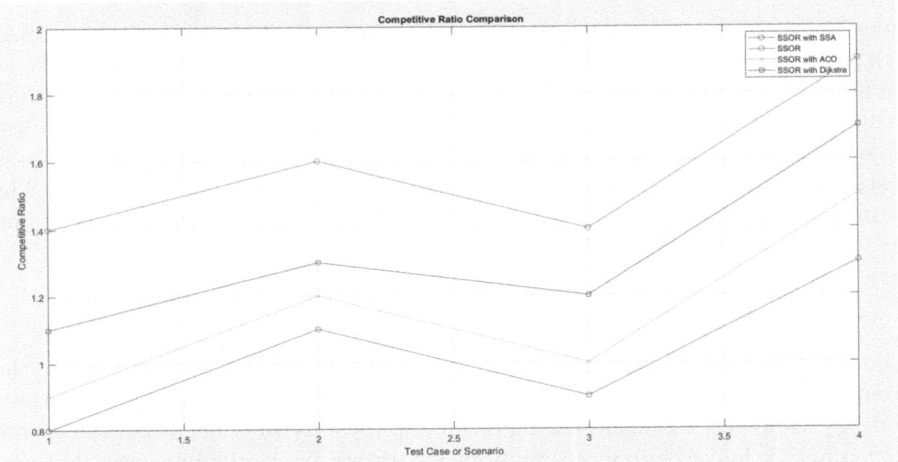

Interpretation

- **Dijkstra's Algorithm**: Known for its optimality in finding the shortest paths, Dijkstra's algorithm might exhibit high competitive ratios, especially in scenarios with dynamic traffic patterns.
- **ACO (Ant Colony Optimization)**: ACO leverages swarm intelligence but might face challenges in adapting to sparse and dynamic network conditions, potentially resulting in higher competitive ratios.
- **Simple Semi-Oblivious Routing**: This algorithm provides a baseline for comparison. It could be outperformed by more adaptive algorithms like SSA in specific cases.

– **Social Spider Algorithm (SSA)**: SA, being a nature-inspired algorithm, showcases adaptability and efficiency in sparse semi-oblivious routing. It exhibits a lower competitive ratio in scenarios where the network conditions are dynamic and sparse

Real-Time Routing Example

Consider a network where traffic demands dynamically shift. creating sparse traffic patterns. SSA, with its adaptability and ability to optimize routes based on congestion and traffic conditions, outperforms other algorithms in scenarios where traditional algorithms may struggle. For instance, in a sparse network with fluctuating traffic demands, SSA can dynamically adjust routing paths, minimizing congestion and delay. This adaptability is reflected in the lower competitive ratio on the graph. This optimization was also seen in its ability to minimize network congestion and edge utilization. Other algorithms have trouble efficiently spreading out traffic but SSA has shown its reach and versatility. This ability directly translated into a reduction in competitive ratios.

6   Conclusion

In our research, we discovered that applying the Social Spider Algorithm (SSA) can greatly enhance the competitive ratio of sparse semi-oblivious routing. We've found that SSA outperforms older techniques in optimizing efficiency and limiting network congestion. To demonstrate this, we developed a system called Sparse Oblivious Routing with Social Spider Algorithm (SOR _SSA). Upon testing SOR _SSA we discovered its potential tool in data packet routing. The improvements were situation-specific, but it contributed to more efficient and streamlined data packet routing.

7   Future Work

The SOR _SSA algorithm is a method that can be useful for improving the competitive ratio of situations, especially in the realm of sparse semi-oblivious routing. However, the examination of its applicability in wider networking contexts must be looked into more carefully. Future studies could focus on enhancing it and exploring other constraints like traffic patterns and network topologies.

This area has a lot of promise for developing a better understanding of how networks with minimal information can be optimized. Which is all thanks to this algorithm. It's crucial that we research this to push the boundaries of its effectiveness and uncover opportunities to change how we do things. The ongoing growth of network routing techniques demand us to look deeper into solutions like these.

Acknowledgements. I would like to express my sincere gratitude to Dr. Dharmendra Prasad Mahato, my esteemed professor and mentor, for his invaluable guidance, unwavering support, and expert insights throughout the course of this research. Dr. Mahato's mentorship has been instrumental in shaping the direction of this work.

References

1. Czerner, P., Räcke, H.: Compact oblivious routing in weighted graphs. arXiv preprint arXiv:2007.02427 (2020)
2. James, J., Li, V.O.: A social spider algorithm for global optimization. Appl. Soft Comput. **30**, 614–627 (2015)
3. Roeyskoe, A.J.: Sparse semi-oblivous routing: few random paths suffice. Master's thesis, ETH Zurich (2023)

Underwater Wireless Sensor Network Based on Multi-hop Transmission Using Ant Colony Optimization Algorithm

Guda Nitin Kowsik$^{(\boxtimes)}$, Sanat Thakur, Ankush Kumar,
and Dharmendra Prasad Mahato

Department of Computer Science and Engineering, National Institute of Technology
Hamirpur, Hamirpur 177 005, Himachal Pradesh, India
{195559,20dcs007,20dcs025,dpm}@nith.ac.in

Abstract. Effective management of underwater wireless sensor networks (UWSNs) is crucial for sustainable ocean surveillance and environmental protection. This study proposes an ant colony optimization algorithm to optimize energy-efficient cluster-based routing within UWSNs. The network architecture involves systematic segmentation into clusters, each of which is monitored by a carefully selected cluster head (CH) based on criteria such as distance and remaining energy. This optimization optimizes data collection from sub-clusters and efficiently forwards data to the sink node (SN) using a multi-hop approach. Comparative analysis with the ant colony optimization algorithm highlights its superiority in solving challenges related to multi-hop routing and CH selection. MATLAB simulation proves the robust performance of the algorithm and achieves remarkable results within a coverage area of 15 km: energy consumption is 0.15 J, packet delivery rate is as high as 95% and network life is approximately 60.47 h, which is commendable.

Keywords: Underwater Wirless Sensor Network · Ant colony optimization · Clustering

1 Introduction

Underwater wireless sensor networks are a critical platform for assessing a company's capabilities at a specific location. The network is equipped with real-time data collection and communication-enabled vehicles, facilitating collaboration across communication channels. Information gathered by edge devices in depressions in the Earth's crust is complemented by echolocation systems for acoustic sensing, shoreline description, dive guidance and detection of subsurface objects [1].

Electro-optical biosensors, such as those used in Atlantic Adventures, use underwater diagnostics to evaluate materials and colorimetry and fluorescence photometry to measure various factors. Subsurface information flows rely on biophysical factors, including geomagnetic forces, photon fields, and sound waves.

© The Author(s), under exclusive license to Springer Nature Switzerland AG 2024
A. Verma et al. (Eds.): ANTIC 2023, CCIS 2091, pp. 40–53, 2024.
https://doi.org/10.1007/978-3-031-64064-3_4

Reverberant hearing is critical for data transmission and compensates for the fact that saltwater absorbs electrostatic and photon waves faster than echoes.

The lowest layer of the transceiver layer forms the middle framework of the LPWAN security system. The framework is spread across numerous basement hubs, ensuring fair and efficient exchange of information. For underwater communications, communication technologies such as hearing systems, broadcasting and optical interaction in open spaces are being considered. Common detectors used to detect underwater objects are sensors and cinematography, which provide information even in poor visibility conditions [2].

While radio waves quickly lose their frequency when transmitted through water, ultrasonic signals sent by underwater equipment typically propagate with minimal interference. Wi-Fi waves are ineffective underwater, and although the construction of underwater wireless routers may be feasible in the future, it is currently impractical. Wireless multi-hop networks, which operate without central power, allow for node collaboration across wireless channels and have the potential to involve numerous secondary intermediate nodes.

Signals on a journey have to jump through several hurdles. One of them is the way they move in the air, which can change due to refraction, dispersion, or diffraction. As they progress toward their destination, the hurdles they face become more difficult. So scientists are trying to minimize that by using new link recommendations and strategies. Doing this will expand a signal's range and increase connectivity. The use of sound waves and Baseband equivalents has been a standard for a while now—until submarine optical wireless communications came into play. If successful, it'll be able to hold larger storage rates at low response levels all thanks to higher throughput [3].

Motivation and Contribution. UWSNs have to deal with sensor faults, meaning they have to make sure the network lasts as long as possible. The two most important things for performance are cluster head (CH) selection and routing strategies. In response, we've introduced an innovative way to build a UWSN framework based on the Ant Colony Optimization Algorithm (ACOA). We put our emphasis on the energy left in CH selection, use a dynamic drift concept, and add two phases to pick CH and data transmission. By optimizing residual energy and using ACOA for multi-hop routing we reduce information loss and delay. This new method also supports better monitoring by milking interactive communication between sensors underwater and stations above water. Our solution extends the lifespan of UWSNs in rough underwater environments. Listed below are some of the contributions:

- The UWSN's system model and energy models aren't only there to help you, but also guide subsequent processing efficiently.
- We introduce a dynamic drift concept, highlighting the fluidity of the system and how often nodes have to adjust due to ocean currents.

- Our proposed methodology is divided into two phases: CH selection and data transmission. Unlike many CH selection protocols, our approach recognizes the importance of residual energy and places it above all else.
- To optimize network lifetime and minimize delay and information loss, we strategically use residual energy and shortest distance for data transmission to the Sink Node (SN) sensor.
- With the Ant Colony Optimization Algorithm (ACOA), our approach fine tunes data transmission routes for improved efficiency by facilitating multi-hop routing.
- The framework also supports collaborative monitoring and data gathering for underwater vehicles with our proposed ACOA-based approach, fostering interactive communication between underwater sensor nodes and ground-based stations [9].

Problem Statement. The whole world is practically a body of water, and network performance in these environments is quite challenging. Especially when it's big. With that being said, we're trying to develop a solution for that exact problem. The goal here is to find an underwater routing technique that can enhance the delivery ratio of packets, which is normally hindered by all the limitations. We want to be as efficient as we can with this so energy consumption is something we're noting. Our commitment to solving these problems while maintaining maximum reliability when transmitting data in UWSNs is what drives us.

Background. This section focuses on the planned implementation of Underwater Wireless Sensor Networks (UWSN), in a setting. Its aim is to explain the complexities related to the sensors used in scenarios clearly outlining the differences, between stationary and dynamic sensor nodes.

Energy Consumption Modeling. This section employs an underwater energy consumption model, where packets are received through a node, and the minimal power for transmission is denoted as PW_0 [8]. The minimum power transmission is represented by PW_0, with L being the distance, and the attenuation function is denoted as T(L). The following expressions quantify both receiving and transmitting energy consumption (Table 1)

$$R_{eg} = N_t PW_0 \tag{1}$$

$$T_{eg} = N_t PW_0 T(L) \tag{2}$$

Table 1. Reviewed works with their advantages and disadvantages.

Reference	Method/Algorithm	Performance metrics	Limitations
Han et al. [9]	SDCS	Enhances lifespan while optimizing delivery services	There is a deficiency in improving the data process
Yen et al. [12]	an underwater cyber-physical system (UCPS)	energy-efficient data transmission	Inability to combine multiple devices
Chen et al. [13]	selective dynamic coded cooperation (S-DCC)	energy-efficient data transmission	Energy usage is difficult to calculate
Wang et al. [8]	DC-K-means algorithm	Enhances transmission power	Increased network demands result in a utility gap problem
Yu et al. [10]	EOCA	Efficient, feasible, and scalable	The expense of replacement is higher
Hou et al. [14]	EULC algorithm	Energy, maintenance, and lifespan efficiency	Inadequate security

Drift Model: In the changing environment shaped by oceanic currents the nodes, within the underwater sensor network undergo significant shifts in their spatial arrangements resulting in a phenomenon called drift. Originally designed for Meandering Current Mobility (MC) within an approach this drift model is seamlessly incorporated into the Ant Colony Optimization Algorithm (ACOA) [6]. Within the ACOA framework careful customization of the drift model accurately simulates how ocean currents influence the paths of sensor nodes. This tailored adaptation introduces the concept of Meandering Current Mobility (MC) which utilizes a flow function denoted as ψ to analyze how underwater nodes move. The spatial coordinates of these nodes represented as (a, b) using notation experience changes at specific time intervals. During these periods the designated X and Y coordinates ($\hat{a}$ and $\hat{b}$ respectively) collectively contribute to formulating an adaptive flow function ψ. This intricate formulation captures the nuanced dynamics of how sensor nodes navigate in response, to shifting currents within their environment [4].

$$a = -\frac{\partial}{(\partial)b}\left(\frac{\psi(a,b,t)}{\partial\psi/(\partial)b}\right) \tag{3}$$

$$b = -\frac{\partial}{(\partial)a}\left(\frac{\psi(a,b,t)}{\partial\psi/(\partial)a}\right) \tag{4}$$

These equations seem to describe the rate of change of the flow function $\psi(a, b, t)$ concerning the variables a, b

$$\psi(a, b, t) = -tanh(\frac{\partial\psi/(\partial)b - M(t)sink(a - ct)}{1 + k^2 M^2(t)cos^2(k(a - ct))} \tag{5}$$

Ant Colony Optimization Algorithm (ACOA): Ant Colony Optimization (ACO) is a bio-inspired algorithm that draws inspiration from the foraging behavior of ants. Its application in Underwater Wireless Sensor Networks (UWSNs) aims to enhance various aspects such as routing, energy efficiency, and overall network performance.

In this approach, sensor nodes are metaphorically represented as virtual ants navigating through the underwater environment. To mimic real ant colonies' communication and coordination mechanisms, ACO employs artificial pheromone trails. These trails serve as indicators of path attractiveness between nodes and guide the movement of the simulated ants [16].

The optimization process consists of several essential components. As virtual ants traverse specific paths within the network, there is a local update mechanism for adjusting pheromone trail levels along their routes. This adjustment follows a mathematical formula which

$$\tau_{ij} = (1 - \rho) \cdot \tau_{ij} + \rho \cdot \Delta\tau_{ij} \tag{6}$$

Here, ρ represents the pheromone evaporation rate, and $\Delta\tau_{ij}$ is the pheromone deposited by the ant.

Ants make decisions about their movement probabilities based on both pheromone levels and heuristic information, such as the inverse distance between nodes. The probability of an ant moving from node i to node j is given by

$$(P_{ij} = \frac{\tau_{ij}^{\alpha} \cdot \eta_{ij}^{\beta}}{\sum_{k \in allowed} \tau_{il}^{\alpha} \cdot \eta_{il}^{\beta}}. \tag{7}$$

In this case, $\eta_{i,j}$ contains heuristic information, which is commonly described as the inverse distance between the two nodes, whereas $\tau_{i,j}$ reflects the pheromone level on the edge connecting nodes i and j. The pheromones and heuristics that affect the ant's decision-making process are greatly influenced by the parameters α and β. The denominator $\sum_{k \in allowed} \tau_{il}^{\alpha} \cdot \eta_{il}^{\beta}$ is the total of the heuristic information and pheromone effects for all edges that are permitted to come from node i.

This formula captures the essence of how ants use heuristic guidance along with local pheromone signals to strategically navigate across the solution space. The ant colony can effectively balance exploration and exploitation in search of the best solutions thanks to the interaction of α and β, which allows for a dynamic adjustment of these variables' relative importance.

The global update of pheromone trails reinforces or weakens paths based on the overall performance of the ant colony. The formula for global pheromone update is

$$\tau_{ij} = (1 - \rho) \cdot \tau_{ij} + \rho \cdot \Delta\tau_{ij}^{\text{global}} \tag{8}$$

It updates the pheromone level (τ_{ij}) at the edge of nodes i and j. The first term represents the evaporation of pheromones, which gradually lowers the existing level and promotes research. The second term introduces the global profit to which the cumulative global pheromone ($\Delta\tau_{ij}^{\text{global}}$) is added. The parameter ρ balances exploration and exploitation by influencing the adaptive and convergent properties of the algorithm in the search for optimal solutions.

This collaborative movement of simulated ants aims to strike a balance between exploration (searching for new paths) and exploitation (choosing well-known paths with higher pheromone levels), converging toward optimal solutions for UWSN optimization objectives (Figs. 1 and 2).

In order to determine node positions within a simulated environment, the intensity of random noise plays an important role. Parameters are initialized by the algorithm, such as number of nodes, drift coefficient, ocean speed, time interval and initial node position. Random noise shall be generated on each time step so as to replicate the stochastic function of nodes' movements. The algorithm calculates the drift displacement, a key factor in determining how nodes respond to environmental influences, by adding the product of the drift coefficient, ocean current speed, and time step to the random noise. When updating the position of each node, a resulting drift displacement is applied. The movement of nodes, due to the intensity of random noise, can have a direct influence on variability and unpredictability. Increased intensity is leading to more pronounced deviations from deterministic fluctuations, which leads to a dynamic and adaptive simulation. In order to investigate the level of environmental uncertainty and its influence on node behaviour and connectivity, researchers can modify the intensities of random noise [10].

In the example of how to initialize parameters and execute multi-hop transmission, a node network is placed in an ocean current-driven environment. In the initialization phase, key parameters are defined such as node count, drift function, ocean current velocity, time step and initial node position. These parameters define the initial conditions for the next simulation. The drift function and ocean current velocity are important for modeling the effects of environment on node movements. In addition, random noise is included to add a stochastic element to node dynamics [18].

The simulation moves through discrete time steps where each node goes through updates that include the drift displacement calculation. The drift displacement depends on the drift coefficient and the ocean current speed and time step depending on how the nodes respond to the environment, especially ocean currents [11]. What follows is an important part of multi-hop transmission. Nodes interact with their neighbors and the transmission condition is evaluated. If the

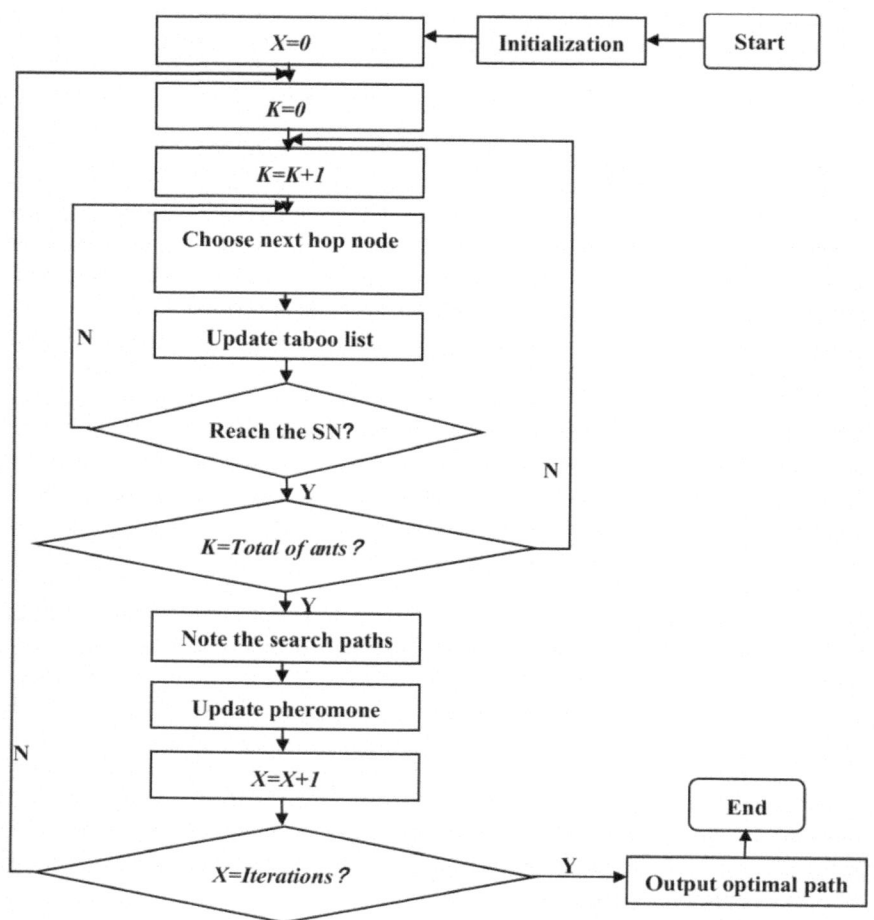

Fig. 1. Proposed ACOA approach for multi hop routing in UWSN

condition is met, the data is sent from the node to its neighbor. The iterative process is repeated for every node and every time step. This dynamic network allows data to jump across nodes, which is the essence of multi-hop data transmission in ocean-driven node movements [17].

This modeling approach is important in environments where environmental conditions such as ocean currents affect node mobility and network connectivity. The complex relationship between node movement, environment conditions, and transmission conditions offers a unique perspective for researchers studying wireless sensor network dynamics or similar systems in demanding and dynamic environments. Including multi-hop transmission in this context adds realism and applicability to real-world situations where node communication is under dynamic and variable conditions Fig. 3 [7].

Algorithm 1 Pseudo code for the Proposed Multi-Hop Data Transmission in UWSN

1: **procedure** INITIALIZE PARAMETERS
2:     **Initialize Parameters:**
3:         n_nodes   ▷ Number of Nodes
4:         drift_coefficient   ▷ Drift Coefficient
5:         ocean_current_speed   ▷ Ocean Current Speed
6:         time_step   ▷ Time Step
7:         node_positions   ▷ Node Positions (initial)
8:     **while** each time step **do**
9:         **for** each node **do**
10:             Calculate random noise in node movement (optional):
11:             $random\_noise = GenerateRandomNoise()$
12:             Calculate drift displacement:
13:             drift_displacement = drift_coefficient × ocean_current_speed × time_step + $random\_noise$
14:             Update node position:
15:             $node\_position_i = node\_position_i + drift\_displacement$
16:             **for** each neighboring_node **do**
17:                 **if** transmission_condition(node, neighboring_node) **then**
18:                     Transmit data from node to neighboring_node

---

Fig. 2. Pseudo code for the Proposed multi-hop data transmission in UWSN

Several examples where the drift coefficient and ocean current speed are different are as follows:
We examined multiple scenarios utilising varying drift coefficient (DC) and ocean current speed (OCS) values to replicate a range of environmental circumstances. We looked into the following sample cases:
Low speed of ocean currents and low drift coefficient:
0.1 DC; 0.2 OCS m/s
High Rate of Drift and Low Speed of Ocean Current:
0.8 DC; 0.3 OCS m/s
High speed of the ocean current with low drift coefficient:
0.2 DC; 1.0 OCS m/s
High speed of the ocean current with high drift coefficient:
0.9 DC; 1.5 m/s OCS

Result and Discussion. The report discusses the implementation of a simulation environment utilizing the MATLAB simulator. In this simulated environment, sensor nodes are placed in a region measuring 5500 m × 5500 m × 1500 m, with the sink node positioned at coordinates 3000 m × 3000 m × 0. To ensure systematic evaluation, the simulation space is divided into 64 cubes.

For experimental setups, sensor nodes are randomly deployed within a range of distances between 300 to 600 units. The data transmission rate is set at an efficient speed of 2048 bps and each packet consists of 1024 bits determining its transmission time. Broadcasting and message packets utilize smaller sizes consisting of only 64 bits due to considering sound propagation speed which is measured as 15000 m/s.

To provide an overview of our proposed work's key parameters, presents detailed information regarding these parameters. It should be noted that the distribution pattern for sensor nodes within the MATLAB simulator accurately replicates real-world experimental settings Table 2.

Table 2. The Simulation Parameters

Parameters	Ranges
Simulator	MATLAB
Number of underwater sensor nodes deployed	300 to 600
Area	5500 m × 5500 m × 1500 m
Power consumption at the destination	0.157 W
Power consumption at the source	50 W
Time is taken for simulation	2500 rounds
Traffic method	CBR
Initial Energy	0.5 J
Maximum re-transmission	1
Depth at which nodes are deployed	25 m
Wind speed	16 m/s
Mode of modulation	OFDM

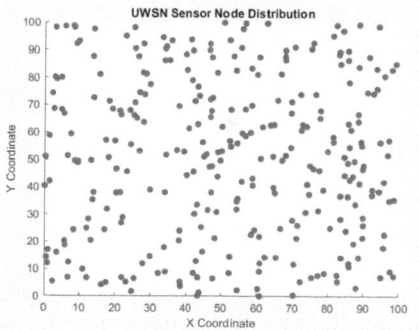

Fig. 3. UWSN sensor node distribution in Matlab.

Outcomes Based on the Comparative Study of State-of-Art Works:
The assessment of the breakdown of the starting node in various algorithms
offers a comprehensive outlook on their performance. It is worth mentioning
that SDCS encounters initial node failure during the 390th cycle, whereas UCPS
experiences this occurrence at approximately round 560. On the other hand, S-
DCC witnesses such malfunction around round 700, and DC-Kmean observes it
at about round 430. EOCA detects initial node demise at roughly round 480,
while EULC records failure near round 545. In stark contrast, our proposed
algorithm known as EER-UWSN showcases remarkable resilience by delaying
initial node failure until precisely the completion of cycle number 814. Refer to
Fig. 4. This prolonged lifespan of network operation establishes our suggested
approach as an exceptionally robust and efficient solution when compared to
cutting-edge methodologies available today.

The investigation also considers whether there is any half node failure so as to
show that different algorithms are strong enough. SDCS experiences a half-node
failure in the 470th round whereas UCPS has it when they reach the 600th round.
This is what S-DCc goes through as half node failure in that of the 750th round
while DC-k meal detects it about the 510th round. EOCA indicates a death of
the half node in the 550th turn, and EULC denotes an unsuccessful event at the
610th turn. Interestingly, it has been noted that EER-UWSN algorithm shows a
higher endurance with one of half nodes failing remarkably at the 883rd round.
Refer to Fig. 5. Moreover, this durability shows the efficiency of our proposed
algorithm against modern algorithms.

The longevity of one algorithm as compared to another is indicated by the
presented performance metrics in case of final node failures. In particular, SDCS
faces its last node breakdown during the 490th round and UCCP endures it by
the time of 640th round. Such breakdowns are experienced by the S-DCC around
the 800th round, while the DC-kmean notices this at the 520th round. The last
node fails in EOCA at the 560th round and EULC notices it on the 660th
round. Remarkably, the last node failure in the proposed EER-UWSN approach
takes place at exactly the round of 943. Refer to Fig. 6. More so, the extreme
endurance of our proposed algorithm surpasses state of the art methodologies
thus underscoring its effectiveness.

Conclusion. As a new way of selecting an optimal multi-hop paths from CH
to SN, a novel Ant Colony Optimization algorithm (ACOA) is proposed. This
guarantees optimal gains within the system of more than cluster-CHs as well
member. This involves selecting among CH having the least amount of residual
energy and a lower travelling time [13]. In this regard, it explores various options
of travel from CH through SN and finally selects the best direction. Employing
MATLAB simulations it shows that the provided ACOA has higher efficiency
compared to similar studies on the same aspect in the domain, as well it boasts
about an improved average packet delivery ratio besides giving a longer lifespan
for the system. The proposed ACOA used only 0,15J energy and as result packet
delivery ratio was 95%. Refer to Table 3 and Table 4 in comparison with, for

Table 3. Comparative study based on Packet Delivery ratio.

Methods	Packet delivery ratio %
SDCS	77.4
UCPS	92
S-DCC	75.7
DC-Kmean	76.5
EOCA	86.8
EULC	82.3
EER-UWSN	95

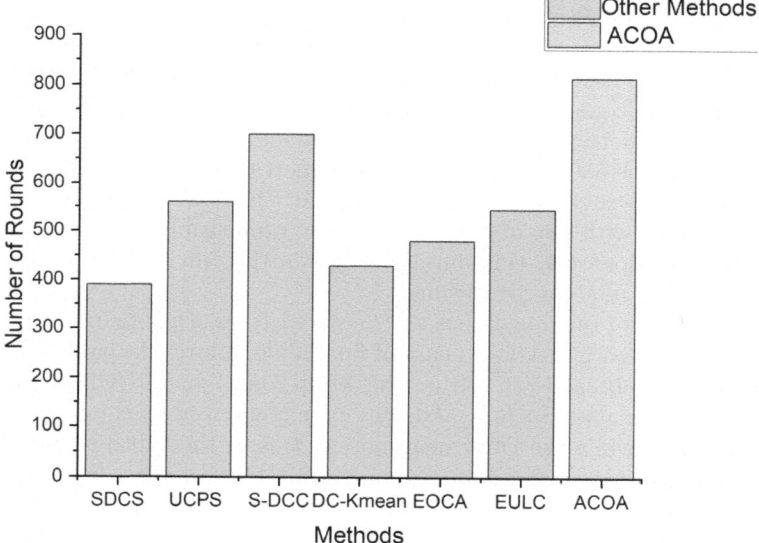

Fig. 4. State of art study based on the initial node dead.

Table 4. Results based on energy consumption.

Methods	Energy Consumption (J) %
SDCS	0.52
UCPS	0.53
S-DCC	0.26
DC-Kmean	1.38
EOCA	0.35
EULC	0.48
EER-UWSN	0.15

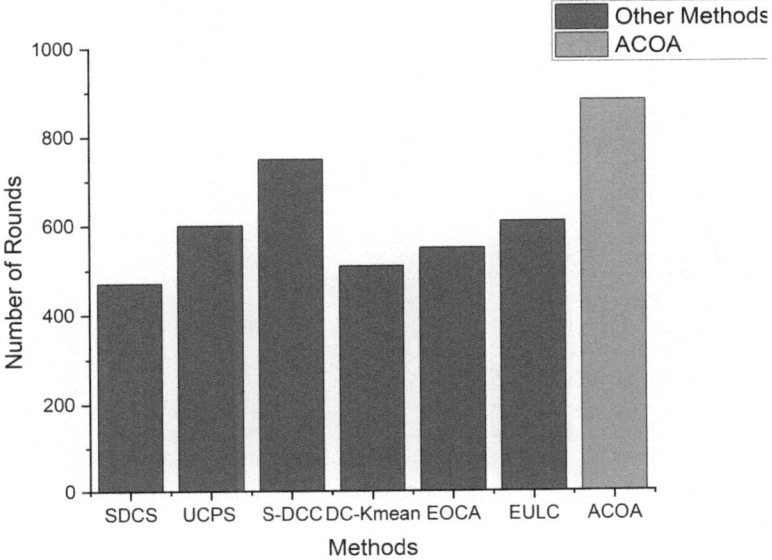

Fig. 5. State of art study based on the Half node dead.

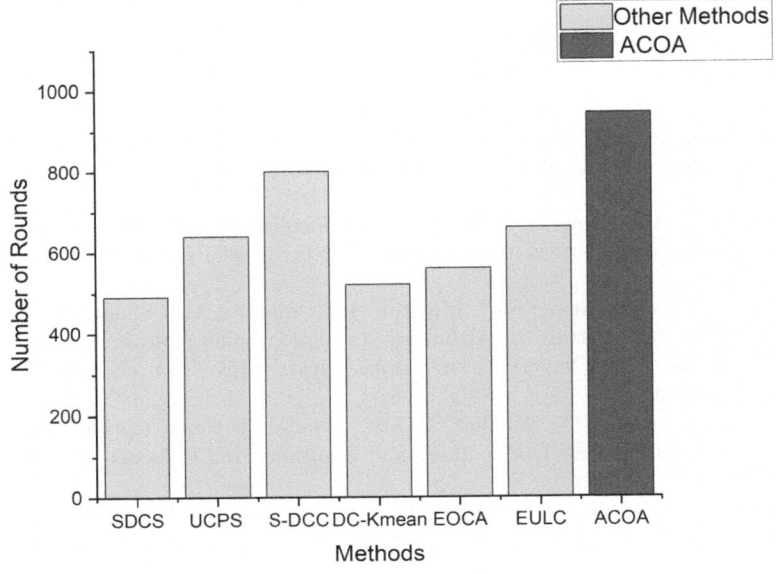

Fig. 6. State of art study based on the Final node dead

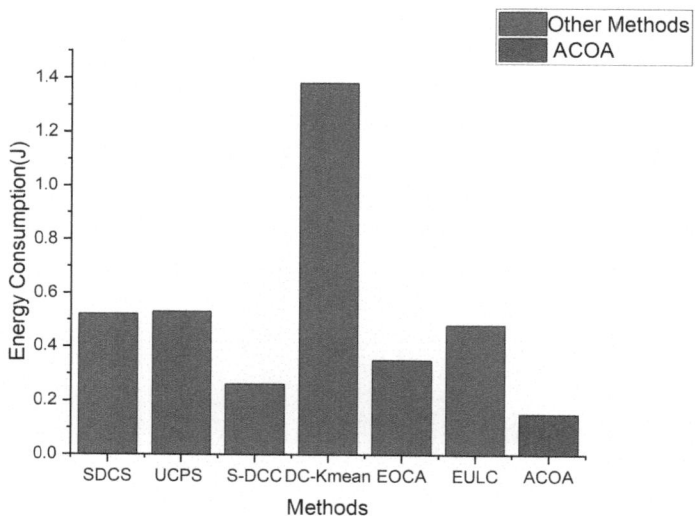

Fig. 7. State-of-the-art study of packet delivery ratio with respect to energy consumption.

example, DC-K-means, SDCS, EOCA or S-DCC. It means that this study shows how acoa can improve the lifespan and functionality of networks. Refer to Fig. 7.

References

1. Vijay, M.M., et al.: Underwater wireless sensor network-based multihop data transmission using hybrid cat cheetah optimization algorithm. Sci. Rep. **13**(1), 10810 (2023)
2. Gong, Z., Li, C., Jiang, F.: AUV-aided joint localization and time synchronization for underwater acoustic sensor networks. IEEE Signal Process. Lett. **25**(4), 477–481 (2018)
3. Othman, Z., Sulaiman, S.I., Musirin, I., Omar, A.M., Shaari, S.: Dolphin echolocation-based sizing algorithm for stand-alone photovoltaic system. In: 2018 IEEE International Conference on Applied System Invention (ICASI), pp. 1284–1287. IEEE (2018)
4. Gimenez, A., Verdu, J., Sánchez, P.D.P.: General synthesis methodology for the design of acoustic wave ladder filters and duplexers. IEEE Access **6**, 47969–47979 (2018)
5. Teshome, A.K., Kibret, B., Lai, D.T.: A review of implant communication technology in WBAN: progress and challenges. IEEE Rev. Biomed. Eng. **12**, 88–99 (2018)
6. Omer, M., Mojabi, P., Kurrant, D., LoVetri, J., Fear, E.: Proof-of-concept of the incorporation of ultrasound-derived structural information into microwave radar imaging. IEEE J. Multiscale Multiphys. Comput. Tech. **3**, 129–139 (2018)

7. Li, B., Zhang, M., Rong, Y., Han, Z.: Transceiver optimization for wireless powered time-division duplex MU-MIMO systems: non-robust and robust designs. IEEE Trans. Wireless Commun. **21**(6), 4594–4607 (2021)

8. Wang, M., Chen, Y., Sun, X., Xiao, F., Xu, X.: Node energy consumption balanced multi-hop transmission for underwater acoustic sensor networks based on clustering algorithm. IEEE Access **8**, 191231–191241 (2020)

9. Han, G., Shen, S., Song, H.: A stratification-based data collection scheme in underwater acoustic sensor networks. IEEE Trans. Veh. Technol. **67**(11), 10671–10682 (2018)

10. Yu, W., Chen, Y., Wan, L.: An energy optimization clustering scheme for multi-hop underwater acoustic cooperative sensor networks. IEEE Access **8**, 89171–89184 (2020)

11. Wan, Z., Liu, S.: An energy-efficient multi-level adaptive clustering routing algorithm for underwater wireless sensor networks. Clust. Comput. **22**(6), 14651–14660 (2019)

12. Yan, J., Yang, X., Luo, X., Chen, C.: Energy-efficient data collection over AUV-assisted underwater acoustic sensor network. IEEE Syst. J. **12**(4), 3519–3530 (2018)

13. Chen, Y., Jin, X., Wan, L.: Selective dynamic coded cooperative communications for multi-hop underwater acoustic sensor networks. IEEE Access **7**, 70552–70563 (2019)

14. Hou, R., He, L., Luo, J.: Energy-balanced unequal layering clustering in underwater acoustic sensor networks. IEEE Access **6**, 39685–39691 (2018)

15. Blum, C.: Ant colony optimization: introduction and recent trends. Phys. Life Rev. **2**(4), 353–373 (2005)

16. He, J., Hou, Z.: Ant colony algorithm for traffic signal timing optimization. Adv. Eng. Softw. **43**(1), 14–18 (2012)

17. Chu, K.C., Horng, D.J., Chang, K.C.: Numerical optimization of the energy consumption for wireless sensor networks based on an improved ant colony algorithm. IEEE Access **7**, 105562–105571 (2019)

18. Al-Khayyat, A.T.A., Ibrahim, A.: Energy optimization in WSN routing by using the K-means clustering algorithm and ant colony algorithm. In: 2020 4th International Symposium on Multidisciplinary Studies and Innovative Technologies (ISMSIT), pp. 1–4. IEEE (2020)

Detection of Malicious Network Traffic Attacks Using Support Vector Machine

Devanshi Dwivedi[(✉)], Aditya Bhushan, Ashutosh Kumar Singh, and Snehlata

Department of Computer Science and Engineering, United College of Engineering
and Research, Prayagraj 211010, Uttar Pradesh, India
devanshidwivedi83@gmail.com

Abstract. Network security plays an important role in an increasingly related society. For the safety and security of information system, detection of network traffic attacks is crucial. This research work focuses on the use of Support Vector Machines (SVM) algorithm as a machine learning tool for the detection of network traffic attacks. SVM is a flexible and adaptable classification algorithm that has shown its fruitfulness in multiple domains, including network security. This paper elaborates the utilization of SVM to observe between normal and malicious network traffic patterns. In this paper, we prepare multiple categories of network attacks, such as Denial-of-Service (DoS), User-to-Root (U2R), and Remote-to-Local (R2L) attacks. For training and evaluation purpose, KDD Cup 99 dataset is used. Several number of performance metrics, like accuracy, precision, recall, as well as F1-score, are also used to evaluate the correctness of the SVM-based intrusion detection system. The results illustrate the capability of SVM in detection of network traffic, attaining high accuracy rates while accurately solving the issues of complex attack patterns where the F1-Score for the Linear kernal and RBF 96.65 and 99.24 respectively. In addition to this, the research also highlights the significance of feature engineering along with hyperparameter engaged in develop SVM models for specified network security. In the end, this study highlights the usefulness of SVM as an essential tool in network security to identify network traffic attacks.

Keywords: Network Security · Support Vector Machine · Performance matrics · Network attacks · Denial-of-service

1   Introduction

Attacks on network traffic are prevalent as well as determined threat in the digital age, causing an important risk to the safeguard and stability of computer networks throughout the world. These attacks, often managed by malicious individuals or groups, include the modification disruption or illegal access to data travel over computer networks. Understanding the nature of attacks on network

A. Bhushan, A. K. Singh and Snehlata—Contributed equally to this work.

traffic is essential for organizations and individuals similar as they try to preserve their confidential data and information and maintain the integrity of their digital infrastructure. These cyberattacks come in many forms, exploiting vulnerabilities in network protocols, software applications, or the infrastructure itself. They can sweep from relatively easy and remote incidents to complex, coordinated attacks on important systems. Popular examples of attacks on network traffic consist of Distributed Denial of Service (DDoS) attacks shown in Fig. 1, which flood a network or server with a flood of traffic, making it unreachable to authorized users, and Man-in-the-Middle (MitM) attacks, where an attacker intercept and possibly change the data transmit between two persons without their knowledge.

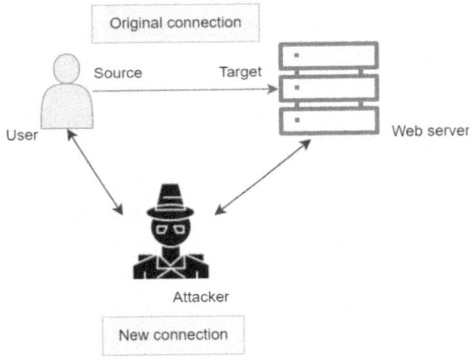

Fig. 1. Man-in-the-middle attack

Machine learning is a sub-field of artificial intelligence (AI) that concentrate on developing algorithms and models that permit computers to learn from data and create predictions or decisions without being clearly programmed. Types of Machine learning:

- **Supervised learning:** In this learning system, Models learn from labeled dataset, create predictions as well as classifications.
- **Unsupervised learning:** In this learning system, Models observe hidden patterns and structures in unlabeled data, like clustering or association.
- **Reinforcement learning:** In this learning system, Agents learn to create series of decisions to increase rewards in a dynamic environment.
- **Semi-supervised Learning:** It unites labeled as well as unlabeled data for training.

The usefulness of ML algorithms for detection of network traffic attacks can be evaluated by multiple quantitative measures along with several attributes. Supervised learning is often employed for threat detection systems, in which the data model comprehends patterns of usual network behavior together with it can detect variations as cyber assault. Explaining dataset for supervised learning strategies can be overwork and also time-taken hence in unsupervised learning approach mitigates the requirements for comprehensive human analysis, forming it a more valuable and beneficial solution. By acquiring from both usual as well as unusual happenings, semi-supervised learning models can potentially decrease false positives. The model becomes more discerning in distinguishing between regular and unusual patterns because it is exposed to a broader representation of the data. Reinforcement learning can be applied to dynamic network security scenarios, where the model learns to adapt its behavior based on the evolving nature of attacks and defenses.

There are several machine learning technique which are reported for network traffic analysis like Deep learning techniques, k-Nearest Neighbour (k-NN) algorithm, Decision trees, Random Forest and Naive Bayes Classifier. It is crucial to comprehend the working idea behind each of these strategies to better understand the advantages and disadvantages of these techniques. So, it is necessary to learn these techniques along with their characteristics.

K-NN is a non-parametric algorithm widely known for traffic classification depend on the likeness of traffic patterns. It allocate a class label to a data point depend on the class labels of its closest neighbors in the feature space. Decision trees are easy as well as explainable models that can be used for traffic classification and decision-making tasks.

Random Forest is a common machine learning algorithm, used for traffic analysis in network. It is especially beneficial for tasks like intrusion detection, anomaly detection in network, as well as classification of network traffic into different classes. Network traffic analysis based on Random forest algorithm are found to be unreliable when the data set is over fit or when there is a huge amount of unreliable features.

Naive Bayes classifier for analysis of network traffic can be an uncomplicated and easy method, particularly for tasks like network intrusion detection as well as network traffic classification into several classes. Also it has some privileges for analysis of network traffic, like the simplicity, speed, along with the capability to process high-dimensional data. Naive Bayesian models are found to be inaccurate as the capability to capture complicated relationships in data is finite as compared to more experienced algorithms. This can result in lack of accuracy when dealing with complicated network traffic patterns.

The major contributions of this paper as follows:

- The paper places a specific focus on the vital task of detecting network traffic attacks as a crucial aspect.
- The paper describes how SVM is employed to differentiate between normal and malicious network traffic patterns.
- The paper extends the scope by addressing multiple categories of network attacks, including Denial-of-Service (DoS).
- In conclusion, the paper emphasizes the utility of SVM as an essential tool in network security, particularly for mitigating network traffic attacks.

The rest of this paper is organized in sections. Section 2 lay out the background as well as related work for the paper. Section 3 explains the experiment and analysis part, also including brief narration of SVM algorithm. The result and discussion part for proposed algorithm approach is demonstrates in Sect. 4, and the paper in concluded in Sect. 5.

2 Related Work

Various researches on the application of SVM for detection of network traffic attacks is presented here. Ngueajio et al. [1] focus on the Intrusion Detection System (IDS) by using SVM and also a system developed to identify and categorize unauthorized or malicious activities in a computer network using the SVM algorithm. SVMs are excellent at binary classification tasks, resulting in them useful for detecting unexpected network traffic patterns [2], give an overview of a novel SVM k-NN group method for intrusion detection system is an innovative techniques that combines SVM and k-NN for detection of network attacks and to enhance overall security. This grouped method of SVM as well as k-NN influences the strengths of SVM as well as K-NN classifiers.

Zhang et al. [3] focus on the design of an intrusion detection systems which make use of neural networks as well as SVMs and also examine their performance. Both of them neural networks and SVMs attained exceptionally high accuracy rates. The pair of two neural networks along with SVM technique reveal a compatible level of performance, and implies that both models can be planned as a viable options for intrusion detection. Khan et al. [4] initiate an IDS that unite SVM and hierarchical clustering for network intrusion detection. This inspect the advantages of hierarchical clustering for feature extraction. Kim et al. [5] introduces a method of applying SVM to network-based Intrusion Detection System and also confer the application of SVMs for network intrusion detection as well as contrast performance of SVM with other machine learning techniques.

Mishra et al. [6] addressed the significance of feature reduction in SVM-based techniques that focuses on dimensionality reduction approaches combined with SVMs for intrusion detection. Kausar et al. [7] involves details about the use of SVMs in intrusion detection. We performed a thorough evaluation of the present state of research in intrusion detection utilizing SVM as classifiers in this study.

Han et al. [8] performed a closed evaluation of the present state of research in intrusion detection which make use of SVM. In addition to this, researchers have been developing a variety of hybrid methods that merge SVMs with other machine learning algorithms, in order to improve detection performance while avoiding false alarms. In this research paper [9], there is the creation of an attack detection algorithm based on the Fuzzy Support Vector Machine. This algorithm undergoes training and evaluation on different types of data to assess its effectiveness in detecting and responding to network intrusions. Park et al. [10] discusses the use of SVMs for network intrusion detection. It compares SVM's effectiveness to various machine learning algorithms and examines its capability for identifying network assaults.

Mhamdi et al. [11] present research discuss the deployment of a system based on deep learning techniques for network detection of attacks. The authors confess that the results from their implemented deep learning algorithm for identifying network intrusions are not yet suitable for use in commercial applications. This suggests that the model's performance could be improved. In spite of recent challenges, researcher also underline that this approach offers better potential and benefits as well as a viable step towards future improvement.

Anwar et al. [12] intention of this research is to carefully design a supervised model for the extraction of necessary cyber threat intelligence concept from unorganized sources of data. Alejandre et al. [13] proposed a new feature selection approach for identifying botnets during the Command and Control (C&C) phase.

In Command and Control phase, Cyber Hackers establish and maintain distinct connections to hacked devices in the target network. The proposed method used the C4.5 classifier to evaluate individuals within the Genetic Algorithm(GA) as an optimizer algorithm and make use of the C4.5 classifier to analyze individuals within the GA. Liu et al. [14] presents a review of techniques based on deep learning for traffic on networks classification, which is essential for malicious traffic detection. For network traffic classification, deep learning approach is better option to examine and classify network traffic data into multiple categories. Network traffic classification based on deep learning approach, may improve network security, enhance Quality of Service (QoS) and also beneficial for identifying and respond to security threats.

Alsubhi et al. [15] presents a review of several machine learning based approaches for the detection and classification of botnets in network traffic. There are different ML algorithms for detection as well as classification of botnets namely SVM, Decision Trees, K-Means Clustering, Naive Bayes. Ahmad et al. [16] focus on the utilization of machine learning approaches to enhance the security of the Internet of Things (IoT) ecosystem. IoT devices are sensitive to different security threats, including data breaches, and network attacks. Machine learning techniques gives appropriate solutions for detecting, preventing, and lighten these threats. Miller et al. [17] describes the function of machine learning techniques in botnet detection. Machine learning approach is essential in botnet detection due to its capacity to analyse as well as categorize network traffic data that is based on formerly learnt patterns and anomalies.

This method is suitable for detecting and minimising botnets. Yassin et al. [18] paper introduce a hybrid model that merge SVM and K- means clustering for intrusion detection in computer networks. A hybrid model merge SVM as well as K-means clustering for intrusion detection in computer networks can advantages the ability of both methods to improve the accuracy of intrusion detection systems. Mulay et al. [19] introduced a hybrid model that merge SVM with hierarchical clustering for detection of network intrusion.

3   Experiment and Analysis

Analyzing traffic attacks in network is important to specification and lightens computer network security threats. Attacks on network traffic can take several forms, and their analysis includes monitoring, gathering, and examine network data to detect and respond to suspicious or malicious activity. Here's a brief description of how to analyze network traffic attacks:

3.1   Different Detection Mechanism

- **Anomaly detection:** In Anomaly detection method, Look for anomalies in network traffic, including sudden spikes in data volume or unexpected communication patterns. Anomaly detection tools as well as techniques can help to automate this process.
- **Signature based detection**: For analyzing network traffic attacks, make use of intrusion detection system (IDS) or intrusion prevention systems (IPS) that use signature-based detection to differentiate network traffic to known attack patterns. These signatures are such as fingerprints of well known attacks.
- **Traffic analysis:** In traffic analysis, inspect packet headers together with payloads to determine doubtful patterns or content. Pay attention to protocol anomalies, uncommon port usage, or traffic from well known venomous IP addresses
- **Behavioral detection**: In behavioral detection technique, implement behavior-based detection systems that examine behavior of network over time as well as identify deviations from expected behavior. This can be more efficient in detecting novel or unknown cyber threats.
- **Continuous monitoring:** In continuous monitoring method, prepare constant monitoring of network traffic to identify as well as answer to new attacks as they emerge. Security is an unfinished process that needs continual and careful observation.

In short, network traffic attack analysis is a complicated process that merges several different techniques and tools to examine, respond to, and reduce network security attacks. It is necessary to stay up-to-date on fresh as well as new threats and continual monitoring increase safety measures to preserve against developing attack techniques.

3.2   Malicious Network Traffic Analysis

Analysis of malicious network traffic is a important cyber security practice that includes observing, inspecting, as well as analyzing data packets sent over a computer network to identify and lighten potential threats, vulnerabilities, and cyber attacks. In today's connected cyberspace world, where organizations depends heavily on networked systems along with the Internet to conduct their business, the identification and avoidance of venomous network activity has become outstanding. The main motive of malicious network traffic analysis is to preserve network infrastructure, data and confidential information from a broad range of cyber threats.

Efficient analysis of malicious network traffic need a combination of skillful security personnel, strong tools as well as technologies, along with up-to-date threat intelligence. It is a continuous process that modifies to developing cyber threats, and makes use of a critical facet of any comprehensive cyber security policy for organizations of all sizes. By carefully identifying and label security issues within their network operations, businesses can reduce the risks associated with cyber attacks and preserve their critical assets and data.

3.3 Algorithm Used

Machine learning algorithms are often used for network traffic analysis to identify anomalies, intrusions, as well as patterns in network data. The selection of algorithm rely on the certain goals of the analysis and the type of dataset available. SVMs are a well liked option for network traffic analysis for different cause:

- **High-dimensional data:** Data in network traffic is always high-dimensional as well as it has several number of features expressing the behavior of network packets. SVMs are systematic when dealing with high-dimensional data together with it can also find complicated decision boundaries in this space.
- **Nonlinearity**: Network traffic patterns can be extremely nonlinear, and SVMs can fruitfully capture nonlinear relationships by using kernel functions like the Radial Basis Function (RBF) kernel. This permit SVM algorithm to model complicated relationships in the data, that one can be demanding for linear models.
- **Support vectors**: SVMs recognize support vectors, and that data points are nearest to the decision boundary. These support vectors play an important role in explaining the decision boundary as well as, it is the most informative data points for recognize class characteristics. This can be valuable for network traffic analysis when trying to know the essential quality of different types of traffic.
- **Flexible to outliers**: Data in network traffic can consist outliers or anomalies that are crucial for detection in cybersecurity applications. SVMs are not so much sensitive to outliers as compared to some other machine learning algorithms, this make it acceptable for anomaly detection.

3.4 Support Vector Machine

SVMs are powerful and adaptable machine learning algorithms commonly used for classification and regression process. It is established by Vladimir Vapnik and his co-worker in the 1960s, SVMs have since become a elementary tool in the area of supervised learning due to their capability to hold both linear as well as nonlinear data separation, robust generalization, together with solid theoretical foundations.

At its centre, the aim of SVM is to detect the optimal hyperplane that better distinct data points in a high-dimensional space. This hyperplane shown in Fig. 2a, act as a decision boundary that differentiate between different classes or conclude numerical values in regression problems. What sets SVM apart from other classifiers is its focus on maximizing the span between data points of different classes shown in Fig. 2b.

The margin is defined as the distance between the hyperplane and the nearest data points, known as support vectors. SVMs appear in different varieties and can be classified based on their particular applications as well as characteristics.

- **Linear SVM**: Linear SVM is a machine learning algorithm commonly used for binary classification as well as regression tasks. It is particularly efficient when the data can be partitioned into two classes by a straight line (or a hyperplane in higher dimensions). The goal of Linear SVM is to find the optimal hyperplane that better divide data points of several classes while maximizing the range between them.
- **Non-linear SVM**: Non-Linear SVM is a dissimilar form of the SVM algorithm planed for processing data sets that are not linearly separable in their original and new feature space. In cases where the decision boundary is not a linear hyperplane, nonlinear SVMs utilize kernel functions to map the data into a higher-dimensional space where the linear hyperplane can efficiently separate classes.
- **One-class SVM**: This type of SVM is commonly used for anomaly detection. It determine a decision boundary around the majority class, as well as any data points drop down outside this boundary are considered anomalies. One-class SVMs are mainly useful when dealing with unbalanced datasets.
- **Multi-class SVM**: While SVMs are naturally binary classifiers, they can be expand to handle multi-class classification issues using several techniques like one-to-all (OvA) or one-to-one (OvO) strategy. In One-to-all, a discrete binary classifier is trained for each class, while in One-to-one, a binary classifier is trained for each pair of classes.

4   Result and Discussion

The Algorithm 1, employed for network traffic analysis utilizing the used dataset will be elucidated categorizing various network activities, including normal behaviors and potential security threats.

4.1   Dataset Description

The KDD Cup 99 dataset is divided into training data, used for training machine learning models with labeled examples, and testing data, used to evaluate the model's ability to generalize to new, unseen data.

The dataset from the Table 1, is the training dataset is used to train machine learning models. It contains a labeled set of network connections, where each connection is categorized as either normal or representing a specific type of attack (e.g., DoS, probe, U2R, R2L).

Table 1. Training dataset class description

Class	Patterns
Normal	67343
DOS	45927
Probe	11656
R2L	995
Total	125921

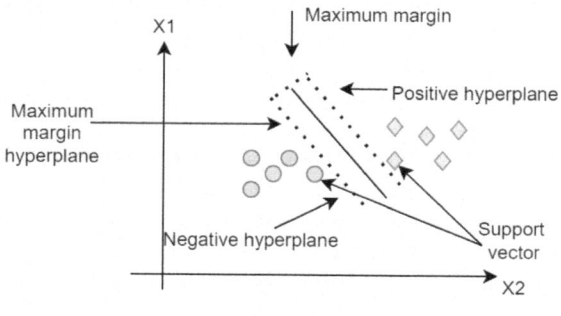

(a) Hyperplane structure

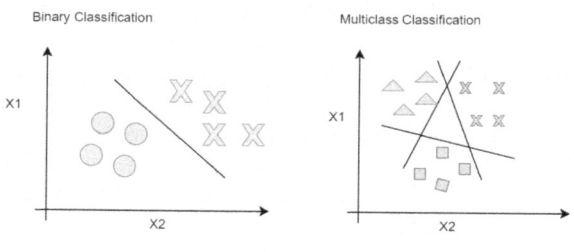

(b) SVM-class classification

Fig. 2. SVM hyperplane and binary classification

Similar to the training dataset, the testing dataset represented in Table 2, consists of network connections with various attributes, but without the associated labels indicating the type of connection.

Table 2. Testing dataset class description

Class	Patterns
Normal	9711
DOS	7458
Probe	2421
R2L	2754
Total	22344

The dataset is used to evaluate the performance of the trained machine learning models on new, unseen data.

4.2   Mean Statistics

For the utilisation of SVMs to detect malicious network traffic attacks, we use a variety of statistics as well as metrics to describe the performance and usefulness of model.

Algorithm 1. Support Vector Machine

Input: Training data D_{train}, Testing data D_{test}
Output: Detected attacks in D_{test}
Training Phase:
Initialize the SVM model
Train the SVM model on D_{train}
Testing Phase:
for each data point x_i in D_{test} **do**
    Predict the label for x_i using the SVM model
    if Predicted label is malicious **then**
        Mark x_i as a detected attack
    else
        Mark x_i as normal network traffic
    end if
end for
Output: Detected attacks in D_{test}

Accuracy indicates the overall correctness of the model's predictions. It symbolize the proportion of correctly or accurately classified events among all events and is usually mentioned as in percentage, calculated with Eq. (1).

$$Accuracy = \frac{TP + TN}{TP + TN + FP + FN} \tag{1}$$

The measure of number of the instances that are concluded as attacks are actually attacks, known as Positive predicted value. Calculated with Eq. (2).

$$Precision = \frac{TP}{TP + FP} \tag{2}$$

The recall metric presented in Eq. (3) provides an indicator to measure completeness.

$$Recall = \frac{TP}{TP + FN} \tag{3}$$

F1 Score is defined as, the harmonic mean of precision and recall, F1 score also gives a balance between precision as well as recall, and beneficial when there is a disturbance between the number of attacks and non-attacks can calculated using Eq. (4).

$$F_1 - score = \frac{2 \cdot \text{precision} \cdot \text{recall}}{\text{precision} + \text{recall}} \qquad (4)$$

4.3 Confusion Matrix

The tabular representation of the performance of a classification model, known as confusion matrix represented in Table 3. It gives a complete breakdown of the model's predictions against with the actual class labels shown in Fig. 3, and helping to evaluate the performance of model.

Table 3. Performance matrix

	Actual Class	
	Positive	Negative
Positive	True Positive (TP)	False Positive (FP)
Negative	False Negative (FN)	True Negative (TN)

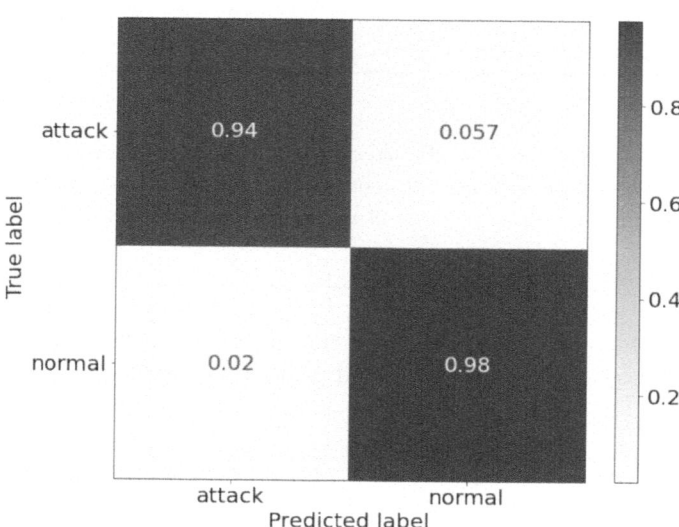

Fig. 3. Confusion matrix

The Table 4, presents a comprehensive analysis of key performance metrics for a classification model. The precision, recall, and F1 score are reported for two classes, "Attack" and "Normal." These metrics offer insights into the model's ability to accurately identify instances of each class, crucial for evaluating its efficacy in distinguishing between normal network behavior and potential security threats.

The overall accuracy of the model is an impressive 99.24%, emphasizing its success in correctly classifying both "Attack" and "Normal" instances.

Table 4. Analysis of attributes

Attribute	Precision	Recall	F1 Score	Support
Attack	0.99237	0.99128	0.99183	14569
Normal	0.99250	0.99344	0.99297	16922
Accuracy	–	–	0.99244	31491

The Table 5, presents the linear kernel training-set score of 96.88% and performs consistently on the test set with scores of 96.66%. In contrast, the RBF kernel outshines with exceptional scores, reaching 99.28% on the training set and maintaining this high performance on the test set with a score of 99.24%. This underscores the superior generalization ability of the RBF kernel.

Table 5. Performance metrics

Kernel Name	Train-set Score	Test-set Score	Recall	Precision	F1-score
Linear	96.88	96.66	96.66	96.67	96.65
RBF	99.28	99.24	99.24	99.24	99.24

The SVM model is arranged with the best values for hyper parameters C and degree, which have been determined through a hyper parameter tuning process. Figure 4a and 4b, describe the visualization of destination (dst)-bytes and source (src)-bytes. It gives beneficial insights into traffic data.

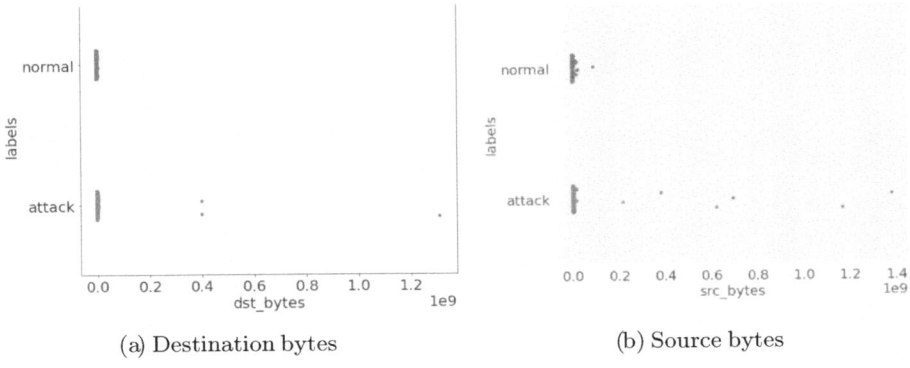

(a) Destination bytes   (b) Source bytes

Fig. 4. Comparison of destination and source bytes

The summary of recall, precision, and F1-score for both kernels reaffirms the significant performance advantage of the RBF kernel, which attains consistent and exceptional results across all metrics.

The findings underscore the effectiveness of the chosen kernel, especially the RBF, in achieving high accuracy and robust performance in the context of network traffic analysis.

A pie chart shown in Fig. 5, based on the unique labels in the DataFrame df's 'labels' column, presenting the arrangement of these labels in a visually pleasing manner. The labels are shown under each pie chart section, and the subtitle is entitled "Labels". The chart exhibit the clear difference between 'Normal Traffic' as well as 'Malicious Traffic.'

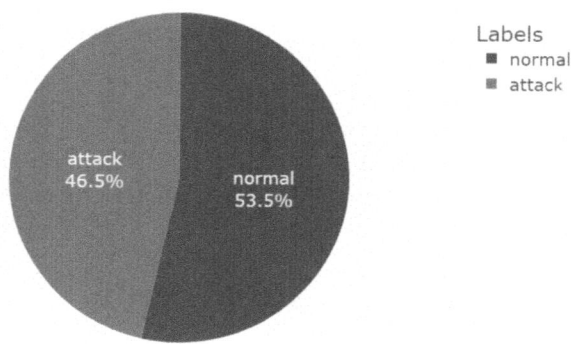

Fig. 5. Attack proportion on KDD dataset

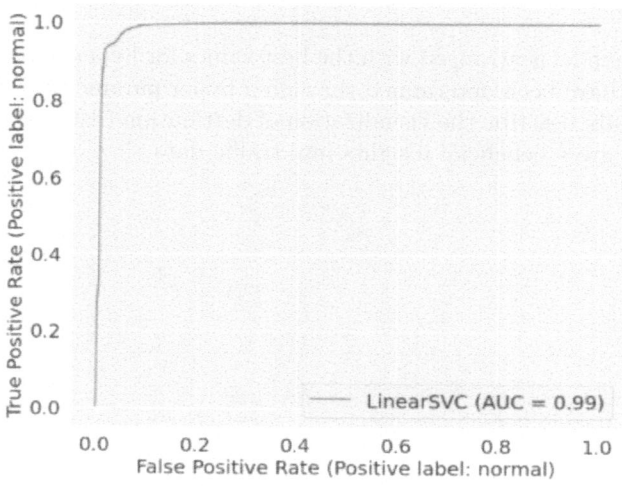

Fig. 6. ROC curve

A Receiver Operating Characteristic (ROC) curve in Fig. 6, the curve explain the trade-off between the true positive rate as well as true negative rate at various probability thresholds. ROC curves are often used to evaluate and visualise the performance of classifiers, such as machine learning models such as SVM and also favorable for determining how effectively the model can differentiate between the positive as well as negative classes.

5   Conclusion

In this article, we implement SVM approach to detect malicious network traffic attacks. It starts with inspecting the KDD Cup99 data set. The feature includes different host rates, server rates, src-bytes and dst-bytes. After this, modelling will be done using SVM, by using multiple kernels (linear and RBF) with custom parameters settings and with the help of parameter tuning using Random Search We can notice that RBF kernel is the best kernel in our problem and gave us very favourable results as the F1 score of linear kernel is 96.65 while F1 score of RBF kernel is 99.24. It shown promising as we achieve very positive result.

In future, we further expand modern techniques for feature engineering, also label the issue of difference between the dataset in network traffic attack detection and add more machine learning approach for detection of network traffic attacks.

References

1. Ngueajio, M., Washington, G., Rawat, D., Ngueabou, Y.: Intrusion detection systems using support vector machines on the KDDCUP'99 and NSL-KDD datasets: a comprehensive survey. In: Proceedings Of SAI Intelligent Systems Conference, pp. 609–629 (2022)
2. Aburomman, A., Reaz, M.: A novel SVM-kNN-PSO ensemble method for intrusion detection system. Appl. Soft Comput. **38**, 360–372 (2016)
3. Li, K., Zhang, Y., Wang, S.: An intrusion detection system based on PSO-GWO hybrid optimized support vector machine. In: 2021 International Joint Conference On Neural Networks (IJCNN), pp. 1–7 (2021)
4. Khan, L., Awad, M., Thuraisingham, B.: A new intrusion detection system using support vector machines and hierarchical clustering. VLDB J. **16**, 507–521 (2007)
5. Kim, D., Park, J.: Network-based intrusion detection with support vector machines. In: Information Networking: International Conference, ICOIN 2003, Cheju Island, Korea, 12–14 February 2003. Revised Selected Papers, vol. 2662, pp. 747–756. Springer, Cham (2003). https://doi.org/10.1007/978-3-540-45235-5_73
6. Mishra, A., Cheng, A., Zhang, Y.: Intrusion detection using principal component analysis and support vector machines. In: 2020 IEEE 16th International Conference on Control & Automation (ICCA), pp. 907–912 (2020)

7. Kausar, N., Belhaouari Samir, B., Abdullah, A., Ahmad, I., Hussain, M.: A review of classification approaches using support vector machine in intrusion detection. In: Abd Manaf, A., Sahibuddin, S., Ahmad, R., Mohd Daud, S., El-Qawasmeh, E. (eds.) Informatics Engineering and Information Science: International Conference, ICIEIS 2011, Kuala Lumpur, Malaysia, 14–16 November 2011, Proceedings, Part III, pp. 24–34. Springer, Cham (2011). https://doi.org/10.1007/978-3-642-25462-8_3

8. Han, W., Xue, J., Yan, H.: Detecting anomalous traffic in the controlled network based on cross entropy and support vector machine. IET Inf. Secur. **13**, 109–116 (2019)

9. Long, Y., Ouyang, J., Sun, X.: Network intrusion detection model based on fuzzy support vector machine. J. Networks **8**, 1387 (2013)

10. Kim, D., Park, J.: Network-based intrusion detection with support vector machines. In: Kahng, H.K. (eds.) Information Networking: International Conference, ICOIN 2003, Cheju Island, Korea, 12–14 February 2003. Revised Selected Papers, vol. 2662, pp. 747–756. Springer, Cham (2003). https://doi.org/10.1007/978-3-540-45235-5_73

11. Tang, T., Mhamdi, L., McLernon, D., Zaidi, S., Ghogho, M.: Deep learning approach for network intrusion detection in software defined networking. In: 2016 International Conference on Wireless Networks and Mobile Communications (WINCOM), pp. 258–263 (2016)

12. Ghazi, Y., Anwar, Z., Mumtaz, R., Saleem, S., Tahir, A.: A supervised machine learning based approach for automatically extracting high-level threat intelligence from unstructured sources. In: 2018 International Conference on Frontiers Of Information Technology (FIT), pp. 129–134 (2018)

13. Alejandre, F., Cortés, N., Anaya, E.: Feature selection to detect botnets using machine learning algorithms. In: 2017 International Conference on Electronics, Communications and Computers (CONIELECOMP), pp. 1–7 (2017)

14. Rezaei, S., Liu, X.: Deep learning for encrypted traffic classification: an overview. IEEE Commun. Mag. **57**, 76–81 (2019)

15. Shinan, K., Alsubhi, K., Alzahrani, A., Ashraf, M.: Machine learning-based botnet detection in software-defined network: a systematic review. Symmetry **13**, 866 (2021)

16. Ahmad, R., Alsmadi, I.: Machine learning approaches to IoT security: a systematic literature review. Internet Things **14**, 100365 (2021)

17. Miller, S., Busby-Earle, C.: The role of machine learning in botnet detection. In: 2016 11th International Conference for Internet Technology and Secured Transactions (ICITST), pp. 359–364 (2016)

18. Muda, Z., Yassin, W., Sulaiman, M., Udzir, N.: Intrusion detection based on K-Means clustering and Naïve Bayes classification. In: 2011 7th International Conference on Information Technology in Asia, pp. 1–6 (2011)

19. Mulay, S., Devale, P., Garje, G.: Intrusion detection system using support vector machine and decision tree. Int. J. Comput. Appl. **3**, 40–43 (2010)

IoT Based Safety Monitoring and Communication System for Underground Coal Mines

Boddu Madan Gopal[1], Yatham Nitish Reddy[1], Chakka Bharghava Siddhartha[1], Shaik Rashmi[1], V. Ravikumar Pandi[2(✉)], Vipina Valsan[2], Soumya Sathyan[2], and Kavya Suresh[2]

[1] Department of Computer Science and Engineering,
Amrita School of Computing, Amrita Vishwa Vidyapeetham, Amritapuri, India
[2] Department of Electrical and Electronics Engineering,
Amrita School of Engineering, Amrita Vishwa Vidyapeetham, Amritapuri, India
ravikumarpandiv@am.amrita.edu

Abstract. Coal, a crucial finite resource responsible for nearly half of the global electricity generation, is obtained via mining activities. Nevertheless, coal mining gives rise to substantial safety risks for individuals. Mining sites are confronted with challenges, such as the existence of combustible gases like methane. Unintentional ignition of these gases leads to catastrophic mine explosions, resulting in fatalities and severe injuries. To address these difficulties, this initiative uses Internet of Things (IoT) for conceiving an all-encompassing oversight mechanism that perpetually oversees critical variables. These variables comprise levels of methane (CH_4) and carbon dioxide (CO_2), alongside indicators such as temperature, humidity, and soil dampness within coal mines. The proposed IoT-based safety system presents a multifaceted approach to enhance human safety in coal mines. By leveraging real-time data collection and analysis, the system can promptly identify dangerous gas levels or adverse environmental conditions. Consequently, the system will issue timely alerts and notifications to workers and supervisors, enabling swift responses and evacuation procedures in the event of escalating danger. By providing comprehensive insights into the mining environment, the system contributes to a safer working environment and a significant reduction in the occurrence of accidents.

Keywords: Carbon dioxide · Coal Mining · IoT · Methane · Warning system · Workers safety

1 Introduction

The process of underground mining is highly unsafe environment where the risks increase in the distance from the ground. Gas leaks, fires, and explosive events serve to exacerbate the risks connected with coal mining. Individuals working within coal mines are frequently subjected to various gases, including methane (CH_4), carbon dioxide (CO_2),

A. Verma et al. (Eds.): ANTIC 2023, CCIS 2091, pp. 69–80, 2024.
https://doi.org/10.1007/978-3-031-64064-3_6

hydrogen sulphide, nitrogen oxides, among others, often lacking full comprehension of the potential dangers carried by these gases. The mining operations with unsafe manners are due to different methodologies utilized by the miners for extricating various minerals [1]. The extraction of the ores through mining still remains an essential resources for modern civilization. An ore is a rock with economic significance for the human civilization. It contains sufficient minerals that can be converted into a saleable product which generates a financially acceptable profit under existing economic conditions. The coal mines have numerous risky stipulations include high temperature and humidity, discharge of destructive gases that make unsafe surroundings for specialists working there [2].

India possesses extensive reserves of deep-seated coal deposits, which necessitate underground mining for extraction in an environmentally responsible manner. The method predominantly employed for mining these coal seams involves the board and pillar technique. Following the extraction of a specific seam, a notable proportion of coal remains unexploited within the pillars. The secure retrieval of these locked coal reserves from the pillars, known as depillaring, hinges on effective roof management and the design of appropriate support systems. Within underground coal mines, the occurrence of accidents stemming from roof collapses, or strata movement, has been a prominent concern, representing a significant contributor to such incidents. Stakeholders have been consistently striving to mitigate the risks associated with strata movement. To minimize this phenomenon, it is imperative to monitor strata conditions closely and formulate robust support system designs, informed by comprehensive assessments of the geomechanically characteristics of the overlying strata. The integration of innovative methodologies and the adoption of enhanced equipment within mining operations hold the potential to improve productivity levels and enhance safety of workers involved [3].

Coal mining operations present numerous safety challenges for human workers, including the risk of gas leaks, collapses, and high temperatures. Communication is another problem in coal mines. An accident or trouble cannot be relied upon by the head office for evacuation procedures or for sending aid to the scene of the accident. The current safety system only concentrates on the area where miners are present and does not give a comprehensive idea about the environment of the whole of coal mines. Coal mines; it is based on the miners' equipment and the health of the miners. It may pose a problem to the miners as they do not know about the trouble in the mines where they are not present. But with a new approach, it needs development of a safety system such that mines are monitored 24/7 so no harm is done to anyone. The number of accidents and deaths in the past years in India is shown in Fig. 1 [4].

The technological advancements have the potential to significantly decrease the occurrences of fatalities and accidents in coal mines. This would greatly enhance the safety of workers, providing them with a more secure working environment.

One prominent challenge in workplace safety is the lack of clarity among workers regarding the severity of problems they encounter. This lack of information hinders their ability to respond promptly and appropriately to potential dangers, jeopardizing both their safety and effective problem resolution. Additionally, communication breakdowns occur when workers exit confined work areas, catching external team members off guard.

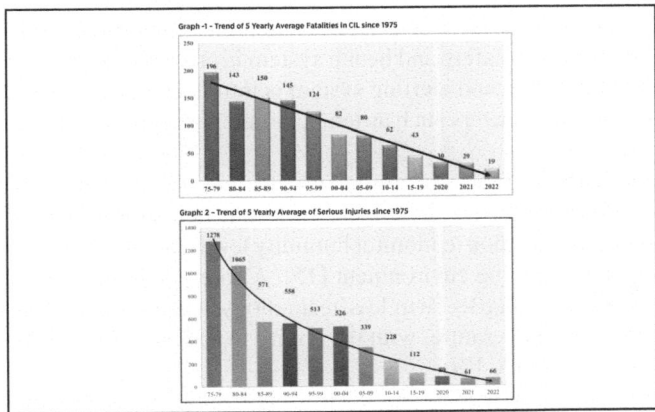

Fig. 1. The records of number of accidents and Deaths in the recent years

This lack of coordination and heads-up communication leads to confusion and ineffi-
ciencies. To address these issues, a dual-pronged solution is required: one that provides
workers with accurate information about the seriousness of situations and simultaneously notifies external teams when workers are exiting, enhancing workplace safety and
communication.

In previous efforts within this field, sensor data has been the primary focus, with
systems monitoring and issuing alerts based on predefined thresholds. This approach
introduces a nuanced response system with distinct danger levels. The first level triggers a responsive LED alert for immediate attention. The second level activates a
buzzer alert, signaling heightened caution. In the most critical situations, the third level
employs advanced communication via WhatsApp to notify external parties promptly.
This multifaceted approach ensures timely response and efficient communication. The
report systematically details the components, methodology, outcomes, and significance,
emphasizing the rigorous research and innovative thinking that define its journey.

2 Literature Review

The development of IoT-based safety systems for coal mines has gained significant
attention in recent years, reflecting the critical importance of ensuring the well-being
of miners working in challenging and potentially hazardous underground environments.
Several research initiatives have explored various aspects of this field, focusing on the
integration of advanced sensor networks and wireless communication technologies to
monitor and alert workers about potential dangers [5].

These initiatives aim to reduce risks, prevent accidents, and create a secure atmo-
sphere for mining operations. However, despite these advancements in worker safety,
there remains a notable gap in terms of communication within coal mines. Efficiently
controlling methane emissions, commonly referred to as Coal Mine Methane (CMM),
is a paramount concern in coal mining due to the potential for catastrophic methane
explosions. Hence an intelligent monitoring system with real time communication is

essential [6, 7]. The importance of IoT based communication protocol for the information exchange for industrial safety and health system is proposed in [8, 9]. An IoT-based coal mine safety monitoring and alerting system is introduced that integrates a network of sensors to measure parameters such as temperature, humidity, gas concentration, and vibration [10–12].

The machine learning tools are useful in detecting the accident severity level in an industry [13, 14]. Similarly, an intelligent coal mine helmet is developed employing Zigbee wireless communication to monitor humidity levels, methane concentrations, and temperature within the mining environment [15]. A safety helmet for miners has been developed by integrating ZigBee wireless technology to monitor gas concentrations, humidity, and ambient temperature, with the ability to activate LEDs and sound alarms as alerts when necessary [16, 17].

Furthermore, the role of technology in ensuring worker safety extends beyond coal mining. An IoT-based automated miner tracking and imperilment observance system has been developed, demonstrating the broader applicability of IoT in mining safety [18]. Similarly a smart coal mine safety and monitoring system has been implemented, emphasizing the importance of technology in enhancing safety across various mining contexts [19].

In conclusion, the ongoing efforts to develop IoT-based safety systems for coal mines and mining operations in general represent a crucial step towards safeguarding miners and improving the sustainability of mining operations. These systems integrate advanced sensor networks and wireless communication technologies, aiming to prevent accidents and reduce risks in hazardous mining environments. The integration of LoRaWAN, Zigbee, and Wi-Fi technologies is at the forefront of these advancements.

3 Methodology

A diverse array of sensors has been thoughtfully integrated into the Arduino system, each serving a distinct purpose to enhance comprehensive data collection as shown in Fig. 2. The initial inclusion is the MQ5 sensor, dedicated to the monitoring of methane ($CH4$) concentration in the surrounding air, quantified in parts per million (ppm). Following this, the MQ135 sensor has been strategically employed to precisely gauge the concentration of carbon dioxide ($CO2$) in the ambient air.

For the measurement of atmospheric conditions, the DTH11 sensor has been ingeniously employed. This sensor, distinguished by its compact size and remarkable accuracy, plays a pivotal role in capturing both temperature and humidity metrics. Its multifunctionality adds a layer of richness to the data tapestry. Notably, the sensor ensemble extends beyond the realms of air analysis. The inclusion of a soil moisture sensor provides insights into the moisture content within the soil, offering valuable information for assessing environmental conditions and optimizing various processes.

In essence, this system encapsulates a spectrum of sensor technologies, each with a specific focus and purpose. The MQ5 and MQ135 sensors meticulously scrutinize air composition, while the DTH11 sensor masterfully captures temperature and humidity data. Meanwhile, the soil moisture sensor delves into the intricacies of soil conditions.

Fig. 2. The prototype with all working components

3.1 Connections to the Arduino for Reading the Sensor Values

(a) Sensor Connections to the Arduino

The connectivity arrangement of sensor network is both strategic and intricate, ensuring seamless data integration into the Arduino microcontroller. Starting with the MQ5 sensor, its analog output finds its home in the A0 pin of the Arduino. Similarly, the MQ135 sensor's analog output interface aligns with the A1 pin, creating a direct channel for data transfer.

Transitioning to the soil moisture sensor, its output is thoughtfully linked to the A2 pin of the Arduino, enriching data collection capabilities further. Moving beyond the analog inputs, the A4 and A5 pins of the Arduino engage in a symbiotic partnership with the SDA and SCL pins of the I2C adapter. This connection proves pivotal in facilitating communication with the 16 × 2 LCD display, forming an integral part of visualization system.

Completing the circuit, the output of the DHT11 sensor finds its home in the digital pin 2 of the Arduino. This strategic linkage not only ensures a dedicated channel for temperature and humidity data but also streamlines the flow of information within sensor network.

(b) Monitoring Device Connections from the Arduino

The setup involves a series of carefully established connections to ensure the functionality of various components. Beginning with the LED, its positive terminal, which is the longer leg, is effectively linked to the digital pin 8. Simultaneously, the negative terminal, or the shorter leg, is securely connected to the ground. This arrangement enables the LED to be controlled through digital pin 8, turning it on and off as required.

Moving on to the buzzer, its positive pin, denoting the side connected to the piezo-electric element, is skillfully integrated with digital pin 9. This strategic connection allows the system to activate the buzzer by sending appropriate signals to digital pin 9. The negative pin of the buzzer, on the other hand, is connected to the ground, thus completing the circuit and ensuring the flow of current required for the buzzer to emit sound.

Lastly, the digital pin 10 serves a unique purpose – it is linked to the Reset (RST) pin of the WiFi module. This connection facilitates the ability to reset or restart the WiFi module as needed. This can be particularly useful in situations where the module encounters errors or connectivity issues, providing a means to quickly address such problems.

3.2 Checking the Abnormalities and Assigning the Danger Levels

The approach to anomaly detection follows a structured hierarchy, ensuring a systematic assessment of deviations as shown in Fig. 3. At the foundational level, initiate by scrutinizing multiple key parameters. Here concentration goes on identifying whether specific requirements have been fulfilled, such as methane (CH4) levels above 15 parts per million (ppm), carbon dioxide (CO2) levels over 4200 ppm, soil moisture percentage above 40, temperature rising above 45 °C, or humidity surpassing 80%. If any of these requirements are met, it suggests that danger level 1 has been triggered.

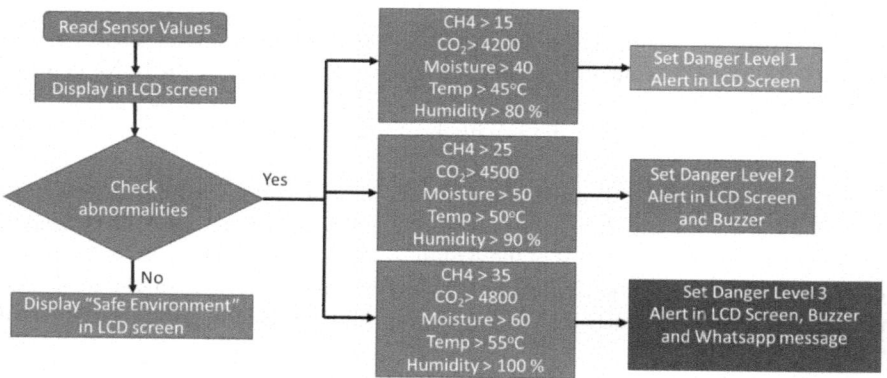

Fig. 3. The flow chart of assigning of danger levels and giving alerts

Building upon this baseline assessment, subsequent layer of analysis delves into relative anomalies. Here, the interplay of multiple factors comes into play. If both the CH4 concentration surges beyond 25 ppm and the CO2 concentration climbs above 4500 ppm, or if the soil moisture percentage ascends past 50% and the temperature and humidity reach 50 °C and 90%, respectively, danger level 2 is promptly triggered.

In highest echelon of scrutiny is evaluating exceptionally elevated threshold values. A multi-faceted examination entails confirming whether the CH4 concentration rises above 35 ppm, the CO2 concentration exceeds 4800 ppm, the soil moisture percentage breaches 60%, the temperature soars above 55 °C, and the humidity reaches 100%. Fulfilling these stringent criteria culminates in the designation of danger level 3.

In essence, the anomaly detection framework is characterized by its layered approach, systematically gauging different tiers of potential hazards. From foundational thresholds to relative interactions and ultimately to extreme parameters, this methodology ensures a comprehensive understanding of potential abnormalities, enabling proactive responses based on varying degrees of risk.

This meticulous tiered approach to anomaly detection embodies the commitment to a holistic understanding of potential risks. By traversing through layers of assessment, it is not only capture overt abnormalities but also uncover subtle interactions and extreme outliers that might otherwise go unnoticed.

At the foundational level, where individual parameter thresholds are evaluated, it establish a baseline for potential hazards. This is akin to a preliminary safety net that catches scenarios where any single parameter breaches its safety limit. These initial triggers prompt a swift response, allowing for pre-emptive actions to mitigate risks before they escalate.

Transitioning to the realm of relative anomalies, it venture into the dynamic interplay between different parameters. This stage recognizes that certain risks might not be apparent when considering parameters in isolation. However, when specific combinations of conditions are met, they can lead to significant hazards. This tier emphasizes the importance of a comprehensive approach to risk assessment, where the collective impact of multiple factors is acknowledged and addressed.

The pinnacle of this approach, evaluating exceedingly high thresholds, is a testament to dedication to thorough analysis. By establishing stringent criteria for danger level 3, it addresses scenarios of extreme environmental conditions that could pose serious threats. These conditions are often rare but have the potential for severe consequences, making their identification and response crucial in maintaining safety.

Collectively, the anomaly detection strategy is a sophisticated blend of precision and comprehensiveness. It recognizes that risks can manifest in various ways, from individual parameter breaches to intricate interactions and extreme outliers. This approach involves multiple aspects which enable us to not just react to obvious threats but also identify concealed hazards. This work aim is to improve safety, reduce interruptions, and promote a better comprehension of the intricate connections within the environment observed.

3.3 Sending Alerts Based on the Danger Levels

Once the detection and categorization of danger levels are accomplished through meticulous analysis of sensor data, the system springs into action with tailored response mechanisms. Based on the severity of the danger level identified, distinct alerts come into play, aligning with the commitment to timely and effective risk mitigation.

For instances flagged as danger level 1, a calculated LED alert is initiated. This luminous cue serves as an immediate visual indicator, drawing attention to the potential risk that requires intervention. This visual alert is both noticeable and discernible, ensuring that the concerned party is promptly informed of the situation at hand.

Stepping up to danger level 2, this approach intensifies with the introduction of a purposeful buzzer alert. The acoustic nature of this alert serves as an even more pronounced indicator of heightened risk. The audible alarm is designed to be attention-grabbing and urgent, making it suitable for scenarios demanding a more immediate response.

In the realm of utmost criticality, characterized by danger level 3, this work executes a strategic approach. Central to this approach is the integration of a WiFi module called

ESP8266, which holds a significant role in the overall functionality. Specifically, this module acts as a bridge for enabling communication over a wireless network.

To realize the objective of sending WhatsApp messages, this work has harnessed the capabilities of an external API service called "callmebot service." This service provides a dedicated interface and protocol through which the system can interact with the WhatsApp platform. When the system detects a situation warranting a danger level 3 response, the ESP8266 module is engaged to establish a connection with the callmebot service's API.

Through this connection, the necessary data and content for the WhatsApp message are relayed, initiating the process of alerting designated recipients about the critical event. This entire sequence of actions highlights the commitment to ensuring rapid and effective communication in scenarios of the utmost seriousness, enabled by the integration of advanced technologies like the ESP8266 module and external API services.

4   Results and Discussion

Significant progress of a data collection system through an array of sensors have been effectively established. The approach adopted to visualize this data revolves around the utilization of a 16×2 LCD display as shown in Fig. 4.

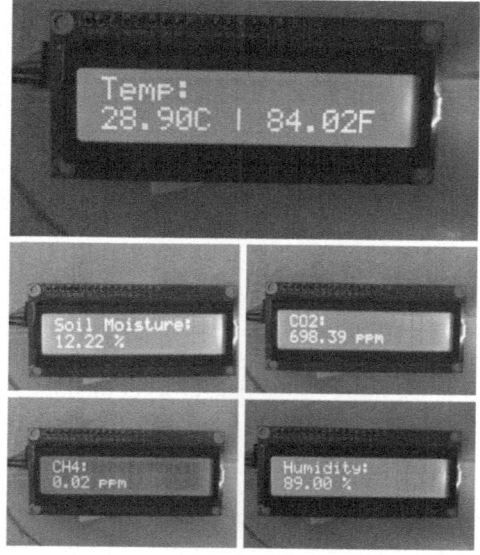

Fig. 4. The images of LCD showing different sensor readings

In addition to the previous accomplishments, the proposed algorithm that was a fundamental component of this design is implemented in the controller. This algorithm serves a crucial purpose: it enables us to determine and assign specific danger levels based on the irregularities or anomalies detected by the sensors.

The algorithmic implementation involves a systematic approach to interpreting the data collected from the sensors. It assesses the readings against predefined thresholds or ranges that define normal operating conditions. When the algorithm identifies readings that deviate beyond these established bounds, it triggers the assignment of corresponding danger levels.

These danger levels are indicative of the severity of the abnormality and serve as a means to prioritize responses or interventions. The danger level 1 will be indicated in LCD screen as preliminary warning to the workers as shown in Fig. 5.

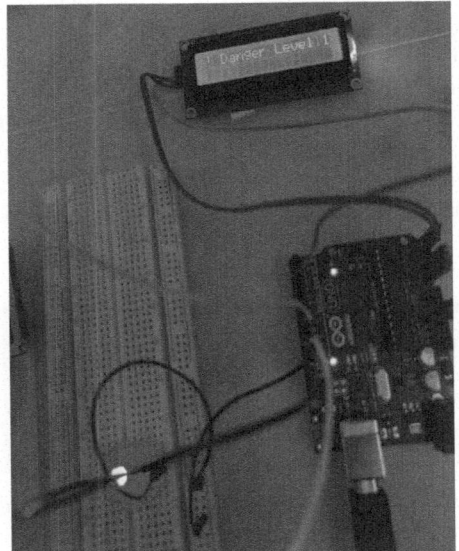

Fig. 5. The danger level 1 indication in an LED light

Fig. 6. The danger level 2 and danger level 3 on the LCD

Furthermore, it achieves significant milestones related to the response mechanisms for danger levels 2 and 3 as shown in Fig. 6. In the context of danger level 2, the key accomplishment lies in the successful implementation of an alert system using a buzzer. This means that whenever the sensor data reaches a threshold indicative of danger level 2, the system efficiently triggers a distinct audible alert through the buzzer. This auditory signal serves as an immediate warning, drawing attention to the moderate level of abnormality detected by the sensors.

Moving on to danger level 3, it has achieved a noteworthy feat by establishing a mechanism to send notifications via WhatsApp as shown in Fig. 7. When the system detects a reading that corresponds to danger level 3, it adeptly initiates the process of sending a notification through the WhatsApp platform. This notification system ensures that designated individuals or parties are promptly informed about the critical nature of the situation as indicated by the sensor data.

By accomplishing these results, it has effectively transformed this work into a comprehensive and responsive system. The integration of alert mechanisms for varying levels of danger enhances the practicality and effectiveness of solution, ensuring that appropriate actions can be taken in a timely manner to address potential issues or anomalies.

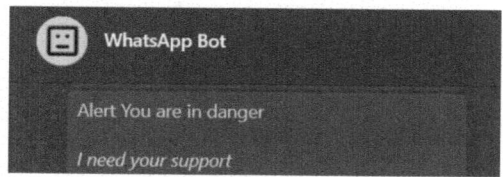

Fig. 7. The screenshot of a sample message sent to a person outside using ESP8266

5   Conclusion

This initiative is focused on a significant goal to improve environmental monitoring and safety procedures in coal mines. In essence, the endeavor revolves around achieving a dual objective – to enhance the well-being of the workforce operating within these mines and to optimize the operational efficiencies that drive the coal mining industry. To materialize this vision, a multifaceted three-stage alert process is meticulously devised that serves as the cornerstone of this innovative solution. This alert system is thoughtfully designed to detect and respond to deviations and irregularities in the mine environment. The tri-stage alert process accommodates not only the needs of the miners working in the heart of the mine but also extends its protective reach to encompass external stakeholders, such as supervisors and dedicated departments responsible for oversight. By catering to varying levels of urgency, the alert process tackles potential hazards head-on, significantly minimizing the risk of accidents and undesirable incidents. At the same time, it streamlines responses, maximizing operational efficiency. By synergizing technology, data analytics, and a well-orchestrated alert system, it aspire to usher in a new era of safety practices that safeguard lives, preserve resources, and propel the coal mining industry toward sustainable success.

Acknowledgement. We would like to convey our gratitude to Amrita Vishwa Vidyapeetham and Chancellor Sri Mata Amritananda Mayi Devi, for providing us a chance to showcase our efforts towards this societal applications.

References

1. Kock, D., Oberholzer, J.W.: The development and application of electronic technology to increase health, safety, and productivity in the South African coal mining industry. IEEE Trans. Ind. Appl. **33**(1), 100–105 (1997)
2. Hamrin, H.: Guide to Underground Mining: Methods and Applications. Atlas Copco (1980)
3. Kumar, D.: Application of modern tools and techniques for mine safety & disaster management. J. Inst. Eng. (India) Ser. D **97**, 77–85 (2016)
4. Xiao, W., Xu, J., Lv, X.: Establishing a georeferenced spatio-temporal database for Chinese coal mining accidents between 2000 and 2015. Geomat. Nat. Haz. Risk **10**(1), 242–270 (2019). https://doi.org/10.1080/19475705.2018.1521476
5. Wang, L., Cao, Q., Zhou, L.: Research on the influencing factors in coal mine production safety based on the combination of DEMATEL and ISM. Saf. Sci. **103**, 51–61 (2018)
6. Narendran, P., Reddy, V., Saju, S., Suriya, L.U., Ravi Kumar Pandi, V.: Smart home with condition monitoring. In: Ranganathan, G., Fernando, X., Shi, F. (eds.) Inventive Communication and Computational Technologies. LNNS, vol. 311, pp. 653–667. Springer, Singapore (2022). https://doi.org/10.1007/978-981-16-5529-6_50
7. Kumar, M.N., Ramesh, M.V.: Accurate IoT based slope instability sensing system for landslide detection. IEEE Sens. J. **22**(17), 17151–17161 (2022). https://doi.org/10.1109/JSEN.2022. 3189903
8. Kumar, K., Chaudhary, S., Anandaram, H., Kumar, R., Gupta, A., Joshi, K.: Industry 4.0 and health care system with special reference to mental health. In: 2023 1st International Conference on Intelligent Computing and Research Trends, ICRT 2023 (2023). https://doi. org/10.1109/ICRT57042.2023.10146640
9. Balasundaram, A., Routray, S., Prabu, A.V., Krishnan, P., Malla, P.P., Maiti, M.: Internet of Things (IoT) based smart healthcare system for efficient diagnostics of health parameters of patients in emergency care. IEEE Internet Things J., 1 (2023). https://doi.org/10.1109/JIOT. 2023.3246065
10. Ansari, A.H., Shaikh, K., Kadu, P., Rishikesh, N.: IoT based coal mine safety monitoring and alerting system. Int. J. Sci. Res. Sci. Eng. Technol. (IJSRSET) **8**(3), 404–410 (2021)
11. Manohara, K.M., Nayan Chandan, D.C., Pooja, S.V., Sonika, P., Ravikumar, K.I.: IOT based coal mine safety monitoring and alerting system. Int. J. Eng. Res. Technol. (IJERT) ICEI **10**(11) (2022)
12. Manasa, T., Kadali, J., Syed, N., Raju, G.S.V.S.K., Jamal, K.: IoT based coal mine safety monitoring and warning system. In: 2022 Sixth International Conference on I-SMAC (IoT in Social, Mobile, Analytics and Cloud) (I-SMAC), Dharan, Nepal, pp. 11–15 (2022). https:// doi.org/10.1109/I-SMAC55078.2022.9987361
13. Rijo George, M., Nalluri, M.R., Anand, K.B.: Severity prediction of construction site accidents using simple and ensemble decision trees. In: Marano, G.C., Ray Chaudhuri, S., Unni Kartha, G., Kavitha, P.E., Prasad, R., Achison, R.J. (eds.) SECON 2021. LNCE, vol. 171, pp. 599–608. Springer, Cham (2022). https://doi.org/10.1007/978-3-030-80312-4_50

14. Chennupati, V.D., Reddy, Y.V., Kanth, B.S.K., Rishwanth, K.V., Karthik, K., Nisha, K.L.: A machine learning-powered web application for accident severity detection. In: Proceedings of the 5th International Conference on Inventive Research in Computing Applications, ICIRCA 2023, pp. 540–545 (2023). https://doi.org/10.1109/ICIRCA57980.2023.10220796

15. Porselvi, T., Ganesh, S., Janaki, B., Priyadarshini, K., Shajitha Begam, S.: IoT based coal mine safety and health monitoring system using LoRaWAN. In: 2021 3rd International Conference on Signal Processing and Communication (ICPSC), Coimbatore, India, pp. 49–53 (2021). https://doi.org/10.1109/ICSPC51351.2021.9451673

16. Qiang, C., Ping, S.J., Zhe, Z., Fan, Z.: Zig bee based intelligent helmet for coal miners. In: Proceedings of the IEEE World Congress on Computer Science and Information Engineering, pp. 433–35 (2009)

17. Mishra, A., Malhotra, S., Singh, H.P.: Real time monitoring & analyzation of hazardous parameters in underground coal mines using intelligent helmet system. In: 2018 4th IEEE International Conference on Computational Intelligence & Communication Technology, pp. 1–5 (2018)

18. Hai, M.A., Jyoty, W.B., Uddin, R.S., Mahfuza, R., Rahman, Y.: IoT-based automated miner tracking and imperilment observance system. In: 2022 IEEE Delhi Section Conference (DELCON), New Delhi, India, pp. 1–6 (2022). https://doi.org/10.1109/DELCON54057.2022.9753002

19. Prabu, A.V., Gayatri, N., Madhuri, J., Rajasoundaran, S., Shaik, M.F., Velliangiri, S.: Smart coal mine safety & monitoring system. In: 2022 6th International Conference on Trends in Electronics and Informatics (ICOEI), Tirunelveli, India, pp. 408–412 (2022). https://doi.org/10.1109/ICOEI53556.2022.9776791

Enhancing Network Security: A Hybrid Approach for Detection and Mitigation of Distributed Denial-of-Service Attacks Using Machine Learning

Nizo Jaman Shohan[(✉)] [ID], Gazi Tanbhir [ID], Faria Elahi, Ahsan Ullah, and Md. Nazmus Sakib

Department of Computer Science and Engineering, World University of Bangladesh, Dhaka, Bangladesh
nizojamanshohan@gmail.com, gazitanbhir@gmail.com, fariae2019@gmail.com
{ahsan.ullah,nazmus.sakib}@cse.wub.edu.bd

Abstract. The distributed denial-of-service (DDoS) attack stands out as a highly formidable cyber threat, representing an advanced form of the denial-of-service (DoS) attack. A DDoS attack involves multiple computers working together to overwhelm a system, making it unavailable. On the other hand, a DoS attack is a one-on-one attempt to make a system or website inaccessible. Thus, it is crucial to construct an effective model for identifying various DDoS incidents. Although extensive research has focused on binary detection models for DDoS identification, they face challenges to adapt evolving threats, necessitating frequent updates. Whereas multiclass detection models offer a comprehensive defense against diverse DDoS attacks, ensuring adaptability in the ever-changing cyber threat landscape. In this paper, we propose a Hybrid Model to strengthen network security by combining the feature-extraction abilities of 1D Convolutional Neural Networks (CNNs) with the classification skills of Random Forest (RF) and Multi-layer Perceptron (MLP) classifiers. Using the CIC-DDoS2019 dataset, we perform multiclass classification of various DDoS attacks and conduct a comparative analysis of evaluation metrics for RF, MLP, and our proposed Hybrid Model. After analyzing the results, we draw meaningful conclusions and confirm the superiority of our Hybrid Model by performing thorough cross-validation. Additionally, we integrate our machine learning model with Snort, which provides a robust and adaptive solution for detecting and mitigating various DDoS attacks.

Keywords: Distributed Denial-of-Service (DDoS) · Machine Learning (ML) · Convolutional Neural Networks (CNNs) · Random Forest (RF) · Multi-layer Perceptron (MLP) · Hybrid Model · Intrusion Detection and Prevention System (IDPS) · Snort

A. Verma et al. (Eds.): ANTIC 2023, CCIS 2091, pp. 81–95, 2024.
https://doi.org/10.1007/978-3-031-64064-3_7

1   Introduction

Distributed denial-of-service (DDoS) attacks pose a significant threat to the security of computer networks. A DDoS attack involves a deliberate effort to disturb the regular flow of traffic to a specific server, service, or network by inundating the target or its associated infrastructure with an excessive volume of Internet traffic [1]. DDoS attacks can wreak havoc in real life, disrupting essential online services and crippling businesses by rendering their websites and applications inaccessible. However, Fig. 1 vividly illustrates the distribution of CVSS Scores. CVSS, an acronym for the "Common Vulnerability Scoring System," represents a standardized framework within the field of cybersecurity. Its primary purpose is to evaluate and categorize the severity of vulnerabilities found within software, systems, and networks. It assigns a numerical score to vulnerabilities, ranging from 0.0 (least severe) to 10.0 (most severe) [2,3].

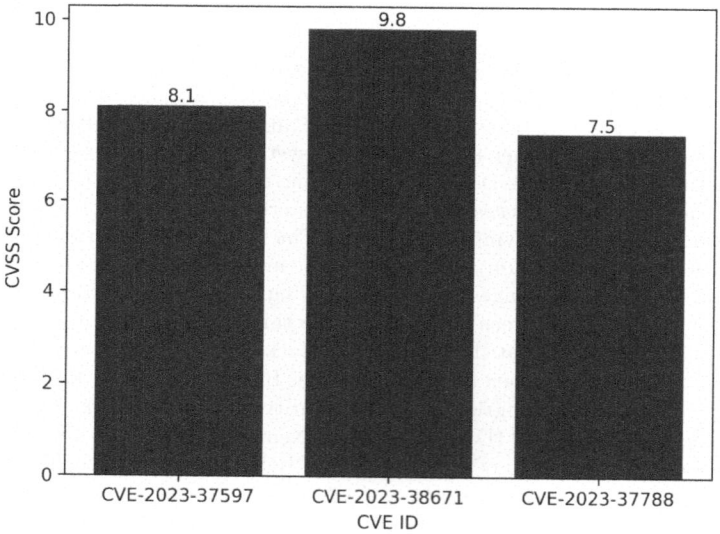

Fig. 1. CVSS scores of various DDoS attacks in 2023 [4–6].

Numerous researchers have historically employed traditional methodologies for detecting DDoS attacks, predominantly relying on signature matching. In this paradigm, the system compares incoming network traffic to a pre-existing database of known attack patterns or signatures [7]. Despite its historical prevalence, this approach exhibits limitations when confronted with emerging and evolving attack types.

Despite the prevalent use of binary detection models by many researchers to identify DDoS incidents, these models may struggle to effectively adapt to evolving threat landscapes [8,9]. Due to their inability to recognize new attack patterns, frequent updates may be required to handle emerging DDoS techniques, rendering them less adaptable over time. In contrast, a multiclass detection model distinguishes attack types (e.g., UDP floods, SYN floods, HTTP floods), offering a comprehensive defense against diverse DDoS attacks. Its adaptability ensures a robust and sustainable defense in the ever-changing cyber threat landscape.

Based on these concerns, we proposed a Hybrid Model to bolster network security by synergizing the feature-extraction capabilities of 1D Convolutional Neural Networks (CNNs) with the classification prowess of Random Forest (RF) and Multi-layer Perceptron (MLP) classifiers. The study utilizes the CIC-DDoS2019 dataset for multiclass classification of various DDoS attacks [10].

Finally, we integrate our machine learning model with Snort, a renowned Intrusion Detection and Prevention System (IDPS). This fusion of machine learning and Snort's Intrusion Prevention System (IPS) capabilities equip us with a robust and adaptive solution for detecting and mitigating DDoS attacks, enhancing the resilience of computer networks against evolving threats.

2   Related Work

Addressing the escalating threat posed by Distributed Denial of Service (DDoS) attacks, an advanced deep learning-based detection methodology is proposed. The approach utilizes Logistic Regression, K-Nearest Neighbor, and Random Forest algorithms with the NSL KDD dataset. However, limitations inherent in this dataset, notably its outdated nature and limited coverage of DDoS attacks, hinder a comprehensive analysis. Despite these constraints, the employed models exhibit marked enhancements in accuracy, particularly with the KNN and Random Forest models outperforming Logistic Regression. This underscores the imperative for future research to access more expansive and current datasets to bolster cybersecurity strategies, advocating for the development of real-time DDoS detection tools [11].

In the landscape of cybersecurity, addressing Distributed Denial of Service (DDoS) attacks remains a critical concern prompting exploration of machine learning applications. However, existing research confronts challenges in achieving robust DDoS detection due to the attack's multifaceted nature. This study introduces a machine learning-based strategy employing XGBoost and Random Forest classifiers, utilizing the CICDDoS2019 dataset. While this approach demonstrates improved accuracy rates compared to previous methodologies, some drawbacks persist. Dataset selection profoundly influences model performance, and despite advancements, the modified XGBoost classifier showcases promising results but doesn't eliminate false positives entirely. Additionally, the training time for sophisticated classifiers like XGBoost remains considerable, limiting real-time applicability. Thus, while this study showcases progress in DDoS detection, challenges in dataset dependency and real-time implementation persist, warranting further refinement in future research endeavors [9].

Within the realm of IoT security, assessing the detection of DDoS attacks holds paramount importance, spotlighting the complexities and evasiveness inherent in these incursions. The use of Machine Learning (ML) stands as a key strategy in thwarting these threats, with researchers examining diverse ML algorithms through the lens of the CICDDoS2019 dataset. They advocate for enriching this dataset to effectively categorize a wider spectrum of attack types, underscoring the pivotal role of implementing novel algorithms to heighten the efficacy and efficiency of detection mechanisms [12].

The domain of network security and the detection and mitigation of DDoS attacks have undergone substantial advancements driven by pioneering research endeavors. Sanmorino and Yazid introduced the flow pattern-based DDoS attack detection by analysing network traffic characteristics, encompassing source and destination IP addresses, traffic types, and volume [13].

Zekri et al. delved into the susceptibility of cloud computing environments to DDoS attacks and propose a DDoS detection system hinging on the C4.5 algorithm, underlining the potential of machine learning techniques in fortifying cloud resources [14].

Idhammad, Afdel, and Belouch introduced an online sequential semi-supervised machine learning approach for DDoS detection, adeptly amalgamating supervised and unsupervised techniques to elevate detection accuracy while curtailing false positives [15].

Mapanga et al. proposed a hybrid neural network design that combines MLP and CNN architectures in order to improve the detection rate of time-delayed assaults. This work focuses on detecting malicious nodes that deliberately or randomly drop packets destined for other target nodes. Furthermore, each packet drop attack is classified according to its attack type by watching and analyzing how each packet drop assault affects network properties. Furthermore, accomplishment in limiting false alarms during the detection of innovative assaults in the MANET environment IDS, spanning several packet dropping attack types such as selfish, sleep deprivation, and Blackhole attacks, is demonstrated [16].

The utilization of Snort and Zeek, integrated with Machine Learning (ML), within Software-Defined Networking (SDN) shows promise in distinguishing between benign and malicious traffic in simulated environments. However, a drawback lies within SDN itself, particularly in its susceptibility to DDoS attacks. Snort's focus primarily on volumetric DDoS attacks within SDN architecture might overlook non-volumetric variations, while also concentrating primarily on the control layer, potentially leaving other layers vulnerable. This highlights the necessity for future advancements in SDN security, encompassing a wider array of attack types and deeper analysis to fortify against diverse DDoS threats [17].

Furthermore, James et al. conducted an in-depth exploration of the effectiveness of 25 time-based features for the detection and categorization of 12 types of DDoS attacks. Their investigation encompassed both binary and multiclass classification. While achieving a notable 99% accuracy in binary DDoS detection, the accuracy experienced a drop to approximately 70% when classifying specific attack types [18]. In continuation of this foundational work, our research introduces a novel model that surpasses the 70% accuracy achieved by existing models in multiclass detection.

3 Methodology

In this part the various steps of our Hybrid Model creation are given. Also, we described the detection and mitigation process of various DDoS attacks based on our hybrid approach.

3.1 Preprocessing

As mentioned, we have the CIC-DDoS2019 dataset, a standard benchmark dataset for our experimental results. We conducted a comprehensive check for missing values within the dataset using Pandas' isnull() function, which identifies missing values in dataset. After that, we dropped irrelevant columns, including one that served as the label for binary detection. Since the goal is to develop a multiclassification model, we retained only the column with multiclass labels.

3.2 1D CNN Feature Extraction

Due to its remarkable capacity for feature extraction, the utilization of 1D CNN is extensive in the analysis of time series data [19]. In the initial stage, we partitioned the dataset into feature (X) and label (y) components to facilitate supervised machine learning. Subsequently, we divided the dataset into training and testing subsets, allocating 80% for training and 20% for testing, while ensuring reproducibility via a random seed of 42. Standardization of the features is performed using the StandardScaler() function from scikit-learn, thereby enhancing model convergence and reliability.

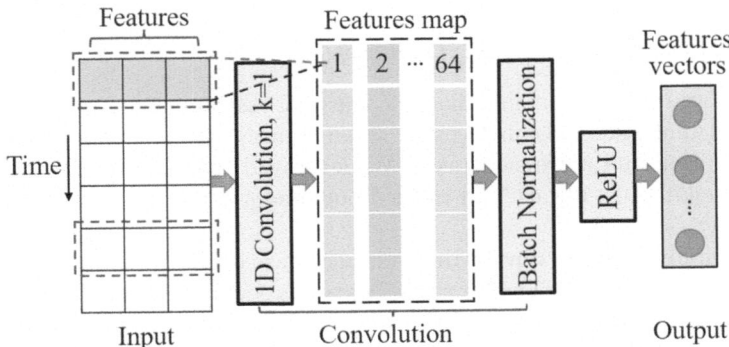

Fig. 2. Feature extraction framework of 1D CNN [20].

Furthermore, to align with the input requirements of our 1D CNN model, we reshaped the data into a 2D tensor using Python's reshape() method. This transformation ensured data compatibility for subsequent feature extraction. Our feature extraction methodology leveraged a 1D CNN model implemented with TensorFlow and Keras, comprising an input layer, a convolutional layer, and a global average pooling layer (Fig. 2). The convolutional layer utilized filters and kernels to capture crucial data patterns, while the global average pooling operation summarized the extracted features, creating a representative feature set.

In 1D CNN, the convolution operation is a fundamental mathematical concept. It involves applying a convolutional kernel (a small filter) to the input signal or feature sequence. The kernel slides over the input and computes the dot product at each position, resulting in feature maps. Equation (1) expresses the 1D convolution operation.

$$Y_i = \sum_{j=1}^{N} X_{i+j-1} W_j \tag{1}$$

Note that in Eq. (1):
'Y_i' is the output feature map at position i.
'X_{i+j-1}' is the input sequence at position $i + j - 1$.
'W_j' is the kernel's weight at position j.
'N' is the kernel size.

The Rectified Linear Unit (ReLU) activation function is commonly applied to the output of the convolution operation in convolutional neural networks to introduce non-linearity. Equation (2) expresses the ReLU activation function.

$$ReLU(x) = \max(0, x) \tag{2}$$

Then the feature extraction model is applied to the reshaped data, resulting in X_train_features and X_test_features.

3.3   Random Forest Model Training

Random Forest is an ensemble machine learning method that combines the predictions of multiple decision trees to enhance accuracy and reduce overfitting in classification and regression tasks. We leveraged the RandomForestClassifier from the scikit-learn library and trained our model using the X_train_features as input.

Gini impurity occurs during the training phase of the Random Forest model when we call model_rf.fit(X_train_features, y_train) and builds a forest of decision trees by making these feature and threshold decisions at each node on the training data. Equation (3) expresses the Gini impurity.

$$Gini(p) = 1 - \sum_{i=1}^{C} p_i^2 \tag{3}$$

Note that in Eq. (3), $Gini(p)$ is the Gini impurity of the node. C is the number of classes. p_i represents the proportion of data points belonging to class i in the node.

Having successfully trained the RF model, we proceeded to the testing phase. In this stage, the RF model made predictions on `X_test_Features` using `predict()` function and calculated the accuracy using `accuracy_score()` function of the `sklearn.metrics` library.

Aggregating predictions by majority voting happens in the testing phase when we make predictions on the test data using the trained Random Forest classifier. Equation (4) expresses the Majority voting.

$$\hat{y} = argmax_y \sum_{i=1}^{n} 1(\hat{y}_i = \hat{y}) \tag{4}$$

Note that in Eq. (4):
$\hat{y}$ is the final prediction.
$\hat{y}_i$ is the prediction of the i-th tree.
n is the number of trees.
$1(\cdot)$ is the indicator function.

3.4 MLP Model Training

MLP is a foundational feedforward neural network architecture known for its capability to model complex non-linear relationships in data, making it a vital tool in various machine learning and pattern recognition tasks. During this training phase, we utilized the `MLPClassifier` from the scikit-learn library, and trained our model using X_train_features.

The MLP architecture consists of multiple layers, each with its set of neurons and weights. Equation (5) expresses the output of a neuron in a hidden layer or the output layer.

$$y_j = \phi(v_j) \tag{5}$$

Note that in Eq. (5):
y_j represents the output of the j-th neuron in the layer.
$\phi(\cdot)$ represents the activation function.
v_j represents the weighted sum of the input connections for the j-th neuron.

As an activation function, we used the ReLU activation function. Then, we proceeded to the testing phase. In this stage, the MLP model made predictions on `X_test_Features` as we did in the Random Forest model's testing phase.

The MLP learning process employs backpropagation, constituting a form of supervised learning. It involves adjusting the connection weights to minimize the error in the network's predictions. Equation (6) expresses the error in an output node (j) for the n-th data point.

$$e_j(n) = d_j(n) - y_j(n) \tag{6}$$

Note that in Eq. (6), $e_j(n)$ is the error at the j-th output node for the n-th data point. $d_j(n)$ is the desired target value. $y_j(n)$ is the actual output produced by the neuron.

The change in each weight (w_{ij}) can be computed using gradient descent. The weight update for a connection from neuron i to neuron j is given by:

$$\Delta w_{ij}(n) = -\eta \frac{\partial \varepsilon(n)}{\partial v_j(n)} y_i(n) \tag{7}$$

Note that in Eq. (7), $\Delta w_{ij}(n)$ represents the change in weight from neuron i to neuron j for the n-th data point. η is the learning rate. $\frac{\partial \varepsilon(n)}{\partial v_j(n)}$ is the gradient of the error with respect to the weighted sum of inputs for neuron j. $y_i(n)$ represents the output of the previous neuron i.

These mathematical expressions underpin the learning process in the MLP, enabling it to adapt and improve its predictions over time.

3.5   Proposed Hybrid Model

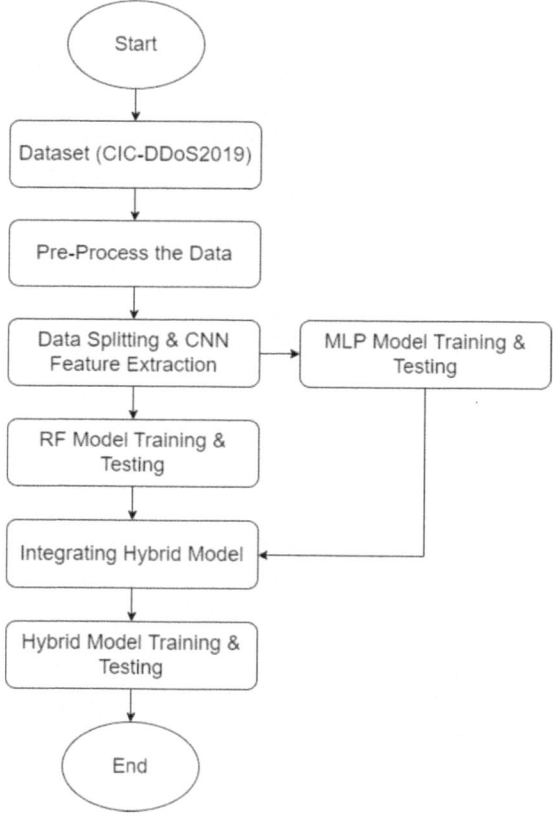

Fig. 3. Integration of proposed Hybrid Model.

In Fig. 3, we initiate our process by employing the CIC-DDoS2019 dataset. The journey begins with data preprocessing and then completes feature extraction using 1D Convolutional Neural Networks (CNNs).

The workflow splits into two main paths: In the first path, we train the Random Forest model, evaluate its performance, and then proceed to the integration point for the Hybrid Model. Concurrently, the second path involves the training and performance assessment of the Multilayer Perceptron (MLP) model, culminating in a similar integration point for the Hybrid Model.

The next stage embodies the culmination of our research and development efforts. At this juncture, the Hybrid Model emerges as the result of our meticulous integration of the strengths of both the RandomForestClassifier and MLP-Classifier. We utilized scikit-learn's StackingClassifier to assemble both models and employ a meta-learner to make final predictions. And the final stage refers to the testing phase of our model.

3.6   Integration of Hybrid Model with Snort

To enhance network security, we introduced custom pre-processor that seamlessly integrate our machine learning-based Hybrid Model with Snort. We developed the custom pre-processor using custom C code to create the necessary pre-processing components. Our process began with defining functions within the custom pre-processor code responsible for packet processing, information extraction, and data transformation.

Subsequently, we integrated our custom pre-processor code with the Snort source code by modifying Snort's configuration files, effectively incorporating our custom pre-processor into Snort's pre-processing pipeline. After that, we recompiled Snort to include our custom pre-processor. This step involved running the appropriate compilation commands to rebuild the Snort executable, now equipped with our enhancements.

This process resulted in the development of a fortified security system, seamlessly blending the strengths of our Hybrid Model with Snort's robust mitigation capabilities.

3.7   Detection and Mitigation Process

In Fig. 4, real-time data is initially captured by Snort from an authorized source. The data goes through a custom pre-processing pipeline, which includes cleaning and formatting the captured traffic data, normalizing numerical features, and extracting relevant information for data transformation. The pre-processed data is then prepared for use with the Hybrid Model.

The Hybrid Model checks whether the traffic is malicious or not. If it identifies malicious characteristics, the pre-processor signals "Yes" to Snort, which proceeds with the mitigation process. If the data analysis does not indicate DDoS characteristics, Snort allows the traffic to pass.

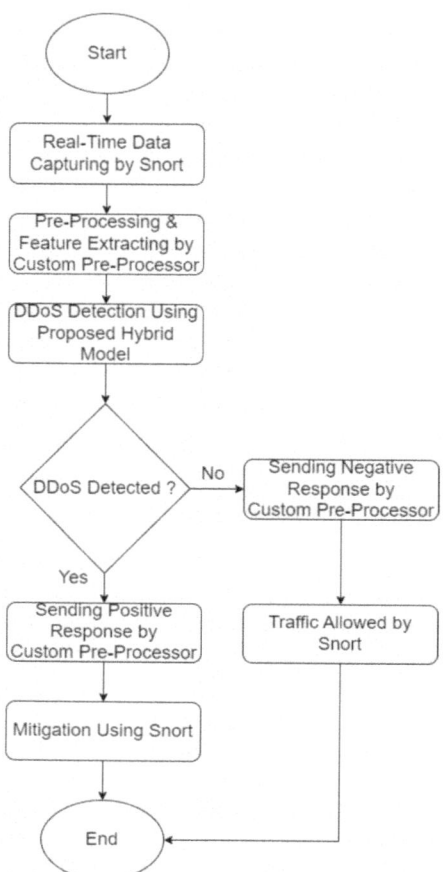

Fig. 4. Proposed hybrid approach for detection and mitigation.

4   Experimental Results

In this segment, we elucidate the proficiency and effectiveness of individual models to emphasize comparisons between the models on evaluation metrics. Furthermore, we confirm the superiority of our Hybrid Model by performing thorough cross-validation.

4.1   Evaluation Metrics

The following metrics are commonly used for evaluating classification models:

- **Accuracy (ACC)** measures the proportion of correctly classified instances in the dataset. It is expressed as:

$$ACC = \frac{TP + TN}{TP + TN + FP + FN} \tag{8}$$

– **Precision (PRE)** quantifies the accuracy of positive predictions and is defined as:

$$PRE = \frac{TP}{TP + FP} \tag{9}$$

– **Recall (REC)**, also known as True Positive Rate (TPR) or Sensitivity, indicates the ability of the model to identify all relevant instances. It is given by:

$$REC = \frac{TP}{TP + FN} \tag{10}$$

– **F1 Score (F1)** is the harmonic mean of precision and recall and balances the trade-off between them:

$$F1 = 2 \cdot \frac{PRE \cdot REC}{PRE + REC} \tag{11}$$

Where:
TP = Accurate Predictions of Positive Instances (True Positives)
TN = Accurate Predictions of Negative Instances (True Negatives)
FP = Inaccurate Predictions of Positive Instances (False Positives)
FN = Inaccurate Predictions of Negative Instances (False Negatives)

These metrics provide a comprehensive view of the model's performance by considering different aspects of classification accuracy as Fig. 5.

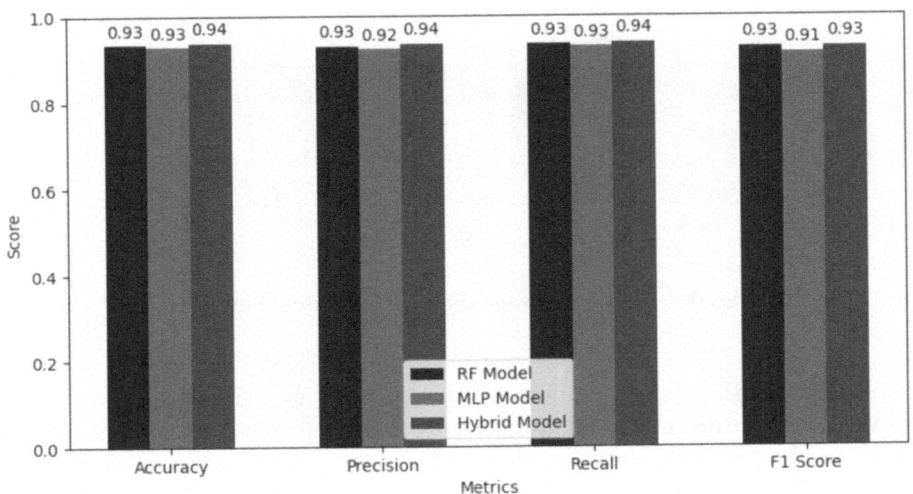

Fig. 5. Performance comparison of individual models in evaluation metrics.

In our performance evaluation, the Hybrid Model, a combination of the Random Forest (RF) and Multi-Layer Perceptron (MLP) classifiers, outperformed both individual models. With an impressive overall average score of around 0.94, the Hybrid Model demonstrated superior accuracy and robustness compared to RF (0.93) and MLP (0.92). These results highlight the Hybrid Model's effectiveness, making it a compelling choice for multiclass predictive models across diverse applications.

4.2   Cross-Validation

Cross-validation stands as a powerful tool for assessing a model's generalization capabilities while identifying potential underfitting and overfitting concerns. Underfitting manifests when a model performs subpar on both training and validation data while overfitting is evidenced by the model excelling in training but faltering during validation in each fold. In contrast, a well-fitted model consistently demonstrates robust performance on both training and validation data.

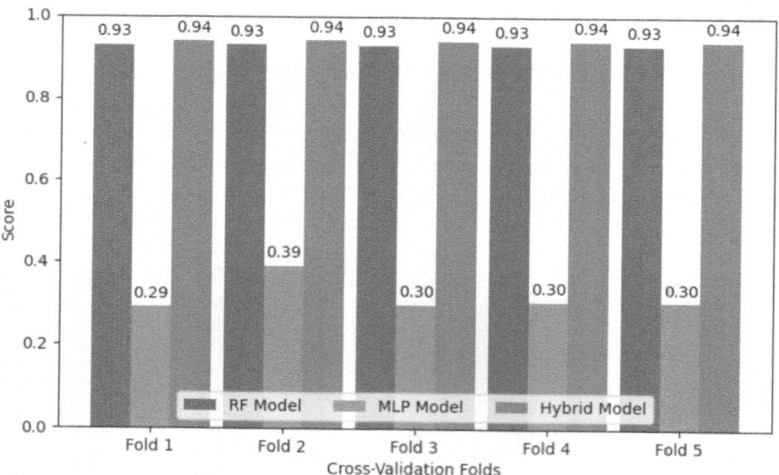

Fig. 6. 5-Fold Cross-validation for individual models.

In our case, the Hybrid Model consistently achieves accuracy scores of 0.94 in every fold during cross-validation shown in Fig. 6, affirming its well-fitted nature and its ability to generalize effectively to new, unseen data. In comparison, while the Random Forest model also demonstrates strong performance with an accuracy of 0.93, there is a noticeable drop in accuracy for the Multi-Layer Perceptron model during cross-validation. This highlights the Hybrid Model's robustness and reliability in maintaining high accuracy across different folds, setting it apart in terms of performance and generalization capabilities.

4.3   Discussion

In the context of network security, the interplay between detection and mitigation is crucial. Improved detection forms the foundation for effective mitigation strategies. The integration of advanced machine learning models with Snort highlights the importance of enhancing the detection phase, which is critical for more effective mitigation.

The performance metrics of all models are summarized in Table 1.

Table 1. Performance Metrics of All Models

Models	Accuracy	Precision	Recall	F1	Avg Cross-Val
RF Model	0.93	0.93	0.93	0.93	0.93
MLP Model	0.93	0.92	0.93	0.91	0.31
Hybrid Model	0.94	0.94	0.94	0.93	0.94

These findings underscore the potential of our proposed Hybrid Model in enhancing network security, opening the door to more robust and accurate DDoS attack detection and mitigation.

Although our research has produced promising results, a crucial aspect remains unexplored-namely, the real-world performance of our model. This uncharted territory stems from the complexities of conducting authentic DDoS attack simulations in controlled environments, where resource constraints, such as the requirement for multiple high-powered PCs, pose significant challenges.

5   Conclusion

This study introduces a robust Hybrid Model for DDoS attack detection, achieving an impressive 94% accuracy in cross-validation and evaluation metrics - surpassing the 70% accuracy of existing models in the case of multiclass detection. The model's capability for multiclass detection signifies a significant advancement in network security, emphasizes the shortcomings of binary models, and advocates for multiclass models in the ever-evolving threat landscape. It is essential to acknowledge the absence of real-world testing in the current study. Moving forward, we will focus on conducting rigorous real-world testing to validate the model's performance in authentic DDoS attack scenarios. This exploration is crucial for translating our promising findings into practical and impactful contributions to network security, ensuring the model's effectiveness in real-world applications.

References

1. CLOUDFLARE, What is a distributed denial-of-service (DDoS) attack. https://www.cloudflare.com/learning/ddos/what-is-a-ddos-attack/. Accessed 25 Nov 2023
2. Mell, P., Scarfone, K., Romanosky, S.: Common vulnerability scoring system. IEEE Secur. Privacy Mag. **4**, 85–89 (2006). https://doi.org/10.1109/msp.2006.145
3. NIST, National Vulnerability Database. https://nvd.nist.gov/vuln-metrics/cvss. Accessed 25 Nov 2023
4. NIST, CVE-2023-37597 Detail. https://nvd.nist.gov/vuln/detail/CVE-2023-37597. Accessed 25 Nov 2023
5. NIST, CVE-2023-38671 Detail. https://nvd.nist.gov/vuln/detail/CVE-2023-38671. Accessed 25 Nov 2023
6. NIST, CVE-2023-37788 Detail. https://nvd.nist.gov/vuln/detail/CVE-2023-37788. Accessed 25 Nov 2023
7. Szynkiewicz, P.: Signature-based detection of botnet DDoS attacks. In: Kołodziej, J., Repetto, M., Duzha, A. (eds.) Cybersecurity of Digital Service Chains. LNCS, vol. 13300, pp. 120–135. Springer, Cham (2022). https://doi.org/10.1007/978-3-031-04036-8_6
8. Kareem, M.I., Jasim, M.N.: DDOS attack detection using lightweight partial decision tree algorithm. In: 2022 International Conference on Computer Science and Software Engineering (CSASE), Duhok, Iraq, pp. 362–367 (2022). https://doi.org/10.1109/CSASE51777.2022.9759824.
9. Santhosh, S., Sambath, M., Thangakumar, J.: Detection of DDOS attack using machine learning models. In: 2023 International Conference on Networking and Communications (ICNWC), Chennai, India, pp. 1–6 (2023). https://doi.org/10.1109/ICNWC57852.2023.10127537
10. Sharafaldin, I., Lashkari, A.H., Hakak, S., Ghorbani, A.A.: Developing realistic distributed denial of service (DDoS) attack dataset and taxonomy. In: 2019 International Carnahan Conference on Security Technology (ICCST) (2019). https://doi.org/10.1109/ccst.2019.8888419
11. Pandey, R., Pandey, M., Nazarov, A.: Enhanced DDoS detection using machine learning. In: 2023 6th International Conference on Information Systems and Computer Networks (ISCON), Mathura, India, 2023, pp. 1–4 (2023). https://doi.org/10.1109/ISCON57294.2023.10112033.
12. Devi, R.S., Bharathi, R., Kumar, P.K.: Investigation on efficient machine learning algorithm for DDoS attack detection. In: 2023 International Conference on Computer, Electrical & Communication Engineering (ICCECE), Kolkata, India, pp. 1–5 (2023). https://doi.org/10.1109/ICCECE51049.2023.10085248.
13. Sanmorino, A., Yazid, S.: DDoS attack detection method and mitigation using pattern of the flow. In: 2013 International Conference of Information and Communication Technology (ICoICT) (2013). https://doi.org/10.1109/icoict.2013.6574541
14. Zekri, M., Kafhali, S.E., Aboutabit, N., Saadi, Y.: DDoS attack detection using machine learning techniques in cloud computing environments. In: 2017 3rd International Conference of Cloud Computing Technologies and Applications (CloudTech) (2017). https://doi.org/10.1109/cloudtech.2017.8284731
15. Idhammad, M., Afdel, K., Belouch, M.: Semi-supervised machine learning approach for DDoS detection. Appl. Intell. **48**, 3193–3208 (2018). https://doi.org/10.1007/s10489-018-1141-2

16. Mapanga, I., Kumar, V., Makondo, W., Kushboo, T., Kadebu, P., Chanda, W.: Design and implementation of an intrusion detection system using MLP-NN for MANET. In: 2017 IST-Africa Week Conference (IST-Africa), Windhoek, Namibia, pp. 1–12 (2017). https://doi.org/10.23919/ISTAFRICA.2017.8102374
17. AbdulRaheem, M., Oladipo, I.D., Imoize, A.L., et al.: Machine learning assisted snort and zeek in detecting DDoS attacks in software-defined networking. Int. J. Inf. Technol. **16**, 1627–1643 (2023). https://doi.org/10.1007/s41870-023-01469-3
18. Halladay, J., et al.: Detection and characterization of DDoS attacks using time-based features. IEEE Access **10**, 49794–49807 (2022). https://doi.org/10.1109/ACCESS.2022.3173319
19. Kiranyaz, S., Avci, O., Abdeljaber, O., et al.: 1D convolutional neural networks and applications: a survey. Mech. Syst. Signal Process. **151**, 107398 (2021). https://doi.org/10.1016/j.ymssp.2020.107398
20. Qin, P., Li, H., Li, Z., et al.: A CNN-LSTM car-following model considering generalization ability. Sensors **23**, 660 (2023). https://doi.org/10.3390/s23020660

A Brief Review on LPWAN Technologies for Large Scale Smart Agriculture

Rashmita Sahu$^{(\boxtimes)}$ ⓘ and Priyanka Tripathi ⓘ

NIT Raipur, Raipur, India
{rsahu.phd2022.mca,ptripathi.mca}@nitrr.ac.in

Abstract. The growing Internet of Things (IoT) use in smart agriculture (SA) requires extensive connectivity between intelligent end devices in large-scale agriculture. The broad intercommunication among IoT devices in the field is hampered by the restricted radio coverage and limited capacity to support many devices in conventional wireless sensor networks. The present emphasis in research and development is on Low-Power Wide-Area Networks (LPWANs) as a potential solution for fulfilling long-distance communication requirements while simultaneously reducing power consumption in end devices. LPWAN has emerged as a widely used communication technology for IoT applications because of its cost-efficiency, ability to prolong battery lifespan, and capacity to facilitate long-distance communication. The authors have presented a brief theoretical review and comparison of LPWAN technologies regarding protocol parameters and features, IoT-related characteristics, and cost requirements for deployment in Smart Agriculture. Three popular LPWAN protocols—Sigfox, LoRaWAN, and NB-IoT—provide a complete description of their technical characteristics needed for the application and have been compared regarding network throughput, device lifetime, and overall cost. Based on the existing literature, Sigfox and LoRaWAN are the clear winners. However, NB-IoT provides superior performance in terms of latency and quality of service.

Keywords: Internet of Things · Low Power Wide Area Networks · LoRaWAN · Sigfox · NB-IoT · Smart Agriculture

1 Introduction

Agriculture is essential for the economic development of countries and the survival of human beings since it enables the production of primary food sources [1]. In the coming years, the agricultural industry will suffer a significant challenge due to decreasing resources, unpredictable weather patterns, a rising population, and a decrease in cultivable areas. According to the FAO, the global population is predicted to reach approximately 10 billion by 2050. To adequately nourish this growing population, a 70% increase in food production will be necessary [2, 3]. The global number of IoT devices is expected to nearly double from 15.1 billion in 2020 to more than 29 billion in 2030. Figure 1 shows the Worldwide IoT connected device count from 2019 to 2023, with projections for 2022 to 2030 (in billions) [2]. And digital twins that can be used in many ways in agriculture [4]. Due to the low cost of production and progress in communications technologies and sensors for farmland, it is now possible to measure and analyse things like soil acidity, temperature, and moisture [1–5]. Appropriate communication technology selection is essential in ensuring the efficacy of distant smart farming. The scientific community has extensively studied communication technologies and protocols used in Smart Agriculture [4]. Research in this area has concentrated chiefly on networking protocols [6], energy efficiency, resilience, scalability, and other related aspects. Specific criteria, such as a broad communication range, low power consumption, and cheap cost, are necessary for IoT-enabled SA applications [1, 6].

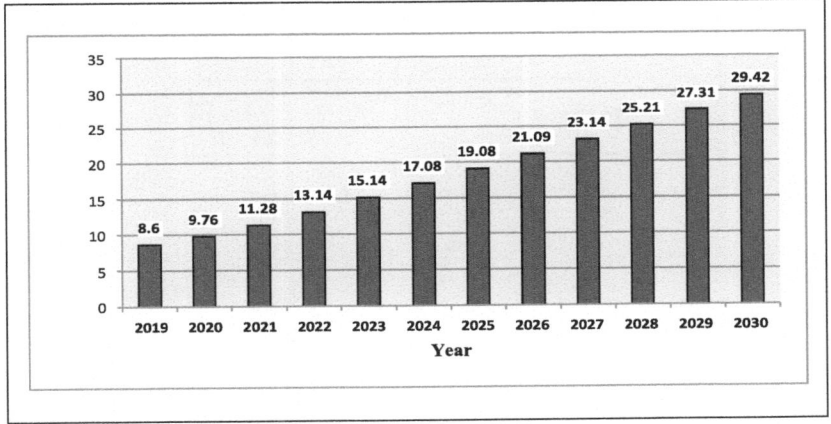

Fig. 1. Worldwide IoT connected device count from 2019 to 2023, (in billions) [2]

Technologies like Bluetooth Low Energy and ZigBee, popular for short-distance communications, cannot meet long-distance transmission needs. Moreover, mobile cellular communication technologies such as 2G, 3G, and 4G might provide a more comprehensive transmission range. Still, this approach has the drawback of exhausting the device's energy resources. Hence, IoT applications demand the development of a LPWAN technology. It has a communication range of up to 40 km in rural areas and 10 km in urban areas, a battery life of up to 10 years, a cost of fewer than five dollars per device, and an annual subscription fee of less than one dollar per device [3]. It was developed specifically for Internet of Things applications, which require transmitting a small number of very brief messages across a wide radio range. Because of these benefits, LPWAN has been the subject of several performance studies in both outdoor and indoor settings [4]. This technology was not introduced until 2013. Many LPWAN systems have emerged in licensed and unlicensed frequency bands. Sigfox, LoRaWAN, and NB-IoT are now considered prominent emerging technologies characterized by significant technological differences. To select the proper protocol for an innovative agricultural application, we have to understand the possible wire-less protocols with their properties, that is explained below in sections.

1.1 Overview of IoT Wireless Communication Technologies for SA

The wireless communication technologies or protocols utilized in IoT applications are broadly categorized into two categories: conventional and LPWAN. Figure 2, which shows the categories of all the protocols used in IoT-based applications. Traditional communication technologies are divided into Cellular, Non-Cellular, and Satellite subcategories. The short-range communication protocols such as RFID, NFC, Zigbee, 6Low-PAN, Bluetooth, and Wi-Fi are coming under the non-cellular subcategory, and the most popular communication technologies such as 2G, 3G, 4G, 5G, and 6G come under Cellular subcategory [6–10].

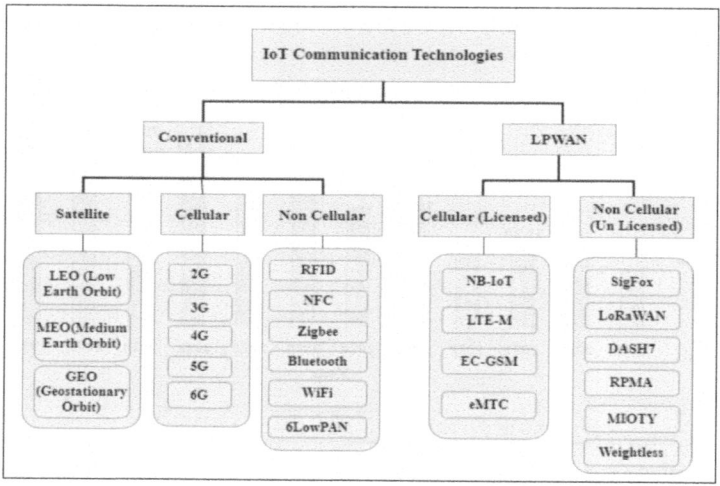

Fig. 2. Category of IoT Communication Technologies

The LPWAN technologies are divided into two subcategories: Cellular (Licensed) and Non-Cellular (UN Licensed). Protocols such as NB-IoT, LTE-M, EC-GSM, and MTC come under the Cellular (Licensed) subcategory. In the Non-Cellular (Un Licensed) subcategory, protocols such as SigFox, LoRaWAN, DASH7, RPMA, MIOTY, and Weightless are coming.

1.2 Categorize Wireless Protocols According to Range for SA

Existing wireless protocols for the Internet of Things may be categorized into three groups according to their respective communication ranges. Bluetooth, radio-frequency identification (RFID), Near-Field Communication (NFC), and ultra-wideband (UWB) are all instances of short-range wireless connectivity technologies that operate within a maximum range of 10 m. ZigBee, LoWPAN, and WiFi [3] are wireless communication technologies with medium-range capabilities, often spanning distances between 10 and 100 m [8]. Cellular networks, networks, such as 2G, 3G, 4G, 5G, and LPWAN, exemplify long-range wireless communication technologies that can carry signals exceeding

100 m. Low-power wide-area networking (LPWAN) is an advanced communication technology specifically developed to cater to the requirements of systems necessitating long-distance networking with minimal power consumption. Figure 3 illustrates an overview of the wireless communication technologies used in IoT-based SA applications, explicitly focusing on short-range and long-range options.

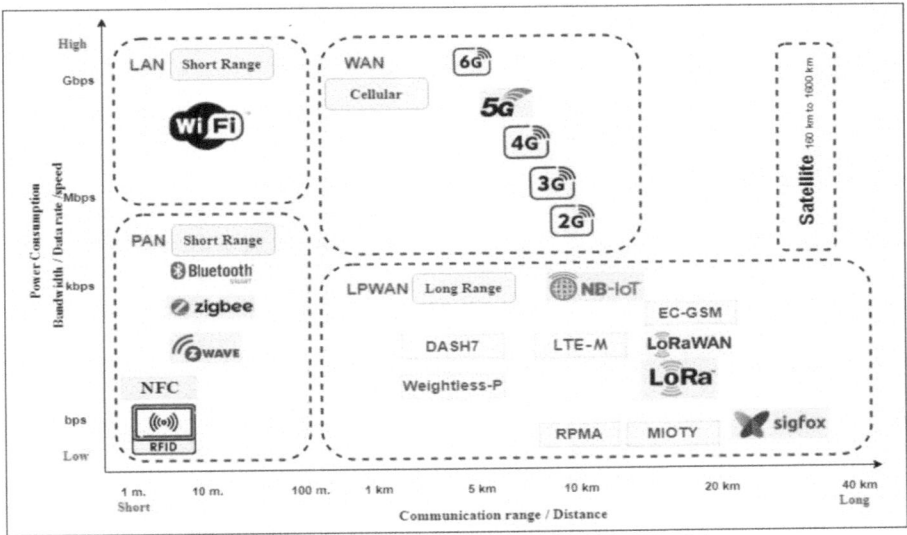

Fig. 3. Wireless Protocols According to Range and Bandwidth [7]

The rest of the article is structured as follows: A Brief Technological overview is given in Sect. 2. The LoRa-based layered architecture for SA is explained in Sect. 3. In Sect. 4, a comparative study of LPWAN protocols such as LoRaWAN, Sigfox, and NB-IoT is performed. We evaluate and conclude the paper in Sect. 5.

2 A Brief Technical Overview of LPWAN

Low-power Wide Area Networks (LPWAN) is a wireless comprehensive area network technology that facilitates the connection of battery-powered devices with limited bandwidth requirements, enabling communication across extensive distances while maintaining low data transfer rates [8]. LPWAN has been specifically designed to cater to the needs of machine-to-machine (M2M) and IoT networks. These networks provide many advantages over typical mobile networks, including reduced operational costs and enhanced power efficiency. Additionally, they can accommodate more interconnected devices throughout a more extensive geographical region. This technology can support a range of packet sizes, typically 10 to 1,000 bytes, while maintaining uplink rates of up to 200 Kbps. The majority of LPWANs exhibit a star topology, whereby each endpoint establishes a direct connection with central access points that are shared across all endpoints, like the structure often seen in Wi-Fi networks [7, 9, 10].

2.1   LPWAN Architecture

The basic structure of LPWAN consists of many vital components, including end devices, gateways, network servers, and an application server, as seen in Fig. 4.

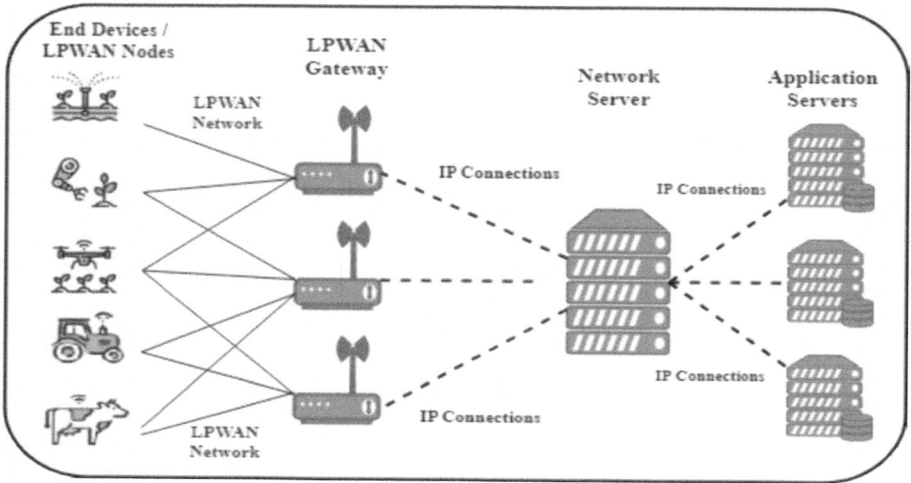

Fig. 4. LPWAN Architecture [9]

2.2   Types of LPWAN

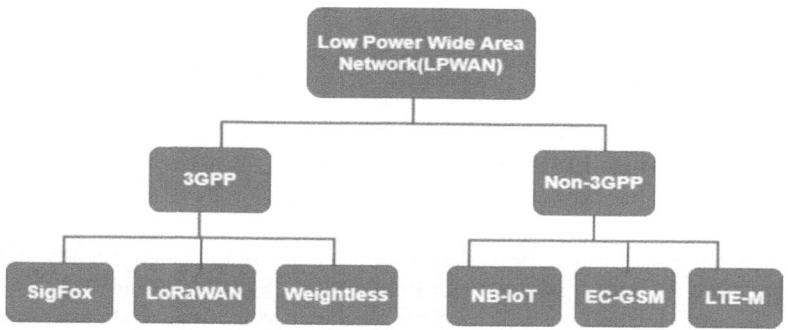

Fig. 5. Types of Most Popular LPWAN

The term LPWAN refers not to a single technology but rather to a collection of several low-power wide area network technologies that may take on a variety of different forms [7, 8]. Figure 5 depicts a categorization of current popular LPWAN technologies.

2.2.1 LoRaWAN (Long Range Wide Area Network)

LoRaWAN, an acronym for Long Range Wide Area Network, is a wireless communication protocol and an LPWAN technology developed explicitly for facilitating low-power, wide-area networking of devices in the context of the Internet of Things (IoT) and machine-to-machine (M2M) applications. Frequently used to establish connections between sensors, actuators, and other devices that need the transmission of limited data quantities over extensive distances while prioritising the preservation of battery energy [4]. The LoRaWAN network operates as a star-of-stars topology, including three essential components: end devices, gateways, and a central network server [6, 8]. However, end devices can transmit signals on many channels to increase their overall data transfer rate, provided that they adhere to the prescribed restrictions for each frequency band [7, 8]. The connection between the network server and the user is established by using one or more gateways, which are also responsible for transmitting downlink messages [10, 11, 14]. The end device exchanges packets with the gateway using the LoRa physical layer. This physical layer establishes a connection with the network server using an IP-based protocol stack. LoRaWAN devices may be categorised into three distinct categories: A, B, and C [8, 17, 18]. Class A and Class B devices are often operated using batteries; however, Class C devices need a connection to the main power supply due to their significant energy consumption [20, 29] (Fig. 6).

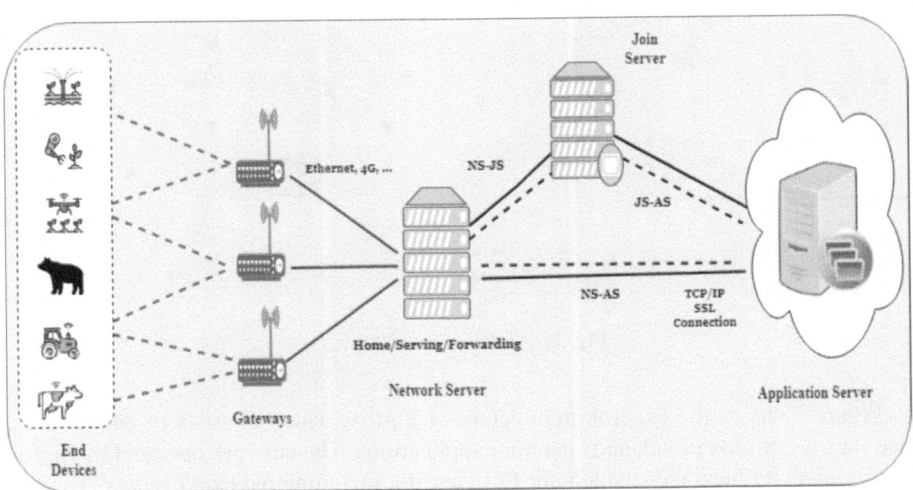

Fig. 6. Architecture of LoRaWAN

The downlink connection can operate in either an asynchronous manner, known as Class C, or in a synchronous method that follows the uplink, referred to as Class A and B. Class A initiates the opening of very concise receiving apertures after transmitting a message, followed by entering a state of dormancy to save energy. In a previous study [11, 24], the authors provide evidence that Class C necessitates 225 times the energy consumption of Class A when considering the static spreading factor (SF) and output power. As a result, our sensor node functions in Class A mode [11].

2.2.2 SigFox

SigFox is a wireless network that operates on the ISM standard. It is unlicensed, operates at low power, has a moderate data throughput, and is cost-effective. It is a unidirectional communication protocol that serves as a specialized end-to-end solution for facilitating connection in the IoT ecosystem. The system uses an Ultra Narrow Band carrier inside the sub-GHz ISM channels in conjunction with the Binary Phase Shift Keying (BPSK) modulation technique [7]. The use of narrow-band technology expands the communication range due to a substantial reduction in noise levels. Sigfox imposes limitations on the communication capabilities of each end device. Specifically, it limits downlink communications to four transmissions, each carrying a payload of eight bytes. Similarly, up-link communications are restricted to a maximum of 140 transmissions, with each transfer delivering a payload of 12 bytes. Many nations have adopted and deployed Sigfox with great success. The usage of Sigfox, however, does not include roaming capabilities while travelling between different countries [11, 20]. The primary drawback of the Sigfox communication system is its need for more suitability for bidirectional communication since it operates only in a unidirectional manner [26, 27].

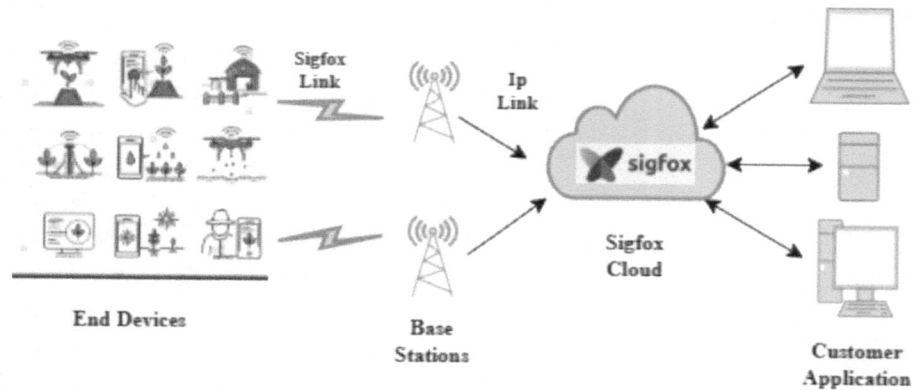

Fig. 7. Architecture of Sigfox

Figure 7 shows the general architecture of Sigfox, which consists of end devices, base stations, Sigfox cloud, and customer applications. The network operated by Sigfox uses lightweight messages, which are 12 bytes, not including payload headers. The end device wakes and transmits a letter to the base station using its wireless antenna with a Sigfox link. The signal is received by several Sigfox base stations in the area; then, base stations send the message to the Sigfox Cloud. Finally, the customer's application system gets the message from Sigfox Cloud [9].

2.2.3 Narrow Band-IOT (NB-IoT)

NB-IoT is a communication protocol designed specifically for Internet of Things (IoT) applications. It operates within a bandwidth of 180 kHz. The downlink data rate of NB-IoT is 250 kbps, but the uplink data rate is 20 kbps [7]. The lack of support for transition renders it unsuitable for mobile IoT applications, presenting a notable drawback. Implementing NB-IoT is a matter of apprehension due to its need to update LTE infrastructure hardware [20]. Furthermore, the successful deployment of this technology is contingent upon using the Internet of Things (IoT) service offered by a telecom operator. Hence, this technology lacks cost-effectiveness and fails to provide comparable openness to other IoT technologies. The Narrowband Internet of Things (NB-IoT), which is a low-power vast area network (LPWAN) technology, can function simultaneously with LTE or GSM bands [26] within the designated frequency range. Expanding upon the Long-Term Evolution (LTE) paradigm, this protocol incorporates the utilisation of elements derived from both the physical and upper layers within the LTE protocol stack [8, 10] (Fig. 8).

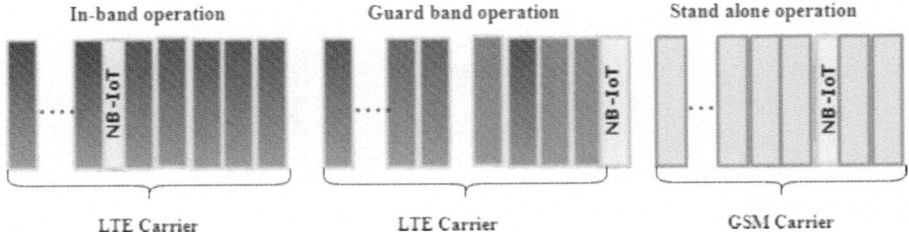

Fig. 8. Operational Modes of NB-IoT

In real terms, NB-IoT technology intends to simplify the LTE protocol stack by adapting it for IoT applications. Compared to the size of a single resource block in LTE and GSM transmission [16], the bandwidth needed for NB-IoT is just 200 kHz. The following figure shows that the frequency spectrum NB-IoT utilises works in various modes. Narrowband Internet of Things (NB-IoT) uses the frequency channels established for the Global System for Mobile Communications (GSM) while operating independently. A previously unused portion of the Long-Term Evolution (LTE) carrier's guard band is used during a guard band operation—in-band operation takes advantage of the LTE carrier's resource blocks [9, 23].

3 LoRa Based Layered Architecture for Smart Agriculture

In a LoRa-based architecture for SA [1, 2, 5], the communication network topology is hierarchical and comprises LoRa nodes that communicate with each other through gateways. The architecture consists of LoRa nodes, LoRa gateways, network servers, and application servers. LoRa nodes and gateways are not directly linked, although any LoRa node within the coverage area of a gateway can transmit messages to it. The primary function of the central network server is to handle the reception of incoming packets, eliminate any duplicate packets, and send the messages to the application servers. Figure 9 depicts the primary components of the network architecture layout for smart farms, which is based on LoRa technology [5].

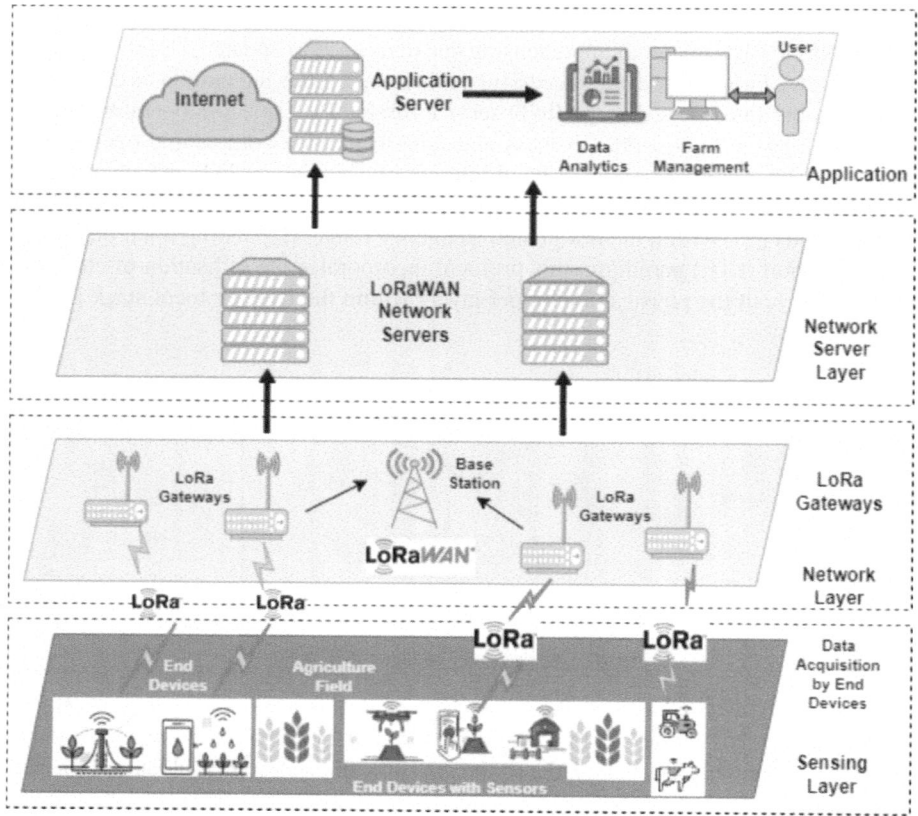

Fig. 9. LoRa Based Layered Architecture for Large scale Smart Agriculture

Data Acquisition: The job of LoRa sensor nodes in the field is to receive sensing data and send it to gateways using the LoRaWAN protocol [5, 6].

Gateways: LoRa gateways are connected to the Internet and handle the reception and transmission of data packets between various LoRa sensor and actuator nodes in the field [5, 6].

Network Server: The network server is involved with controlling the management of the LoRa gateways, and the handling of duplicate received packets [1]. Moreover, it is accountable for dispatching and arranging data and acknowledgement to be transferred to selected nodes [5].

Application Server: The application server in the LoRa architecture for SA controls the LoRaWAN application layer. It does tasks like encoding, decoding downlink, uplink data, and encrypting and decrypting data [5].

4 Comparative Study of LPWAN Technologies

Different types of LPWAN technologies are used for various IoT applications according to their basic requirements. Here, we have taken the three most popular LPWAN technologies, LoRaWAN, Sigfox and NB-IoT, for comparison based on their cost, IoT features and parameters.

4.1 Methodology Used for the Comparative Study of LPWANS

In this work, the comparative study of three LPWAN protocols was done based on Previous literature review only. This is a theoretical comparison; we have not performed any simulation-based experiments.

4.2 Comparison Based on the IoT Factors

A. QoS (Quality of Service)
Using the ALOHA protocol, Sigfox and LoRaWAN utilise unlicensed sub-GHz frequency channels and employ asynchronous communication [8]. They are good at preventing interference and fading/multipath but don't offer quality service. The licenced frequency and LTE-based synchronous protocol used by NB-IoT are best for quality of service (quality of service), but they are more expensive. (We say that the prices for LTE radio bands are more than 500 million euros per MHz [9]). Considering the tradeoff between quality of service (quality of service) and cost, NB-IoT is the recommended choice for applications requiring a guaranteed service level. On the other hand, applications that do not have this restriction can go for LoRaWAN or Sigfox [9].

B. Latency and Battery Life
In Sigfox, LoRaWAN, and NB-IoT, end devices mainly operate in sleep mode unless the application requires active participation. This approach minimises energy consumption to the greatest extent possible. However, the NB-IoT end device needs more power because it communicates and handles quality of service in real-time, and its OFDM/FDMA access modes need more peak current [9]. Higher energy consumption reduces the lifespan of NB-IoT end devices in comparison to Sigfox and LoRaWAN. Moreover, NB-IoT offers a connection solution with reduced latency for IoT devices.

   Contrary to Sigfox, LoRaWAN has class C functionality, which allows for lower bidirectional latency but requires more energy usage. Therefore, Sigfox and LoRaWAN-Class-A are the most suitable options for applications that are not latency-sensitive. For IoT applications that need fast and responsive connection, NB-IoT and LoRaWAN-Class-C are the optimal options [8, 9].

4.3 Tabulated Comparison Based on Other IoT Features and Parameters

Table 1. Parameter Wise Comparative Study of SigFox, LoRaWAN and NB-IoT [1–18]

S. No.	Parameters/Features	Wireless Technologies		
		SigFox [1, 7–9, 11, 20, 26, 27]	LoRaWAN [6–14, 17, 18, 20, 29, 34]	NB-IoT [6–8, 10, 20, 26]
1	Frequency bands	Unlicensed	Unlicensed	Licensed (paying)
2	Range	10 km (urban), 40 km (rural)	5 km (urban), 20 km (rural)	1 km (urban), 10 km (rural)
2	Operating Frequency	865–924 MHz	433, 868, 780, 915 MHz	700–900 MHz
3	Power Consumption	Medium	Very Low	Medium
4	Security	Medium	Very High	Medium
5	Battery Lifetime	7–8 years	>10 years	7–8 years
6	Message Bandwidth	100 Hz	7.8–500 kHz	180 kHz
7	Packet Size	12 Byte	19–250 B	16–2536 bits
8	Licensed	NO	NO	YES
9	Cellular	NO	NO	YES
10	Standardization Group	SigFox	LoRa Alliance	3 GPP
11	Modulation	Uplink - DBPSK Downlink - GFSK	CSS	QPSK
12	Network Topology	Star	Star-of-stars	Star
13	Scalability	50k/cell	50k/cell	100k/base station
14	Uplink data rate	0.1–0.6 kbps	0.3–50 kbps	0.3–62.5 kbps
15	Downlink data rate	0.6 kbps	0.3–50 kbps	<300 kbps
16	Maximum payload length	12 byte (UL) 8 byte (DL)	243 bytes	1600 bytes
17	Maximum messages/day	140 (UL), 4 (DL)	Unlimited	Unlimited
18	Interference Immunity	Very High	Very High	Low
19	Allow Private Network	No	Yes	No

(*continued*)

Table 1. (*continued*)

S. No.	Parameters/Features	Wireless Technologies		
		SigFox [1, 7–9, 11, 20, 26, 27]	LoRaWAN [6–14, 17, 18, 20, 29, 34]	NB-IoT [6–8, 10, 20, 26]
20	Localization	Yes (RSSI)	Yes (TDOA)	No (under specification)
21	Deployment model	Operator based	Operator based and private	Operator based
22	Adaptive Data rate	No	Yes	No

Table 1 presents a comprehensive comparison of the primary LPWAN technologies, viz. LoRaWAN, Sigfox, and NB-IoT focus on many factors relevant to the IoT based on previous literature reviews. The attributes that are compared include range, data rate, power consumption, scalability, security, cost, coverage, etc. The LoRaWAN protocol performs better than other technologies like NB-IoT and Sigfox. When evaluating the characteristics of NB-IoT, LoRa, and Sigfox, NB-IoT and LoRa provide some advantages over Sigfox [13]. The cost is relatively affordable, the battery capacity exhibits a notable magnitude, and the battery life is extended by using unlicensed LoRa technology [14]. When comparing LoRaWAN, NB-IoT (Narrowband IoT), and Sigfox, it's essential to consider various factors, including device cost, network infrastructure cost, and ongoing operational expenses [12]. According to research, it has been shown that licensed Narrowband Internet of Things (NB-IoT) technology has superior range capabilities and simultaneously offers improved Quality of Service (quality of service) [10, 15–27].

A comparative Study of LPWANs in terms of Features of the IoT is outlined in Table 2. Considering the facts shown in the table enables us to make an informed choice about selecting the finest LPWAN protocol for SA application implementation.

The LoRaWAN protocol is superior to other technologies like NB-IoT and Sigfox, according to a quick comparison of the significant LPWAN technologies based on actual discussion [9–15]. When considering the different characteristics of these technologies, NB-IoT and LoRa may be beneficial [13]. Censed LoRa technology is inexpensive, has a large battery capacity, and extends battery life. The benefits of unlicensed NB-IoT include a higher range and concurrent Quality of Service (quality of service) [20]. Figure 10 shows the Comparison Graph of LPWANs concerning various IoT system parameters. The graph is drawn by considering the IoT parameters above Tables 1, 2, and 3. This comparison graph concludes the tables above, which can visually describe the IoT features of Sigfox, LoRaWAN and NB-IoT.

Table 2. Comparative Study of LPWANs in terms of IoT Features [1, 3, 12]

Features	LoRaWAN [6, 8, 10, 11, 14, 17, 18, 20, 29, 34]	Sigfox [8, 11, 20, 26, 27]	NB-IoT [8, 10, 20, 26]
Range and Coverage	LoRaWAN has a shorter range as compare to sigfox, specifically less than 20 kms,	Sigfox provides the advantage of extensive coverage throughout a whole city using only one base station, which has a range of over 40 km	The range and coverage of NB-IoT are the lowest (less than 10 km). Its main job is to connect end devices that can't connect to cell phone networks (like those that are indoors or deep indoors)
Data Rate	Low data rates (0.3 kbps to 50 kbps) make it ideal for apps that need to send small amounts of data on a regular basis	Provides data rates up to 1000 bps, making it suitable for low-bandwidth applications like environmental monitoring	Offer higher data rates compared to LoRaWAN and Sigfox, ranging from 100 kbps to several Mbps, allowing for more data-intensive applications
Power Consumption	The device uses very little power, which makes it perfect for battery-powered devices that need to last for a long time, from a few months to many years	Like LoRaWAN devices, Sigfox devices don't need a lot of power, which means their batteries last longer	While more energy-intensive than Lo-RaWAN and Sigfox, these protocols are designed for low power usage, resulting in longer battery life for IoT devices
Scalability	Highly scalable, supporting thousands of devices per gateway, making it suitable for large-scale IoT deployments	Designed for massive IoT deployments, supporting a large number of devices, but may have limitations in terms of data transmission and network congestion	Scalable solutions capable of handling a significant number of devices, leveraging existing cellular infrastructure for seamless integration

(continued)

Table 2. (*continued*)

Features	LoRaWAN [6, 8, 10, 11, 14, 17, 18, 20, 29, 34]	Sigfox [8, 11, 20, 26, 27]	NB-IoT [8, 10, 20, 26]
Security	Offers strong end-to-end encryption and device authentication, ensuring data security and privacy	Provides security features like message integrity checks and device authentication but may have limitations in comparison to LoRaWAN	Utilize cellular network security standards, providing robust encryption and authentication mechanisms
Cost	Lower deployment costs due to the absence of cellular subscription fees and the use of unlicensed spectrum	Lower deployment costs due to the absence of cellular subscription fees and the use of unlicensed spectrum	Higher initial deployment costs, It could be more cost-effective for large-scale deployments due to existing cellular infrastructure and competitive pricing from cellular providers

Table 3. Comparative Study of LPWANs in terms of Cost [6, 8, 10, 11, 14, 17, 18, 20, 26, 27, 29, 34].

Cost Parameters	LoRaWAN	Sigfox	NB-IoT
Device Cost	LoRaWAN devices are usually not too expensive, and there are a lot of different brands to choose from. Different LoRaWAN devices and sensors have different prices, but there are numerous options that are both affordable and efficient	Sigfox devices have been designed to be economically efficient, with a range of choices offered at different pricing levels. Sigfox modules are often priced competitively	Narrowband Internet of Things (NB-IoT) modules and devices are often more cost-effective compared to conventional cellular devices, primarily because they prioritise affordable connectivity for Internet of Things (IoT) applications

(*continued*)

Table 3. (*continued*)

Cost Parameters	LoRaWAN	Sigfox	NB-IoT
Network Infrastructure	Setting up a private LoRaWAN network can require an initial investment in gateway hardware and network server infrastructure. However, many regions also have public LoRaWAN networks that can reduce infrastructure costs	Sigfox provides a global LPWAN network infrastructure, which reduces the need for organizations to invest in building their own LPWAN networks. This can be cost-effective for businesses with international IoT deployments	It relies on existing cellular infrastructure, which can reduce network deployment costs compared to building a new LPWAN infrastructure. However, this can vary by region and mobile network operator
Operational Costs	LoRaWAN's low-power design helps minimize operational costs, as devices can run on batteries for extended periods. There are also no recurring subscription fees for using public LoRaWAN networks	Sigfox devices are known for their low power consumption, resulting in extended battery life and lower operational costs. Sigfox typically charges subscription fees for connectivity, which can vary by usage and region	NB-IoT devices tend to be power-efficient, leading to longer battery life and lower operational costs. Mobile network operators may charge subscription fees for connectivity

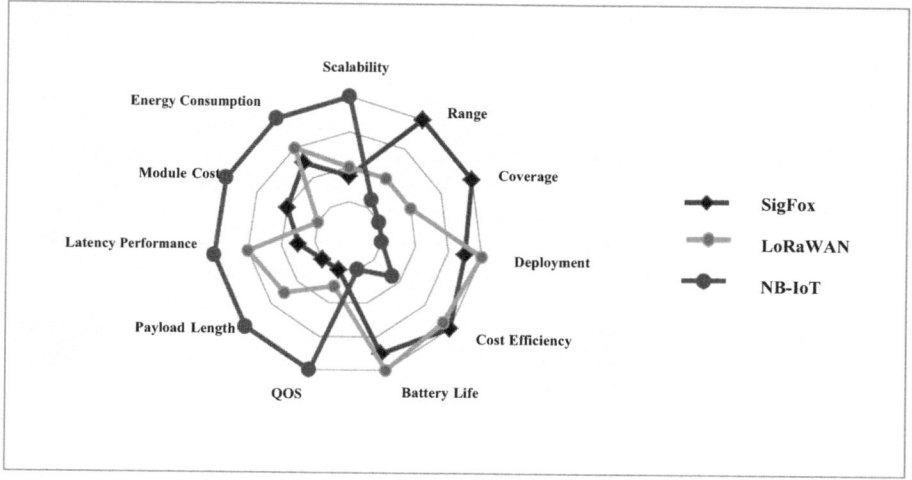

Fig. 10. Comparison Graph of LPWANs with respect to various IoT system parameters

5   Conclusion

This article provides a brief technical overview and comparative study of several LPWAN technologies required for a large-scale smart agriculture application. Considering several factors, this study analyses the most well-known LPWAN technologies, including LoRa, Sigfox, and NB-IoT. All three LPWAN technologies–LoRaWAN, NB-IoT, and Sigfox— offer cost-effective IoT deployment options. The choice of the most cost-effective option depends on several factors, including the application's specific requirements, geographical coverage, available infrastructure, and the scale of the deployment. Organizations should conduct a detailed cost analysis to determine which LPWAN protocol best aligns with their budget and project needs. LoRaWAN is known for its long-range capabilities and community-driven support, while NB-IoT offers cellular integration and higher data rates. Sigfox provides global coverage at a lower cost but with data rate and payload size limitations. The selection of the appropriate LPWAN protocol for Smart Agriculture applications requires careful evaluation of these parameters. LoRa and NB-IoT, two competing technologies, provide better support for real-time monitoring and other essential tasks in agricultural areas. In the future, we can enhance this study by performing simulation-based experimental co comparisons of more LPWAN protocols by using different popular IoT-based simulators such as such as NS3, LoRaSim, MATLAB, Omnet++, etc.

References

1. Pagano, A., Croce, D., Tinnirello, I., Vitale, G.: A survey on LoRa for smart agriculture: current trends and future perspectives. IEEE Internet Things J. **10**(4), 3664–3679 (2022)
2. https://www.statista.com/statistics/1183457/iot-connected-devices-worldwide/
3. Avşar, E., Mowla, Md.N.: Wireless communication protocols in smart agriculture: a review on applications, challenges and future trends. Ad Hoc Netw., 102982 (2022)
4. Prakash, C., Singh, L.P., Gupta, A., Lohan, S.K.: Advancements in smart farming: a comprehensive review of IoT, wireless communication, sensors, and hardware for agricultural automation. Sens. Actuators A Phys., 114605 (2023)
5. Shaikh, F.K., Karim, S., Zeadally, S., Nebhen, J.: Recent trends in internet of things enabled sensor technologies for smart agriculture. IEEE Internet Things J. (2022)
6. Ahmed, M.A., et al.: LoRa based IoT platform for remote monitoring of large-scale agriculture farms in Chile. Sensors **22**(8), 2824 (2022)
7. Miles, B., Bourennane, E.-B., Boucherkha, S., Chikhi, S.: A study of LoRaWAN protocol performance for IoT applications in smart agriculture. Comput. Commun. **164**, 148–157 (2020)
8. Chilamkurthy, N.S., Pandey, O.J., Ghosh, A., Cenkeramaddi, L.R., Dai, H.-N.: Low-power wide-area networks: a broad overview of its different aspects. IEEE Access (2022)
9. Mekki, K., Bajic, E., Chaxel, F., Meyer, F.: Overview of cellular LPWAN technologies for IoT deployment: Sigfox, LoRaWAN, and NB-IoT. In: 2018 IEEE International Conference on Pervasive Computing and Communications Workshops (PerCom Workshops), pp. 197–202. IEEE (2018)
10. Hossain, M.I., Markendahl, J.I.: Comparison of LPWAN technologies: cost structure and scalability. Wirel. Pers. Commun. **121**(1), 887–903 (2021)

11. Marini, R., Mikhaylov, K., Pasolini, G., Buratti, C.: Low-power wide-area networks: comparison of LoRaWAN and NB-IoT performance. IEEE Internet Things J. **9**(21), 21051–21063 (2022)

12. Garlisi, D., Pagano, A., Giuliano, F., Croce, D., Tinnirello, I.: A coexistence study of low-power wide-area networks based on LoRaWAN and Sigfox. In: 2023 IEEE Wireless Communications and Networking Conference (WCNC), pp. 1–7. IEEE (2023)

13. Gonçalves, L.R., Volpato, R.M., Pimenta, T.C.: A comparison of low power wireless technologies for SmartGrid networks. In: 2021 International Conference on Microelectronics, ICM, pp. 228–231. IEEE (2021)

14. Singh, R.K., Puluckul, P.P., Berkvens, R., Weyn, M.: Energy consumption analysis of LPWAN technologies and lifetime estimation for IoT application. Sensors **20**(17), 4794 (2020)

15. Jradi, H., Nouvel, F., Samhat, A.E., Prévotet, J.-C., Mroue, M.: A seamless integration solution for LoRaWAN into 5G system. IEEE Internet Things J. (2023)

16. Islam, N., Ray, B., Pasandideh, F.: IoT based smart farming: are the LPWAN technologies suitable for remote communication? In: 2020 IEEE International Conference on Smart Internet of Things (SmartIoT), pp. 270–276. IEEE (2020)

17. Gurubaran, K., et al.: Real time experimental calibration of ultrasonic sensor and LoRa communication module in LoRaWAN architecture. In: 2023 2nd International Conference on Vision Towards Emerging Trends in Communication and Networking Technologies (ViTECoN), pp. 1–6. IEEE Xplore (2023). https://doi.org/10.1109/ViTECoN58111.2023.10156966

18. Haxhibeqiri, J., et al.: A survey of LoRaWAN for IoT: from technology to application. Sensors **18**(11), 3995 (2018). www.mdpi.com. https://doi.org/10.3390/s18113995

19. Mekki, K., Bajic, E., Chaxel, F., Meyer, F.: A comparative study of LPWAN technologies for large-scale IoT deployment. ICT Express **5**(1), 1–7 (2019)

20. Kadusic, E., Ruland, C., Hadzajlic, N., Zivic, N.: The factors for choosing among NB-IoT, LoRaWAN, and Sigfox radio communication technologies for IoT networking. In: 2022 International Conference on Connected Systems & Intelligence (CSI), pp. 1–5. IEEE (2022)

21. Aras, E., Ramachandran, G.S., Lawrence, P., Hughes, D.: Exploring the security vulnerabilities of LoRa. In: 2017 3rd IEEE International Conference on Cybernetics (CYBCONF), pp. 1–6. IEEE (2017)

22. Petajajarvi, J., Mikhaylov, K., Hamalainen, M., Iinatti, J.: Evaluation of LoRa LPWAN technology for remote health and wellbeing monitoring. In: 2016 10th International Symposium on Medical Information and Communication Technology (ISMICT), pp. 1–5 (2016)

23. Matthews, V.O., Ajala, A.O., Atayero, A.A., Popoola, S.I.: Solar photovoltaic automobile recognition system for smart - green access control using RFID and LoRa LPWAN technologies. J. Eng. Appl. Sci. (2017)

24. Kumar, S., Rangan, P.V., Ramesh, M.V.: Pilot deployment of early warning system for landslides in eastern Himalayas. In: Proceedings of the Tenth ACM International Workshop on Wireless Network Testbeds, Experimental Evaluation, and Characterization (2016)

25. WiNTECH 2016, vol. 03-07-October, pp. 97–99. ACM Press, New York (2016)

26. Petric, T., Goessens, M., Nuaymi, L., Toutain, L., Pelov, A.: Measurements, performance and analysis of LoRa FABIAN, a real-world implementation of LPWAN. In: 2016 IEEE 27th Annual International Symposium on Personal, Indoor, and Mobile Radio Communications(PIMRC), pp. 1–7. IEEE (2016)

27. Lauridsen, M., Nguyen, H., Vejlgaard, B., Kovacs, I.Z., Mogensen, P., Sorensen, M.: Coverage comparison of GPRS, NB-IoT, LoRa, and SigFox in a 7800 km^2 area. In: 2017 IEEE 85th Vehicular Technology Conference (VTC Spring), Sydney, NSW, pp. 1–5 (2017)

28. Vejlgaard, Lauridsen, M., Nguyen, H., Kovacs, I.Z., Mogensen, P., Sorensen, M.: Coverage and capacity analysis of Sigfox, LoRa, GPRS, and NB-IoT. In: 2017 IEEE 85th Vehicular Technology Conference (VTCSpring), Sydney, NSW, pp. 1–5 (2017)

29. Dos Reis, B.R., Easton, Z., White, R.R., Fuka, D.: A LoRa sensor network for monitoring pastured livestock location and activity. Transl. Anim. Sci. **5**(2), txab010 (2021)
30. Jiang, X., et al.: Hybrid low-power wide-area mesh network for IoT applications. IEEE Internet Things J. **8**(2), 901–915 (2020)

OpenGNN: Augmenting Graph Neural Networks for Open-Set Node Prediction in Complex Networks

Binon Teji [ID] and Swarup Roy[(✉)][ID]

Network Reconstruction and Analysis (NETRA) Lab, Department of Computer Applications, Sikkim University, Gangtok, India
`bteji.20pdca01@sikkimuniversity.ac.in`, `sroy01@cus.ac.in`

Abstract. Traditional classification approaches, grounded in closed-set frameworks, face limitations in their ability to handle novel, unseen instances that frequently arise in dynamic real-world systems. The open-set classification framework plays a crucial role in addressing this challenge. In the context of node prediction within complex networks, the task of open-set prediction for unseen or unknown nodes remains a relatively unexplored frontier. The presence of these unseen nodes, capable of disrupting network dynamics, carries significant implications across various network domains.

In this study, we introduce an open-set classification paradigm using Graph Neural Networks (GNNs), presenting a novel dimension to the field. The proposed framework effectively isolates unseen nodes that do not belong to any labeled training classes. Our approach enhances the vigilance, effectiveness, and robustness of GNNs that heavily rely on graph convolutions. We experimentally validate the proposed framework using three popular real-world complex networks. Importantly, our method outperforms contemporary frameworks. The `OpenGNN` code for reproducing the results is available for download (https://github.com/Netralab/OpenGNN).

Keywords: Open-set classification · Graph Neural Networks · Unknown node prediction · Complex networks · Node embedding

1 Introduction

Network or graph-structured data represents the mathematical formulation of various complex real-world systems, including social networks (e.g., Facebook and WeChat), biological networks (e.g., Protein-Protein Interaction) [1], citation networks (e.g., Cora and Citeseer), and many others. Node classification is a fundamental task in network analysis, involving the assignment of predefined class labels to new nodes. This task has witnessed significant advancements in network science. For instance, labeling web pages with semantic classes enables more precise internet searches [2], categorizing users into specific age groups or

A. Verma et al. (Eds.): ANTIC 2023, CCIS 2091, pp. 114–128, 2024.
https://doi.org/10.1007/978-3-031-64064-3_9

interests for targeted ad delivery in online advertising networks [3], or categorizing proteins into functional categories based on their molecular structure [4].

Classical node classification problems follow a *closed-set* framework, limiting them to assigning elements or nodes to known classes exposed during training. In reality, real-world systems are dynamic and often present the challenge of encountering novel elements or nodes that do not belong to any of the classes seen (previously *unseen*) by the classifier during training. There is a growing need for an *Open-set* learning framework [5] to address such situations. Open-set recognition (OSR) has primarily been developed for Euclidean data spaces [6]. However, the problem of detecting unseen nodes in a dynamic network remains a relatively unexplored research area.

In recent years, there has been a significant upsurge in interest surrounding Graph Deep Learning (GDL) [7]. More precisely, Graph Neural Network (GNNs) has demonstrated remarkable success in various tasks, such as node classification [8,9], edge or link prediction [10–12], and subgraph isolation [13]. The key to GNNs' success lies in their framework, which integrates graph convolutions and neural message passing strategies [8,14]. These strategies facilitate the flow of information within the graph structure through graph links, further optimized for specific downstream tasks. In simpler terms, GNNs are designed to gather and update information for each node at every layer by considering the structures of their neighboring nodes.

The classical framework of GNN is not designed to detect unseen or unknown nodes in a network. Typically, it adheres to a closed-set learning paradigm and misclassifies any novel node into existing classes for which it was trained. For instance, the introduction of a foreign or unknown node to a network disrupts the overall network organization and often mislabels an unseen node as one of the predefined known classes. The rearrangement of network topology can sometimes enhance or deteriorate the performance of even the most robust GNNs [15].

The GNNs' lack of consideration for network-related perturbations is a significant concern, as it can potentially be exploited in sensitive areas. For instance, it may contribute to financial fraud [16], aid in the dissemination of malware [17], or even result in biased recommendations within recommendation systems [18]. Therefore, it is crucial to equip GNNs for open-set classification scenarios, where the presence of unknown nodes can be appropriately classified as belonging to the 'Unknown' class. Figure 1 illustrates the node classification task in both closed and open-set scenarios.

In summary, we make the following contributions:

- We introduce a straightforward extension of the GCN model and its variants for the open-set node classification task.
- We present a meta-recognition model based framework for classifying unknown nodes using graph-based latent node embeddings.
- Our empirical results demonstrate the superiority of our approach in achieving higher accuracy compared to the other baseline models.

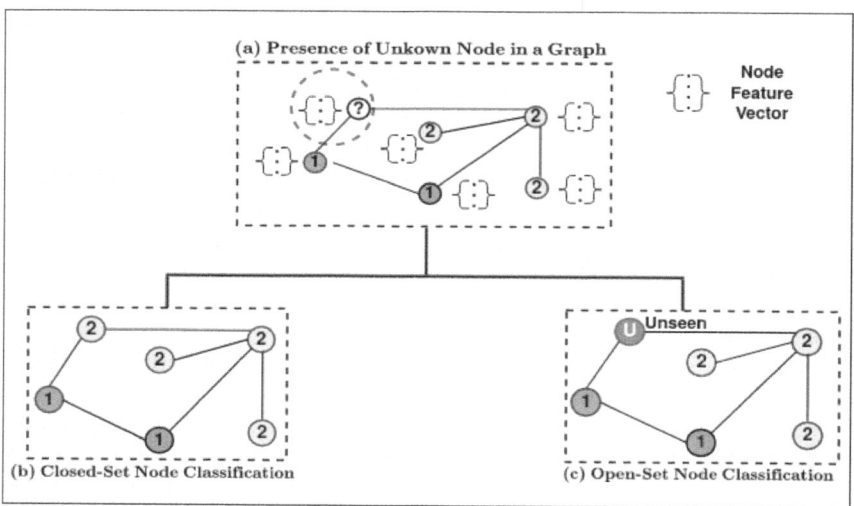

Fig. 1. Closed vs. Open Set Node Classification: **(a)** Input graph with known labelled nodes and its features. White node (encircled in dotted-red line) actually not belongs to any of the known labels. **(b)** Traditional node classifier misclassifies the node **?** into either of the known classes (1 or 2). **(c)** Open-set classifier should label it as Unseen/ Unknown, not belongs to either 1 or 2. (Color figure online)

2   Prior Works on Open-Set Learning

The majority of efforts in open-set classification have primarily focused on the domain of Euclidean space, where the challenge lies in effectively classifying data points to identify novel classes. Traditional anomaly detection methods laid the initial foundation; however, they often struggled with the complexities of diverse data distributions. Seminal works, following Vapnik's principle, emerged as extensions of Support Vector Machines (SVMs) for unlabeled data [19]. Notable examples include the Isolation Forest (iForest) method [20], which explicitly isolates anomalies instead of profiling normal instances, and the Mahalanobis distance [21], which, when applied to pre-trained neural classifiers, has shown strong performance in detecting out-of-distribution (OOD) and adversarial examples.

Moreover, open-set learning has gained substantial interest in the field of Natural Language Processing (NLP). Fei et al. [22] introduced a learning system capable of incremental learning for new classes in a fully labeled document collection housing a large number of classes. The *DOC* framework [23] proposed deep open classification, constructing a multi-class classifier with a 1-vs-rest final layer of sigmoids, effectively tightening decision boundaries through Gaussian fitting.

Xu et al. [24] presented an open-world learning approach based on meta-learning, allowing the addition or removal of classes without requiring model re-training.

In the realm of computer vision (CV), Scheirer et al. [25] introduced the concept of 1-vs-set, which draws decision boundaries from the marginal distances of a 1-class or binary SVM with a linear kernel. This approach was applied to challenging problems such as facial recognition on datasets like Caltech 256 and ImageNet. Wu et al. [26] harnessed attention-based graph convolutional networks for zero-shot learning with pre-training tailored for unseen classes, enhancing the model's generalization capabilities. The CAP method [27] made significant strides in improving open-set recognition for object detection tasks by introducing a decreasing probability value of class membership as data points transition from known data to open space.

While these pioneering works predominantly focused on grid-data structures, the domain of open-set learning in graph structures remains relatively unexplored. In the upcoming sections, we delve into the formulation of the open-set learning problem within the context of node classification tasks in graph data.

3 Preliminaries and Problem Formulation

Given a graph $\mathcal{G} = (\mathcal{V}, \mathcal{E}, \mathbf{X}, \mathcal{Y})$, where $\mathcal{V}$ represents the set of vertices or nodes and $\mathcal{E}$ is the set of edges or links connecting these nodes, represented as pairs of nodes (u, v). The topological structure of the graph $\mathcal{G}$ can be described using an adjacency matrix, where $\mathbf{A}_{u,v} = 1$ if there is an edge from node u to node v, and $\mathbf{A}_{u,v} = 0$ otherwise. $\mathbf{X}$ is a feature matrix of dimensions $|\mathcal{V}| \times \mathcal{D}$, where $\mathcal{D}$ represents the number of features associated with each node in the graph. $\mathcal{Y}$ is a single-column label matrix of $\mathcal{G}$, containing discrete ground-truth values that correspond to the $C = \{C_1, C_2, \cdots, C_n\}$ classes, resulting in a dimension of $|\mathcal{V}| \times 1$.

In the context of a closed-set node classification framework, the goal of the classifier is to optimize a learning function f (based on training samples from C) to map each test node into one of the C classes. Consequently, $\hat{\mathcal{Y}}_u = f(\mathbf{A}, \mathbf{X})$ represents the label prediction for node u. In our specific case, the learning function f is equivalent to $\hat{\mathcal{Y}}_u = GCN(\mathbf{A}, \mathbf{X})$. If a node $u \in \mathcal{V}$ is associated with the label $C_i \in C$, then $\mathcal{Y}_u^{C_i} = 1$, and $\mathcal{Y}_u^{C_j} = 0$ for $j = 1 \cdots n$ and $j \neq i$.

Moving to the node classification task within an open-set learning framework, the objective is twofold: to classify the seen nodes into existing C classes and to categorize unseen or novel nodes (those dissimilar to any nodes in C) into a separate label, denoted as "Unseen (U)." In other words, for a given graph $\mathcal{G}$, we assume the adjacency matrix $\mathbf{A} = \mathbf{A}_{Train} \bigcup \mathbf{A}_{Test}$ and the corresponding feature matrix $\mathbf{X} = \mathbf{X}_{Train} \bigcup \mathbf{X}_{Test}$ for $\mathcal{G}$. Here, $\mathbf{A}_{Train}$ and $\mathbf{X}_{Train}$ represent the input adjacency matrix and node features for training. The $\mathbf{A}_{Train}$ consists of labeled nodes represented as $V_l \in \mathcal{V}$. After training model is tested using $\mathbf{A}_{Test}$. The open-set classifier, denoted as $GCN' : \mathbf{A}_{Test} \mapsto C \bigcup U$, maps the test set to either C (the seen class) or U. In practice, the open-set learning model may perform the open-set classification task as described below:

$$\hat{\mathcal{y}}_u = \begin{cases} C_i, & \text{if } P(\mathcal{Y}_u = C_i | \mathbf{A}_{Test}) > \tau, \exists C_i \in C \\ \text{U}, & \text{otherwise} \end{cases} \tag{1}$$

Here, $P(\mathcal{Y}_u = C_i | \mathbf{A}_{Test})$ represents the probability that the testing node u belongs to either class C_i or the "Unseen" class (U).

The above equation (Eq. 1) effectively captures the essence of open-set classification, where nodes that cannot be confidently assigned to any of the known classes are categorized as "Unseen." The threshold τ is often set to control the confidence level required for classification, allowing for flexibility in determining what constitutes a confident classification. However, any alternative confidence measure can be adapted instead of any user-given threshold τ. Next, we discuss how we model OpenGNN.

4   Methodology

We employ a straightforward approach to enhance the capabilities of the conventional Graph Convolutional Network (GCN) [8] for classifying both known and unknown nodes within a graph simultaneously. GCN, or any standard classifier in its original form, lacks the capacity to detect such unseen nodes. To address this limitation, we introduce an unsupervised open-set detection layer alongside the conventional GCN during classification (testing), creating what we refer as OpenGNN. Our approach unfolds in two main steps. We adhere to the conventional node classification framework to train on an input graph, encompassing all known nodes. During testing, we make use of the embeddings obtained during training to predict both seen and unseen nodes. Here, we introduce probabilistic approach that hinges on meta-recognition framework which distinguishes both seen and unseen nodes effectively. Figure 2 illustrates the proposed OpenGNN framework for open-set node classification.

4.1   Learning Node Embeddings with GCN

We primarily generate node embeddings for each graph node by employing GCN (Graph Convolutional Network) [8], which is a message-passing framework for generating latent-vector node embeddings. These embeddings are generated through multi-layer transformations as follows:

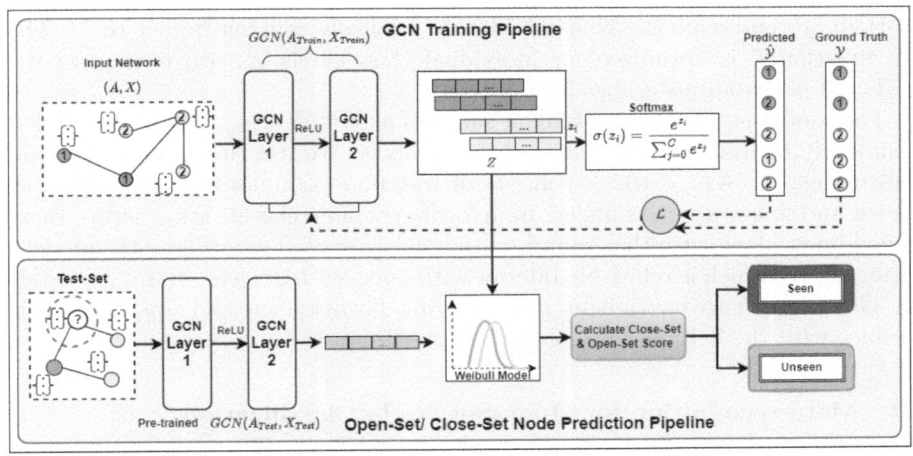

Fig. 2. Proposed OpenGNN framework for Open-Set Node Classification

$$H^{(l+1)} = \sigma(\tilde{D}^{-\frac{1}{2}}\tilde{\mathbf{A}}\tilde{D}^{-\frac{1}{2}}H^{(l)}W^{(l)}), \tag{2}$$

Here, $\tilde{\mathbf{A}}$ represents the adjacency matrix of $\mathcal{G}$, augmented with the identity matrix I_N. $W^{(l)}$ is a trainable weight matrix in layer l, $\sigma(.)$ is an activation function, and $\tilde{D}_{ii} = \sum_j \tilde{A}_{ij}$. The first layer $H^{(0)} = \mathbf{X}$ uses node features as the raw input matrix.

In the closed-set paradigm for node classification tasks, the model takes the simple form as:

$$Z = GCN(\mathbf{A}, \mathbf{X}) = \hat{A} \cdot \text{ReLU}(\hat{A} \cdot \mathbf{X} \cdot W^{(1)}) \cdot W^{(2)}, \tag{3}$$

Here, $\hat{A} = \tilde{D}^{-\frac{1}{2}}\tilde{\mathbf{A}}\tilde{D}^{-\frac{1}{2}}$. Z is the latent-vector matrix for the training node samples. $W^{(1)}$ and $W^{(2)}$ are the learning parameters of the model.

The predicted class probabilities are computed as follows:

$$\hat{y} = softmax(Z) \tag{4}$$

Finally, the model parameters are learned in a semi-supervised manner by minimizing the cross-entropy error on the output of the labeled nodes, defined as follows.

$$\mathcal{L}(\mathcal{Y}, \hat{\mathcal{Y}}) = -\sum_{i=1}^{N} y_i \cdot \log(\hat{y}_i) \tag{5}$$

Here, $\mathcal{Y}$ represents the true class labels, typically ranging from 1 to N. The loss function $\mathcal{L}$ is optimized for individual class labels y_i with respect to the predicted probabilities $\hat{y}_i$ for all N classes.

The model is trained on training samples as $GCN(\mathbf{A}_{Train}, \mathbf{X}_{Train})$ until it confidently converges on the ground-truth labels. We use this model to obtain embeddings for $\mathbf{A}_{Test}$, which consists of test node samples consisting of both known and unknown class nodes. In an ordinary node classification setup, these embeddings, along with the ground-truth labels, are used to evaluate the model's performance, which is relatively inferior with open-set test cases. Here, we enable the GCN model to be vigilant in classifying both known and unknown node samples with the help of meta-recognition techniques.

4.2   Meta-recognition for Open-Set Node Classification

We augment the standard GCN model to be more attentive to the open-set node classification framework. Motivated from meta-recognition [28] approaches designed for text classification [29] we tune it for graph-structured data.

Meta-recognition involves considering post-recognition scores, where predictions are made based on the scores/distances generated by a base algorithm across a dataset of known class examples. Furthermore, the emphasis can be placed on modeling the tail of the non-match distribution scores to enable open-set node classification. This necessitates a statistical classifier capable of automatically determining success or failure for a test instance without requiring prior information.

Drawing inspiration from a substantial body of work in text and vision [28,30,31], we employ the Weibull model [32], which accurately fits the graph data in open-set node classification [30]. The Weibull distribution offers a flexible and versatile framework for modeling the uncertainty associated with open-set classification. It enables the quantification of the inclusion or exclusion of data points from known classes, which is essential for open-set classification where unseen or outlier data may be present. We compute the inclusion probability, denoted as $P(Z_i \in \text{Class}_k)$, for each test node Z_i with respect to the kth class, based on its embedding generated by the trained GNN. The Weibull distribution is employed to calculate this probability as follows.

$$P(Z_i \in \text{Class}_k) = 1 - e^{-(\frac{d(Z_i, \mu_k)}{\lambda_k})^c}, \tag{6}$$

where $d(Z_i, \mu_k)$ is the distance between embedding Z_i and the mean embedding vector μ_k of Class k. λ_k is the scale parameter (scale factor) and c is the shape parameter (shape factor) for the Weibull distribution of class k. Accordingly, for each class k, we gather the trained embeddings, Z_k, generated during training. Subsequently, we derive a representative feature vector for each class with M embeddings as follows.

$$\mu_k = \frac{1}{M} \sum_{i=1}^{M} Z_{k_i}. \tag{7}$$

We use Mahalanobis distance [33] for distance calculation between node i's embeddings, Z_{k_i} and μ_k resulting in M distances per class. Closer distance reports in lower Mahalanobis distance score, which is calculated as follows.

$$d(Z_{k_i}, \mu_k) = \sqrt{(Z_{k_i} - \mu_k)^T Cov^{-1}(Z_{k_i} - \mu_k)} \tag{8}$$

where, Cov is the covariance matrix which are pre-computed trained embeddings of particular class. Finally, the sum of all inclusion probabilities contributes towards total close set probability (CSP). The open set probability (OSP) is calculated by subtracting the total closed-set probability from 1.

$$OSP = 1 - \sum_i P(Z_i \in \text{Class}_k) \tag{9}$$

Based on this intuition, the Eq. (1) for classifying nodes in both close-set and open-set classification framework which can be adjusted as follows:

$$\hat{y} = \begin{cases} \mathbf{U}, & \text{if } \max_k(\sum_i P(Z_i \in \text{Class}_k)) < OSP \\ \mathbf{C}, & \text{otherwise} \end{cases} \tag{10}$$

Equation (10) classify a test case as *known* (C) category or *unknown* node category (U) by comparing the maximum of close-set density score and the total open-set density score for classification task. If the maximum of close-set density score is greater than open-set score, we label the specific query embedding as known, otherwise, it is termed as unknown. We adjust the threshold and tail-size of Weibull model throughout our experiments.

5   Experiments

We assess our model's performance through a series of experiments involving node classification tasks for both known and unknown classes of network nodes.

5.1   Datasets

We test our model on three network datasets [34–37]—Cora, Citeseer, and WikiCS. Various dataset specific statistics are reported in Table 1.

Table 1. Popular Benchmarking Network Dataset Used

Network	#Nodes	#Edges	#Features	#Labels
Cora	2708	10556	1433	7
Citeseer	3327	9104	3703	6
WikiCS	11701	431726	300	10

5.2 Experimental Set-Up

We train our model using two message-passing GCN layers with selected sub-networks of known nodes. Predictions are made on the remaining classes, which serve as testing node samples. Our input network is divided into a 70% training set, a 20% validation set, and a 10% testing set. Notably, the testing set comprises both a few known class node samples and unknown node samples that the model has not previously encountered. This deliberate arrangement ensures a thorough evaluation of the model's generalization and adaptability to new, unencountered class nodes. The ultimate objective is to accurately classify instances from both known and unknown classes.

We initialize the network weights as described in [38]. A dropout rate of 0.5 and 256 hidden dimensions are used. The model is trained for a maximum of 200 epochs using the Adam optimizer [39] with a learning rate of 0.01. We employ accuracy as the evaluation metric for multi-class classification. All experiments are conducted on Google Colaboratory.

5.3 Results

To assess the performance of OpenGNN, we conduct a series of experiments. As discussed before, OpenGNN utilizes a meta-recognition technique that involves analyzing post-recognition scores obtained by calculating the distances between the trained gallery of embeddings and their corresponding cluster centers. As depicted in Fig. 3, the plot illustrates clearly distinguished clusters of trained embeddings in a 2-D space. Each cluster center, representing a specific class distribution, is precisely located at the center of its respective cluster.

We fit the obtained distances to a Weibull model for each correctly classified class. Figure 4 illustrates the Weibull distribution generated using the Mahalanobis distance with a tail size of 90 for the three candidate network datasets. The plot indicates the degree to which a data point is distanced from the center in relation to the inclusion probability, which later aids in the inference of a test example.

Furthermore, we calculate the overall accuracy, considering both known and unknown classes, for the test nodes. Figure 5 displays the overall accuracy for the three network datasets, each containing unseen classes ($U = 1, 2, 3$). From the figure, it is evident that OpenGNN achieves higher accuracy when $U = 1$. For the Cora network, it reaches 76.50%. Similarly, for Citeseer it is 75.09%, and for WikiCS it is 76.27%. Additionally, we observe that as the number of unseen classes increases, there is a slight decrease in the overall accuracy for each of the network datasets, though this decrease is not very significant. Following a

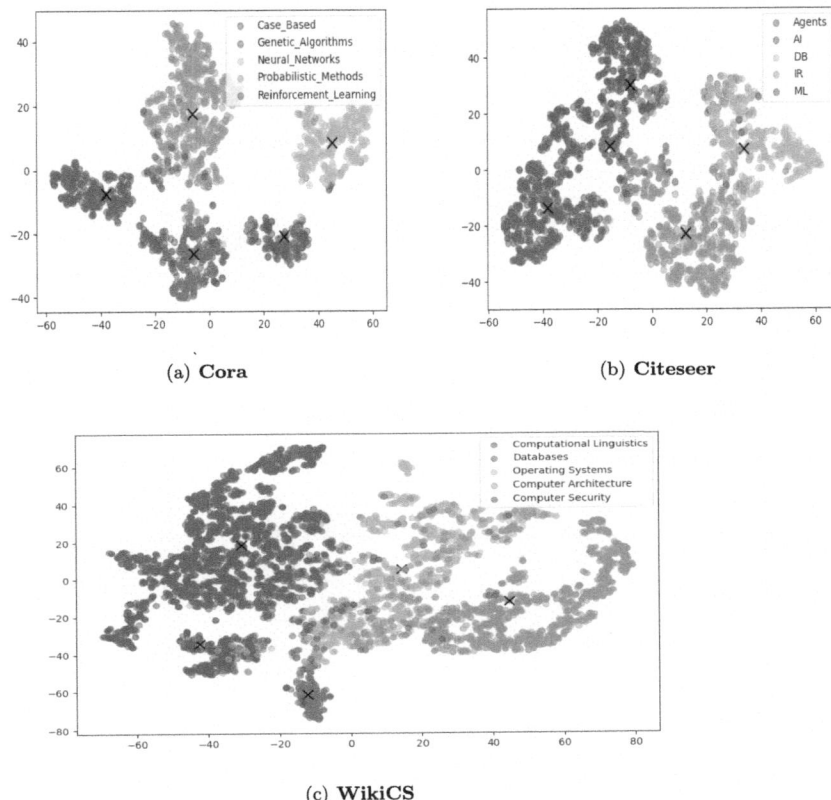

Fig. 3. Embeddings of 5 known classes in 2D space with cluster centers (×) representing the mean vector for the candidate network datasets.

similar line of results, we separately calculate the accuracy for both known and unknown nodes within each category of nodes. Figure 6 presents the separate accuracy scores for both known and unknown categories of nodes across the candidate network datasets. We observe that, in most cases, the accuracy of unknown nodes exceeds that of known nodes, except for the combination of $U = 2$ for the Citeseer and WikiCS networks, and $U = 3$ for the WikiCS network. In fact, the OpenGNN model excels in distinguishing unseen class nodes from the known category with noteworthy accuracy. However, accurately classifying within the known multi-class classification setting remains a challenge for a few combinations of test cases.

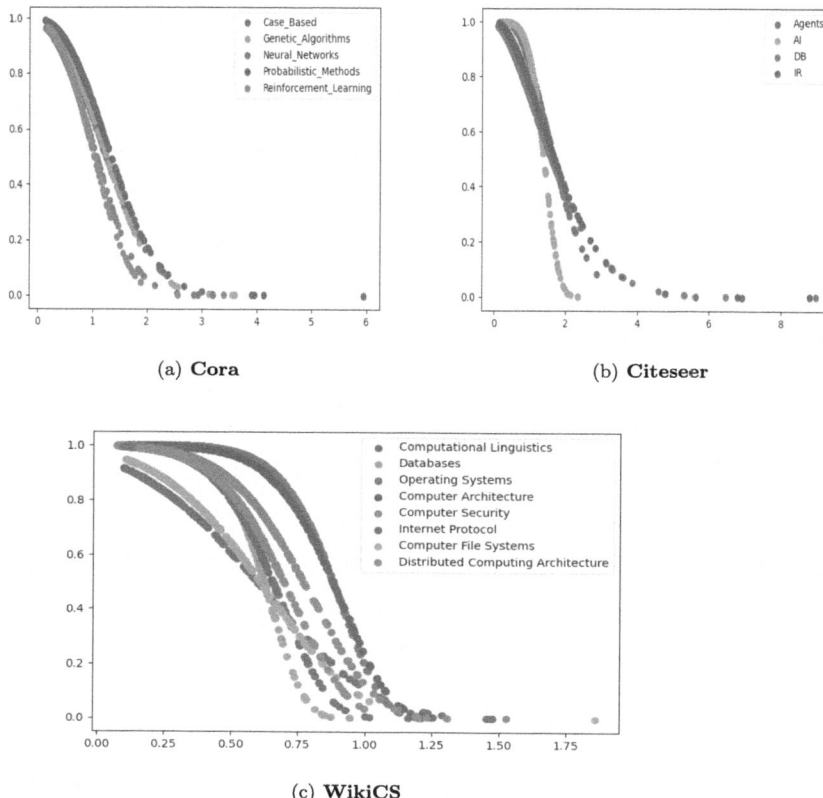

(a) **Cora**   (b) **Citeseer**

(c) **WikiCS**

Fig. 4. Weibull distribution generated using *libMR* over Mahalanobis distance for two unseen class with tail-size of 90 for *Cora*, *Citeseer* and *WikiCS* network. *x-axis shows the probability of inclusion and y-axis shows distance from the center.*

Finally, we compare `OpenGNN` with other baseline models. Table 2 presents the accuracy of `OpenGNN` compared to other models in the open-set node classification setting for three unseen classes. In all the test cases, we observe that `OpenGNN` outperforms other models, achieving higher accuracy. This further demonstrates that the meta-recognition-based GNN model for the open-set node classification excels at differentiating unseen class nodes with greater proficiency than existing methods.

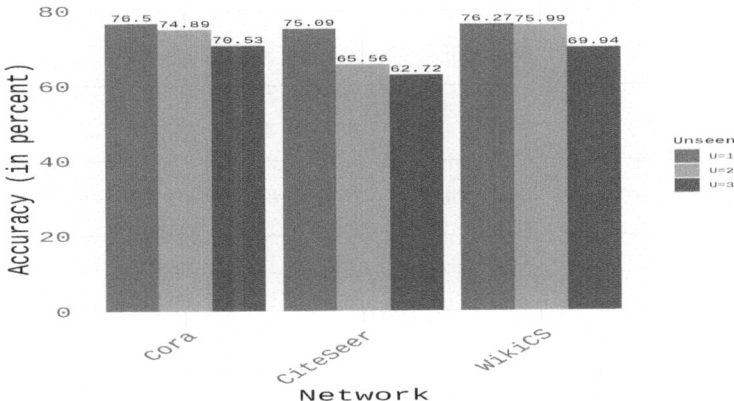

Fig. 5. Overall accuracy achieved over candidate test network with different number of unseen classes (U) and rest introduced as known classes.

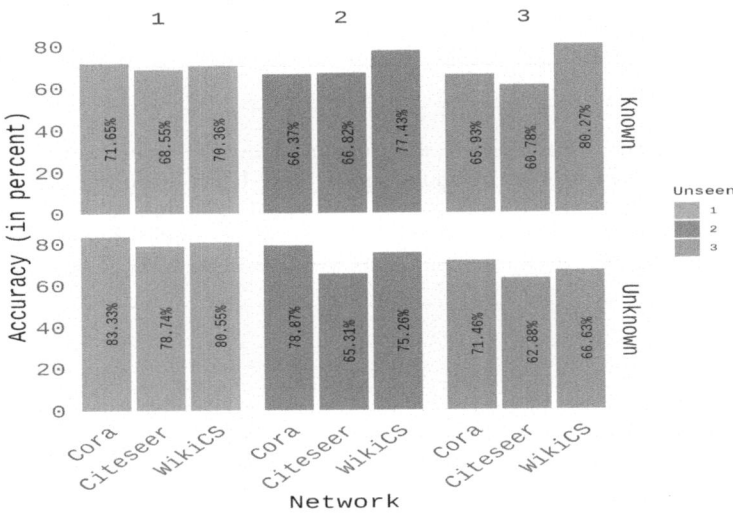

Fig. 6. Prediction accuracy of OpenGNN for Known and Unknown nodes with different test subnetworks.

Table 2. Benchmarking of OpenGNN with various baselines for varying number of unseen classes U. Best scores in network highlighted in bold.

Network	Method	$U = 1$	$U = 2$	$U = 3$
Cora	OpenGNN	**76.50**	**74.89**	**70.53**
	GCN	54.38	27.96	0.15
	MLP	45.85	25.11	0.14
	GCN_Sigmoid	08.98	26.96	15.19
Citeseer	OpenGNN	**75.09**	**65.56**	**62.72**
	GCN	29.20	13.11	0.06
	MLP	26.80	11.91	06.03
	GCN_Sigmoid	26.54	13.18	06.38
WikiCS	OpenGNN	**76.27**	**75.99**	**69.94**
	GCN	34.16	28.95	21.29
	MLP	34.41	27.36	21.13
	GCN_Sigmoid	33.18	27.11	20.52

6   Conclusion

In this work, we introduced OpenGNN, a meta-recognition-based probabilistic approach that augment existing GNN models in the open-set node classification setting. Experiments on three network datasets demonstrate the effectiveness of the proposed method. The approach can be seamlessly integrated with graph convolution-based dominant GNN models for the open-set node classification task.

Acknowledgement. This research was supported by the Department of Science & Technology (DST), Govt. of India under DST-ICPS Data Science program [DST/ICPS/Cluster/Data Science/General], carried out at NetRA Lab, Sikkim University. We thank Amardeep Sharma, Kirtan Sharma Ghimire, and Niten Rai for getting involved in implementation of the preliminary version of the work.

References

1. Guzzi, P.H., Roy, S.: Biological Network Analysis: Trends, Approaches, Graph Theory, and Algorithms. Elsevier, Amsterdam (2020)
2. Edelman, B., Gilchrist, D.S.: Advertising disclosures: measuring labeling alternatives in internet search engines. Inf. Econ. Policy **24**(1), 75–89 (2012)
3. Ullah, I., Boreli, R., Kaafar, M.A., Kanhere, S.S.: Characterising user targeting for in-App mobile Ads. In: 2014 IEEE Conference on Computer Communications Workshops (INFOCOM WKSHPS), pp. 547–552. IEEE (2014)
4. Deng, M., Zhang, K., Mehta, S., Chen, T., Sun, F.: Prediction of protein function using protein-protein interaction data. In: Proceedings. IEEE Computer Society Bioinformatics Conference, pp. 197–206. IEEE (2002)

5. Bendale, A., Boult, T.E.: Towards open set deep networks. In: Proceedings of the IEEE Conference on Computer Vision and Pattern Recognition, pp. 1563–1572 (2016)
6. Geng, C., Huang, S., Chen, S.: Recent advances in open set recognition: a survey. IEEE Trans. Pattern Anal. Mach. Intell. **43**(10), 3614–3631 (2020)
7. Monti, F., Boscaini, D., Masci, J., Rodola, E., Svoboda, J., Bronstein, M.M.: Geometric deep learning on graphs and manifolds using mixture model CNNs. In: Proceedings of the IEEE Conference on Computer Vision and Pattern Recognition, pp. 5115–5124 (2017)
8. Kipf, T.N., Welling, M.: Semi-supervised classification with graph convolutional networks. arXiv preprint arXiv:1609.02907 (2016)
9. Yue, X., et al.: Graph embedding on biomedical networks: methods, applications and evaluations. Bioinformatics **36**(4), 1241–1251 (2020)
10. Teji, B., Roy, S., Dhami, D.S., Bhandari, D., Guzzi, P.H.: Graph embedding techniques for predicting missing links in biological networks: an empirical evaluation. IEEE Trans. Emerg. Topics Comput. **12**(1), 190–201 (2023)
11. Teji, B., Das, J.K., Roy, S., Bhandari, D.: Predicting missing links in gene regulatory networks using network embeddings: a qualitative assessment of selective embedding techniques. In: Udgata, S.K., Sethi, S., Gao, X.Z. (eds.) Intelligent Systems. LNNS, vol. 431, pp. 143–154. Springer, Cham (2022). https://doi.org/10.1007/978-981-19-0901-6_14
12. Teji, B., Roy, S.: Missing link identification from node embeddings using graph auto encoders and its variants. In: 2022 OITS International Conference on Information Technology (OCIT), pp. 1–6. IEEE (2022)
13. Ashoor, H., et al.: Graph embedding and unsupervised learning predict genomic sub-compartments from HiC chromatin interaction data. Nat. Commun. **11**(1), 1173 (2020)
14. Gilmer, J., Schoenholz, S.S., Riley, P.F., Vinyals, O., Dahl, G.E.: Neural message passing for quantum chemistry. In: International Conference on Machine Learning, pp. 1263–1272. PMLR (2017)
15. Pereira, G.T., de Carvalho, A.C.P.L.F.: Bringing robustness against adversarial attacks. Nat. Mach. Intell. **1**(11), 499–500 (2019)
16. Richardson, B., Williams, D., Mikkelsen, D.: Network Analytics and the Fight Against Money Laundering. McKinsey and Company, Charlotte (2019)
17. Queiruga-Dios, A., Encinas, A.H., Martín-Vaquero, J., Encinas, L.H.: Malware propagation models in wireless sensor networks: a review. In: International Joint Conference SOCO 2016-CISIS 2016-ICEUTE 2016: San Sebastián, Spain, 19th–21st October 2016 Proceedings 11, pp. 648–657. Springer, Cham (2017)
18. Wei, T., Feng, F., Chen, J., Wu, Z., Yi, J., He, X.: Model-agnostic counterfactual reasoning for eliminating popularity bias in recommender system. In: Proceedings of the 27th ACM SIGKDD Conference on Knowledge Discovery & Data Mining, pp. 1791–1800 (2021)
19. Schölkopf, B., Platt, J.C., Shawe-Taylor, J., Smola, A.J., Williamson, R.C.: Estimating the support of a high-dimensional distribution. Neural Comput. **13**(7), 1443–1471 (2001)
20. Liu, F.T., Ting, K.M., Zhou, Z.-H.: Isolation forest. In: 2008 Eighth IEEE International Conference on Data Mining, pp. 413–422. IEEE (2008)
21. Kamoi, R., Kobayashi, K.: Why is the Mahalanobis distance effective for anomaly detection? arXiv preprint arXiv:2003.00402 (2020)

22. Fei, G., Wang, S., Liu, B.: Learning cumulatively to become more knowledgeable. In: Proceedings of the 22nd ACM SIGKDD International Conference on Knowledge Discovery and Data Mining, pp. 1565–1574 (2016)
23. Shu, L., Xu, H., Liu, B.: DOC: deep open classification of text documents. arXiv preprint arXiv:1709.08716 (2017)
24. Xu, H., Liu, B., Shu, L., Yu, P.: Open-world learning and application to product classification. In: The World Wide Web Conference, pp. 3413–3419 (2019)
25. Scheirer, W.J., de Rezende Rocha, A., Sapkota, A., Boult, T.E.: Toward open set recognition. IEEE Trans. Pattern Anal. Mach. Intell. **35**(7), 1757–1772 (2012)
26. Xuefei, W., Liu, M., Xin, B., Zhu, Z., Wang, G.: Attention-based graph convolutional network for zero-shot learning with pre-training. Math. Probl. Eng. **1**–**13**, 2021 (2021)
27. Scheirer, W.J., Jain, L.P., Boult, T.E.: Probability models for open set recognition. IEEE Trans. Pattern Anal. Mach. Intell. **36**(11), 2317–2324 (2014)
28. Scheirer, W.J., de Rezende Rocha, A., Parris, J., Boult, T.E.: Learning for meta-recognition. IEEE Trans. Inf. Forensics Secur. **7**(4), 1214–1224 (2012)
29. Prakhya, S., Venkataram, V., Kalita, J.: Open set text classification using CNNs. In: Proceedings of the 14th International Conference on Natural Language Processing (ICON-2017), pp. 466–475 (2017)
30. Scheirer, W.J., Rocha, A., Micheals, R.J., Boult, T.E.: Meta-recognition: the theory and practice of recognition score analysis. IEEE Trans. Pattern Anal. Mach. Intell. **33**(8), 1689–1695 (2011)
31. Lyu, Z., Gutierrez, N.B., Beksi, W.J.: MetaMax: improved open-set deep neural networks via Weibull calibration. In: Proceedings of the IEEE/CVF Winter Conference on Applications of Computer Vision, pp. 439–443 (2023)
32. Weibull, W.: A statistical distribution function of wide applicability. J. Appl. Mech. (1951)
33. Mahalanobis, P.C.: On the generalized distance in statistics. Sankhyā: Indian J. Stat. Ser. A (2008-) **80**, S1–S7 (2018)
34. Sen, P., Namata, G., Bilgic, M., Getoor, L., Galligher, B., Eliassi-Rad, T.: Collective classification in network data. AI Mag. **29**(3), 93–93 (2008)
35. Bojchevski, A., Günnemann, S.: Deep Gaussian embedding of graphs: unsupervised inductive learning via ranking. arXiv preprint arXiv:1707.03815 (2017)
36. Pan, S., Jia, W., Zhu, X., Zhang, C., Wang, Y.: Tri-party deep network representation. Network **11**(9), 12 (2016)
37. Mernyei, P., Cangea, C.: Wiki-CS: a Wikipedia-based benchmark for graph neural networks. arXiv preprint arXiv:2007.02901 (2020)
38. Glorot, X., Bengio, Y.: Understanding the difficulty of training deep feedforward neural networks. In: Proceedings of the Thirteenth International Conference on Artificial Intelligence and Statistics, pp. 249–256. JMLR Workshop and Conference Proceedings (2010)
39. Kingma, D.P., Ba, J.: Adam: a method for stochastic optimization. arXiv preprint arXiv:1412.6980 (2014)

Optimizing Amazon SageMaker Workloads with Predictive Compute Type Selection Strategies

Kavita Srivastava[1]([✉])(iD) and Manisha Agarwal[2]

[1] Institute of Information Technology and Management, Delhi, India
srivastava.kavita1507@gmail.com
[2] Banasthali Vidyapith, Tonk, Rajasthan, India

Abstract. Effective resource provisioning is a critical aspect of optimizing cloud infrastructure, ensuring efficient resource allocation, and managing costs judiciously. One key element in this process is predicting the most suitable "Compute Type" for various workloads, as different types exhibit varying efficiencies in handling specific tasks. The precision in selecting the appropriate compute type not only leads to enhanced performance but also contributes to cost savings. AWS offers a broad range of compute types designed to satisfy various requirements about cost, scalability, and performance. Because these instances are suitable for specific use cases and workloads, choosing the right compute type is essential. Effective compute type selection is essential for managing costs and allocating resources as efficiently as possible. Precise forecasts lead to enhanced functionality, financial savings, and increased energy efficiency. In this paper, we have four kinds of compute types available in AWS - Accelerated Compute Types, Compute Optimized Instances, Memory Optimized Instances, and Standard Instances. We have proposed an automated approach for prediction of most appropriate compute types for specific workloads, reducing the manual configuration. In order to create the predictive model, we have used the Support Vector Machines (SVM) classifier and the ensemble methods. The SVM model balances F1-scores across classes and obtains an amazing overall accuracy of 84.49%. Conversely, AdaBoost performs worse, ranking 69.10% accurate and having comparatively lower F1-scores, particularly for "Memory Optimized Instances." With a remarkable accuracy of 99.42% and high F1-scores across all classes, XGBoost is particularly good at classifying 'Compute Type' using the features that are provided.

Keywords: Resource Provisioning · AWS · Compute Types · Ensemble Methods · Support Vector Machines (SVM) · XGBoost · AdaBoost

1 Introduction

AWS provides a range of compute types to accommodate varying demands on cost, scalability, and performance. These compute types are intended to support a broad spectrum of workloads, ranging from high-performance computing clusters to basic web apps [6]. The type of compute types you choose will rely on your particular use case, workload demands, and budgetary constraints. From fully managed serverless solutions to conventional virtual machines and container-based services, AWS provides a broad range of options to meet diverse compute demands. Selecting the appropriate instance type for your application's needs is crucial since different AWS instance types are tailored for particular use cases and workloads. Accelerated Compute Types are significant for Workloads requiring a lot of processing capacity, such as data processing, scientific simulations, and machine learning, are the target audience for accelerated computing instances. To speed up compute-intensive tasks, these instances have FPGAs (Field-Programmable Gate Arrays) and GPUs (Graphics Processing Units). Their use cases include video encoding, deep learning, artificial intelligence (AI), scientific computing, and other jobs where GPU acceleration is advantageous. Workloads requiring a lot of CPU power but not a lot of RAM or GPU capacity are best suited for compute-optimized instances, which are optimized for great computational performance [6, 9]. They offer a high vCPU to RAM ratio. Their use cases include batch processing, data analytics, high-performance web servers, and compute-intensive applications involving data manipulation and number crunching. Instances with memory optimization are built for tasks requiring a large quantity of RAM. Large in-memory databases, caching, data analytics, and apps with a high memory footprint are among the uses for them that work best. Their use cases include large-scale memory-intensive applications, in-memory databases, real-time big data analytics, and in-memory caching. Standard instances offer a well-balanced combination of CPU, memory, and network performance [9]. They are a solid option for applications with moderate resource requirements because they are adaptable and appropriate for a variety of workloads. Their use cases include numerous general-purpose workloads, content management systems, development and test environments, small to medium-sized web apps, and more. Predicting the most suitable "Compute Type" helps optimize resource allocation and cost management in the cloud, as different types may be better suited to specific workloads. In fact, the accurate compute type selection leads to performance enhancements. Proper selection of "Compute Type" can lead to improved performance and faster execution of machine learning models and data processing tasks. By choosing the most cost-effective "Compute Type" based on workload requirements, organizations can save money on cloud computing expenses. In this paper we present an automated approach to compute type prediction, reducing the need for manual selection and configuration [8]. Precise prediction of the suitable compute types for specific workloads holds great importance in cloud computing, especially on services such as AWS, for multiple reasons. Predictive modeling [5] of compute type can help in the efficient scaling of resources up or down based on demand, ensuring that resources are available when needed. Furthermore, optimizing resource usage based on workload characteristics contributes to green computing by reducing unnecessary energy consumption and environmental impact. Real-life applications of compute type predictions include cloud resource management in various industries, including e-commerce, web hosting, media streaming, big data analytics, machine learning, healthcare, finance, and research. It is relevant in scenarios where cloud computing resources are extensively used, and efficient resource allocation is critical [6]. The findings from this study can be adapted for various cloud platforms and services beyond Amazon SageMaker.

The paper is organized as follows: Sect. 2 presents a literature review. Section 3 describes the methodology used, including data collection, preprocessing, data cleaning and the training and assessment processes. Section 4 presents results of predictions using Support Vector Machines (SVM) classifier and ensemble methods. A critical analysis of both of these methods is also presented.

2 Literature Review

The importance of a data-driven framework for cloud computing management, with a focus on optimization and deep learning, is discussed by S. Karim et al. in 2022 [1]. To manage uncertainty in cloud networks, especially in data centers like Amazon Web Services and Wikipedia, it suggests a model-based, data-driven strategy. An Artificial Neural Network model is used to manage cloud workload and enable real-time resilience, debugging, and availability analysis, ultimately boosting cloud platform performance. During the pandemic, greater data input has resulted in data quality reduction. The difficulty of reducing the total cost of ownership for cloud services is covered in Y. Sfakianakis et al., 2020 [2], who emphasize the significance of altering the type, quantity, size, and provider of VM instances at runtime to achieve cost efficiency. The authors provide DyRAC, an adaptive resource assignment technique for cloud services, which is tested with real VM configurations from well-known providers (AWS, GCP, Azure) and four resource assignment policies. It has been demonstrated that DyRAC can cut expenditures by up to 33% compared to traditional methods. According to A. Guptha et al., 2021 [3], several levels of reliability are available for cloud computing services including storage, servers, and databases sent via the internet thanks to the security precautions taken by suppliers like Microsoft Azure, AWS, and GCP. Customers are unsure about these providers' distinct security strategies, pricing, and features that guard against cyberattacks. To assist clients in making more informed decisions and to increase their trust when choosing a cloud service provider, the paper compares and contrasts the security services offered by these providers. 2018: Y. Xue et al. [4] explores how the market for cloud computing is growing for media services as a result of the increased demand for picture and video applications. The current service level agreements do not appropriately reflect performance needs, despite the fact that cloud services offer stability and performance. The approach for evaluating image and video services across different cloud platforms is suggested in the article, with a focus on features like facial recognition, image analysis, OCR, VOD, live streaming, and video transcoding. To provide information for choosing a media cloud service, extensive tests are run on platforms including Google Cloud, Microsoft Azure, AWS, Alibaba Cloud, Baidu Cloud, and Tencent Cloud. According to E. Yildirim et al., 2023 [5], forecasting data transfer performance in cloud networks is difficult because short-term network changes make it difficult to perform resource optimization activities such replica selection, load balancing, and auto-scaling. End-system characteristics, network characteristics, and dataset characteristics are among the factors affecting throughput. By relying on information from network layer devices and memory-to-memory transfers, existing research frequently ignores end-system and dataset properties. This study gathered multivariate time series data from AWS, including end-system and network measurements, and produced accurate estimates of network and disk throughput that outperformed previous models. Noviani et al., 2022 [6] highlights how cloud servers are in high demand, particularly among enterprises, because of their affordability and quick response times. The study analyzes the CPU processing, latency, and throughput performance of AWS and GCP using the Golang Framework and a SQLite database. Helping consumers select the best cloud provider is the goal. When load testing using the GET method, the study used JMeter and discovered that AWS had a better success rate than GCP. Bermudez et al., 2013 [7] demonstrated an examination of Amazon Web Services (AWS), a well-known cloud provider with a range of services, which is presented in this research. The study looks at AWS's EC2, S3, and CloudFront services using passive measures to show their traffic allocation, content distribution, and infrastructure strategies. The results show that a single Amazon datacenter in Virginia serves the majority of material on EC2 and S3, which results in network slowness and possible user outages. On the other hand, CloudFront's content delivery network, which serves most of the traffic from the closest cache, provides improved performance with dynamic load balancing and effective cache selection. Researchers working on improving cloud design and developers considering AWS for content deployment will find this information useful. In the context of e-commerce applications, Bommannavar et al., 2019 [8] addresses how cloud computing affects software development and testing. It highlights how difficult it is to allocate resources for the best possible performance and usage under a variety of circumstances. The optimum resource estimation policy is the main emphasis of the study, which also includes experiments on AWS and a cloudsim simulator. Because there are no trace logs, workload modeling is difficult. Therefore, it creates workloads using an e-commerce application model and creates a resource utilization model for policy selection. Xue et al., 2018 [4] discusses how the demand for picture and video applications is driving the increasing presence of media services in the cloud market. The performance needs for media cloud services are not well represented by the existing service level agreements, despite the fact that cloud services have great stability and performance. In this study, a performance evaluation approach for image and video services—which include OCR, live streaming, video transcoding, facial recognition, image analysis, and VOD—across many cloud platforms is presented. Its objective is to offer insights into efficient media cloud service selection based on cloud QoS and media application needs. To that end, it undertakes comprehensive evaluations on platforms such as Google Cloud, Microsoft Azure, AWS, Alibaba Cloud, Baidu Cloud, and Tencent Cloud. The significance of a data-driven paradigm for managing cloud computing is covered in Karim et al., 2022 [1], with an emphasis on optimization and deep learning. In order to overcome data quality issues, the research suggests a model-based strategy, particularly when considering data centers such as Amazon Web Services. Because of the impact that resource allocation is having on data quality in the pandemic scenario, an Artificial Neural Network (ANN) model is used for workload management and time allocation with the goal of enhancing performance and lowering overhead on the cloud platform. For resource optimization tasks, cloud network data transfer throughput prediction is essential, but difficult because of transient network oscillations (Yildirim et al., 2023 [5]). Three groups of parameters affect throughput: end-system, network, and dataset characteristics. Neural network models that are now in use frequently overlook dataset and end-system considerations. Multivariate time series data, including network performance and end-system indicators, were gathered for this research via AWS. Their neural network models outperform models with less correlated variables and univariate models with transfer learning, achieving remarkable forecasts with about 3.7% error for network performance and 6.1% for disk throughput.

Research Gap. In essence, Amazon SageMaker is a machine learning solution that streamlines the creation, training, and large-scale implementation of machine learning models. There isn't a thorough investigation of methods for choosing the right compute type in Amazon SageMaker in the current literature. This involves taking into account various instance types, configurations, and resource allocation that are especially designed with SageMaker workloads in mind. While optimization, cost minimization, security, and performance evaluation have all been explored in the context of cloud computing by previous researchers, none of them have specifically focused on the difficulties and solutions associated with identifying the best compute type for Amazon SageMaker applications. The difficulties in determining the best compute type from workload parameters, past data, or other pertinent variables are not covered in any of the research. For machine learning workloads to utilize resources efficiently, predictive modeling is essential. While AWS, GCP, and Azure are among the cloud service providers covered in several articles, the integration of Amazon SageMaker with these platforms and the optimization of compute type selection in this context are not particularly explored. The proposed work focuses on creating predictive models for choosing the best compute type for particular Amazon SageMaker workloads in order to fill this research gap. This study would make a significant contribution to the field of cloud machine learning, especially in relation to Amazon SageMaker.

3 Methodology

3.1 Data Collection and Preprocessing

We have used AWS pricing data (AmazonSageMaker.csv) from Kaggle website1[1]. In order to predict the Compute Type, we have chosen three attributes – PricePerUnit, V CPU, and Memory. We have chosen these attributes for several reasons:

Resource Allocation: The main goal of compute type selection is to allocate the appropriate number of computing resources to a given activity or workload. Since they directly relate to the cost and available processing power and memory associated with a specific instance type, PricePerUnit, VCPU, and Memory are crucial properties.

Cost Optimization: PricePerUnit is important since it shows how much a certain Compute Type costs. Budgetary restrictions may apply to certain jobs or workloads, thus it's important to consider the costs involved while selecting a compute type.

Resource Requirements: The two most important technological requirements for compute types are memory and virtual CPU (VCPU). Different workloads require different amounts of memory and computing power. Matching these requirements with the right instance types is made easier by the VCPU and Memory characteristics.

---

[1] https://www.kaggle.com/datasets/annpastushko/amazon-web-services-pricing?select=AmazonSageMaker.csv.

Performance: A compute type's performance is directly impacted by its VCPU and memory. A large number of VCPUs may be required for parallel processing in some workloads, while plenty of memory may be needed for data-intensive operations in others. The overall effectiveness and performance are impacted by the combination of these characteristics.

Resource Scaling: To ensure that your workload or application operates efficiently, selecting the appropriate compute type is crucial. PricePerUnit, VCPU, and Memory give information about how well a compute type fits the particular scaling needs.

Trade-offs between economic and technical aspects: Cost and technical capabilities are frequently areas where decision-makers must compromise. These qualities aid in striking the ideal balance between financial limitations and technical appropriateness.

Compatibility and Suitability: Two of the most important measures of a compute type's compatibility and suitability for a particular task are its memory and Vcpu. Some workloads might not operate well if these characteristics don't meet their needs.

Further, as the dataset has many missing values in the Compute Type field, we have handled the missing values. The resulting values for each kind of Compute Types are shown below (Fig. 1).

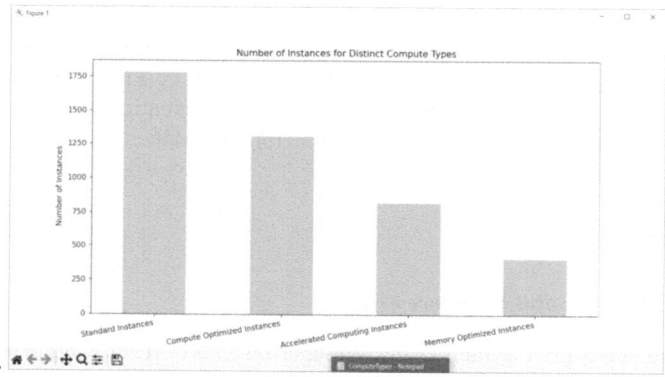

Fig. 1. Compute Types in the Dataset

3.2 Support Vector Machines (SVM) Classifier

We have used SVM classifier for several reasons:

Effective in High-Dimensional Space: SVMs are effective in high-dimensional feature spaces, which is often the case when you have multiple attributes (features) to consider when predicting Compute Types. Attributes such as PricePerUnit, VCPU, Memory, and others can form a high-dimensional feature space.

Non-Linearity Handling: While linear SVMs are commonly used, SVMs can also handle non-linear data through the use of different kernel functions. This flexibility allows SVMs to capture complex relationships between attributes and Compute Types.

Robust Against Overfitting: SVMs are less prone to overfitting, making them suitable for cases where you have a limited dataset or want to avoid overfitting due to noise in the data. This robustness helps in generalizing well to new, unseen data.

Optimal Hyperplane: SVMs aim to find the optimal hyperplane that best separates different classes. When predicting Compute Types, this means finding a hyperplane that effectively separates the instances belonging to different Compute Types, helping in accurate classification.

Margin Maximization: SVMs aim to maximize the margin between the classes. This helps in finding a clear boundary between different Compute Types, reducing the risk of misclassification.

Effective with Small to Medium Datasets: SVMs can perform well with small to medium-sized datasets, which is often the case in cloud computing environments where you have a finite number of Compute Types.

Tolerant of Outliers: SVMs are less sensitive to outliers in the data, which can be important in real-world datasets where data anomalies can exist.

3.3   Ensemble Methods (AdaBoost and XGBoost)

Using Ensemble Methods like AdaBoost and XGBoost for predicting Compute Types offers several advantages in the context of machine learning and prediction tasks:

Improved Prediction Accuracy: Ensemble methods combine multiple weaker models to create a stronger, more accurate predictor. This is particularly beneficial when dealing with complex and non-linear relationships in the data, as is often the case when predicting Compute Types.

Robustness to Overfitting: Ensemble methods are less prone to overfitting, which can be crucial when working with data that has noise or when the model needs to generalize well to unseen instances.

Handling Class Imbalance: In the case of Compute Type prediction, there may be imbalances in the dataset with some Compute Types being more prevalent than others. Ensemble methods can effectively handle class imbalances by assigning more weight to minority classes during training.

Feature Importance: Ensemble methods, especially XGBoost, provide valuable insights into feature importance. Understanding which features (e.g., PricePerUnit, VCPU, Memory) are most influential in predicting Compute Types can aid in model interpretability and feature selection.

Flexibility: Ensemble methods can work with a variety of base models, making them adaptable to different types of data and prediction problems. This flexibility is essential when dealing with real-world datasets that may have varying characteristics.

Robustness to Noisy Data: Real-world datasets can be noisy or contain outliers. Ensemble methods can handle such situations by giving less weight to models that perform poorly on noisy data points.

Hyperparameter Tuning: Both AdaBoost and XGBoost allow for tuning hyperparameters to optimize the model's performance. This flexibility is valuable when finetuning the model for Compute Type prediction.

Consolidation of Weak Models: In some cases, base models may have individual shortcomings. Ensemble methods can consolidate the strengths of these models to create a more robust predictor.

Ensemble Diversity: The diversity of base models in an ensemble is essential for its effectiveness. Ensemble methods can ensure that diverse models are used, reducing the risk of making the same prediction errors across all base models.

State-of-the-Art Performance: XGBoost, in particular, is known for its state-of-the-art performance and speed. It is often used in machine learning competitions and industry applications where predictive accuracy and efficiency are paramount.

In the context of predicting Compute Types, which involves multiple attributes and potentially complex relationships, using ensemble methods like AdaBoost and XGBoost can lead to more accurate, robust, and reliable predictions, helping in resource allocation and management in cloud computing environments.

3.4 Motivation and Applicability of Ensemble Methods

The proposed approach on predictive compute type selection for Amazon SageMaker is motivated by the use of ensemble methods because of their significant advantages in managing dynamic and complicated scenarios. Improved predictive accuracy is ensured by ensemble methods, such as Random Forests, which regularly outperform individual models. This is especially important for SageMaker workloads, where the best compute type selection depends on a number of criteria and precise forecasting is required for efficient resource use. Furthermore, ensemble approaches are inherently robust, guaranteeing the prediction strategy's efficacy in a variety of workload conditions. By merging predictions from models trained on several data subsets, they reduce overfitting and encourage generalization to new SageMaker workloads. Because of the intricate relationships seen in SageMaker workloads, ensemble approaches are excellent at capturing complex patterns and describing various data features using a variety of models. Because of their innate flexibility, they may adjust to shifting workload patterns by adding fresh training data, which helps to sustain the strategy's efficacy over time. In SageMaker, where workload uncertainties exist, ensemble methods offer a measure of prediction uncertainty that helps decision-makers evaluate prediction reliability for well-informed re-source allocation. Additionally, by employing ensemble approaches, we are able to uncover critical aspects impacting the best compute type selection and obtain insights into the significance of features. Decision-makers can more easily allocate resources according to the most important characteristics thanks to this transparency. By combining predictions from many models, ensemble methods also significantly contribute to the reduction of model bias and promote an accurate and well-rounded prediction strategy. Overall, the proposed predictive compute type selection strategy for Amazon SageMaker workloads is more robust, flexible, and comprehensible now that ensemble methods have been added.

4 Results and Discussion

We start by loading the dataset of Amazon SageMaker instances. Missing values in the feature set (X) are addressed using a SimpleImputer, which replaces missing values with the mean of the respective column. Feature scaling, specifically standardization, is applied to the training and testing data using a StandardScaler. This step ensures that all features have similar scales, which is crucial for some machine learning algorithms. First, we select an SVM classifier (Support Vector Machine) with a linear kernel and a regularization parameter C = 1.0. The accuracy and classification report is given below: Accuracy: 0.8449074074074074 (Table 1).

Table 1. SVM Classification Report

	Precision	Recall	F1-score	Support
Accelerated Computing Instances	0.91	0.79	0.85	170
Compute Optimized Instances	0.97	0.74	0.84	259
Memory Optimized Instances	0.88	0.71	0.78	72
Standard Instances	0.76	0.97	0.85	363
Accuracy			0.84	864
Micro avg	0.88	0.80	0.83	864
Weighted avg	0.87	0.84	0.84	864

4.1 Discussion

"Accelerated Computing Instances": The model correctly predicted 85% (0.85) of instances for this class. The precision is 0.91, meaning that when the model predicted this class, it was correct 91% of the time.

"Compute Optimized Instances": The model correctly predicted 84% (0.84) of instances for this class. The precision is 0.97, indicating a high level of precision.

"Memory Optimized Instances": The model correctly predicted 78% (0.78) of instances for this class. The precision is 0.88.

"Standard Instances": The model correctly predicted 85% (0.85) of instances for this class. The recall is 0.97, indicating a high level of recall.

This classifier is chosen for its capability to handle both binary and multi-class classification tasks. The SVM model is reasonably accurate at predicting the "Compute Type" of Amazon SageMaker instances (Figs. 2 and 3).

Next, we have applied ensemble method on the given dataset and we get the following output: AdaBoost Accuracy: 0.6909722222222222 and XGBoost Accuracy: 0.9942129629629629 (Table 2 and Figs. 4, 5).

The SVM model performs reasonably well, achieving a good overall accuracy of 84.49% and balanced F1-scores for each class. AdaBoost struggles in comparison, with

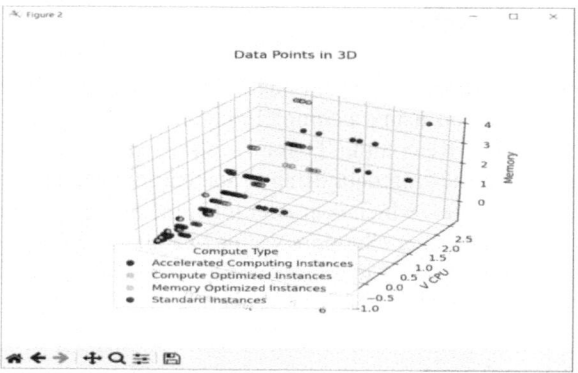

Fig. 2. Scatter Plot Obtained by applying SVM Classifier

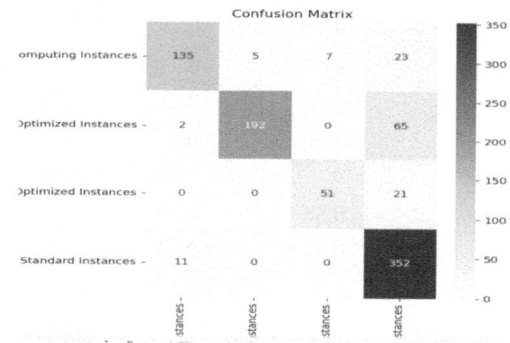

Fig. 3. Confusion Matrix Obtained from SVM Classifier

Table 2. XGBoost Classification Report

	Precision	Recall	F1-score	Support
Accelerated Computing Instances	0.97	1.00	0.99	170
Compute Optimized Instances	1.00	1.00	1.00	259
Memory Optimized Instances	1.00	1.00	1.00	72
Standard Instances	1.00	0.99	0.99	363
Accuracy			0.99	864
Macro avg	0.99	1.00	0.99	864
Weighted avg	0.99	0.99	0.99	864

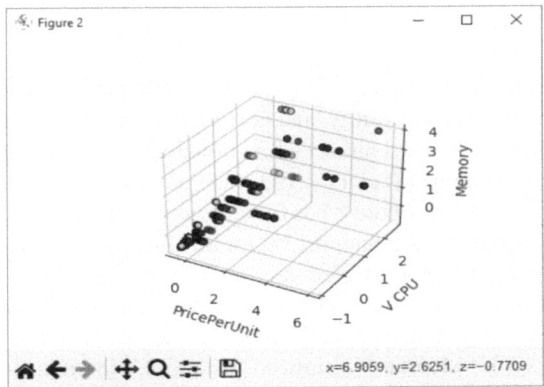

Fig. 4. Scatter Plot Obtained by applying Ensemble Techniques

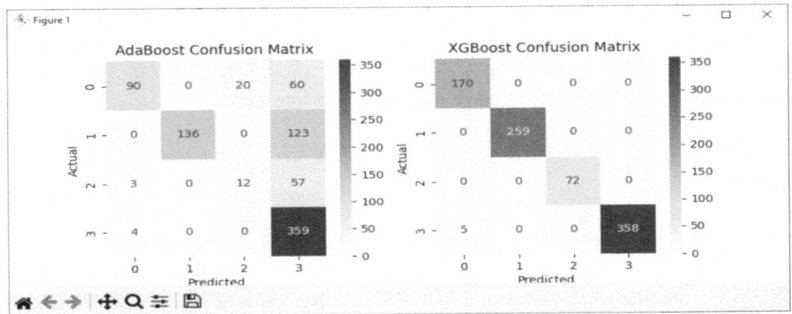

Fig. 5. Confusion Matrix Obtained from Ensemble Techniques

an accuracy of 69.10% and relatively low F1-scores, particularly for the 'Memory Optimized Instances.' XGBoost performed well with an exceptional accuracy of 99.42% and high F1-scores for all classes. It indicates that it is highly effective in classifying 'Compute Type' based on the given features. Table 3 provides a performance comparison of the proposed approach with existing state of the art methods.

Table 3. Performance Comparison

Classifier	Naïve Bayes	Neural Network	SVM	AdaBoost	XGBoost
Accuracy	0.45	0.36	0.85	0.69	0.99

5 Conclusion

In this paper, the importance of selecting the right AWS compute type to meet specific requirements related to cost, scalability, and performance has been highlighted. Precise compute type selection not only enhances functionality and financial savings but also contributes to increased energy efficiency. The study presents an automated approach for predicting the most suitable compute types for various workloads, reducing the need for manual configuration. Leveraging Support Vector Machines (SVM) and ensemble methods, the predictive models demonstrated varying levels of accuracy. The SVM model showcased an impressive overall accuracy of 84.49%, effectively balancing F1-scores across classes. Conversely, AdaBoost performed with a lower accuracy of 69.10%, particularly struggling with "Memory Optimized Instances." In contrast, XGBoost stood out with a remarkable accuracy of 99.42% and high F1-scores across all classes, making it exceptionally proficient in classifying 'Compute Type' based on the provided features. These findings underscore the potential of machine learning techniques, particularly XGBoost, in streamlining compute type selection processes, ultimately leading to improved resource allocation and cost efficiency within AWS environments.

Disclosure of Interests.   The authors have no competing interests.

References

1. Karim, S., He, H.: Optimization: data-driven management using deep learning in cloud computing. In: 2022 23rd Asia-Pacific Network Operations and Management Symposium (APNOMS), Takamatsu, Japan, pp. 1–4 (2022). https://doi.org/10.23919/APNOMS56106. 2022.9920000
2. Sfakianakis, Y., Marazakis, M., Bilas, A.: DyRAC: cost-aware resource assignment and provider selection for dynamic cloud workloads. In: 2020 IEEE 26th International Conference on Parallel and Distributed Systems (ICPADS), Hong Kong, pp. 502–509 (2020). https://doi.org/10.1109/ICPADS51040.2020.00071
3. Guptha, A., Murali, H., Subbulakshmi, T.: A comparative analysis of security services in major cloud service providers. In: 2021 5th International Conference on Intelligent Computing and Control Systems (ICICCS), Madurai, India, pp. 129–136 (2021). https://doi.org/10.1109/ICICCS51141.2021.9432189
4. Xue, Y., Zhang, H., Ma, H.: Performance evaluation of image and video cloud services. In: 2018 IEEE 20th International Conference on High Performance Computing and Communications; IEEE 16th International Conference on Smart City; IEEE 4th International Conference on Data Science and Systems (HPCC/SmartCity/DSS), Exeter, UK, pp. 733–741 (2018). https://doi.org/10.1109/HPCC/SmartCity/DSS.2018.00126
5. Yildirim, E., Akon, A.: Predicting short-term variations in end-to-end cloud data transfer throughput using neural networks. IEEE Access 11, 78656–78670 (2023). https://doi.org/10.1109/ACCESS.2023.3299311
6. Noviani, E.F., et al.: Performance analysis of AWS and GCP cloud providers. In: 2022 IEEE International Conference on Cybernetics and Computational Intelligence (CyberneticsCom), Malang, Indonesia, pp. 236–241 (2022). https://doi.org/10.1109/CyberneticsCom55287.2022.9865484

7. Bermudez, I., Traverso, S., Mellia, M., Munafò, M.: Exploring the cloud from passive measurements: the Amazon AWS case. In: 2013 Proceedings IEEE INFOCOM, Turin, Italy, pp. 230–234 (2013). https://doi.org/10.1109/INFCOM.2013.6566769
8. Bommannavar, P.A., Krishnan, R., Shahedha, S.: Optimal resource estimation policy selection for ecommerce applications in cloud. In: 2019 1st International Conference on Advanced Technologies in Intelligent Control, Environment, Computing & Communication Engineering (ICATIECE), Bangalore, India, pp. 236–242 (2019). https://doi.org/10.1109/ICATIECE45860.2019.9063825
9. Garfinkel, S.: An evaluation of Amazon's grid computing services: EC2, S3, and SQS (2007)
10. Saini, R., Behl, R.: An introduction to AWS—EC2 (elastic compute cloud), 99–102 (2020). https://doi.org/10.15439/2020KM4
11. Masood, A., Sherif, A.: Automated Machine Learning: Hyperparameter Optimization, Neural Architecture Search, and Algorithm Selection with Cloud Platforms. Packt Publishing (2021)

K-Means Clustering Based VM Placement Using MAD and IQR

Akanksha Tandon, Aditya Jena, and Sanjeev Patel$^{(\boxtimes)}$

Department of Computer Science and Engineering, National Institute of Technology Rourkela, Rourkela 769008, Odisha, India
patels@nitrkl.ac.in

Abstract. Cloud Data Centers (CDCs) have been developed into a virtual computing platform for businesses. Nevertheless, CDCs require significant power, which is essential for processor speed, particularly for Internet of Things (IoT) activities. Despite the existence of a significant amount of research in the green allocation of resource methodologies, it has been carried out to minimize the usage of the CDCs. Traditional systems mainly seek to minimize the number of physical machines (PMs) and rarely tackle the problems of overload and energy efficiency of the virtual machines (VMs) regulations concurrently. Furthermore, present systems cannot evaluate and redirect traffic from relevant sources to maximize the quality of service (QoS) supplied by CDCs. To improve energy saving, we attempt to enhance the adaptive four thresholds energy-aware framework for VM deployment energy efficiency (AFED-EF) scheme to improve energy savings. That is a unique adaptive energy-aware VM allocation and deployment technique for different applications to address these issues. We conducted a comprehensive exploratory program utilizing an authentic workload of over a million Planet Lab VMs. The research results demonstrate that our modified approach outperforms the AFED-EF and other existing traditional approaches, such as median absolute deviation (MAD), interquartile range (IQR), and overload detection using exponentially weighted moving average.

Keywords: SLA violation · Energy Consumption · Cloud data centers · Virtual Machines · Energy Efficiency · virtual machine allocation (VMA) · and Median absolute deviation

1 Introduction

Cloud computing solutions allow the client to access a centralized repository with programmable resources anytime. Generally, cloud computing systems are classified into infrastructure as a Service (IaaS), Software as a Service (SaaS), and Platform as a Service (PaaS) [1]. PaaS primarily offers cloud consumers infrastructure enabling development and implementation, leaving individuals to install and manage the necessary Linux kernel and applications. In case of IaaS, each licensed system contains a Linux kernel and the essential frameworks. However,

A. Verma et al. (Eds.): ANTIC 2023, CCIS 2091, pp. 142–154, 2024.
https://doi.org/10.1007/978-3-031-64064-3_11

SaaS delivers technology upon request, implying that customers do not need to pay for the product's unique licensing. Through the very last couple of short decades, Kaur et al. [2] have proposed that cloud technology has already become increasingly popular as a reduced functionality information technology, enabling local firms to sublet decentralized configurable assets (super-computing and connectivity) made available as a large-scale service model without making capital stakes in maintenance and management. Among all cloud platform types, IaaS is now the most extensively used. Throughout this prototype, a network operator could indeed rent agreement virtual computing technical guidance assets (computation, flash memory, internet connectivity, and packet forwarding assistance) through one or even more virtual servers, cloud service providers (CPs) wrapped into intertwined VMs and constructed as just a network virtualization recommendation, to construct nonhomogenous Virtualization, offering personalized customer application forms to its end customers.

This paper deals with how VM allocation policies can be changed to reduce energy consumption in a data center while maintaining a reasonable QoS for its applications. This study aims to investigate the relationship between VM allocation policies, energy consumption, and QoS and identify optimal VM allocation policies that reduce energy consumption while maintaining a reasonable QoS. The study will use simulation-based approaches to evaluate the impact of VM allocation policies on energy consumption and QoS in a data center. The results of this study will provide guidelines for data center operators to make appropriate decisions regarding VM allocation policies, resulting in a more sustainable and efficient data center. This paper proposes a VM allocation method and a VM selection policy method to satisfy the above-mentioned objectives. VM consolidation consists of the following four sub-processes: VM Placement, host overloading monitoring under-load discovery, VM Selection for migrating from the overloaded server identification, and VM placement for supplying chosen VMs on such a fresh set of servers. This work precises four VM consolidation sub-components: VM placement, host overloading, VM selection, and migration. However, a few writers have concentrated exclusively on VM consolidation in their studies. Powering data center resources may be accomplished in two phases. The first stage is to position VMs efficiently, and step two is to optimize the resources allocated to them in the initial phase by employing VMs migration as resource consumption increases.

We have tried to implement K-Means-MAD-IQR and medium fit power efficient algorithm to determine the threshold for over-utilization and choice of host for migration, which are paramount in deciding energy consumption.

1.1 Contribution

We have followed the paper presented by author Zhou et al. [3]. In which authors have determined four thresholds based on the K-Means-MAD-IQR. Though the authors have developed a new VM deployment mechanism based on the four thresholds determined, our contribution is to study these two approaches for determining the threshold values and VM placement mechanism. We have observed that the identification of new threshold values will play a significant role during the VM placement. It improves the performance of adaptive four threshold energy aware for deploying VM allocation (AFED-EF). We have modified the VM placement scheme by introducing new energy efficiency parameters. We have implemented K-Means-MAD-IQR and Medium fit power efficient algorithms to determine the threshold for over-utilization and choice of host for migration.

This paper has been presented in the following order. Section 2 presents related work. Section 3 highlights the system model of the complete VM placement structure, and the results are presented in Sect. 4. In the last section, we have concluded and stated the future direction of the result.

2   Related Work

The process of consolidating virtual machines, which entails three crucial steps: (i) identifying overloaded hosts, (ii) choosing which virtual machines to pick for consolidation, and (iii) deciding where to deploy these virtual machines, has been thoroughly studied by many academics. A thorough summary of related work in VM consolidation is given in Table 1. In this Table, Beloglazov et al. [4] and Xu et al. [5] have looked at the goals, methods, standards for measuring performance, and simulators used by different writers in this field. The Best Fit Decreasing (BFD) method for deploying virtual machines was introduced by Beloglazov et al. The four VM selection strategies they proposed were migration minimization (MM), static threshold (ST), high-performance growth (HPG), and random choice (RC). Researchers and engineers are working to increase the efficiency and advantages of cloud computing in response to its rising popularity. When cloud infrastructure is used efficiently and economically, cloud computing becomes viable, allowing organizations of all sizes to become stable. Cloud computing allows users to provide resources on demand and execute programs in a way that suits their demands by picking virtual resources that meet their application's resource requirements. It is therefore up to cloud resource providers to transform virtual resources into physical resources in order to accommodate these virtual resources on physical resources. Despite considering the providers' optimization aims and resource suppliers, the author discovers particular inherent challenges in cloud computing [6].

Kulshrestha et al. [12] have proposed that only one variable exponential weight moving average (EWMA) uses the mean of time-proportionally weighted information as its foundation. Hussain et al. [13] have proposed a technique to conserve resources using an audiovisual public cloud. Its primary goal is identifying appropriate hosts to close down to conserve energy. Li et al. [14] created a novel VMP approach called Modified Particle Swarm Optimization (MPSO) that depends on several resources. The MPSO method foregoes local optimization.

Table 1. Comparative review of VM placement

Author	Objective	Methodology	Performance Evaluation Metrics	Simulator
Beloglazov et al. [4]	1) VMP 2) VM selection	1) Modified Best Fit Decreasing (BFD) 2) Utilization thr related dynamic policies - MM, ST, HPG, RC	a) Energy consumption b) SLAV c) VMM count	CloudSim
Wang et al. [7]	1). Host overload detection 2). Based on Host susceptibility	1). Based on Resource utilization correlation (RUC) for allocated VMs.	a). VM migration count b). Hot/cold spot count c). SLA violation d). Performance degradation	CloudSim
Moges et al. [8]	1) VMP	1) MBFD 2) PABFD 3) PEFFD 4) PEBFD 5) MFPED	a) Energy consumption b) overload time fraction c). VMM count	CloudSim
Kulkarni et al. [9]	1) VMP 2) VM Placement Optimization 3) Host Overload Detection 4) VM Selection	1) Power Aware Best Fit Decreasing (PABFD) 2) Global Workload Scheduler 3) THR	a) Energy Consumption b) Overall SLA Violation c) VM Migration d) Total Host (PM) Shutdown e) Mean VM Allocation Time Mean Host Selection policy	CloudSim
Fu et al. [10]	1) VM Placement 2) VM Selection	1) PABFD, minimum correlation coefficient (MCC) 2) Utilization threshold-based dynamic policies - MMT, MU, MC, RC	a) Energy Consumption b) Overall SLA Violation c) VM Migration	CloudSim
Melhem et al. [11]	1) VM Placement 2) Host overload detection.	1). Markov chain model	a) Energy consumption b) PlanetLab, c) Random	CloudSim

3 System Model

3.1 Working of K-Means-MAD-IQR

We have used two methodologies in this work by combining power usage, SLA breaches, and the host's energy efficiency and naming them K-Means-MAD-IQR Algorithm and Medium Fit Power Efficient Decreasing (MFPED). Our approach involves two parts: finding a threshold to determine the overutilization of the host and finding a suitable host for VMs that need to be migrated from an overutilized or an underutilized host. To determine the overutilization threshold, we use the K-Means-MAD-IQR Algorithm.

Algorithm 1. K-Mean-MAD-IQR [3]

Require: The past utilization set, $T = T_1, T_2, \ldots, T_n$.
Ensure: IQR value of Host Utilization.
    pastCpuUtilization = host.getUtilizationHistory()
    k = 7
    clusters = KMeansClusters(pastCpuUtillization, k)
    for $i = 1$ to k **do**
    $MC[i] \leftarrow MAD(C[i])$ /* Using eq.(5) and(6)*/

    end for
    IQR value of Host Utilization

---

we calculate medium absolute deviation and IQR to determine the overutilization threshold. We use the K-Means-MAD-IQR Algorithm. The K-Means-MAD-IQR Algorithm takes in the utilization history of all the host VMs, T = T1, T2, . . . , Tn, and formed clusters using the K-Means clustering algorithm. Thereafter, the median absolute deviation (MAD) is calculated for each cluster, and the results are put in the form of an array, MC. Median absolute deviation of a cluster C as shown in Eq. (1).

$$MAD(C) = Median(|C_i - median(C)|) \tag{1}$$

after that, the array MC's interquartile range value, IQR, is found. Using this IQR value, the host is checked for overutilization. The IQR range of array MC is determined using Eq. (2):

$$IQR(MC) = Q_3(MC) - Q_1(MC) \tag{2}$$

The threshold for over-utilization P is determined as Eq. (3),

$$P = (1 - s * IQR), \tag{3}$$

where s is the safety parameter. Thereafter, we calculate the host utilization threshold, U_{Thr} using Eq (4),

$$U_{Thr} = \frac{\sum_{j=1}^{M} R_i}{Host_{MIPS}}, \tag{4}$$

where, R_j is the requested MIPS for j^{th} VMs. M is the total number of VMs. $Host_{MIPS}$ is the total MIPS the cost currently provides.

3.2 Working of Medium Fit Power Efficient Decreasing

VM placement problem can be transformed into a bin-packing problem. A bin-packing problem is an allocation problem where user requests will be mapped to available resources subject to minimize wastage. This process is known as the fitting approach. There are many versions of the fit model that are available in the literature [8]. Researchers have widely used bin packing techniques and their variants for VM placement problems. The interested one may refer [8] for detailed discussion.

The following is the medium-fit bin-packing rule: Letting L_h be a host's ideal resource utilization rate, which is provided as [8].

$$L_h = \frac{overload_{thr} + underload_{thr}}{2} \tag{5}$$

where L_h denotes the required levels of resource utilization in a host.
Moges et al. [8] proposed the Medium Fit Power Efficient Decreasing (MFPED) algorithm, incorporating a novel bin-packing heuristic called MFrule. The operational process of the MFPED algorithm is illustrated in Fig 1.

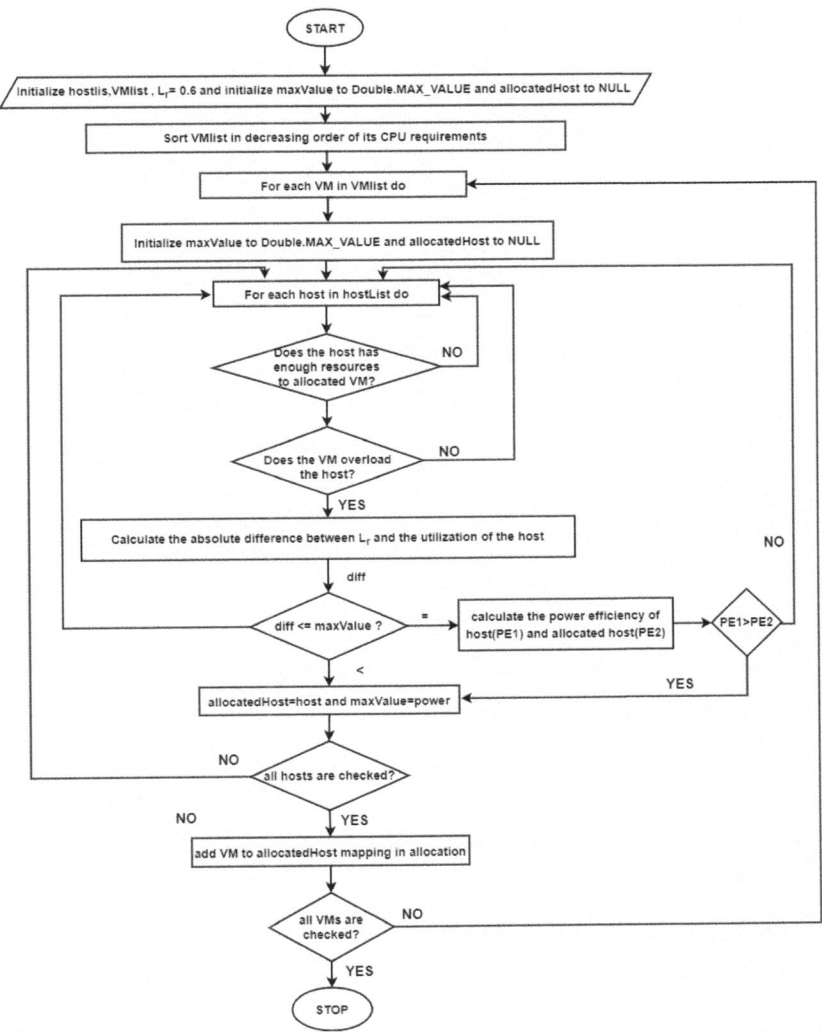

Fig. 1. Flowchart of medium fit power efficient decreasing (MFPED) [15]

In this approach, a physical machine is considered more suitable for VM placement than others if it exhibits a minimal difference in CPU utilization from the desired level, which is set at 0.6 in this paper. In cases where two physical machines have equivalent utilization levels, the selection is based on the superior power efficiency of the respective machines. Fig 2 represents the system model of the proposed algorithm.

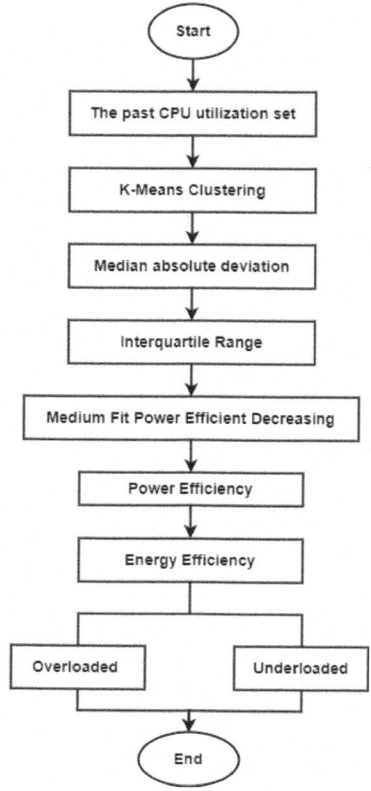

Fig. 2. Working flow of system model

4   Results and Discussions

In the following sections, we will carry out several exercises to assess the effectiveness of the AFED-EF algorithm. The suggested computation benefits are embodied in the MEEVMP [15], EWMA [12], THR-0.8 [16], MAD 2.5 [16], and IQR-1.5 [16]. These methods are chosen to compare in regards to the energy usage, SLA violation time per active host (SVTH), performance degradation due to migration (PDCM), and a variety of VM migrations. The MMT and MU are used to compare the VM selection policy. We examine the proposed algorithm findings for different measures during the initial set of experiments by modifying the values of criterion c. We adjust the parameter c between 0.5 to 3.0 with a difference of 0.5. The primary outcome of this investigation assists us in determining the ideal amount of parameter estimate c for the proposed algorithm. In the following research, we evaluate the effectiveness of the recommended method with an energy-efficient VM selection and without an energy-efficient VM selection.

4.1   Performance Metrics

This paper uses three performance metrics: Energy Efficiency, SLA violations, and several VM migrations.

Energy Consumption

We calculated energy consumption in order to calculate energy efficiency. The data center holds the power values for every host, using which we can calculate the total energy consumption. The total energy consumption (EC) is thus given by:

$$EC = \sum_{h=0}^{H_{count}} \sum_{t_1}^{t_2} E_h(v(t)) \tag{6}$$

where $E_h(v(t))$ is the power of a host at any given time interval, t and EC may be understood as energy consumed between time t_1 to t_2 (Energy(t_1, t_2)); h represents the host number in the range $[0, H_{count}]$; t_1 is the start time taken as 0; t_2 is end time taken as τ.

Service Level Agreement

The concept of SLA violation as defined by [3] indicates the situations in which a host is incapable of providing a specific VM with the requested number of instructions (MIPS) at a given moment. The measurement of SLA violation can be conducted either from the perspective of hosts or VMs, with both approaches yielding identical results. SLA violations are calculated as:

$$SLA = \text{PDCM} \times \text{Time per active host} \tag{7}$$

where PDCM denotes the performance degradation caused by VM migration.

Average Service Level Agreement

Average SLA violations are calculated as [12]:

$$\text{Average SLA violations} = \sum_{w=1}^{V_{count}} \left(\frac{\sum_{t=0}^{t=T} req(w,t) - alloc(w,t)}{V_{count}} \right) \tag{8}$$

where req(w, t) is the MIPS requested by VM v at time t, and alloc(w, t) represents the MIPS allocated to the VM at that time.

VM Migration

The associated metrics to VM migration is calculated as:

$$VMM = \text{The number of VM migrations in the data center each day.} \tag{9}$$

4.2   Simulation Set-Up

We have used the setup provided by Beloglazov et al. [16] described in their research, depicted in Table 2. In this, configuration are 800 physical computers with two distinct power models, and 1024 physical machines. Four distinct kinds of virtual servers. The workload samples were created randomly and derived using existing cloud records (PlanetLab). Research has proven that computer processors seriously influence server power consumption in data centers. Server processors, storage, disk, and throughput all impact how much power they use. We use the significant energy consumption data from the SPECpower benchmarking [17]. We choose two servers with two cores each. Table 3 shows CPU utilization.

Table 2. Parameters and configurations for simulation

Parameters	Configuration
Host type	HP ProLiantML110G4(2*1800MIPS)
Host type	HP ProLiantML110G5(2*2600MIPS)
Number of host	800,400 of each host type
VM type	2500MIPS, 2000MIPS, 1500MIPS, 1000MIPS
Workloads	PlanetLab(10 days of traces)

Table 3. CPU utilization

CPU Usages %	Threshold G4(Watt)	Threshold G5(Watt)
0	86	93.7
10	89.4	97
20	92.6	101
30	96	105
40	99.5	110
50	102	116
60	106	121
70	108	125
80	112	129
90	114	133
100	117	135

4.3   Workloads

We used a windows computer with an Intel i7-6700 3.4 GHz processor and 8 GB of memory for the tests, as the computer's high processing power and sufficient memory allowed for the smooth running of the experiments. The experiment group's composition of 10 instances of intake workload traces collected via PlanetLab on 10 separate days provided a diverse sample that accounted for any variations in workload over time. Gathering input workload information through 800 physiological nodes and 1,000 virtual machines is significant as it indicates the actual usage of PlanetLab cloud servers. This large sample size accurately represents the workload more accurately than a smaller sample size. Configuration of VMs is shown in Table 4.

Table 4. Configurations of VM

Virtual Machine	core	Capacity(MIPS)	RAM(GB)
High Instance	1	2500	0.85
Large Instance	1	2000	3.75
Small Instance	1	1000	1.7
Micro Instance	1	500	0.61

4.4   Results Analysis

We ran the analysis using datasets taken from PlanetLab, a real-world cloud. The PlanetLab is a powerful research platform supported by CoMon [18], a monitoring and controlling system that collects footprints. The data contains the CPU usage in percentage of over 100 virtual machines running on global hosts. These statistics were collected on various days in March and April of 2010. Table 5 and Table 6 show ten days of planate-lab workload. Table 7 shows the comparison of proposed algorithm power consumption, the average SLA breach, and the VMs migration. Results show that the proposed algorithm achieves the best results in terms of energy consumption, and the following techniques perform better in the sequence MEEVMP, EWMA, THR-0.8, MAD-2.5, and IQR-1.5. In terms of average SLA, EWMA outperforms the other compared techniques, while MFPED performs best in terms of VM migration. It has been observed that there is a tradeoff between various output performance measures such as energy consumption, ASLA, and VM migrations.

Table 5. QoS parameters of medium fit decreasing on various workloads using MMT

Date	Energy Con.(KWH)	SLA(%)	VM Mig
03/03/2011	100.70	0.01581	20447
06/03/2011	74.53	0.01426	15252
09/03/2011	84.41	0.02122	19317
22/03/2011	101.59	0.02034	25375
25/03/2011	88.69	0.01841	20286
03/04/2011	136.66	0.01662	26523
09/04/2011	106.83	0.01768	22979
11/04/2011	103.97	0.01812	21852
12/04/2011	90.57	0.01929	19809
20/04/2011	73.21	0.02851	19821

Table 6. QoS parameters of medium fit decreasing on various workloads using MU

Date	Energy Con.(KWH)	SLA(%)	VM Mig
03/03/2011	99.21	0.03392	37117
06/03/2011	73.17	0.03398	30302
09/03/2011	82.67	0.04902	37963
22/03/2011	100.03	0.04837	48686
25/03/2011	87.07	0.03995	37510
03/03/2011	134.8	0.04434	53721
09/03/2011	105.1	0.04165	43732
11/04/2011	102.42	0.04303	43515
12/04/2011	90.57	0.01929	19809
20/04/2011	89.02	0.042187	37414

Table 7. Comparison of various algorithms

Algorithim	Energy Con.(KWH)	ASLA(%)	VM Mig
MEEVMP	111.77	10.98	17639
EWMA	129.7	8.87	14684
IQR1.5	188.86	9.98	26476
MFPED	110.93	3.62	10975
Mad2.5	184.88	10.18	26292
THr0.8	163.33	9.10	45517
EEVMP	112.56	11.07	18860
Proposed Algo	100.70	9.52	20447

5   Conclusion

This study offers AFED-EF, an individual VM allocation and positioning technique, in order to properly manage changes and achieve optimized energy effectiveness for IoT systems in a CDC. Our paper gives more weightage to energy efficiency than SLA violation. The proposed algorithm, when compared with the VM placement algorithm MEEVMP, reduces the energy consumption by 9.85%, and the average SLA violation by 13.2%. As a result, researchers want to use AFED-EF to expand VM optimizations and assessment methods inside this OpenStack public cloud in the future. This effort will also encompass micro services IoT requirements that operate on virtualized back-end platforms and gateways to describe various heterogeneity in temporal and spatial IoT requirements. This medium enables the proposed technique to continuously regulate the hosts and activate transducers to move some parts of the requests to neighboring hosts to conserve resources and power to prevent violating the customers' SLA.

Further, our attempt would be made to select appropriate clustering techniques to improve the quality of services. We will use different clustering algorithms in order to determine appropriate thresholds for the identification overloaded and underloaded VMs that leads to better performance.

References

1. Liu, X., Cheng, B., Wang, S.: Availability-aware and energy-efficient virtual cluster allocation based on multi-objective optimization in cloud datacenters. IEEE Trans. Netw. Serv. Manage. **17**(2), 972–985 (2020)
2. Kaur, P.D., Chana, I.: A resource elasticity framework for QoS-aware execution of cloud applications. Futur. Gener. Comput. Syst. **37**, 14–25 (2014)
3. Zhou, Z., Shojafar, M., Alazab, M., Abawajy, J., Li, F.: AFED-EF: an energyefficient VM allocation algorithm for IoT applications in a cloud data center. IEEE Trans. Green Commun. Netw. **5**(2), 658–669 (2021)
4. Beloglazov, A., Buyya, R.: Energy efficient allocation of virtual machines in cloud data centers. In: 2010 10th IEEE/ACM International Conference on Cluster, Cloud and Grid Computing, pp. 577–578 (2010). IEEE
5. Zhou, Z., et al.: Fine-grained energy consumption model of servers based on task characteristics in cloud data center. IEEE Access **6**, 27080–27090 (2018). https://doi.org/10.1109/ACCESS.2017.2732458
6. Tripathy, A.K., Sarkar, M., Sahoo, J.P., Li, K.C., Chinara, S. (eds.): Advances in Distributed Computing and Machine Learning. LNNS, vol. 127. Springer, Singapore (2021). https://doi.org/10.1007/978-981-15-4218-3
7. Wang, J.V., Ganganath, N., Cheng, C.-T., Chi, K.T.: Bio-inspired heuristics for VM consolidation in cloud data centers. IEEE Syst. J. **14**(1), 152–163 (2019)
8. Moges, F.F., Abebe, S.L.: Energy-aware VM placement algorithms for the OpenStack neat consolidation framework. J. Cloud Comput. **8**(1), 2 (2019)
9. Kulkarni, A.K., Annappa, B.: Context aware VM placement optimization technique for heterogeneous IaaS cloud. IEEE Access **7**, 89702–89713 (2019)
10. Fu, X., Zhou, C.: Virtual machine selection and placement for dynamic consolidation in cloud computing environment. Front. Comp. Sci. **9**, 322–330 (2015)

11. Melhem, S.B., Agarwal, A., Goel, N., Zaman, M.: Markov prediction model for host load detection and VM placement in live migration. IEEE Access **6**, 7190–7205 (2017)
12. Kulshrestha, S., Patel, S.: An efficient host overload detection algorithm for cloud data center based on exponential weighted moving average. Int. J. Commun. Syst. **34**(4), 4708 (2021)
13. Hussain, M., Wei, L.F., Lakhan, A., Wali, S., Ali, S., Hussain, A.: Energy and performance-efficient task scheduling in heterogeneous virtualized cloud computing. Sustain. Comput. Inform. Syst. **30**, 100517 (2021)
14. Liu, X., Li, W., Zhang, X.: Strategy-proof mechanism for provisioning and allocation virtual machines in heterogeneous clouds. IEEE Trans. Parallel Distrib. Syst. **29**(7), 1650–1663 (2017)
15. Sunil, S., Patel, S.: Energy-efficient virtual machine placement algorithm based on power usage. Computing, 1–25 (2023)
16. Beloglazov, A., Buyya, R.: Optimal online deterministic algorithms and adaptive heuristics for energy and performance efficient dynamic consolidation of virtual machines in cloud data centers. Concurrency Comput. Pract. Experience **24**(13), 1397–1420 (2012)
17. Zhou, Z., Hu, Z., Song, T., Yu, J.: A novel virtual machine deployment algorithm with energy efficiency in cloud computing. J. Cent. South Univ. **22**(3), 974–983 (2015). https://doi.org/10.1007/s11771-015-2608-5
18. Park, K., Pai, V.S.: CoMon: a mostly-scalable monitoring system for PlanetLab. ACM SIGOPS Oper. Syst. Rev. **40**(1), 65–74 (2006)

On Designing an Intelligent Shipping Algorithm for Decentralized E-Commerce Systems

Suneel Kumar[1,2(✉)], Sarvesh Pandey[2], and Umesh Bhatt[2,3]

[1] Department of Computer Science, Institute of Science, BHU, Varanasi, UP, India
suneel@bhu.ac.in
[2] Computer Science, MMV, BHU, Varanasi, UP, India
sarveshpandey@bhu.ac.in
[3] Indian Institute of Technology Madras, Chennai, India

Abstract. The foundation of online shopping lies in the efficient and timely delivery of products from sellers to customers directly through a streamlined (and user-friendly) digital platform. However, transitioning to the online shopping platform leads to the following two problems: higher shipping charges and product handling fees levied by these platforms. The shipping charge is typically exempted if the order value is equal to or higher than the predetermined threshold value. The existing shipping charge exemption rule does not favor customers with low and mid-range budgets who often place orders valued lower than the threshold. To address the inherent biasness, we propose the History Informed Shipping (HIShip) method, establishing a fair business environment for all parties involved – the online shopping platform provider, sellers, and customers. HIShip intelligently utilizes the order history data, i.e., the cumulative sum of orders' value placed in the recent past, to make the shipping charge exemption rule friendly to low and mid-budget customers. Furthermore, it reduces biasness against vendors selling products that cost less than the threshold amount. Such a win-win scenario for the seller and customer eventually generates more revenue for the online shopping platform. We simulate the blockchain environment and use the TPC-H dataset to assess the performance. Our algorithm outperforms the threshold-based traditional approach.

Keywords: Blockchain · E-Commerce · Intelligent Shipping · Smart Contract · TPC-H

1 Introduction

In the last few years, the technology underlying Bitcoin, called blockchain, has received remarkable attention from the industry and academia. Blockchain technology uses distributed records called a ledger, integrates consensus mechanism, decentralized data storage, encryption algorithm, peers, and use of computers to build new technology. Each peer in the network has a copy of all records. The concept of a chained structure within the blockchain renders the system immutable and transparent. Recently, blockchain technology has predominantly focused on the financial sector. Still, it also has led to tremendous changes in the non-financial sectors like e-commerce, e-government, supply chain, and credit evaluation.

A supply chain is a network of organizations and individuals involved in producing products and their delivery to the end user. The network is built with the producer, warehouse IN, transportation, warehouse OUT, retailers, and end-users (consumers). Nowadays, the network is spread worldwide. Supply chain management is the strategic and systematic coordination of the various components within the supply chain to ensure efficient, effective, and cost-effective operations. Several aspects could be explored regarding information related to security, transparency, and trustworthiness among users, retailers, suppliers, and manufacturers. The lack of transparency in the supply chain information results in a trust deficit between parties and hampers operations. Product tracking becomes challenging, particularly in cases where counterfeit and substandard products emerge. To encounter such types of problems, blockchain technology is best suited. Blockchain technology, while facilitating information transmission, ensures traceability and authenticity and provides a secure transaction in a distributed environment.

With the rapid development of online shopping, e-commerce platforms try to attract more and more consumers to purchase products from their respective shopping websites [1–3]. Suppliers promise to fulfill the user's requirements to reach their primary objectives. The E-commerce industry is predicted to surpass sales of $8 Trillion in 2026. India's e-commerce market is expected to reach 200 billion by 2026 [4], which is 2.5% of the total e-commerce industry value. Since 2020, the global COVID-19 pandemic-induced lockdowns have significantly catalyzed the expansion of the e-commerce sector. The analysis of data from the U.S. Department of Commerce shows that online consumer expenditure increased by 32.4% year over year in 2020. The transition from the traditional grocery system to the online grocery system is that online grocery shopping serves customers and manages home delivery. The consumers find the platform where they can get maximum benefits in terms of product price, quality, services, and delivery charges. In a traditional pricing model, users are entitled to complimentary delivery services when placing orders for high-priced products. When users engage in multiple transactions involving low-cost items, they are subject to incurring delivery charges with each order. Why do they not receive incentives in terms of delivery charges?

Milton asserts that the prevailing practice among online grocery retailers involves soliciting a delivery fee that amounts to only 80% of the total delivery cost. Undoubtedly, online grocers will not charge handling costs and internal shipping with customers. For instance, Whole Foods Market (WFM) announced free delivery for 2 h in 2017 through Amazon Prime. Since October 25, 2021, WFM has been charging a delivery fee of $ 9.95 on every order to cover the handling cost associated. The shipping policy used by the grocer directly impacts the consumer's behaviors. The report [4] indicates that 95% of purchase decisions made by online consumers in the United States are influenced by shipping costs, with 63% of these decisions identified as primarily attributable to the abandonment of their shopping carts.

The online grocer uses a different strategy to mitigate the impact of shipping costs and motivate and retain more customers. For example, the goods and food delivery company Gopuff, which operates in the U.S. and England, charges a flat fee of $1.95 for each delivery. Walmart Grocery and Kroger Delivery charge flat fees depending on the user's location and speed. Yamibuy, Wee, Hungryroot, Walgreen, etc., are online grocers implementing the CFS (contingent free shipping). According to this policy, consumers are exempt from the delivery fee when their order value surpasses a specified threshold; otherwise, they incur a fixed-rate shipping fee. The marking analysis says that consumers typically do not make decisions about purchasing based on total price when product cost, handling cost, and shipping fee are separately charged.

A database benchmark is a crucial instrument for assessing the performance of research and practitioner data. These tools compare the performance of the different databases, software, hardware, and configurations to answer the common question of which system performs best in the specified domain for specific applications. Transaction Processing Performance Council (TPC-H) is a decision support benchmark. The TPC-H dataset is a synthetic dataset intentionally crafted to emulate real-world database datasets. It contains customers, orders, line items, and more to benchmark the business operations [5]. To assess the system's performance under varying workloads, we ingested different sizes of TPC-H order data, specifically sorting and ingesting 10K, 50K, 100K, and 500K orders based on the purchase date.

Smart Contract
A simple contract is a legally binding agreement between two or more parties wherein they mutually commit to specific obligations or actions in the future. An ordinary contract is called a "smart contract" when it incorporates automated and self-executing functionalities by the terms and conditions specified in the agreement. Its primary characteristic is its capacity to eliminate the need for third-party intermediaries and establish trust through self-execution. For instance, John obtained a loan from a bank and entered into a contractual agreement with the bank. This agreement stipulates that the bank automatically deducts a predetermined sum from his account when his salary is deposited in his account at the end of each month. The computer program responsible for automatically deducting John's salary from his account by verifying and executing all the terms and conditions of the agreement is referred to as a smart contract [6]. The primary characteristics of blockchain technology (BT)— security, transparency, inalterability, immutability, and decentralization—have drawn the interest of the computing research community [7].

We developed a blockchain simulation using Python and Flask, with Flask providing a user-friendly interface. Python was used to develop the core components of the blockchain, including block creation, transaction validation, and chain management. The system was tested under varying workloads by ingesting different sizes of TPC-H order data. The 'free_delivery' attribute was computed for each transaction recorded on the chain. The PoW consensus algorithm was used for block validation and mining, ensuring security and immutability. The resulting blockchain was visualized to represent its structure and transactions. Tests were conducted with varying transaction volumes and complexity to assess the system's performance. The HIShip algorithm is implemented to determine eligibility for free delivery using a Solidity smart contract on the Remix IDE. We used dummy data of 20 customers and tested our algorithm on that, obtaining the same results as we did in the case of the Python-based blockchain simulation.

2 Related Work

In this part of the paper, we will describe the literature on e-commerce, explicitly addressing the optimization of delivery charges.

Shipping policy is a crucial entity in the online retailing system operations. The paper discusses the impact of different shipping policies and how they affect customers and retailers. In scenarios with several competing stores, the models are developed to observe how the quantity competes when shipping is free and how prices compete when shipping is computed. Retailers who shift their operations online and use a calculated shipping policy get nothing as an advantage. Smaller local merchants gain by going online and offering free shipping. In the e-commerce market with several competitive retailers, customers and suppliers both prefer the free shipping policy over the calculated policy. The experiment result shows that larger retailers are harmed by free delivery, while smaller stores may profit from it [8].

One crucial challenge among the several challenges in e-commerce is communicating with the logistic companies incorporating the delivery services. To encounter such type of a problem, the paper presents the design of a system that evaluates the websites to help logistic companies in serving product delivery. Swift, an open-source object-oriented language, and HTML (Hypertext Markup Language) are used to develop the last-mile delivery system. The system used Firebase, a Google-backed real-time database, for streamlining development [9].

The rapid growth in communication technology development is driven by the increasing demand for sharing information and data across various sectors. The tourism sector requires communication technology to share views and data about tourist destinations so that new tourists can experience finding their intended destinations. However, the information and data related to the ranking of tourist places are exchanged through a central server. Centralized architecture has many limitations that are required to improve. The research article represents a TDRS (Tourism Destination Rating System), which has 6As (Accessibility, Attractions, Available Packages, Amenities, Activities, and Ancillary Services) T.D. metrics to assess the tourism destination. The review of the destinations is shared on each traveler's mobile device connected to the blockchain network. The model has been tested on many tourists [10].

Today's publishing system suffers from many issues, like long publishing delays and no fair financial credit distribution among the contributors. EUREKA is an open-access publishing platform with blockchain technology that provides fair credits to all publishing contributors directly via smart contracts. There are different interfaces for the authors and reviewers; the writer can submit the article. The judges who review the articles can give their opinions on the acceptance or rejection of the articles, and all the events will be executed through the Ethereum smart contract [11].

A circular economy focuses on the regeneration of resources rather than possession and suggests leveraging shared resources to build new economies and supply networks. Before collaborating on the circular economy, each entity must have the credit rating of the other. In this referenced paper, blockchain technology has been applied to transactions corresponding to the economic entity, and a confidence level method estimates the credit rating of each entity. The system provides a decentralized environment to optimize third-party involvement costs and enables the effective conduct of credit ratings [12].

Selecting a reliable shopping website is a challenging task for a user. The supplier and users may have different points of view regarding the product quality, leading to disputes between users and merchants. Purchasing the product based on images of the product or purchasing the product based on the merchant's claim to have a high-quality product may cause disputes. This dispute cannot be removed completely but can be optimized up to a certain limit, no matter what reputable companies a user selects, even Amazon.com and Alibaba.com. In all analysis conclusions, this problem is because the merchants do not evaluate the product based on the ratings. This paper proposes a grading system, BPGS (Blockchain-based Product Grading System), through which a customer can purchase a genuine product dealing with big data of business. Additionally, under the planned BPGS, 51% of assaults cannot be successful unless 51% of the alliance's retailers and e-commerce businesses are concurrently penetrated [13].

Extensive research and analysis have been conducted to comprehend customers' moods and behavior in online shopping. Researchers systematically analyze and endeavor to ascertain the factors influencing shoppers' behavior. These factors have a direct and immediate impact on the sales quantities. Two ordinary models have been developed with the dataset taken from the Kaggle repository, which estimates the effect of online revenue collections and visiting time in deciding to purchase the products. The result shows that, although time spent on the website was completely insignificant, time spent on the mobile application did have a minor impact on sales ($R2 = 0.249$) [14].

Online shopping users' personal information is important in driving an eCommerce business. It can be proved a significant element in differentiation among the organizations in the competition of business and may provide a well-defined strategy to provide more profits for the organizations. However, there is a challenging worry about the requirement of consumer data and the security of the user's desire for privacy. This research article explains the favorable and adverse effects on consumers' perceptions of privacy and trust. Also, a model of 301 online users has been tested who go through two online shopping websites and use one of them. The result is more oriented toward the positive effects on trust in privacy and websites. The idea of a positive mood in users' behavior toward the website's features has the potential to direct the creation of websites for efficient data collecting and information sharing [15].

An organization has sensitive data like corporate information, its staff's information, and customers' information, which can harm reputation and revenues tremendously. The paper highlights blockchain's value in safeguarding e-commerce data, surpassing traditional methods in securing the data, and providing transparency to maintain trust in the organization. It has integrated blockchain technology into the database of the e-commerce organization system to protect the data from breaching issues.

E-commerce faces challenges in transactions, data security, and transparency. Companies like MultiChain, Elinext, Eligma, Coupit, and Ravain are developing blockchain solutions. Blockchain improves efficiency with transparent, low-cost, and secure payment systems, empowering customers [2].

This paper presents a blockchain-based framework designed to address the product traceability challenge in cross-border e-commerce supply chains. The contributions of the paper are: 1. The introduction of a blockchain-based product traceability framework for cross-border e-commerce supply chains, offering theoretical and methodological contributions to the fields of blockchain technology and supply chain management theories. 2. Introduction of an innovative multi-chain structural model for blockchain system design. It involves an analysis of data characteristics to support the partitioning of multiple chains, making valuable contributions to the research areas of blockchain-based system design and data management [16].

This study explores how online shopping motivation and the type of product impact user behavior on e-commerce websites. It conducted a 2×2 factorial experiment with goal-oriented/experiential shopping motivations and hedonic/utilitarian product types. The results indicate an interactive effect: goal-oriented shoppers can buy hedonic products without guilt or regret concerning their budget [17].

3 Methodology

This section explores the methods and dataset to discuss our proposed work. The section is divided into three sub-major sections - existing work, proposed work, and implementation.

3.1 Existing Work

Many e-commerce websites use different policies to provide the product to the customers so they can easily get it. However, the shipping fee is always a challenging task to handle. Many online grocery stores use the CFS (contingent free shipping) policies, hich are based on the threshold value [18]. Koukova et al. explain how the customers respond to shipping policies that differ from flat-rate policies regarding threshold-based free shipment [19]. Under this scheme, only all those customers who order the product above a threshold can get a free delivery charge product. The customer who orders the product at a meager price has to pay the shipping fee on each order, regardless of what amount they have ordered many times. This existing traditional method charges the shipping fee to those customers who make the orders at low prices but very frequently.

3.2 Proposed Work

E-commerce websites face several challenges, one of which pertains to implementing a free delivery policy for the selection of customers to provide the product without a shipping fee. The current policy dictates that products are eligible for free delivery only when customers place orders exceeding a specified threshold amount. To encounter such a problem, we have proposed an HIShip algorithm that selects the customers to give the shipping charge free delivery product so that both retailers and customers can get benefits. The HIShip algorithm is based on the customer's previous order history. When a customer initiates an order for a product, our algorithm conducts an analysis of the customer's historical order data, performs requisite processing, and subsequently determines whether said customer qualifies for complimentary delivery or if they will incur shipping charges. The algorithm follows the blockchain paradigm to store the transaction into blocks and check into the transaction records whether the next transaction's product will be delivered without a shipping charge. To see the performance of our work, we have considered the TPC-H standard dataset. We have considered the varying number of records, e.g., 10K, 50K, 100K, and 500K, to test our proposed model and showed how our proposed algorithm performs better than the naïve approach.

3.2.1 Workflow Components

In Fig. 1, how our work will be performed is briefly described, along with the associated components.

1. **Users** – It is a person who initiates the order by any device connected to the internet.
2. **Initial Order** – It contains data related to user orders.
3. **Final Order** – Besides the initial order, it contains a free delivery field.
4. **Blockchain** is a chain of block containing orders as transactions.

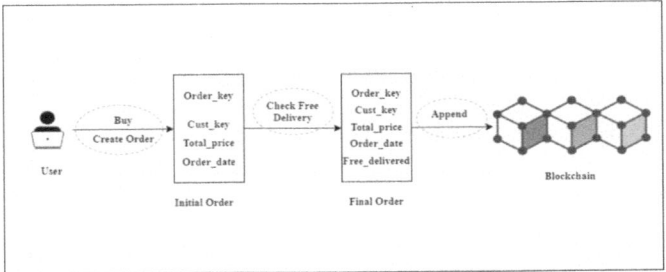

Fig. 1. The workflow of the proposed work

3.2.2 Workflow

1. **Buy** – A user buys an item by sending order data using the buy function and creates an initial order that contains the attributes –

   - Order_key
   - Cust_Key
   - Total_price
   - Order_date

2. **Check** – The buy function will call the Check_delivery function sending (Cust_id, Price, Datework) to check whether the order is eligible for free delivery.
3. **Append** – The buy function will call the append function to append the transaction to the chain.

3.2.3 HIShip Algorithm Pseudocode

```
Input:      Order(Cust_ID,  Price, Time)
1           total ← 0; flag←0;
2           For each Tx in Chain
3               If ( Order. time - Tx.time ) ≤ (1 Year)
4                   If ( Order.cust_ID ==Tx.cust_ID)
5                       If Order.Free_delivered==FALSE
6                           total← total+Tx.price
7                       Else
8                           flag←1
10                  Else
11                      flag←1
12                  If (flag==1)
13                      break
14              If total + Order.price ≥ Threshold
15                  Return TRUE
16              Else:
17                  Return FALSE
```

3.3 Implementation

3.3.1 Python-Based Blockchain Simulation Framework

Our blockchain simulation is implemented using Python and Flask as the primary technologies, with Flask providing the necessary web framework for creating a user-friendly interface for interacting with the blockchain simulation. The core components of the blockchain, including block creation, transaction validation, and chain management, were developed in Python. To assess the system's performance under varying workloads, we ingested different sizes of TPC-H order data, specifically sorting and ingesting 10K, 50K, 100K, and 500K orders based on the purchase date. One of the key functionalities of our blockchain simulation was to compute the 'free_delivery' attribute for each transaction recorded on the chain, a crucial feature for evaluating the free delivery option for customers. Our blockchain simulation implemented the PoW consensus algorithm [20] for block validation and mining, ensuring the security and immutability of the blockchain by requiring participants to solve computationally intensive puzzles before adding a new block to the chain. The resulting blockchain is visualized to represent its structure and the recorded transactions, as illustrated in Fig. 2. To evaluate the performance and scalability of our blockchain simulation, we conducted tests with varying transaction volumes and complexity, essential for assessing the system's ability to handle a growing number of transactions while maintaining performance.

3.3.2 Smart Contract-Based Blockchain Simulation Framework

In addition to the Python simulation, we also implemented our algorithm HIShip to determine the eligibility for free delivery using a Solidity smart contract on the Remix IDE [21].

```
{
    "o_orderkey": "12324",
    "o_custkey": "722",
    "o_totalprice": "159631.71",
    "o_orderdate": "1998-08-02",
    "o_freedelivery": "no",
    "timestamp": 1697550204.0087574
},
{
    "o_orderkey": "12384",
    "o_custkey": "818",
    "o_totalprice": "179483.63",
    "o_orderdate": "1998-08-02",
    "o_freedelivery": "yes",
    "timestamp": 1697550204.0115414
},
{
    "o_orderkey": "20195",
    "o_custkey": "7",
    "o_totalprice": "86096.41",
    "o_orderdate": "1998-08-02",
    "o_freedelivery": "no",
    "timestamp": 1697550204.0141273
}
],
"timestamp": 1697550204.5558403,
"previous_hash": "0f5e9254d03c11f7be6c01556896e84243cd53d9f9729000fbbe62408821e487",
"nonce": 18,
"hash": "0746d98546501c13996cd4678b430e9ddc6f6c738c3083849afdb1fa8f6fd855"
}
],
"peers": []
```

Fig. 2. Python-based Blockchain

```
"Orders": {
    "value": [
        {
            "value": {
                "o_orderkey": {"length": "0x1", "raw": "0x30", "type": "string", "value": "0"},
                "o_custkey": {"length": "0x3", "raw": "0x303030", "type": "string", "value": "C000"},
                "o_itemkey": {"length": "0x3", "raw": "0x303030", "type": "string", "value": "I0000"},
                "o_totalprice": {"value": "0", "type": "uint256"},
                "o_freedelivery": {"value": false, "type": "bool"},
                "timestamp": {"value": "1697785116", "type": "uint256"}
            },
            "type": "struct HIShip.Order"
        },
        {
            "value": {
                "o_orderkey": {"length": "0x1", "raw": "0x31", "type": "string", "value": "1"},
                "o_custkey": {"length": "0x4", "raw": "0x43343031", "type": "string", "value": "C401"},
                "o_itemkey": {"length": "0x5", "raw": "0x4930313231", "type": "string", "value": "I0121"},
                "o_totalprice": {"value": "148", "type": "uint256"},
                "o_freedelivery": {"value": false, "type": "bool"},
                "timestamp": {"value": "1697785140", "type": "uint256"}
            },
            "type": "struct HIShip.Order"
        },
        {
            "value": {
                "o_orderkey": {"length": "0x1", "raw": "0x32", "type": "string", "value": "2"},
                "o_custkey": {"length": "0x4", "raw": "0x43353932", "type": "string", "value": "C592"},
                "o_itemkey": {"length": "0x5", "raw": "0x4930313332", "type": "string", "value": "I0132"},
                "o_totalprice": {"value": "452", "type": "uint256"},
                "o_freedelivery": {"value": false, "type": "bool"},
                "timestamp": {"value": "1697785156", "type": "uint256"}
            },
            "type": "struct HIShip.Order"
        },
```

Fig. 3. Smart contract-based blockchain

This intelligent contract was tested using a set of 20 dummy data orders, and the resulting blockchain is depicted in Fig. 3. This complementary aspect of our project extended the functionality of the blockchain simulation, enabling the verification of free delivery eligibility through a secure and decentralized approach within the blockchain network.

4 Performance Results

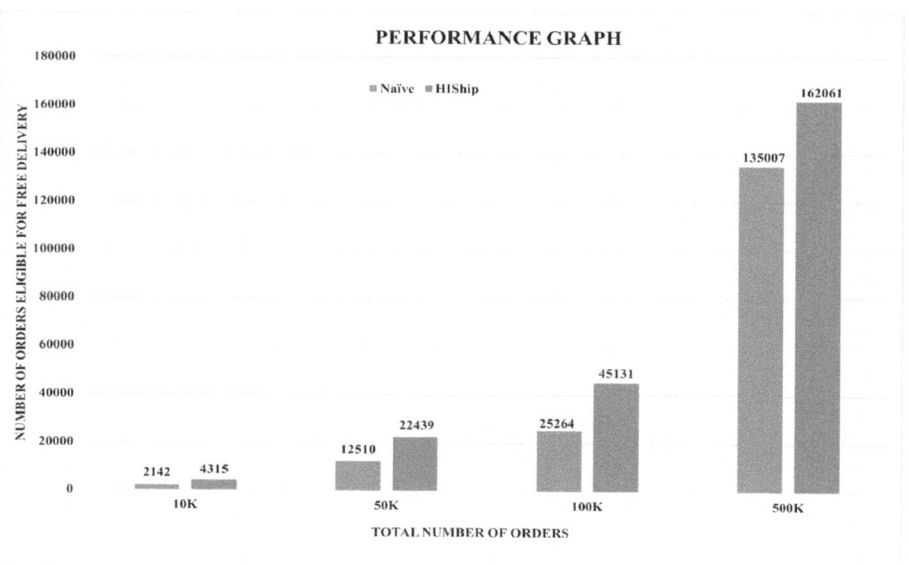

Fig. 4. Performance comparison of our proposed algorithm HIShip with the Naïve algorithm.

In Fig. 4, we have compared the total number of orders eligible for free delivery assigned by both algorithms. The blue column represents the naïve algorithm, while the orange column represents our proposed algorithm. In the Bar graph, we have considered the total number of orders on the X axis, and the Y axis signifies the total number of orders eligible for free delivery. The graph depicting performance data reveals that our newly proposed algorithm outperforms the current algorithm for delivering free services to customers. When examining the specific instances within a set of orders, it becomes evident that our proposed approach consistently demonstrates superior performance in each instance. In the initial instance involving 10,000 orders, the naïve algorithm confers the benefit of free delivery upon 2,142 orders. In contrast, our proposed algorithm surpasses this by extending this advantage to a more extensive set of orders, encompassing 4,315 orders.

In the same way, at the 50K number of orders, the naïve algorithm delivers 12510 ordered products without shipping fees. On the other hand, our proposed algorithm delivers 22439 ordered products without paying any delivery charges, which is nearly double in number to the existing naïve method. On running both algorithms at 100K orders, we found the free delivery on 25264 and 45131 orders by naïve and our approach. Out of a dataset comprising 500K orders, it is observed that the naïve approach results in 135,007 products being delivered without incurring shipping charges. At the same time, the HIShip algorithm exhibits a superior performance by facilitating the shipment of 162,061 ordered products without imposing shipping fees.

We have tested the performance of the HIShip algorithm and naïve algorithm on the 10K, 50K, 100K, and 500K orders separately. The primary purpose of running our algorithm in isolation is to conduct a performance analysis of the algorithm. We have divided each set of records into three categories: High, Middle, and Low values orders.

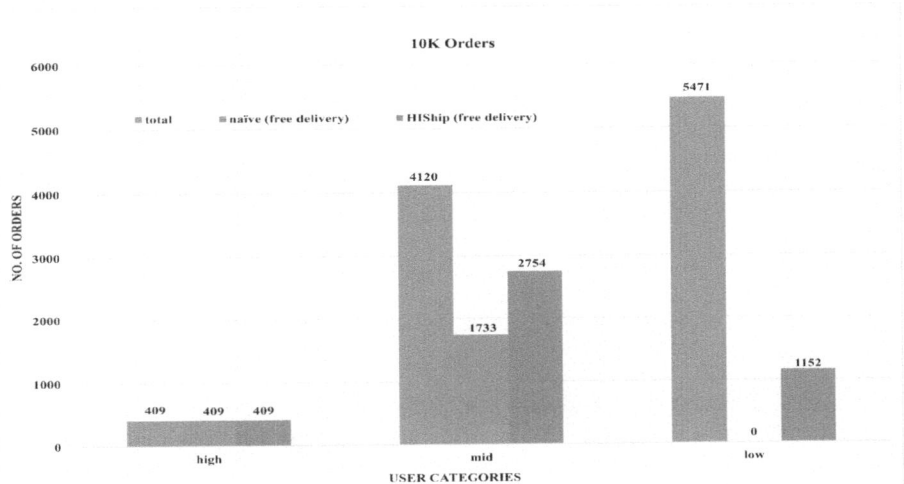

Fig. 5. 10K Orders Classification & Delivery Eligibility: HIShip vs Naive

In Fig. 5, a dataset of 10K orders is divided into three categories based on the number of transactions: the first category contains high-value orders, the second store's middle-value orders, and the remaining orders fall into low-value orders. In the bar graph, sky blue represents the total orders, orange shows the naïve approach to giving free delivery, and the green bar depicts the number of orders that provided free delivery in the case of our proposed algorithm. In this instance of a set of orders in the high category, there are 409 orders, and both the algorithm (the naïve approach and our proposed approach). But in the middle category, out of 4120 orders, the naïve approach provides 1733 orders without any shipping charge, while our proposed algorithm HIShip gives 2754 transactions as delivery charge-free products, which is 1021 more orders and is nearly 25% orders of the total orders. Hence, our proposed algorithm is more efficient than the naïve approach in the middle category. However, if we look at the data of the third category, which is the low amount category, we found that out of 5471 orders, the naïve algorithm does not provide any of the products without shipping charges. In comparison, our proposed method exempts 1152 orders with the shipping charge, which is an excellent performance of our proposed approach. Our algorithm's remarkable point and achievement is that it focuses on frequently ordered low-priced products and provides them with fee-free product shipping.

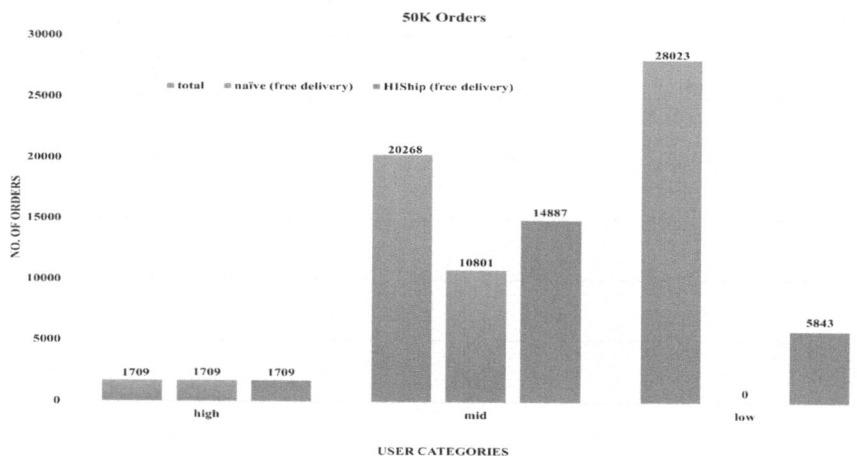

Fig. 6. 50K Orders Classification & Delivery Eligibility: HIShip vs Naïve

In Fig. 6, a dataset of 50K orders has been categorized into three distinct groups based on their transaction amounts. The first category comprises high-value orders, the second encompasses mid-value orders, and the remainder falls under the low-value order category. In our graphical representation, the sky blue bars denote the total number of orders, while the orange bars represent the conventional approach of providing free delivery. In contrast, the green bars illustrate the number of orders benefiting from our proposed algorithm's free delivery system. In this instance of 50K orders, In the uppermost order category (high category), it is noteworthy that both algorithms yield identical results, specifically, the provisioning of 1709 free delivery orders out of a total of 1709. In the middle category of orders, we found that the naïve approach delivers 10,801 products without the shipping fee. At the same time, the proposed algorithm provides 14,887 orders without delivery charges in 20268 mid-category orders. Our approach shows an exciting result in low-budget orders, and the naïve approach charges a shipping charge for every order. At the same time, the proposed algorithm provides 5843 orders, which is more efficient than the naïve approach.

In Fig. 7, a dataset of 100K is classified orders into three distinct categories based on transaction value: high-value, mid-value, and low-value. The graph presents this stratification, with sky blue bars indicating total order counts, orange bars representing counts of orders eligible for free delivery using a traditional approach, and green bars depicting orders qualifying for free delivery under our innovative algorithm. This visual representation offers valuable insights into order distribution and the potential enhancements our proposed algorithm brings to our delivery strategy, enabling us to make more informed decisions for optimizing delivery efficiency. In the high-order category, both algorithms perform the same results. But in the case of the mid category, the naïve algorithm gives 55% of orders without imposing any shipping fee, while our proposed algorithm provides 74% of products without delivery fees. The proposed algorithm offers significant advantages, particularly for orders falling within the third category, making it notably

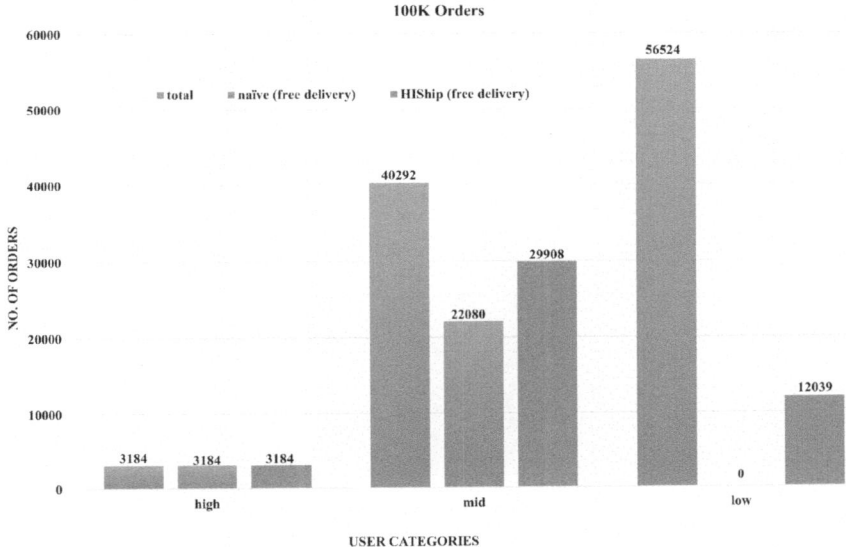

Fig. 7. 100K Orders Classification & Delivery Eligibility: HIShip vs Naïve

remarkable in this context. In the low-budget segment encompassing 100K instances, our proposed methodology facilitated the successful fulfillment of 12,039 orders without incurring any shipping charges for the distribution of products. At the same time, in the same category, the naïve algorithm does not provide a single order without a shipping fee. Our proposed algorithm is low-budget.

In Fig. 8, a dataset of 500K orders is divided into three distinct categories based on their transaction amounts. The initial category encompasses high-value orders, the second category comprises mid-value orders, and the remaining orders are categorized as low-value orders. In our graphical representation, we use sky blue to represent the total order count, while orange corresponds to the conventional or 'naïve' approach of offering free delivery. The green bars in the graph illustrate the number of orders for which free delivery was granted when employing our proposed algorithm. In this instance of 500K orders, we applied both algorithms to ascertain the number of orders that realize the advantage of exempted shipping charges. We get the same results in the high-budget category for both approaches. Within the mid-budget order category, the conventional or "naïve" approach resulted in 70.5% of the total orders being fulfilled without incurring shipping fees. In contrast, our innovative proposed approach achieved a rate of 73% of the total orders, demonstrating an improvement in this aspect. Our approach is more efficient in the last low-budget category of orders. For this category of orders, the naïve algorithm is not more efficient. It provides non-customers with free delivery of products, while our approach provides 7% orders of the total orders without paying any shipping fee.

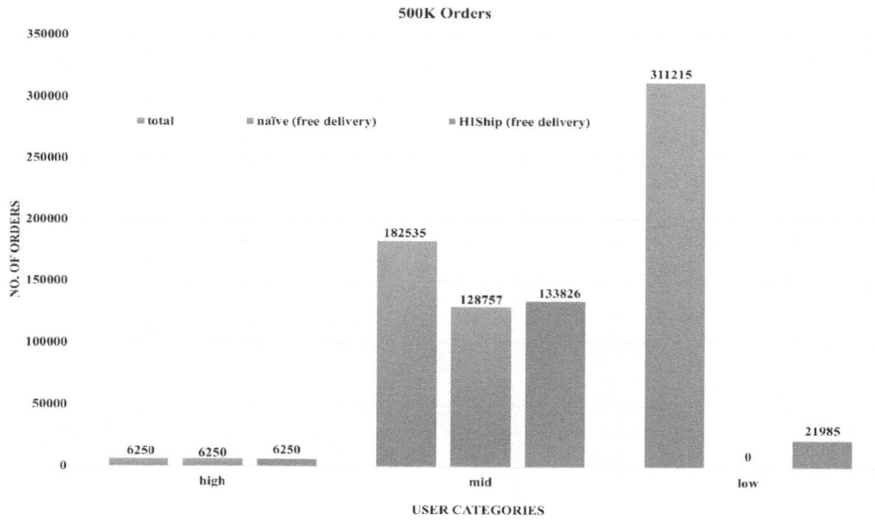

Fig. 8. 500K Orders Classification & Delivery Eligibility: HIShip vs Naive

5   Conclusion

We developed the HIShip method to provide users with free delivery based on their past orders. The test of our algorithm on the TPC-H dataset demonstrated excellent performance, with a significant increase in free-delivery orders. HIShip method has led to an increase in the free delivery orders by 21.5% in the mid-budget orders. Furthermore, it improved th free delivery orders by 21.06% in the low-budget category. It has stimulated customer engagement by incentivizing those who place lower-priced orders, thus fostering increased free delivery. At the same time, HIShip is fair to those sellers who want to sell their products online but whose products are in the low-cost range (less than the set threshold). In the end, integrating HIShip with existing online shopping platforms could also benefit the platform owner as they would attract more traffic.

References

1. India Brand Equity Foundation: E-commerce Industry in India. https://www.ibef.org/industry/ecommerce. Accessed 1 Sept 2023
2. Bulsara, H.P., Vaghela, P.S.: Blockchain technology for e-commerce industry. Int. J. Adv. Sci. Technol. **29**, 3793–3798 (2020)
3. Teo, M.X., Maen, T.A., Qusay, A.-M.: Blockchain technology in e-commerce platform. Int. J. Manag. **11**, 1688–1697 (2020)
4. Hotea Solutions: TPC-H Vesion 2 and Version 3, 14 September 2023. https://www.tpc.org/tpch/
5. Barata, M., Bernardino, J., Furtado, P.: An overview of decision support benchmarks: TPC-DS, TPC-H and SSB. In: Rocha, A., Correia, A., Costanzo, S., Reis, L. (eds.) New Contributions

in Information Systems and Technologies. AISC, vol. 353, pp. 619–628. Springer, Cham (2015). https://doi.org/10.1007/978-3-319-16486-1_61

6. Gavin, W.: Ethereum: a secure decentralised generalised transaction ledger. Ethereum project yellow paper (2014)

7. Kamal, K., Sarvesh, S., Shankar, U.: A journey from commit processing in distributed databases to consensus in blockchain. In: IEEE 38th International Conference on Data Engineering (ICDE), Kuala Lumpur, Malaysia (2022)

8. Guang, L., Lifei, S., Dongyuan, Z.: Free or calculated shipping: Impact of delivery cost on supply chains moving. Int. J. Prod. Econ. (2023)

9. Alkhalifah, A., Alorini, F., Alturki, R.: Enhancement of e-commerce service by designing last mile delivery platform. Comput. Syst. Sci. Eng. **42** (2022)

10. Yunifa, M.A., Hani, N., Sri, H., Supeno, M.S.N., Mochamad, H.: Decentralized tourism destinations rating system using 6AsTD framework and blockchain. In: 2020 International Conference on Smart Technology and Applications (ICoSTA), Surabaya, Indonesia (2020)

11. Andreas, S., et al.: EUREKA – a minimal operational prototype of a blockchain-based rating and publishing system. In: 2019 IEEE International Conference on Blockchain and Cryptocurrency (ICBC), Seoul, Korea (South) (2019)

12. Wu, H.-T., Yi-Jen, S., Wu-Chih, H.: A study on blockchain-based circular economy credit rating system. In: International Conference on Security with Intelligent Computing and Big-data Services (2017)

13. Ching-Nung, Y., Yi-Cheng, C., Shih-Yu, C., Song-Yu, W.: A reliable e-commerce business model using blockchain based product grading system. In: 2019 IEEE 4th International Conference on Big Data Analytics (ICBDA), Suzhou, China (2019)

14. Valerii, S., Maxim, B.: Stay some more and buy? Modeling the effects of visit time on online shopping purchases. In: International Workshop on Data Mining and Knowledge Engineering, pp. 111–118 (2020)

15. Robin, W.: The influence of user affect in online information disclosure. J. Strateg. Inf. Syst. **22**(2), 157–174 (2013)

16. Liu, Z., Li, Z.: A blockchain-based framework of cross-border e-commerce supply chain. Int. J. Inf. Manag. **52** (2020)

17. Chiou, J.-S., Ting, C.-C.: Will you spend more money and time on internet shopping when the product and situation are right? Comput. Hum. Behav. **27**(1), 203–208 (2011)

18. Rafael, B.-A., Leng, M., Mahmut, P.: Online retailers' promotional pricing, free-shipping threshold, and inventory decisions: a simulation-based analysis. Eur. J. Oper. Res. **230**, 272–283 (2013)

19. Koukova, N.T., Srivastava, J., Steul-Fischer, M.: The effect of shipping fee structure on consumers' online evaluations and choice. J. Acad. Mark. Sci. **40**, 759–770 (2012)

20. Satoshi, N.: Bitcoin: a peer-to-peer electronic cash system. Decentralized Business Review (2008)

21. Ethereum Foundation: Remix. https://remix-project.org/. Accessed 3 Sept 2023

PwnShield: An Automated Approach to Detect and Exploit Buffer Overflows and Bypassing Modern Mitigation Techniques

Jamai Badr Eddine[1]($\boxtimes$), Abderrahim Abdellaoui[1], and Bouchnafa Anass[2]

[1] Engineering Sciences Lab, ENSA, Ibn Tofail University, Kenitra, Morocco
{badreddine.jamai,abderrahim}@uit.ac.ma
[2] Engineering Sciences Lab, ENSIAS, Mohammed V University, Rabat, Morocco

Abstract. In the dynamic realm of cybersecurity, the perpetual struggle between security systems and malicious exploits persists. Among these threats. buffer overflow vulnerabilities remain a persistent challenge continually adapting to evade modern mitigation techniques such as NX, RELRO, Stack canaries and PIE. To confront these sophisticated threats, our research introduces PwnShield as an advanced program designed to detect and exploit buffer overflow vulnerabilities effectively and bypass modern mitigation methods. Leveraging the robust capabilities of Python's Pwntools and r2pipe libraries, PwnShield excels in exploitation by combining fuzzing and static binary analysis compared to existing tools like BofAEG and autoBOF, PwnShield demonstrates superior performance and showcases its ability to handle buffer overflow exploitation and bypass a comprehensive range of modern mitigation techniques. PwnShield represents a significant advancement in cybersecurity in an environment where detecting and exploiting buffer overflows presents formidable challenges. With limited research dedicated to addressing these complexities, we are pushing the boundaries of buffer overflow detection and exploitation automation, heralding a new era of progress in the field.

Keywords: Buffer Overflow Attacks · Mitigation Technique · Dynamic Detection · Exploit Generation

1 Introduction

Buffer overflow attacks exploit the lack or the absence of bounds checking in the programming languages, which when manipulated can lead to arbitrary code execution and in worst-case scenarios complete system compromise. Modern mitigation techniques like Address Space Layout Randomization (ASLR) in addition to Non-Executable Stack (NX bit) and Stack Canaries have been developed to counter these attacks. However, like any defense mechanism these techniques are not completely impervious, skilled attackers have demonstrated how these protections can be bypassed leading to successful exploitation. The automation of buffer overflow attacks poses a serious threat to the security of contemporary systems. Attackers can use automated tools to swiftly and easily exploit software flaws and because of this it is challenging for defenders to keep up with the

A. Verma et al. (Eds.): ANTIC 2023, CCIS 2091, pp. 170–191, 2024.
https://doi.org/10.1007/978-3-031-64064-3_13

increasing amount of vulnerabilities. This paper offers several important contributions to the field of cybersecurity particularly in relation to the automated exploit generation of stack buffer overflow vulnerabilities. Firstly, our research delves into the complexities and unique attributes of automating the process of exploit generation for stack buffer overflow vulnerabilities. As a result of our in-depth investigation, we have developed PwnShield a comprehensive solution designed specifically to tackle these challenges. Our second contribution is the rigorous testing and experimentation conducted using CTF (Capture The Flag) challenges and programs listed in the common vulnerabilities and exposures (CVEs) database. The results of these tests show the efficacy of PwnShield in automating the detection and exploit generation for stack buffer overflow vulnerabilities. When juxtaposed with existing solutions, PwnShield's performance stands out as it can handle a wider range of scenarios and generate exploits more rapidly, Table 1 presents the most notable attacks caused by Buffer Overflow (BOF).

Table 1. Most notable attacks caused by Buffer Overflow (BOF).

Exploit	Vulnerable Software	Targeted OS	Year	Infected Host
The Morris Worm	Finger Service Exploited	BSD UNIX (VAX OS)	1988	6000
Stack Smashing Attack	Program	Unix	1996	–
Melissa	Microsoft Outlook email	Microsoft Windows	1999	–
Red Worm	Microsoft IIS Server	Microsoft Windows (2000, XP server)	2001	359,000
Slammer	Microsoft And SQL Server	Microsoft Windows	2003	75,000
The Shellshock Bug	Bash Shell	Linux	2014	Millions
Heartbleed	OpenSSL Cryptographic Library	ALL	2014	144,000
Adobe Flash Player	Adobe Flash Player	Windows, macOS, Linux And Chrome OS	2016	–
EternalBlue	SMB Protocol	Windows	2017	–
WhatsApp VoIP	WhatsApp	Smartphones	2019	1,400

Lastly, we have implemented and examined six distinct exploit techniques for stack buffer overflow vulnerabilities. The results of our exploration highlight the significant degree of risk that these vulnerabilities present. Importantly, this research introduces PwnShield as an innovative automated tool designed to detect buffer overflow vulnerabilities through fuzzing and static analysis and generate exploits capable of bypassing these modern mitigation techniques for ELF binaries. We present an extensive evaluation of PwnShield, demonstrating its effectiveness in identifying and exploiting buffer overflow vulnerabilities, and the results highlight PwnShield's potential for substantial improvements in software security measures and application development practices, underscoring its value in enhancing cybersecurity. A significant number of security breaches have occurred as a result of buffer overflow vulnerabilities. Table 2 lists some of the most notable CVEs of buffer overflow vulnerabilities.

Table 2. The most prominent CVE of buffer overflow vulnerabilities since 2020 to 2023.

CVEs of Software	Vulnerability	Target	Year	Vulnerable version	Version Patched
CVE-2020-14871 On Oracle Solaris	Stack-Based Buffer Overflow	Oracle Solaris Products	2020	11.4 Version And Earlier	11.5 Version And Later
CVE-2022-48196 On Netgear	Buffer Overflow By An Unauthenticated Attacker	Netgear Devices	2022	Versions Before ($<$) 1.0.11.136	Versions After ($>$) 1.0.11.136
CVE-2022-3602 On OpenSSL	Buffer Overflow Lead To Remote Code Execution	All Operating Systems	2020	Version 1.1.1g And Earlier	Version 1.1.1h And Later
CVE-2023-41064 On Apple System	Buffer Overflow With Improved Memory Handling	MacOS, iOS, iPadOS, and watchOS	2023	macOS v13 and iOS v16, iPadOS v16, watchOS v9	macOS v13.1, iOS v16.1, iPadOS v16.1, watchOS v9.1
CVE-2023-4863 On Libwebp	Critical Buffer Overflow Vulnerability	Electron-based applications And Chromium - Based Browsers	2023	Libwebp 2.0.0-2.0.5	Libwebp 2.0.6

2 Literature Review

Buffer overflow vulnerabilities have been a persistent issue in software security for decades, resulting in the compromise of software applications or systems. The most prevalent form of this vulnerability is stack overflow, which attackers can exploit to gain remote administrative privileges and execute shell code [1].

Information leakage and buffer overflow vulnerabilities may now be automatically found and exploited, as well as combined, using a special tool known as Marten. This tool demonstrates proficiency in circumventing memory randomization and exploiting remote processes. Furthermore, Marten has showcased its ability to create concise and robust Return-Oriented Programming (ROP) chain exploits and successfully bypass contemporary defensive measures such as address space layout randomization [2].

A technique along with a corresponding instrument has been introduced that can autonomously identify buffer overflow vulnerabilities in binary programs and generate corresponding exploits. This instrument employs symbolic execution to examine the target software for potential vulnerabilities. Subsequently, it attempts to circumvent system protection by opting for various exploitation techniques depending on the level of security [3].

A solution called BofAEG has been developed utilizing symbolic execution and dynamic analysis and can automatically find stack buffer overflow attack vulnerabilities and create corresponding exploits. Compared to current Automated Exploit Generation (AEG) solutions, BofAEG can effectively detect vulnerabilities and generate exploits based on mitigation furthermore operate more quickly. [4].

Despite the development and implementation of several mitigation techniques, attackers persistently discover methods to bypass these protective barriers. Among the most prevalent vulnerabilities that can impact a binary executable are stack-based buffer overflows. In the current era, due to the enforcement of numerous protection mechanisms by the operating system and at the executable level, exploiting buffer overflow has become increasingly challenging, in other words, to successfully exploit the vulnerability and control the execution flow of the examined executable, and it often necessitates the use of multiple bypassing techniques [5].

In conclusion, while significant progress has been made in the detection and the exploitation of buffer overflow vulnerabilities, these vulnerabilities remain a significant challenge due to the ability of attackers to bypass existing mitigation techniques.

3   Modern Mitigation Techniques

Modern mitigation is essential in the constantly changing field of cybersecurity and plays an integral role in defending systems against various types of attacks, including the notorious buffer overflow attacks. In this section, we will delve into the details of these mitigation techniques, including their operations, strengths, weaknesses, and potential vulnerabilities.

1. Non-Executable (NX) Bit Utilization: CPUs use a mechanism called the NX bit, also referred to as the Non-Executable bit, to divide up memory space for either storing processor instructions (code) or storing data. In the context of buffer overflow protection, marking the stack as non-executable means that even if an attacker manages to inject malicious code into the stack, the system will not execute it [6].
2. Read-only Relocations (RELRO) Implementation: Full RELRO is a security measure used to mitigate exploits that attempt to overwrite the ".got.plt" section of a binary, and in a full RELRO scenario, the entire Global Offset Table (GOT) is marked as read-only after the loader has resolved all dynamic symbols, so this prevents potential buffer overflows from overwriting the GOT [7].
3. Integration of Stack Canaries: A renowned and effective strategy for identifying and thwarting stack overflow attacks is the employment of stack canaries so this approach entails positioning a random value known as a canary on the stack and this value is

verified prior to a function's return so if this value has been modified the program presumes a buffer overflow has transpired and halts execution however this method is not flawless and we will explain later why so the reference canary value for programs compiled with gcc is randomly established at the moment of program start-up and stay unaltered during program execution. Additionally for programs running under Linux the canary value are passed down from the parent process and are only modified when the child process initiates a different program using the exec() function [8].

4. Adherence to the Position Independent Executable (PIE) Principle: Position Independent Executable (PIE) is a characteristic that can be enabled during a program's compilation resulting in the executable emulating the behavior of a dynamic external library during the linking and loading phases. In fact this feature adds an extra degree of randomization to these processes and it's noteworthy that Address Space Layout Randomization (ASLR) was conceived prior to PIE and does not require the activation of PIE for its effective operation [9].

5. Application of Address Space Layout Randomization (ASLR): Address Space Layout Randomization is a security mechanism that entails the random allocation of key data regions including the base of the executable and the positions of the stack, heap and libraries within a process's address space so this randomness complicates an attacker's ability to forecast the target addresses and this unpredictability diminishes the probability of a buffer overflow attack [10].

4   Buffer Overflow Attacks

This section delves into the intricate details of buffer overflow attacks, providing an in-depth overview of their operation types and the potential impact they may have on a system. The focus of this study is buffer overflow (BOF), a vulnerability that, despite its three-decade existence, still continues to be a major contributor to security breaches. Once dubbed the "vulnerability of the decade" for the period of 1988–1998, its persistence is evident. In 2021 it was the most frequently cited vulnerability in the Common Vulnerabilities and Exposures (CVE) list. As of May 2023, the CVE database maintained by MITRE has documented an alarming number of over 14,120 buffer overflow vulnerabilities, signaling an upward trend in the occurrence of this type of vulnerability over time.

4.1   Understanding Buffer Overflow Attacks

At its core, a buffer overflow attack takes advantage of a program's lack of bounds checking. Buffers, which are temporary storage locations in memory, have a fixed size defined at the time of their creation, and a buffer overflow occurs when more data than the buffer's capacity is written into it. The excess data overflows into the adjacent memory this is known as a buffer overflow. In a buffer overflow attack, this overflowing data is carefully crafted to overwrite crucial information in memory such as return addresses or function pointers by doing this attackers can alter the program's execution flow which might result an arbitrary code execution or privilege escalation or even worst complete system compromise (Fig. 1).

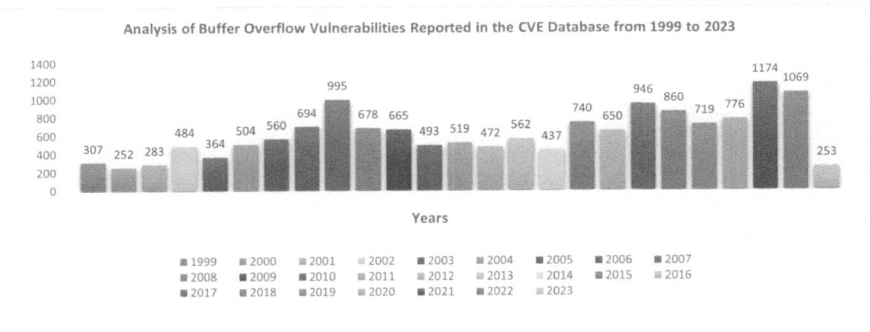

Fig. 1. Buffer overflow statistics in CVEs.

4.2 Types of Buffer Overflow Attacks

Buffer overflow attacks can be categorized into several types, primarily based on the area of memory they target:

1. Stack-based Buffer Overflow Attacks: A stack-based buffer overflow attack is a type of security exploit where an attacker can manipulates and overwrites the return address selectively by exploiting vulnerabilities in the memory stack which allows them to gain control over a system or even worst compromise entire system and launch more potent attacks [11].
2. Heap-based Buffer Overflow Attacks: In contrast to stack-based attacks, heap-based attacks involve overflowing a buffer in the heap data structure so this can lead to an arbitrary code execution, data manipulation or other malicious activities and this kind of attack happen when an attacker exploits vulnerabilities in the dynamic memory management of a program's specifically in the heap data structure [12].
3. Integer Overflow Attacks: When an arithmetic operation tries to produce a numeric value that is outside the range that can be represented with a certain number of bits it is know as an integer overflow attack. Consequently a value that is unexpectedly small or large may cause unexpected behavior such as memory corruption or the execution of malicious code [13].

4.2.1 Stack-Based Buffer Overflow Attacks

Stack-based buffer overflow attacks are among the most common forms of buffer overflow attacks. These attacks target the stack a region of memory that stores data and procedural information such as function call information and local variables.

In a stack-based buffer overflow attack an attacker seeks to overflow a buffer located on the stack writing beyond the buffer's boundaries and overwriting adjacent memory locations. This overwritten information may include return addresses function pointers or security-related information which when manipulated can lead to unauthorized access or even worst execution of malicious code as remote code execution (RCE).

In Figure 2 illustrates an example of a buffer overflow exploit where a cyclic pattern string is injected into a stack buffer so the existing return address is overwritten with the characters "ENSA" which can be located at offset 16 from the beginning of the cyclic pattern string consequently 16 bytes of padding must be inserted to overwrite the values of the return address.

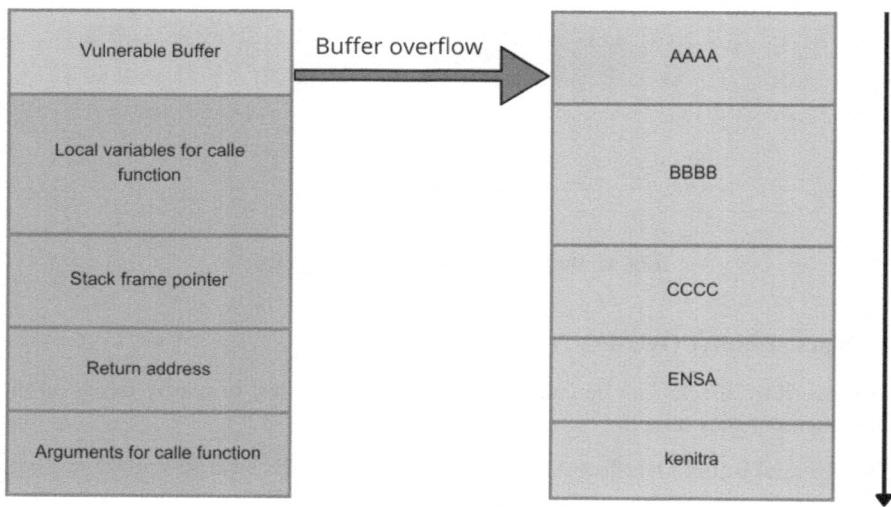

Fig. 2. Overwriting return address

```
Procedure  VulnerableFunction(input:  String)
    Declare  buffer:  Array[8]  of  Character
    Copy(input,  buffer)
End  Procedure

Procedure  Main(argc:  Integer,  argv:  Array  of  String)
    If  argc  > 1  Then
        Call  VulnerableFunction(argv[1])
    End  If
    Return  0
End  Procedure
```

Fig. 3. A code review of vulnerable function to buffer overflow

A classic example of a stack-based buffer overflow attack is the "stack smashing attack" demonstrated in a seminal 1996 paper by Aleph One "Smashing the Stack for Fun and Profit" [14]. In this attack the vulnerability lies in the use of unsafe functions like gets() in C language that do not check the length of input and while a program using these functions accepts more data than it should so the excess data overflows into other areas of the stack and attacker can take advantage of that.

In Fig. 3 the strcpy function copies the input string into the buffer array without checking if the input is longer than the buffer or not for example an attacker provides an input string longer than 8 characters so the excess data overflows into adjacent memory on the stack like in Fig. 5 we overwrite the buffer with the value "AAAABBBBCMasterSsiEnsaKenitra" to determine the offset at which the EIP register points.

```
pwndbg> disassemble vulnerable_function
Dump of assembler code for function vulnerable_function:
   0x08049156 <+0>:     push   ebp
   0x08049157 <+1>:     mov    ebp,esp
   0x08049159 <+3>:     push   ebx
   0x0804915a <+4>:     sub    esp,0x14
   0x0804915d <+7>:     call   0x80491bf <__x86.get_pc_thunk.ax>
   0x08049162 <+12>:    add    eax,0x2e92
   0x08049167 <+17>:    sub    esp,0x8
   0x0804916a <+20>:    push   DWORD PTR [ebp+0x8]
   0x0804916d <+23>:    lea    edx,[ebp-0xe]
   0x08049170 <+26>:    push   edx
   0x08049171 <+27>:    mov    ebx,eax
   0x08049173 <+29>:    call   0x8049040 <strcpy@plt>
   0x08049178 <+34>:    add    esp,0x10
   0x0804917b <+37>:    nop
   0x0804917c <+38>:    mov    ebx,DWORD PTR [ebp-0x4]
   0x0804917f <+41>:    leave
   0x08049180 <+42>:    ret
End of assembler dump.
```

Fig. 4. The assembly of vulnerable_function function in arch 32 Bit

```
pwndbg> run AAAABBBBCMasterSsiEnsaKenitra"
Starting program: /home/badr/Desktop/ensa/research/Python_shield/test/vuln_1 AAAABBBBCMasterSsiEnsaKenitra"
[Thread debugging using libthread_db enabled]
Using host libthread_db library "/lib/x86_64-linux-gnu/libthread_db.so.1".

Program received signal SIGSEGV, Segmentation fault.
0x61736e45 in ?? ()
LEGEND: STACK | HEAP | CODE | DATA | RWX | RODATA
────────────────────────────────────[ REGISTERS / show-flags off / show-compact-regs off
 EAX  0xffffd3fa ◂— 0x41414141 ('AAAA')
 EBX  0x65747361 ('aste')
 ECX  0xffffd680 ◂— 0x61736e45 ('Ensa')
 EDX  0xffffd40c ◂— 0x61736e45 ('Ensa')
 EDI  0xf7ffcb80 (_rtld_global_ro) ◂— 0x0
 ESI  0x804bf04 (__do_global_dtors_aux_fini_array_entry) —▸ 0x8049120 (__do_global_dtors_aux) ◂— endbr32
 EBP  0x69735372 ('rSsi')
 ESP  0xffffd410 ◂— 0x696e654b ('Keni')
 EIP  0x61736e45 ('Ensa')
```

Fig. 5. The return ddress is being overwritten with the value'Ensa' and with an offset of 18.

By carefully crafting the input an attacker can overwrite the return address stored on the stack with the address of the malicious code (usually included in the input string itself) as Fig. 5 (Fig. 4).

While modern systems have defenses to prevent such attacks (like non-executable stacks and address space layout randomization), stack-based buffer overflow attacks are still a concern especially in systems that use outdated or misconfigured software. These attacks underscore the importance of secure coding practices such as avoiding unsafe functions and always checking the length of input data.

4.2.2 Heap-Based Buffer Overflow Attacks

Although less frequent than stack-based attacks, heap-based overflow attacks never-theless constitute a significant security threat. Unlike the stack which mainly handles function call operations the heap is a region of memory used for dynamic memory allo-cation during the run-time of a program. In a similar way to a stack-based attack an attacker targets a buffer located on the heap and overflowing it however because of the different nature of heap memory these attacks can be more complex and harder to exploit. Illustration of the heap based buffer overflow that could occur with the code example shown in the Fig. 6.

```
Procedure vulnerable_function(input: String)
    size <- SizeOf(char)
    buffer <- AllocateMemory(128 * size)
    Copy ( input  ,          buffer)
    FreeMemory(buffer)
End Procedure


Procedure Main(argc: Integer, argv: Array of String)
    Call vulnerable_function(argv[1])
    Return 0
End Procedure
```

Fig. 6. Depiction of a potential heap-based buffer overflow in the code example specifically within the vulnerable_function.

In this code the vulnerable_function the function allocates a buffer of 128 bytes on the heap using malloc so it then copies the string from input into buffer variable using the function strcpy as with the stack-based overflow in Fig. 6 the issue here is that the function Copy does not check the length of input for example if the input is longer than 127 characters (remember one byte is needed for the null-terminating character) so copy will write beyond the end of buffer overflowing into other data on the heap (Figs. 7 and 8).

Heap-based buffer overflow exploits can be more complex than stack-based ones as the layout of the heap because is generally less predictable than the layout of the stack so that why make it more difficult to exploit. Nevertheless a skilled attacker might use tech-niques like heap spraying or manipulating heap metadata to exploit these vulnerabilities potentially leading to unauthorized access or code execution.

```
pwndbg> disassemble vulnerable_function
Dump of assembler code for function vulnerable_function:
   0x0000000000401146 <+0>:     push   rbp
   0x0000000000401147 <+1>:     mov    rbp,rsp
   0x000000000040114a <+4>:     sub    rsp,0x20
   0x000000000040114e <+8>:     mov    QWORD PTR [rbp-0x18],rdi
   0x0000000000401152 <+12>:    mov    edi,0x80
   0x0000000000401157 <+17>:    call   0x401050 <malloc@plt>
   0x000000000040115c <+22>:    mov    QWORD PTR [rbp-0x8],rax
   0x0000000000401160 <+26>:    mov    rdx,QWORD PTR [rbp-0x18]
   0x0000000000401164 <+30>:    mov    rax,QWORD PTR [rbp-0x8]
   0x0000000000401168 <+34>:    mov    rsi,rdx
   0x000000000040116b <+37>:    mov    rdi,rax
   0x000000000040116e <+40>:    call   0x401040 <strcpy@plt>
   0x0000000000401173 <+45>:    mov    rax,QWORD PTR [rbp-0x8]
   0x0000000000401177 <+49>:    mov    rdi,rax
   0x000000000040117a <+52>:    call   0x401030 <free@plt>
   0x000000000040117f <+57>:    nop
   0x0000000000401180 <+58>:    leave
   0x0000000000401181 <+59>:    ret
End of assembler dump.
pwndbg> b *0x0000000000401173
Breakpoint 1 at 0x401173
```

Fig. 7. Setting a breakpoint prior to the program crash.

```
pwndbg> run $(python -c "print('a'*150)")
Starting program: /home/badr/Desktop/ensa/research/Python_shield/test/heap $(python -c "print('a'*150)")
[Thread debugging using libthread_db enabled]
Using host libthread_db library "/lib/x86_64-linux-gnu/libthread_db.so.1".
```

Fig. 8. Overwriting the heap memory.

4.2.3 Integer Overflow Attacks

Integer overflow attacks are another category of security vulnerabilities related to programming and memory management. Unlike buffer overflows which involve overflowing a memory buffer so integer overflows involve numeric operations that result in a value that's too large (or too small in the case of underflow) for the intended storage space. In an integer overflow attack an attacker manipulates the application to perform an operation that results in such an overflow. As result this may lead to unexpected behavior including memory corruption and incorrect computations or bypassing of security checks (Figs. 9 and 10).

Then when the function CopyMemory tries to copy length bytes into buffer it will overflow the small buffer leading to a heap-based buffer overflow therefore an attacker could exploit this vulnerability to overwrite arbitrary memory and potentially leading to unauthorized access or even worst code execution.

```
0x405250    0x0000000000000000    0x0000000000000000    ................
0x405260    0x0000000000000000    0x0000000000000000    ................
0x405270    0x0000000000000000    0x0000000000000000    ................
0x405280    0x0000000000000000    0x0000000000000000    ................
0x405290    0x0000000000000000    0x0000000000000091    ................
0x4052a0    0x6161616161616161    0x6161616161616161    aaaaaaaaaaaaaaaa
0x4052b0    0x6161616161616161    0x6161616161616161    aaaaaaaaaaaaaaaa
0x4052c0    0x6161616161616161    0x6161616161616161    aaaaaaaaaaaaaaaa
0x4052d0    0x6161616161616161    0x6161616161616161    aaaaaaaaaaaaaaaa
0x4052e0    0x6161616161616161    0x6161616161616161    aaaaaaaaaaaaaaaa
0x4052f0    0x6161616161616161    0x6161616161616161    aaaaaaaaaaaaaaaa
0x405300    0x6161616161616161    0x6161616161616161    aaaaaaaaaaaaaaaa
0x405310    0x6161616161616161    0x6161616161616161    aaaaaaaaaaaaaaaa
0x405320    0x6161616161616161    0x6161616161616161    aaaaaaaaaaaaaaaa     <-- Top chunk
```

Fig. 9. Overwriting of the top chunk potentially leading to a'house of force attack 'or overwriting other chunks value.

```
Procedure VulnerableFunction(input: String, length: Unsigned Integer)
    bufferSize <- length * SizeOf(char)
    buffer <- AllocateMemory(bufferSize)
    CopyMemory(input, buffer, bufferSize)
    FreeMemory(buffer)
End Procedure

Procedure Main(argc: Integer, argv: Array of String)
    length <- ToUnsignedInteger(atoi(argv[2]))
    Call VulnerableFunction(argv[1], length)
    Return 0
End Procedure
```

Fig. 10. Illustration of how integer overflows can lead to security vulnerabilities by causing buffer overflows.

4.3 Impact of Buffer Overflow Attacks

The consequences of a successful buffer overflow attack can be severe and may have catastrophic implications. If an attacker manages to execute arbitrary code they might gain unauthorized access to the system and escalate their privileges or even worst take complete control over the system specifically by acquiring root user privileges within the system. In the worst-case scenario they could leverage this control to launch additional attacks and steal sensitive information or disrupt the system's operation.

4.4 Countermeasures and Their Limitations

Even though many defenses against buffer overflow attacks have been developed to mitigate buffer overflow attacks including ASLR, NX bit, Stack Canaries, CFI and CPI however none of them are completely effective. Each countermeasure has its limitations and skilled attackers have demonstrated time and again that these defenses can be bypassed.

4.5 Advanced Buffer Overflow Bypass Techniques

Over time buffer overflow vulnerabilities and the corresponding mitigation techniques have evolved, leading to the development of several advanced bypass techniques. These techniques exploit specific aspects of a system's memory or leverage certain flaws in a system's mitigation measures. PwnShield has been designed to effectively exploit these bypass techniques. The following section provides a detailed look into these techniques and how PwnShield exploit them.

4.5.1 Return to Function Bypass

The return-to-function is a technique used to exploit buffer overflow vulnerabilities by changing the return address of a function call to redirect execution to an existing function within the binary as shown in Fig. 11. This technique is particularly useful in scenarios where code execution is prevented by mitigation technologies such as NX or when the exact addresses of needed gadgets for a full ROP chain are unknown or easily discoverable. In PwnShield this technique is supported by using r2pipe to conduct a thorough static analysis of the binary file enumerating all functions contained within it and this process provides the user with a comprehensive list of potential targets to which execution could be redirected. The user can then select a desired function to use in the exploit and PwnShield will automate the process of crafting the payload with ROP chain to change the return address accordingly with the address of the function selected by the user.

4.5.2 Non eXecutable (NX) Bypass

The NX bit is a technology used in CPUs to divide areas of memory into sections for the storing of processor instructions (code) or for data. In essence it marks certain areas of memory as non-executable meaning that even if an attacker injects code into these areas the system will not execute it. The primary method of bypassing NX is through a technique known as Return-Oriented Programming (ROP). ROP exploits the fact that while an attacker cannot execute their own code so they can manipulate the execution of existing code like return to system function in libc library (get a shell) instead of injecting shell code.

PwnShield leverages the capabilities of the Pwntools library which incorporates integrated Return-Oriented Programming (ROP) functionalities so this facilitates the automated generation of ROP chains which are instrumental in hijacking the control flow of any software, thereby bypassing Non-eXecutable (NX) protections. Consequently this provides the user with the flexibility to select the function name to which they want to return or alternatively to ret2libc (get a shell) all that without the necessity of injecting shell code.

We can see the structure of the stack in Fig. 12 which provide an example of a buffer overflow attack utilizing return-oriented programming we observe the stack's structure. The stack is divided into different regions: the purple areas represent gadgets, the yellow areas store values used for register manipulation and the green area houses a system call and it is important to keep in mind that the purple areas on the stack actually hold the addresses of the gadget instructions rather than the values of the instructions themselves as demonstrated in this illustration.

The technique known as return-to-libc (ret2libc) is frequently employed in projects involving function calls. It allows the invocation of known functions once the necessary

High address

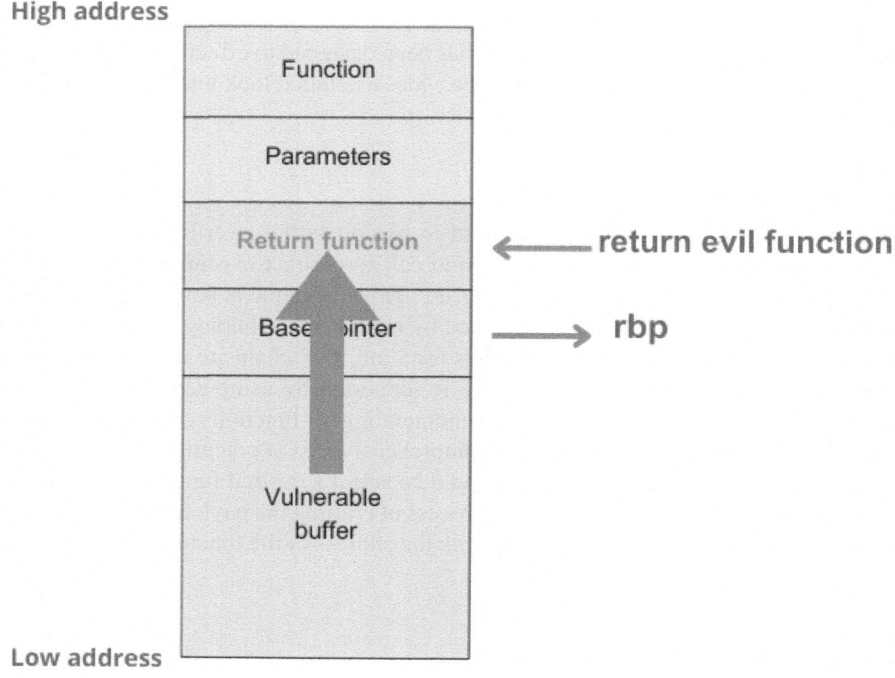

Fig. 11. Overwrite the return address to evil function.

function arguments have been set up. By utilizing ret2libc the protection provided by a non-executable stack which is implemented to counter the execution of shellcode on the stack can be bypassed. In this attack the adversary does not attempt to run injected shellcode on the stack so thus evading the mitigation measures against buffer overflows. The method of mitigating buffer overflows through the utilization of a non-executable stack is discussed in a later section of this chapter.

4.5.3 Stack Canary Bypass

Stack canaries are random values placed on the stack to detect a stack buffer overflow before execution of malicious code can occur. If a canary value is changed the program will abort preventing the exploit. To bypass stack canaries, PwnShield attempts to leak the canary's value then includes it in the overflow payload leaving the canary undisturbed and avoiding detection. Pwntools provides leak finding primitives that help in automating this process making PwnShield capable of bypassing stack canary protections effectively.

4.5.4 Address Space Layout Randomization (ASLR) Bypass

Important data regions within a process such as executable base, the location of the stack, heap and libraries are modified by ASLR in their address space position and because of this it is challenging and more difficult for an attacker to predict target addresses.

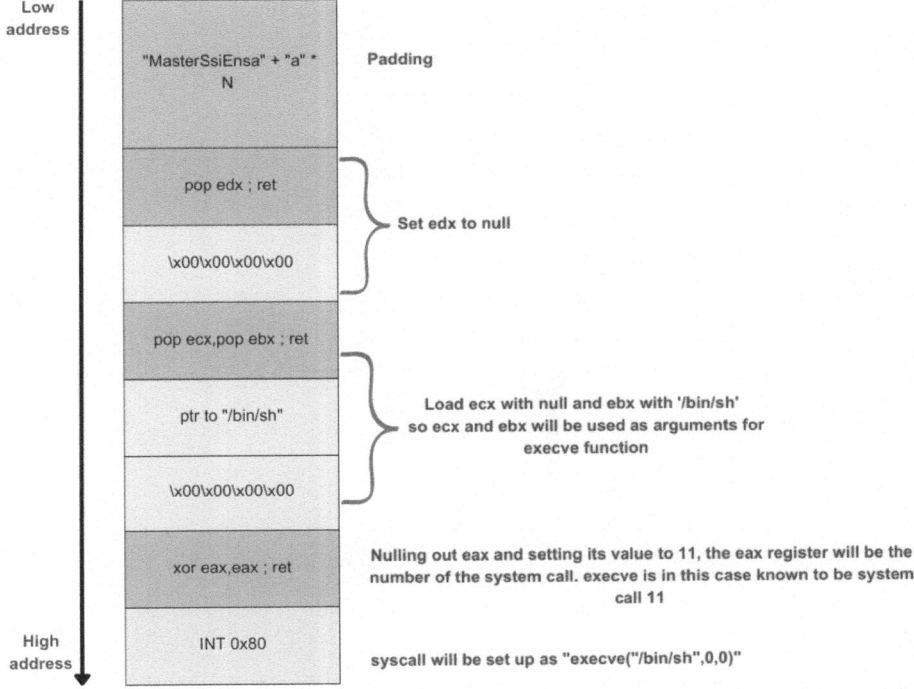

Fig. 12. Using ROP for bypassing NX.

PwnShield bypasses ASLR by using information leaks, where a program inadvertently reveals the addresses of variables or code segments (Fig. 13).

Once these addresses are known so ASLR is no longer efficient. PwnShield supported by Pwntools library can automate the process of identifying and exploiting these leaks addresses.

4.5.5 Partial RELocation Read-Only (RELRO) Bypass

RELRO servers as a mitigation strategy designed as a safeguard of specific memory sections and particularly the Globale Offset Table (GOT) from write operations so just read only, they are two types of Relro:

Partial RELRO: the elf loader will make the GOT section as read only after relocation the beginning of program execution however the procedure linkage table (PLT) can still write GOT, PwnShield uses the Pwntools library to generate an exploit that overwrites a function pointer in the GOT, effectively redirecting the program's execution flow to the return address of the function selected by the user or ret2libc (get shell).

Full RELRO: both the PLT and GOT are marked as read-only for the entire execution of the program preventing any modifications. This significantly hardens the binary against attacks that aim to overwrite the GOT however PwnShield can still exploit condition by leveraging a memory leak to find addresses of the GOT entries and once the

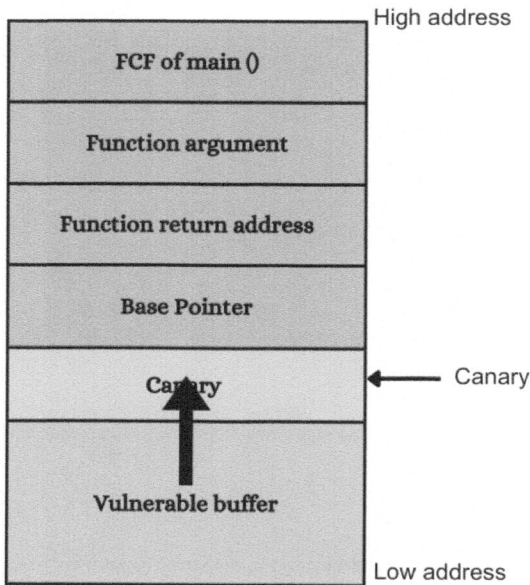

High address

Low address

Canary

Fig. 13. Stack with Canary word.

addresses are known PwnShield can overwrite the ".fini_array" or the "free_hook" or "malloc_hook" function pointers in case if they are used in the binary to redirect the program's execution flow to the function selected by the user or ret2libc (get shell).

4.5.6 Position Independent Executable (PIE) Bypass

PIE is another mitigation technique that enables Address Space Layout Randomization (ASLR) by allowing a program's code section to be loaded at a random memory address. Just as with ASLR PwnShield bypasses PIE by exploiting information leaks so by locating and using these leaks PwnShield can accurately target the executable's code even when its location is randomized. By combining the power of fuzzing and static analysis addition to the robust capabilities of Pwntools as well as r2pipe, PwnShield has proven highly efficient in exploiting these advanced bypass techniques thereby extending the limits of automated vulnerability detection and exploit generation.

5 Methodology

The methodology of this research is founded upon the development and analysis of PwnShield a tool that utilizes multiple libraries to automate the process of detecting and exploiting buffer overflow vulnerabilities while bypassing mitigation techniques such as NX, RELRO, Stack Canaries and PIE. Its primary goal is to streamline the process of identifying vulnerabilities, improving the robustness of software and enhancing the overall cybersecurity posture of systems notably PwnShield is capable of exploiting vulnerabilities in both 32-bit and 64-bit architectures.

5.1 PwnShield Overview

The following sections delineate the core steps of the methodology, detailing how various libraries were employed in the creation and functionality of PwnShield.

1. PwnShield Development: PwnShield was designed as a Python program leveraging the capabilities of the Pwntools library. Pwntools is a CTF (Capture The Flag) framework and exploit development library it's was chosen for its powerful utilities and its ability to simplify the creation of exploits and the primary advantage of Pwntools is its ability to interact with binaries and network services also automate common tasks in exploit development and simplify the process of writing and testing exploits.

2. Static Analysis: The first phase in PwnShield's is to perform a static analysis of the binary file to identify potential security vulnerabilities, this is done using the r2pipe library a set of Python bindings for the Radare2 reverse engineering framework. The primary role of r2pipe in PwnShield is to inspect the binary code without execution to find patterns that may indicate a buffer overflow vulnerability, it's used to examine various components of the binary with a focus on identifying vulnerable functions.

3. Fuzzing for Detection: Following the static analysis phase, the second phase in PwnShield's workflow is to perform fuzzing in order to automatically detect potential buffer overflow vulnerabilities so this is achieved using the Pwntools library which is well-suited for this task due to its capabilities in handling binary data and interfacing with network services, fuzzing is conducted through an automated iterative process that inputs a wide variety of data into the targeted software and observes for any unexpected behavior indicative of potential vulnerabilities.

4. Mitigation Checks: Simultaneously r2pipe is used to inspect the security mitigations applied to the binary, these checks include examining if Non-eXecutable (NX) stack, Partial RELocation Read-Only (RELRO), Stack Canaries or Position Independent Executable (PIE) have been employed so this information is essential as it influences the exploit generation phase.

5. Exploit Generation: Upon the successful detection of a buffer overflow vulnerability and the identification of the associated mitigation techniques so PwnShield then utilizes Pwntools again to craft an exploit, the exploit is generated in a way that takes into account the specific mitigation applied to the binary effectively bypassing them. Each generated exploit is tailored to the specific detected vulnerability thus maximizing the potential for successful exploitation and refer to the Fig. 14 for a comprehensive understanding of the program's structure. Through this well-structured methodology PwnShield is able to automate a complex process that would traditionally require significant manual effort and expertise thereby establishing itself as a significant asset in the field of cybersecurity. The use of robust reliable libraries like Pwntools and r2pipe enhances the effectiveness of PwnShield enabling it to successfully detect and exploit a wide array of buffer overflow vulnerabilities.

5.2 Evaluation of Mitigation Techniques

The effectiveness of PwnShield is evaluated through rigorous testing against various modern mitigation techniques commonly employed to counter buffer overflow

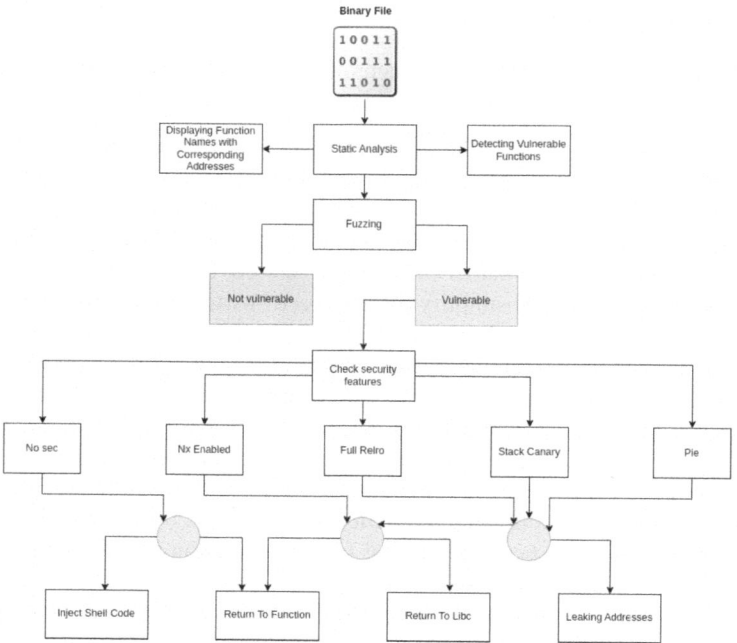

Fig. 14. Visualizing the Workflow of PwnShield

attacks including NX (Non-Executable memory), RELRO (Relocation Read-Only), Stack Canaries and PIE (Position Independent Executable). PwnShield's automated approach ensures that it can bypass these mitigation techniques and successfully exploit buffer overflow vulnerabilities. By extensively testing PwnShield's capabilities against each mitigation technique we can assess its effectiveness in generating exploits that evade protection mechanisms so the evaluation includes measuring the success rate of exploit generation the efficiency of detection and the ability to bypass these techniques in real-world scenarios.

5.3   Ethical Considerations

Throughout the research and evaluation process strict ethical guidelines are adhered to ensuring that the tools and techniques developed are used responsibly and for legitimate purposes so any vulnerabilities discovered are reported to relevant parties for timely patching and improvement of software security. In conclusion the methodology employed in this research harnesses the power of Pwntools to develop PwnShield an automated tool for buffer overflow detection and exploit generation by combining fuzzing, static analysis and exploit generation techniques so PwnShield effectively demonstrates its proficiency in bypassing modern mitigation techniques and accurately detecting vulnerabilities. Through a rigorous evaluation process PwnShield's capabilities are thoroughly assessed and offering valuable insights into its efficiency and potential for enhancing software security.

6   PwnShield Evaluation and Results

This research implementation involved the development of a methodology comprising approximately 700 lines of Python code. The specific libraries employed were pwntools v4.9.0 for automated exploitation and fuzzing, as well as radare2 v5.8.4 for static analysis. The experiments were conducted on a Kali Linux 64-bit machine equipped with an 11th Gen Intel(R) Core(TM) i5-1135G7 processor operating at 2.40 GHz, 8 GB of RAM, and the 6.1.0-kali7-amd64 kernel version. To assess the effectiveness of the methodology a selection of CTF (Capture The Flag) and CVE (Common Vulnerabilities and Exposures) programs with stack buffer overflow vulnerabilities were utilized. These programs were primarily sourced from prominent platforms such as HackTheBox or CTFTime. CTF programs serve as simplified representations of real-world applications specifically designed to concisely demonstrate and illustrate vulnerability principles. It is worth noting that CTF programs are specifically tailored for competition scenarios ensuring the vulnerability exploitation can be successfully achieved. In contrast real-world programs tend to exhibit higher complexity where even the presence of a vulnerability does not necessarily guarantee its exploitability. The implemented methodology leveraged the chosen libraries and experimental environment to analyze and exploit the identified vulnerabilities so by utilizing automation tools and techniques, the research aimed to enhance the overall understanding of buffer overflow vulnerabilities, improve software resilience and fortify system cybersecurity. The performance and effectiveness of PwnShield were evaluated through a series of extensive tests with the results compared against other notable tools in the field specifically BofAEG and autoBOF.

6.1   Comparison with BofAEG

BofAEG is a well-known tool that utilizes symbolic execution to detect and exploit buffer overflow vulnerabilities. However PwnShield demonstrated several advantages over BofAEG in our testing:

1. Struggles with Stack Canary Protection: BofAEG has difficulty exploiting binaries with stack canary protection enabled so compared to PwnShield is designed to bypass such modern mitigation techniques, including stack canaries and making it potentially more effective against a wider array of binaries.
2. Slow and Computationally Intensive: BofAEG's use of symbolic execution can be slow and computationally intensive. PwnShield on the other hand uses a combination of fuzzing and static analysis which may result in faster detection and exploit generation times.
3. Limitations in Return-to-Function Bypass: An inherent limitation of BofAEG is based on the premise of Capture The Flag (CTF) examples which contain a 'win' function designed just to display the CTF flag. However in real scenarios there is no 'win' function. This is opposed to PwnShield which it is capable to provide all the functions in the software by using static analysis with r2pipe library and gives the user the flexibility to select the function they want to return to as we can see in the representative structure of PwnShield in the Fig. 14 (Table 3).

Table 3. Results of BofAEG and PwnShield on CTF and CVE programs.

Program	NX	CANARY	PIE	Win	BofAEG	PwnShield	Exp Tech
redpwnctf2020_coffer	✓	×	×	✓	6 s	4 s	Ret2Win
csictf2020_pwn0x1	✓	×	×	✓	5 s	3 s	Ret2Win
csictf2020_pwn0x2	✓	×	×	✓	6 s	4 s	Ret2Win
csictf2020_pwn0x3	✓	×	×	✓	6 s	4 s	Ret2Win
dctf2021_sanity	✓	×	×	✓	4 s	3 s	Ret2Win
umdctf2021_jne	✓	×	×	✓	6 s	6 s	Ret2Win
csawctf2021_password	✓	×	×	✓	60 s	54 s	Ret2Win
hacktivityctf2021_retcheck	✓	×	×	✓	8 s	5 s	Ret2Win
downunderctf2021_deadcode	✓	×	×	✓	6 s	5 s	Ret2Win
downunderctf2021_out	✓	×	×	✓	5 s	5 s	Ret2Win
csawctf2020_roppity	✓	×	×	×	6 s	6 s	Ret2libc
downunderctf2020_return	✓	×	×	×	7 s	5 s	Ret2libc
dctf2021_babybof	✓	×	×	×	5 s	5 s	Ret2libc
umdctf2021_jnw	✓	×	×	×	6 s	4 s	Ret2libc
tamilctf2021_name	✓	×	×	×	4 s	3 s	Ret2libc
sharkyctf2020_give	✓	×	✓	×	4 s	3 s	Ret2libc
dctf2021_hotelrop	✓	×	✓	×	5 s	4 s	Ret2libc
lexingtonctf2021_gets	✓	×	✓	✓	11 s	7 s	Ret2Win

6.2 Comparison with AutoBOF

AutoBOF automates a process that security researchers could manually undertake when searching for buffer overflows. The underlying methodology of the program can be summarized in the following steps:

Fuzzing the target with the aim of inducing a program crash, if a crash is successfully induced, the exact number of bytes required to cause the crash is determined if no crash occurs the program terminates.

The program identifies "bad" characters - characters that are processed differently than expected or differently than other valid characters so this could include newlines, null-bytes and various other characters.

The program searches for a ROP (Return-Oriented Programming) gadget containing a "jmp esp" instruction. This is used to redirect the program flow to the shellcode placed on the stack.

The payload is assembled from the shellcode and the ROP gadget with the "jmp esp" instruction [15] however these capabilities of AutoBOF has several limitations when compared to PwnShield :

1. Limited Use Cases: AutoBOF is designed to detect a simple type of overflow which may not be commonly found in real-world scenarios. In contrast PwnShield is designed to detect and exploit a wider range of buffer overflow vulnerabilities and making it potentially more useful in practical applications.
2. Lack of Cross-Platform Support: AutoBOF is not currently cross-platform limiting its applicability. PwnShield on the other hand being built with Python and has the potential for broader platform compatibility.
3. Inability to Bypass Mitigations: AutoBOF cannot bypass mitigation techniques which limits its effectiveness against protected programs. PwnShield is designed to bypass modern mitigation techniques enhancing its effectiveness.
4. Time-Consuming Shell Dropping Phase: autoBOF's shell dropping phase which involves sending the shell and then eliminating bad character and that can be time-consuming so PwnShield's approach which involves automated exploitation and fuzzing may potentially be more efficient. In conclusion while autoBOF and BofAEG offer valuable tools for automating the exploitation of buffer overflow vulnerabilities, PwnShield's unique combination of automation static and dynamic analysis and ability to bypass modern mitigation techniques potentially provides a more advanced and efficient solution to buffer overflow detection and mitigation.

6.3 Limitations of PwnShiled

1. Usability Challenges: PwnShield faces usability challenges as improving the user interface and experience involves complex task in design, implementation and user acceptance.
2. Symbolic Execution and Efficiency: May experience limitations in efficiency due to increased computational overhead when incorporating symbolic execution for large-scale software.
3. Expanding to Heap Memory Exploitation: Lack capabilities in identifying and exploiting heap memory vulnerabilities, presenting a limitation in handling these more intricate vulnerabilities compared to stack-base ones.
4. Implementation Challenges: Implementing specific techniques to exploit both stack and heap vulnerabilities is a non-trivial task, involving intricate details and potential security risks.

7 Decusion

In this research, we discovered the threat of buffer overflow and how dangerous it is even with the implementation of modern mitigations, it can still be a real menace in the cyber-security field, as a result there is a vital need for more efficient and advanced detection and exploitation systems. The development and evaluation of our tool PwnShield has provided significant insights and promising results. Our tool's design incorporates a multi-stage process of fuzzing, static analysis and exploit generation depends in the mitigation implemented, showing an innovative approach to identifying and exploiting vulnerabilities another point is that our comparison of PwnShield with existing tools like BofAEG and autoBoof emphasized its superior performance especially in terms of speed and detection range and the ability to bypass modern mitigation techniques such as Stack Canaries, NX, RELRO and PIE.

8 Future Work

Throughout the progression of this research several potential areas for future exploration and development have been identified so the limits of the current PwnShield version as well as the rapid advancement and developing trends in the cybersecuriyt industry have an impact on these prospective paths. From a usability perspective the user interface and experience with PwnShield could see enhancements, in fact PwnShield may become more approachable and user-friendly through creation of more intuitive user interface or the integration with popular cybersecurity platforms so that code make our tool more accessible. In large-scale software, adding symbolic execution can enhance the efficiency of detecting buffer overflow and if we combine it with our current existing static analysis and fuzzing techniques it could become a significantly powerful tool. Expanding the tool's capabilities by exploiting heap memory as well as the stack and this requires identifying all of these vulnerabilities and implementing specific techniques to exploit them which is not simple.

9 Conclusion

This paper introduces PwnShield, a program that can automatically find and exploit stack buffer overflow vulnerabilities in ELF binaries and bypass modern mitigation techniques by using a combination of fuzzing and static binary analysis to identify buffer overflow vulnerabilities and generate exploits. PwnShield can handle a variety of scenarios and exploit techniques such as ROP chains, shellcode injection, GOT overwrite and stack pivoting. Crucially, Pwnshield evaluated using CTF challenges and CVEs, the results show that PwnShield can successfully exploit buffer overflow vulnerabilities and bypass mitigation techniques such as NX, ASLR, RELRO, Stack Canaries, PIE and it outperforms existing tools such as BofAEG and autoBOF in terms of speed and coverage.

References

1. Butt, M.A., Ajmal, Z., Khan, Z.I., Idrees, M., Javed, Y.: An in-depth survey of bypassing buffer overflow mitigation techniques. Appl. Sci., 6702 (2022)
2. Gadient, A., Ortiz, B., Barrato, R., Davis, E., Perkins, J., Rinard, M.: Automatic exploitation of fully randomized executables (2019)
3. Xu, L., Jia, W., Dong, W., Li, Y.: Automatic exploit generation for buffer overflow vulnerabilities. In: 2018 IEEE International Conference on Software Quality, Reliability and Security Companion (QRS-C), pp. 463–468 (2018)
4. Xu, S., Wang, Y.: BofAEG: automated stack buffer overflow vulnerability detection and exploit generation based on symbolic execution and dynamic analysis. Secur. Commun. Netw. (2022)
5. Nicula, Zota, R.D.: Exploiting stack-based buffer overflow using modern day techniques. Procedia Comput. Sci., 9–14 (2019)
6. Pierce, P.: The nx/2 operating system, pp. 384–390 (1988)
7. Jeong, S., Hwang, J., Kwon, H., Shin, D.: A CFI countermeasure against got overwrite attacks. IEEE Access, 36267–36280 (2020)

8. Hawkins, W.H., Hiser, J.D., Davidson, J.W.: Dynamic canary randomization for improved software security, pp. 1–7 (2016)
9. Position independent executables (pie). www.redhat.com/en/blog/position-independent-executables-pie
10. Howard, M.: Address space layout randomization in windows vista. Microsoft Corporation 26 (2006)
11. Gadaleta, F., Younan, Y., Jacobs, B., Joosen, W., De Neve, E., Beosier, N.: Instruction-level countermeasures against stack-based buffer overflow attacks, pp. 7–12 (2009)
12. Gadaleta, F., Younan, Y., Joosen, W.: BuBBle: a Javascript engine level countermeasure against heap-spraying attacks. In: Massacci, F., Wallach, D., Zannone, N. (eds.) ESSoS 2010. LNCS, vol. 5965, pp. 1–17. Springer, Heidelberg (2010). https://doi.org/10.1007/978-3-642-11747-3_1
13. Duan, L., Sun, Y., Zhang, K., Ding, Y.: Multiple-layer security threats on the ethereum blockchain and their countermeasures. Secur. Commun. Netw. (2022)
14. One, A.: Smashing the stack for fun and profit. Phrack Mag., 14–16 (1996)
15. Ytrehus, I.: Detecting buffer overflows using python (2020)

Analysis of the Impacts of Flooding-Based DDoS Attacks on SDN-Enabled Cloud

Jasmeen Kaur Chahal[1]([envelope]) [iD], Abhinav Bhandari[1], and Sunny Behal[2]

[1] Department of Computer Science and Engineering, Punjabi University, Punjab, India
jasmeenkaur2592@gmail.com
[2] Shaheed Bhagat Singh State University, Punjab, India

Abstract. Software-defined Networking (SDN) is a promising networking paradigm that reformulates traditional architecture by altering the networking paradigm from hardware to software-based. SDN has benefits for engineers to have complete supervision of the network through the centralized controller, successful in identifying the network faults, malicious entities, etc. in an efficient way. Similarly, SDN architecture for a cloud environment provides easy cloud services and data centre management. Although SDN is beneficial in numerous ways, the architecture is vulnerable to DDoS attacks that can terminate the activities of the whole network. Authors in the literature proposed a variety of detection and mitigation techniques against DDoS attacks in SDN-enabled cloud, but most of them evaluated their results based on the features that are extracted from a dataset of traditional networks. The novel features of SDN architecture such as packet_in count and flow table entries are missing in non-SDN datasets and therefore, the experimental results based on these datasets can't be accurate. The major contribution of this paper is to find out the features of DDoS in SDN-enabled cloud. A benchmark dataset is employed to find out the unique features of DDoS attacks and normal traffic in the SDN-enabled cloud.

Keywords: Software-defined Networking · DDoS Attack Detection · Novel features of SDN · SDN-enabled Cloud

1 Introduction

Software-defined Networking (SDN) [1] is a networking architecture based on software, i.e. in SDN, the software controls the traffic between network hosts. Traditional network traffic control is hardware based where switches, routers and networking devices supervise the whole network. On the other hand, in centralised SDN architecture, the SDN switches include only the data plane and the whole control plane is shifted to the centralized authority called a controller. The controller is the only entity that is a brain for the whole network and an entity responsible for taking all decisions for traffic, switches and hosts. Examples of these controller includes POX [2], Floodlight [3], Ryu [4], OpenDayLight [5], NOX , etc.

SDN provides a solution to many problems of traditional networks [6]. Separating the data and control planes enables the logical configuration in hardware network architecture. The advancements in technology, also put forward security issues. Distributed

Denial of Service Attack (DDoS) is a hazardous attack that compromises the various points in SDN architecture including the controller by overburdening it and data-control communication link congestion with requests. Similarly, for SDN-enabled cloud, DDoS attacks are a threat to cloud applications and data centres.

Moreover, DDoS attacks has been executed using various bots [7] that produce a large amount of traffic towards the target, as shown in Fig. 1. The result of this is the target gets overwhelmed with the traffic and unable to execute the desired operations. In SDN, DDoS target various spots in the architecture, mentioned below:

- *DDoS Attack on Application Layer*: There are multiple applications related to network management that are working on this layer. Attackers exploit these applications to launch the attack. The malicious applications exhausts the resources fo the network in order to discontinue the service to the legitimate users.
- *DDoS Attack on Control Layer:* The attacker transmits a huge number of packets from spoof IP addresses, which causes a large number of packet_in messages to be produced. In the worst case scenario, it depletes the controller's resources, making it slow and ineffective.
- *DDoS attack on Communication Link:* Attack traffic between the switch and the controller clogs up the communication channel between the application and the control plane.
- DDoS Attack on Data Plane: By overflowing the flow table kept at the switch, the attacker can target the data plane and cause a flow-table overflow.

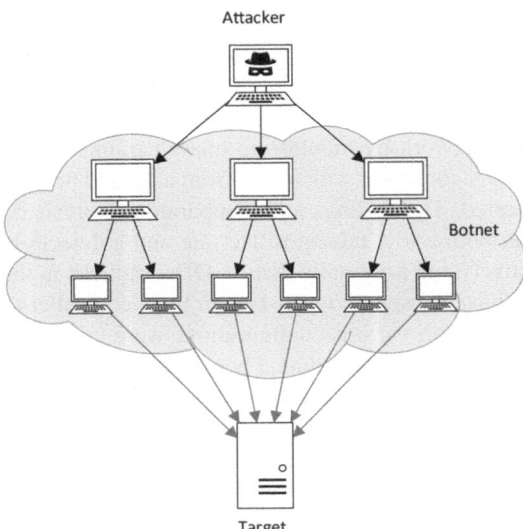

Fig. 1. DDoS Attack: An example

With the passage of time, DDoS attacks have become highly destructive and disrupted a wide range of network services. It has become a major issue for researchers to defend against this attack quickly and efficiently. A number of authors have worked to mitigate DDoS attacks in the SDN environment, but these works implemented their defense systems using non-SDN datasets and unrealistic topologies. Also, the features that they have used to detect DDoS attacks in SDN are based on the parameters of traditional network-based DDoS attacks. Therefore, it is highly crucial to find out the DDoS features based on SDN based dataset so that the proposed defense technique results can be more valuable and reliable. The contributions of this article are mentioned below:

- A thorough analysis of SDN-based DDoS attack Dataset.
- Find out the unique DDoS features based on the parameters of SDN-based DDoS Attack. These features include average packet count per flow (APCPF), average packet count per switch (APCPS) and Port Bandwidth.
- Detailed graphs mention the prominent difference between the obtained results of normal and attack traffic in SDN.

The rest of the paper is categorized into different sections as follows, Section 2 mentions the Related Work and Section 3 mentions the description of the data set used in the work. Section 4 discusses the unique features of DDoS attacks and Normal Traffic is SDN-enabled Cloud. Section 5 shows the results and finally, Section 6 ends in the conclusion of the paper.

2   Related Work

This section represents relevant studies that proposed defense against DDoS attacks based on particular features. Using the session IP counter and IP Payload analysis, Bhayo et al. [8] proposed a secure Internet of things architecture based on SDN that can detect malicious traffic generated by IoT devices or vulnerabilities in IoT devices. Even with huge traffic volumes, the aforementioned methods can easily detect the DDoS assault in the SD-IoT network by monitoring many parameters. These tactics, which involve flooding an SDN controller with traffic from a hacked node and then identifying and alerting it, are tested. The findings and comparative analysis demonstrate that the proposed framework, with a low false-positive rate and a detection rate ranging from 98% to 100%, effectively and accurately detects DDoS attacks in their early stages.

Badotra et al. [9] have chosen two well-known SDN controllers (ODL and ONOS). Four different machines with various configurations were taken into consideration for the experiment. Different scenarios included bombarding the ONOS controller and the ODL-3 node cluster controller. Open-source software was employed to produce malicious DDoS traffic that barraged the targeted controller. Both SDN controllers were discovered to be susceptible to DDoS attacks, and it was found that the ODL-3 node cluster outperformed other configurations in terms of CPU, memory, and disk utilization. The ODL-3node cluster controller experienced a high rate of controller failures.

Aladaileh et al. [10] Examine the effectiveness and consequences of an entropy-based DDoS attack detection technique for detecting high- and low-rate DDoS attacks against the controller, as indicated by the false-positive rate (FPR) and detection rate (DR), which are started by one or more host attacks that target one or more victims. Eight simulated scenarios representing low and high DDoS attack traffic rates on the controller were used to evaluate the efficacy of an entropy-based DDoS attack detection system. According to the testing results, the entropy-based approach increases the average DR for detecting high-rate DDoS attack traffic in comparison to low-rate DDoS attack traffic by 6.25%, 20.26%, 6.74%, and 8.81%. It also reduces the average FPRs for detecting a high DDoS assault traffic rate by 67.68%, 77.54%, 66.94%, and 64.81 when compared to a mild DDoS attack.

Tonkal et al. [11] Using machine learning techniques, a dataset taken from the SDN environment was utilized to categorize legitimate and malicious traffic. The specialized SDN-based dataset contains TCP, UDP, and ICMP traffic that is malicious as well as valid. In the dataset, statistical features like byte_count, duration_sec, packet rate, and packet per flow are present, apart from features that indicate source and target devices. Using the NCA algorithm, the best features were selected, and a successful classification was achieved. After 22 network features were analyzed utilizing NCA approaches, 14 useful features were selected and fed into machine learning algorithms. The kNN, DT, ANN, and SVM algorithms were used to classify over 100,000 network data following preprocessing and feature selection. The trial's results show that, at 100%, DT outperforms the other algorithms in terms of accuracy.

3   Dataset Description

The extraction of features of DDoS attack in SDN-enabled cloud in this work is done using a benchmark dataset "DDoS attack SDN Dataset" [12]. It is SDN specific Dataset generated using a testbed having 10 topologies, where switches are connected to single Ryu controller. The dataset comprising the normal traffic of TCP, UDP and ICMP and attack traffic of TCP SYN attack, UDP flood attack and ICMP attack. Total 23 features are available in the dataset includes both primary and derived. Table 1. is showing the detailed description of the dataset.

4   Unique Features of DDoS Attacks and Normal Traffic in SDN-Enabled Cloud

This section shows the unique features of attack and normal traffic that are present in the dataset. These features can be significantly used to differentiate both traffic in the SDN-enabled cloud [13]. A description of these features is given below:

4.1   Average Packet Count (APC)

The number of packets recorded is not only an important parameter for the detection of DDoS attacks in traditional networks but also plays a vital role in DDoS defense in SDN-enabled networks. In the case of normal traffic, the packet count is relatively low as the legitimate users are sending requests randomly at different times. On the other hand, in attack traffic, the traffic sent by zombies becomes significantly increases at one time which shows a rise in packet count that slows down the network.

To analyse this feature critically, this feature is analysed in two ways – Average Packet Count per Flow (APCPF) and Average Packet Count Per Switch (APCPS).

Table 1. .

Specification	Details
Total number of features in the Dataset	23
Total Number of Records	104,345
Number of Attack Records	40,784
Number of Normal Records	63,561
Total instances of TCP Traffic	29,436
Total instances of normal TCP traffic	18,897
Total instances of TCP-SYN Flood traffic	10,539
Total instances of UDP Traffic	33,588
Total instances of normal UDP traffic	22,772
Total instances of UDP Flood traffic	10,816
Total instances of ICMP Traffic	41,321
Total instances of normal ICMP traffic	24,957
Total instances of ICMP Flood traffic	16,364

Primary Features		
S. No.	Feature	Description
1	Dt	This shows date and time which has been converted into number
2	Switch_id	A number assigned to each switch in a topology
3	Pktcount	The total number of packet count
4	bytecount	The total number of Byte count
5	dur	The total duration in seconds
6	dur_nsec	The duration in nano seconds
7	tot_duration	sum of duration_sec and duration_nsec
8	src	Source IP address
9	dst	Destination IP address
10	port_no	The port number of switch
11	tx_bytes	The number of bytes transferred from the switch port.
12	rx_bytes	The number of bytes received on the switch port.
13	Protocol	TCP, UDP or ICMP

Derived Features		
S. No.	Feature	Description
1	Pkt_rate	Number of packets sent per second
2	Pkt per flow	Packet count during a single flow
3	Bytes per flow	Byte count during a single flow
4	Packet rate	Number of packets sent per second
5	Number of packet_ins	Number of Packet_IN messages
6	Flow_id	Total flow entries in the switch
7	tx_kbps	Data transfer rate
8	rx_kbps	Data receiving rate
9	tot_kbps	Sum of data transfer and receivibg rate

4.1.1 Average Packet Count Per Flow (APCPF)

A flow is defined as a collection of packets referencing the same source IP address. APCPF increases in case of attack and decreases in case of normal traffic as the number of packets sent in an attack is more. APCPF can be defined with packet count during a flow w.r.t. the frequency of each flow. APCPF can be expressed as:

$$APCPF = \sum_{x=1}^{x=y} p_x/f \tag{1}$$

Here, p is the count of packets sent during a flow and x ranges from flow1 to flowy and f is the frequency of each flow.

4.1.2 Average Packet Count Per Switch (APCPS)

Packet Count per switch is the total number of packets sent by a switch in attack as well as normal traffic. Similar to APCPF, it gets increased in case of attack and decreased in case of normal traffic as the malicious users under switches are bombarding the switch with multiple requests. APCPS can be defined with packet count during a flow w.r.t. the number of flow entries in a switch. APCPS can be expressed as:

$$APCPF = \sum_{x=1}^{x=y} p_x/e \tag{2}$$

Here, p is the count of packets sent during a flow and x ranges from flow1 to flowy and e is the number of flow entries in a switch.

4.2 Port Bandwidth

It is defined as the sum of received bytes rx_bytes (r) and transmitted bytes tx_bytes (t). The statistics are collected from the switch ports at periodic intervals. In case of attack, attackers send more requests and less data, so the consumption of bandwidth is less as compared to normal traffic. The port bandwidth is mentioned below:

$$PortBandwidth = \frac{t*8}{1000} + \frac{r*8}{1000} \tag{3}$$

Here tx_bytes and rx_bytes are the extracted Port statistics from the switch.

5 Experimental Results and Evaluation

The features proposed for distinguishing between DDoS traffic and Normal traffic in the above section are investigated and verified by the analysis of the dataset viz. "DDoS Attack SDN Dataset" [12]. The results are based on the primary parameters of the dataset, which include switch_id, pktcount, flow_id, packetins, tx_kbps and rx_kbps.

5.1   Average Packet Count Per Flow (APCPF)

It is defined in equation no. (1), that it is packet count during a flow w.r.t. the frequency of each flow Fig. 2. The results are based on two primary attributes namely pktcount and flow_id. Figure 4 is showing the APCPF for both normal and attack traffic. The maximum value of packet count is between 80000 and 85000 and the minimum is between 500 to 1000. As already mentioned, APCPF increases in case of an attack and decreases in case of normal traffic as the number of packets sent in an attack is more. It is proved in Figs. 5 and 6, where the maximum value for flow 2 in the case of normal traffic (Fig. 5) is 57356.2 whereas for attack traffic (Fig. 6) it is 95443.4, i.e. approximately 66.40% higher than legitimate traffic. Similarly for each flow, the packet count in case of attack traffic is higher than the normal traffic. Figure 7 is showing the comparison of both traffic, it is clearly proved that the APCPF for normal traffic is significantly less than the attack traffic throughout each flow. This results that the feature is providing a notable difference between normal and attack traffic Fig. 3.

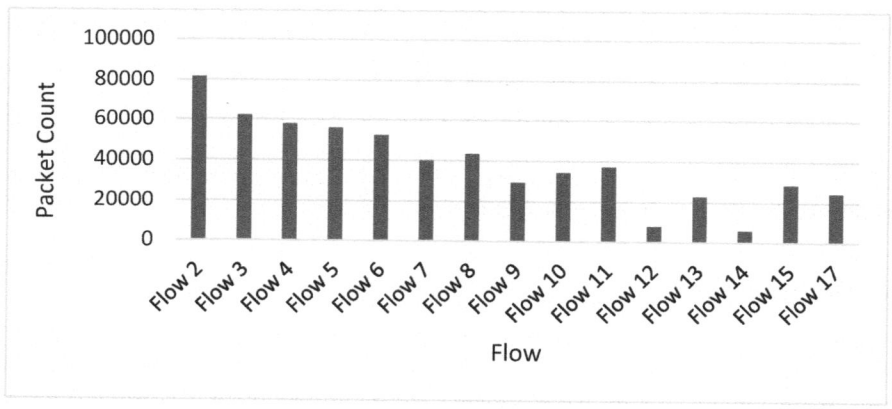

Fig. 2.   APCPF for the complete dataset

5.2   Average Packet Count Per Switch (APCPS)

It is defined in equation no. (2), that it is packet count during a flow w.r.t. the number of flow entries in a switch. The results are based on two primary attributes namely pktcount and switch_id. Figure 8 is showing the APCPS for both normal and attack traffic. The maximum value of packet count is approximately 55000 and the minimum is 4000. As already mentioned, APCPS increases in case of an attack and decreases in case of normal traffic as the number of packets sent in an attack is more. It is proved in Figs. 9 and 10, where the maximum value for Switch1 in the case of normal traffic (Fig. 9) is 52547.2 and for the rest of the switches, the value lies between 23000 to 37000. On the other hand, for attack traffic (Fig. 10), the value lies between 70000 to 84000 except for Switch 1 i.e. approximately twice the APCPS for normal traffic. Similarly for maximum switches, the

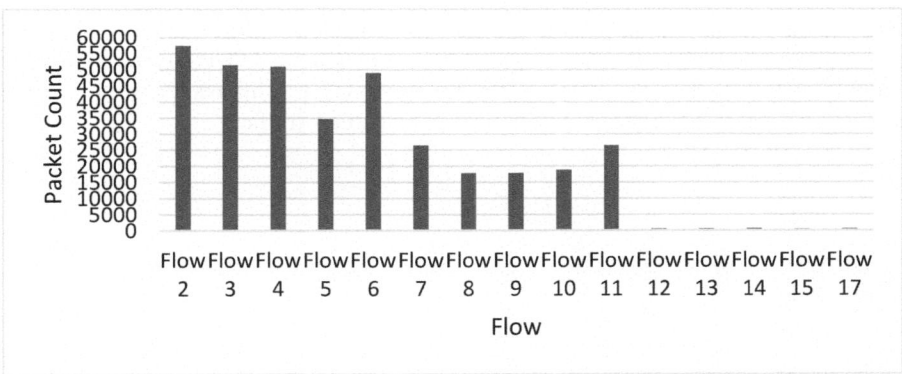

Fig. 3. APCPF for Normal Traffic

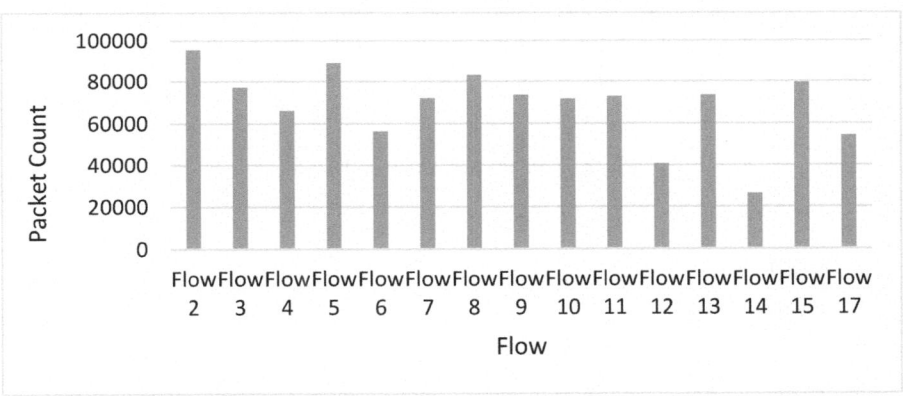

Fig. 4. APCPF for Attack Traffic

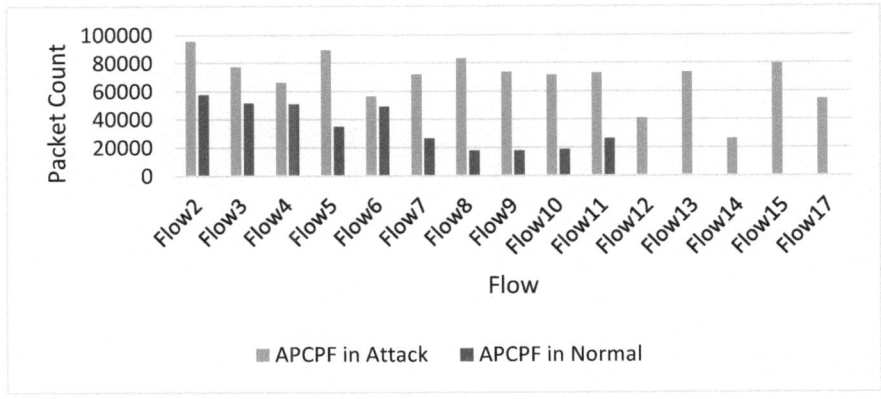

Fig. 5. APCPF for Attack and Normal Traffic

packet count in case of attack traffic is higher than the normal traffic. Figure 11 shows the comparison of both traffic, and it is clearly proved that the APCPS for normal traffic is significantly less than the attack traffic for each switch. This results in the feature providing a notable difference between normal and attack traffic.

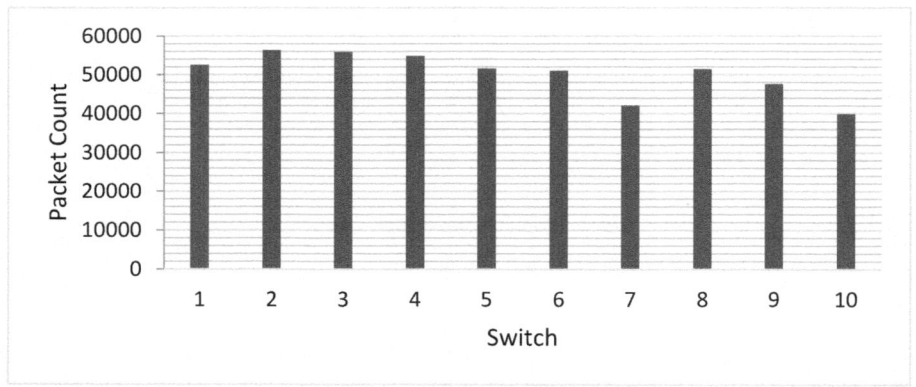

Fig. 6. APCPS for Complete Dataset

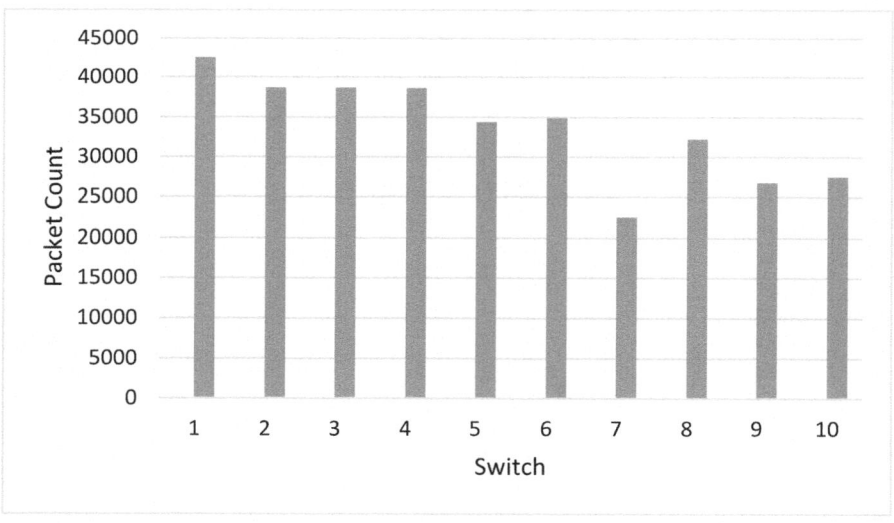

Fig. 7. APCPS for Normal Traffic

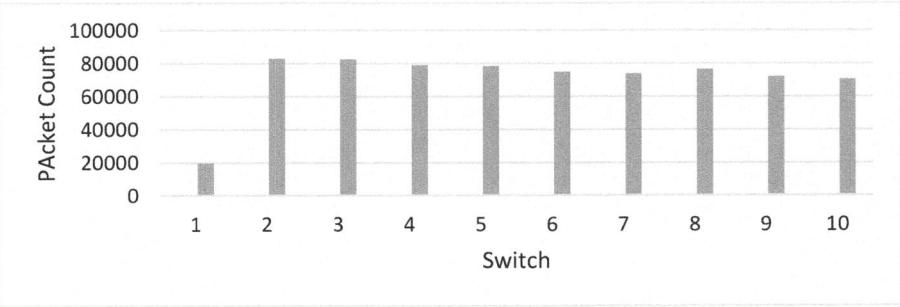

Fig. 8. APCPS for Attack Traffic

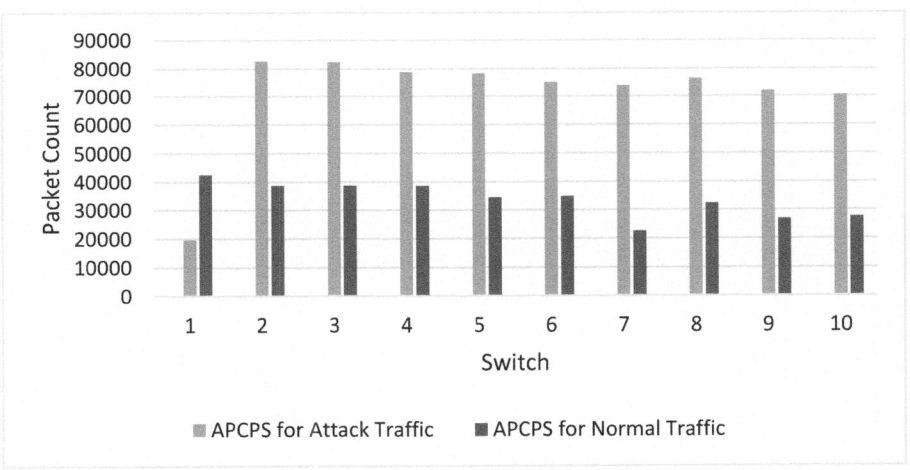

Fig. 9. Comparison of APCPS in Attack and Normal Traffic

Port Band width. For port bandwidth, tx_bytes and rx_bytes are the extracted Port statistics from the switch. Figs. 10 and 11 are showing the Port Bandwidth for both normal and attack traffic. It is clear in both cases that the transmitted bytes in Normal traffic are higher as compared to Attack traffic. This is true for receiving bytes as well. The reason is attackers focus on overwhelming the target with a huge traffic and therefore, they send large number request packets, consume less bandwidth as compared to data packets. Similarly, Fig. 12 is showing the port bandwidth of attack and normal traffic that is quite parallel to individual result of attack and normal traffic.

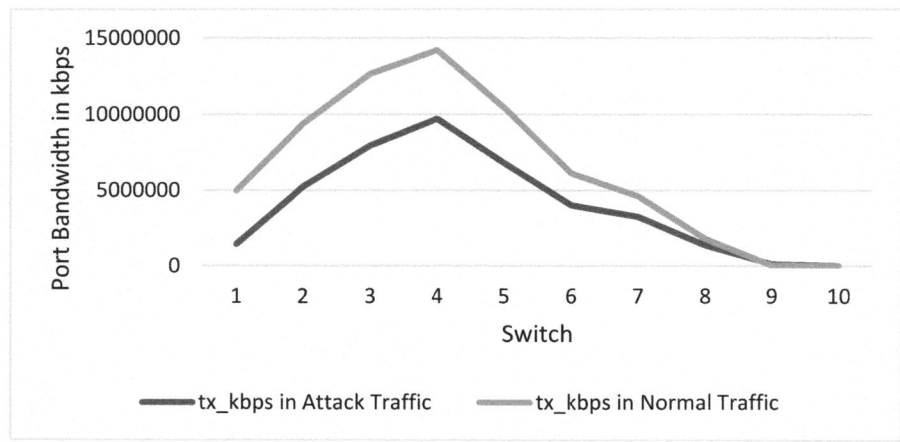

Fig. 10. tx_kbps comparison for Attack and Normal Traffic

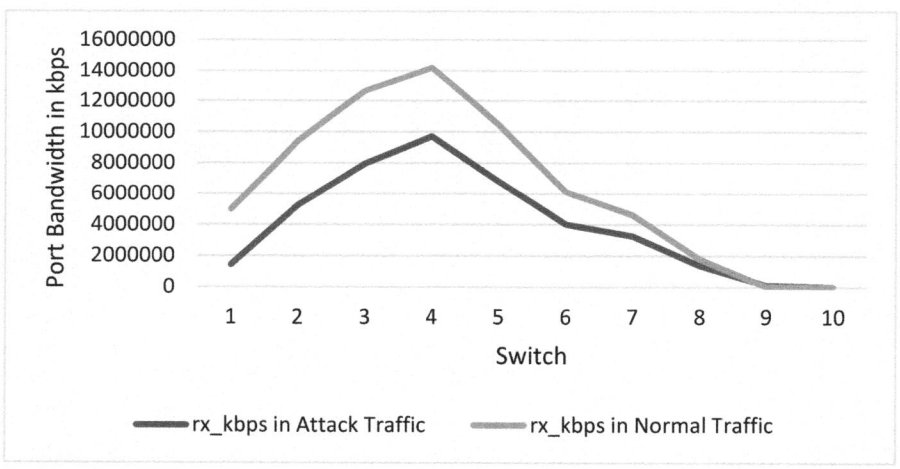

Fig. 11. rx_kbps comparison for Attack and Normal traffic

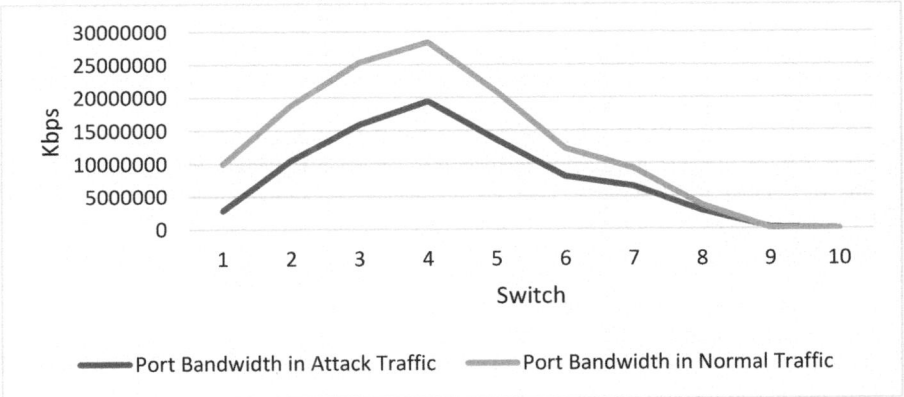

Fig. 12. Port Bandwidth for Attack and Normal Traffic

6 Conclusion and Future Work

SDN is beneficial in numerous ways, the architecture is vulnerable to DDoS attacks that can terminate the activities of the whole network. Authors in the literature proposed a variety of detection and mitigation techniques against DDoS attacks in SDN-enabled cloud, but most of them evaluated their results based on the features that are extracted from a dataset of traditional networks. The novel features of SDN architecture such as packet_in count and flow table entries are missing in non-SDN datasets and therefore, the experimental results based on these datasets can't be accurate. The major contribution of this paper is to find out the features of DDoS in SDN-enabled cloud.

In this work, the unique DDoS features based on the parameters of SDN-based DDoS Attacks have been identified. These features include average packet count per flow (APCPF), average packet count per switch (APCPS) and Port Bandwidth. APCPF increases in case of attack and decreases in case of normal traffic as the number of packets sent in an attack is more, in results it shows that attack traffic is 66.40% higher than legitimate traffic. Similarly, for APCPS increased in case of attack and decreased in case of normal traffic as the malicious users under switches are bombarding the switch with multiple requests, the results show the clear difference.

For Port bandwidth, it is lower for attack traffic as attackers send more requests and less data, so the consumption of bandwidth is less as compared to normal traffic, the graph result shows this clearly. In future work, we aim to propose a robust DDoS detection scheme for SDN-enabled cloud based on machine learning approach.

References

1. Deb, R., Roy, S.: A comprehensive survey of vulnerability and information security in SDN. Comput. Netw. **206**, 108802 (2022). https://doi.org/10.1016/j.comnet.2022.108802
2. POX. https://github.com/noxrepo/pox. Accessed 31 Oct 2018
3. Floodlight. http://www.projectfloodlight.org/. Accessed 31 Oct 2018
4. Ryu. https://osrg.github.io/ryu/. Accessed 31 Oct 2018

5. OpenDaylight. https://wiki.opendaylight.org/view/Main_Page. Accessed 31 Oct 2018
6. Chen, J., Zheng, X., Rong, C.: Survey on software-defined networking. In: Qiang, W., Zheng, X., Hsu, C.-H. (eds.) CloudCom-Asia 2015. LNCS, vol. 9106, pp. 115–124. Springer, Cham (2015). https://doi.org/10.1007/978-3-319-28430-9_9
7. Silva, S.S.C., Silva, R.M.P., Pinto, R.C.G., Salles, R.M.: Botnets: a survey. Comput. Netw. **57**(2), 378–403 (2013). https://doi.org/10.1016/j.comnet.2012.07.021
8. Bhayo, J., Jafaq, R., Ahmed, A., Hameed, S., Shah, S.A.: A time-efficient approach toward DDoS attack detection in IoT network using SDN. IEEE Internet Things J. **9**(5), 3612–3630 (2022). https://doi.org/10.1109/JIOT.2021.3098029
9. Badotra, S., et al.: A DDoS vulnerability analysis system against distributed SDN controllers in a cloud computing environment. Electron. (Switz.) **11**(19), 3120 (2022). https://doi.org/10.3390/electronics11193120
10. Aladaileh, M.A., et al.: Effectiveness of an entropy-based approach for detecting low- and high-rate DDoS attacks against the SDN controller: experimental analysis. Appl. Sci. (Switz.) **13**(2), 775 (2023). https://doi.org/10.3390/app13020775
11. Tonkal, Ö., Polat, H., Başaran, E., Cömert, Z., Kocaoğlu, R.: Machine learning approach equipped with neighbourhood component analysis for ddos attack detection in software-defined networking. Electron. (Switz.) **10**(11), 1227 (2021). https://doi.org/10.3390/electronics10111227
12. Ahuja, N., Singal, G., Mukhopadhyay, D.: DDOS attack SDN Dataset. Mendeley Data V1 (2020)
13. Ahuja, N., Singal, G., Mukhopadhyay, D., Kumar, N.: Automated DDOS attack detection in software defined networking. J. Netw. Comput. Appl. **187**, 103108 (2021). https://doi.org/10.1016/j.jnca.2021.103108

Tree Topologies and Node Covers for Efficient Communication in Wireless Sensor Networks

D. Angel[1](✉) ⓘ, R. Mary Jeya Jothi[2] ⓘ, and M. Vidhya[1]

[1] Department of Mathematics, Sathyabama Institute of Science and Technology, Chennai, Tamil Nadu, India
angel.zara1001@gmail.com
[2] Division of Mathematics, Saveetha School of Engineering, SIMATS, Chennai, Tamil Nadu, India

Abstract. Locating positions of the sensors is a primary concern for WSNs as these are susceptible to multiple forms of attacks. The problem of detecting the position of placement of sensor nodes so that the entire communication area is covered is called the sensor deployment problem. This problem is equivalently the classical NP-complete optimization graph problem called the node cover. The node cover problem finds application across a range of WSN scenarios, including sensor deployment and the monitoring of communication links. In this paper, the node coverage and link coverage problems are solved in tree-based networks and the exact values of the node and edge covers for trees such as n-centipedes, paths, stars, spike trees and banana trees are determined. Furthermore, a use case of node cover within WSNs is presented in the context of disaster response and emergency management in earthquake early warning systems.

Keywords: Node cover · tree-based topologies · wireless sensor networks · graph theory

1 Introduction and Background

Wireless Sensor Networks (WSNs) serve as infrastructure-free networks and are susceptible to multiple forms of attacks, such as eavesdropping and spoofing. Deploying sensors (monitors) at the secure points to oversee communication links is a crucial measure against these threats. Additionally, deploying monitors offers the advantage of establishing a virtual communication backbone, enhancing network efficiency [14]. Graph theory forms a robust basis for addressing the evolving challenges in WSNs, particularly through the utilization of the node cover concept [2, 5, 6]. For basic definitions in graph theory [16] is referred. Node cover sets play a pivotal role in optimizing the deployment of sensor nodes in a WSN. The objective is to position sensor nodes in a way that they collectively form a node cover, guaranteeing that every area of interest within the network's coverage area is monitored. By optimizing the node cover, backup paths can be established, reducing the risk of network disruptions in the event of link failures. This is essential for maximizing the effectiveness of the WSN.

Network topologies play a critical role in the performance and efficiency of various network systems, including wireless sensor networks, computer networks, and communication networks. A network topology diagram provides a visual depiction of a

A. Verma et al. (Eds.): ANTIC 2023, CCIS 2091, pp. 205–214, 2024.
https://doi.org/10.1007/978-3-031-64064-3_15

network's devices, interconnections, and communication pathways, offering a way to visualize the interconnectedness of devices and their communication within the network. Provides an overview of various topology control algorithms found in the existing literature [15]. Tree-based topologies are the most convenient model in comparison to a ring or concentric circle networks or other network topologies. Additionally, tree-based structures enable the definition of a node neighborhood in a network where there is a bidirectional information exchange and the deployed nodes can be modeled by a set of points V representing nodes and lines E representing links. The trees are structures such that data flows are feasible between any pair of nodes. Moreover, the communication range is larger than maximum node distance. In WSN applications that involve event detection or monitoring, tree-based structures ensure efficient data transmission and reporting [7]. When an event occurs, data is forwarded up the tree, and the central sink node can quickly identify and process the information, facilitating timely responses.

The concept of optimizing the utilization of sensor nodes to mitigate energy depletion within the network has captured the attention of researchers and scientists. [1, 4]. Recently, the sensor deployment problem was solved using the revised versions of the Particle Swarm Optimization (PSO) algorithm in [3]. Construction of a Secure Tree-Based Coverage Scheme for Wireless Sensor Networks was obtained in [9]. Node cover problem has been studied for certain tree-based structures, like, X-trees, 1-sibling trees, slim trees, k-rooted sibling trees and hyper trees [8]. Algorithms that incorporate breadth-first search trees for vertex cover in wireless sensor networks serve for both link monitoring and routing purposes were proposed in [11]. [12] has introduced a distributed and localized algorithm designed to identify a vertex cover within distributed systems. An algorithm for improving scalability and fault tolerance within a tree topology is presented in [13]. Vertex cover on the basis of sensor deployment algorithm to find utmost number of sensors with optimal sensor positioning was suggested in [17]. Using the vertex cover, message-passing techniques were analyzed in [19]. A detailed review of the distributed algorithms on node cover problem is provided in [18]. The number of guards required for successfully defending a graph was reviewed and summarized in [20]. This paper investigates the significance of the node cover concept in the context of tree-based networks such as n-centipedes, paths, stars, spike trees and banana trees.

2   Node Cover Set

A node cover **S** for a graph is a subset of vertices in which every is covered by at least one node in S, that is $S \subseteq V$ and for all $e \in E$, one has $u \in S$ or $v \in S$ where e is the edge connecting the node pair u and v. The node cover problem is to identify a cover with the least possible size and $|S|$ is called the node covering number $\beta(G)$. For the example graph in Fig. 1, the red colored nodes form the node cover set and so the node covering number $\beta(G) = 3$. On the other hand, a link cover set is a set of links or lines in a network that cover all the nodes of its network. The link cover of the least possible size is called the link covering number $\beta'(G)$. For the graph in Fig. 2, the blue colored links form the link cove set and so the link covering number $\beta'(G) = 3$.

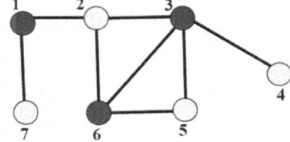

Fig. 1. Least possible node cover set = $\{1, 3, 6\}$

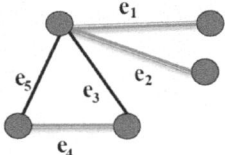

Fig. 2. Link cover set of least size = $\{e_1, e_2, e_5\}$

3 Tree-Based Structures

A tree is a graph with no cycles with a unique path between any two nodes. Trees are commonly used in communication networks for efficient routing and data transmission. A tree structure can facilitate efficient data distribution, as information flows from the root node to the leaves (end nodes) along unique paths. This can help in reducing data collisions and congestion in the network, making trees a suitable choice for organizing network topologies in scenarios like broadcasting, multicasting, and routing in hierarchical network architectures [10]. In this section various trees like centipedes, spike trees, paths, stars and banana trees are considered. The strategic selection of the node cover set for tree-based topologies (refer Fig. 3) can significantly improve the performance and reliability of tree-based networks in terms of coverage, reduced energy consumption, and fault tolerance.

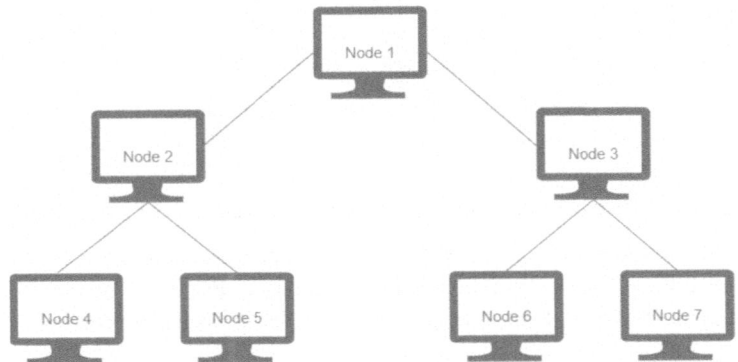

Fig. 3. A Tree Topology with Least Node Cover Set = $\{Node2, Node3\}$

Theorem 3.1. If T is a tree containing a perfect matching, then $\beta(T) = \beta'(T) =$ half of the number of nodes in T.

Proof. Assume that G T has a perfect matching. Since T is bipartite, by Konig's Theorem [16], the node covering and the independence numbers of T are the same. By our assumption, G T has a perfect matching, that implies the matching number equals half the number of nodes in T. Since a perfect matching is always a least link cover and by applying Gallai's Theorem [16], $\beta'(T) = \beta(T) = \frac{n}{2}$.

Initially, Theorem 3.1 is applied for trees with perfect matching which are considered in the next two sections.

3.1 n-Centipede Graph

A caterpillar is a n-leaf tree for which any leaf is at a distance exactly one from a central path called spine. A n-centipede is a n-leaf caterpillar, in which the edges incident to the leaves produces a perfect matching. In other words, the n-centipede is the tree on $2n$ nodes and $2n - 1$ edges obtained by joining the bottoms of n copies of the path graph P_2 laid in a row with edges. The following theorem shows that n-centipede graph satisfies the equality $\beta(G) = \beta'(G)$. A 5-centipede graph is shown in Fig. 4 and 3-centipede graph as a bus topology in Fig. 5.

Fig. 4. 5-centipede graph

Fig. 5. 3-centipede graph as a bus topology

Theorem 3.2.1. Every centipede with 2n number of vertices has $\beta(G) = \beta'(G) = $ n.

Proof. Let G be a centipede graph. As G contains a perfect matching for all n, the proof of this result follows from Theorem 3.1. For example, in Fig. 6, the node covering set of a 5-centipede graph on 10 vertices is denoted by the red colored vertices.

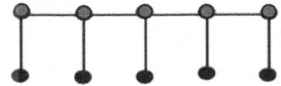

Fig. 6. β(5-centipede) = 5

3.2 Spike Trees

A spike tree is a tree with a perfect matching obtained from an arbitrary tree T by adding a pendent edge to each vertex of T. The following example (refer Fig. 7(a) and Fig. 7(b)) shows how a spike is constructed from an arbitrary tree by adding a pendent edge. The red colored nodes in Fig. 7(b) are the nodes formed by these pendent edges. The exact value of the node covering number and the relation between node cover and link cover on spike trees are explained in the results below.

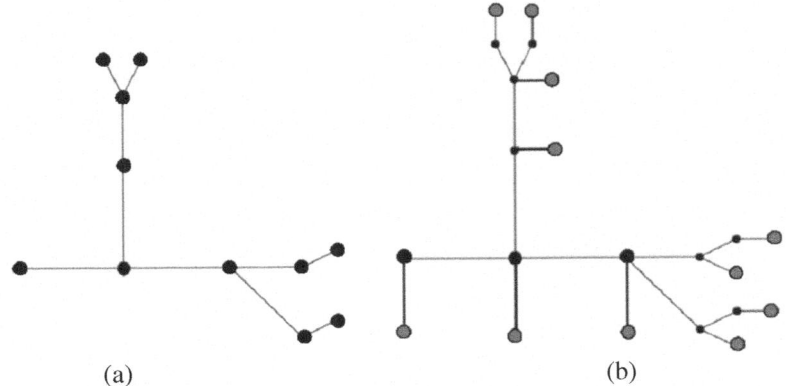

(a)   (b)

Fig. 7. (a) An arbitrary tree topology. (b) Sike tree of Fig. 7(a)

Theorem 3.3.1. If T is a spike tree then $\beta(T) = \frac{n}{2}$.

Proof. Given that T is a spike tree. Since by construction spike trees are trees with a perfect matching and T is bipartite by Theorem 3.1, $\beta(T) = \frac{n}{2}$

Theorem 3.3.2. If T is any tree, then $\beta'(T) \geq \beta(T)$. Equality holds if T is a spike tree.

Proof. To prove: $\beta'(T) \geq \beta(T)$, if T is any tree. Suppose if $\beta'(T) < \beta(T)$. Then $\beta'(T) < |V| - \alpha(T)$. Thus $\beta'(T) + \alpha(T) < |V|$. This is not possible, as T is bipartite. Hence $\beta'(T) \geq \beta(T)$ for any tree T. Suppose if T is a spike tree, then T contains a perfect matching. Hence from Theorem 3.1, $\beta(T) = \beta'(T)$.

In the following section certain trees which contain both a near perfect matching and a perfect matching are considered. A path graph P_n is an example for such a tree.

3.3 Path Graphs

Paths are fundamental concepts in graph theory with many applications (see Fig. 8 and Fig. 9). A path graph P_n is a tree that can be drawn so that all of its vertices and edges lie on a single straight line. It is a tree with two vertices of degree 1, and the other $n - 2$ vertices of degree 2. The length of a path is the number of edges in that path and the length can be zero for the case of a single vertex. Path graphs with even length contains perfect matching whereas paths of odd length contain near perfect matching.

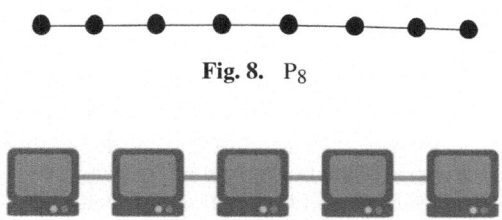

Fig. 8. P_8

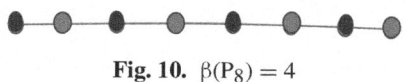

Fig. 9. P_5 as a line topology

Theorem 3.4.1. If G is a path graph P_n then $\beta(G) = \frac{|V|}{2}$ for all n.

Proof. Let G be a path graph P_n. If n is even then G contains a perfect matching. Therefore, by Theorem 3.1, $\beta(G) = \frac{|V|}{2}$. If n is odd, then P_n contains a near perfect matching. This implies $\beta'(G) = \alpha(G) = \frac{|V|}{2}$ and so $\beta(G) = \frac{|V|}{2}$. Hence for all n, $\beta(G) = \frac{|V|}{2}$. For example, in Fig. 10, the node covering set of a path graph on 8 vertices is denoted by the red colored vertices.

Fig. 10. $\beta(P_8) = 4$

Theorem 3.4.2. If G is a path graph P_n, with even number of vertices then, $\beta(G) = \beta'(G)$.

Proof. Let G be a path graph P_n, with even number of vertices, then P_n will contain a perfect matching. Since P_n is bipartite, by Theorem 3.1 we have, $\beta(G) = \beta'(G)$.

Theorem 3.4.3. Let G be a path graph P_n, having odd number of vertices then, $\beta'(G) = \beta(G) + 1$.

Proof. Let G be a path graph P_n. If n is odd, then P_n contains a near perfect matching. Hence $\beta'(G) = \beta(G) + 1$.

3.4 Star Topology

A star topology is the fastest tree structure and is most popular in WSN. The star topology S_n of order n, where $n \geq 1$ is a tree on n nodes with one node having degree $n - 1$ and the other $n - 1$ nodes having degree 1. The star S_n is therefore isomorphic to the complete bipartite topology $K_{1,n-1}$. These are trees with no perfect matching [8]. A star topology with 9 nodes is shown in Fig. 11 and stars as tree topology in Fig. 12. The purpose of employing a star topology is to mitigate the consequences of a line failure by establishing a connection between all existing systems and a central node or hub.

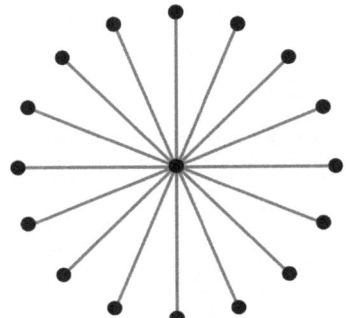

Fig. 11. Star graph with 16 vertices

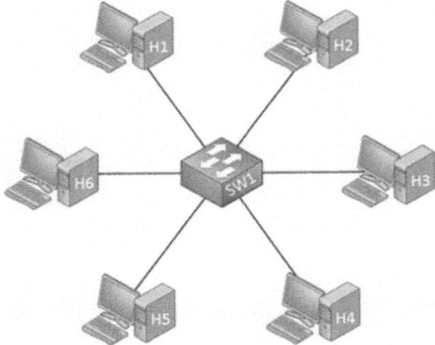

Fig. 12. Star graph with 9 vertices

Theorem 3.5.1. Let T be a tree with $n > 1$, then $\beta(T) = 1$, if and only if T is a star.

Proof. Let T be a star. To prove: $\beta(T) = 1$. Since all the edges of T are incident on the middle vertex, we have $\beta(T) = 1$. Conversely let $\beta(T) = 1$. To prove: T is a star graph. Since $\beta(T) = 1$, and $n > 1$, T must be a complete bipartite graph $K_{1,n}$, which is isomorphic to the star graph S_n.

Theorem 3.5.2. Let T be a tree. Then $\beta'(T) = n - 1$ if and only if T is a Star where n is the number of nodes of T.

Proof. Let T be a star. Since all the edges of T are incident on a single middle vertex, $\beta'(T) = n - 1$. Conversely, let $\beta'(T) = n - 1$. This implies that the minimum edge cover set contains all the edges of T which means that T must be a star.

We now define a banana tree which is obtained from a star graph.

3.5 (n, k)-Banana Tree

An (n, k)-banana tree, is a graph obtained by connecting one leaf of each of n copies of a k-star graph with a single root vertex that is distinct from all the stars. A banana tree of $(3, 5)$ dimension is shown in Fig. 13 and a banana tree with $(2, 4)$ dimension as a tree topology in Fig. 14.

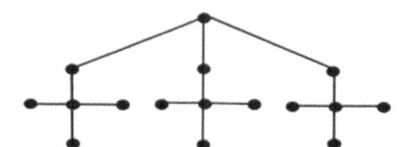

Fig. 13. $(3, 5)$-banana tree

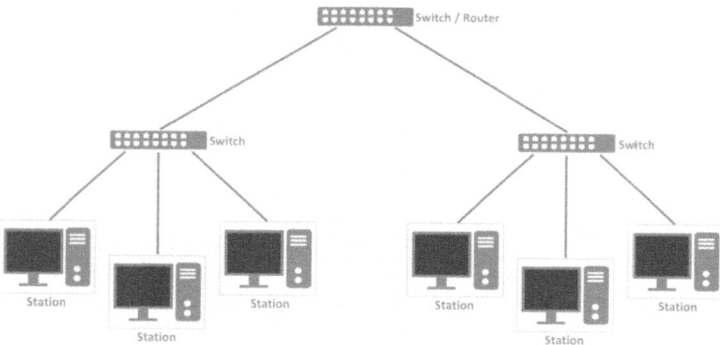

Fig. 14. $(2, 4)$-banana tree as a communication network

Theorem 3.6.1. Let G be a (n, k)-banana tree, then for all n and k, (i) $\beta(G) = n + 1$ (ii) $\beta'(G) = n(k - 1)$ (Fig. 14).

Proof. Let G be a (n, k)-banana tree. Case (i) Suppose $\beta(G) \neq n+1$. Then $\beta(G) < n+1$ say $\beta(G) = n$ or $\beta(G) > n + 1$ say $\beta(G) = n + 2$. But these cases are not possible as the least node cover set of G consists of $n + 1$ vertices. This is because to cover all the edges of G we choose one vertex from each copy of a k-star and the common vertex connecting all k-stars. Thus $\beta(G) = n + 1$. Case (ii) Similarly, to find the least link cover, we choose $k - 1$ edges from each k-star to cover all the vertices of G. There are n copies of k-star and hence $\beta'(G) = n(k - 1)$ for all n, k.

4   Application of Node Cover in Earthquake Early Warning Systems

One specific application of a node cover in WSNs is in disaster response and emergency management, particularly for earthquake early warning systems. In earthquake-prone regions, WSNs are deployed to detect seismic activities and provide early warning signals to minimize the impact of earthquakes on communities. Node cover strategies play a vital role in ensuring reliable and widespread communication within the network. When an earthquake is detected, the sensors (placed on the positions given by a proficiently structured node cover set) collect data about its magnitude and location, and this information is transmitted through a resilient network to a central server. The early warning system then generates alerts that are sent to residents, government agencies, and first responders, allowing for timely evacuation and response measures. The node cover strategy ensures the reliability and fault tolerance of the WSN, ensuring that critical seismic data reaches the intended recipients during moments of crisis.

5 Conclusion

In this paper, the node covering and link covering numbers are determined for certain tree-based topologies. Solving the NP-Complete node cover problem is equivalently the sensor deployment problem. Although there are many algorithms in the existing literature that address this issue, determining the precise values of the least node covers remains an unresolved challenge for tree-based topologies found in WSNs. The results in this paper present an exact solution for obtaining the smallest node cover set on trees. The findings of this research not only contribute to the understanding of network optimization but also provide valuable insights for network engineers and designers, by highlighting the advantages of node cover sets in tree-based networks. Additionally, an instance of utilizing node cover in WSNs is demonstrated within the domain of earthquake early warning systems, specifically in the context of disaster response and emergency management.

References

1. Barthwal, S., Pundir, S., Wazid, M., Singh, D.P., Pundir, S.: Design of an energy aware cluster-based routing scheme to minimize energy consumption in wireless sensor networks. In: Woungang, I., Dhurandher, S.K., Pattanaik, K.K., Verma, A., Verma, P. (eds.) ANTIC 2022. CCIS, vol. 1797, pp. 16–28. Springer, Cham (2023). https://doi.org/10.1007/978-3-031-28180-8_2
2. Angel, D.: Protection of medical information systems against cyber attacks: a graph theoretical approach. Wirel. Pers. Commun. **126**, 3455–3464 (2022)
3. Yarinezhad, R., Hashemi, S.N.: A sensor deployment approach for target coverage problem in wireless sensor networks. J. Ambient Intell. Humanized Comput. **14**, 5941–5956 (2023)
4. Chitnis, R., Cormode, G.: Towards a theory of parameterized streaming algorithms. In: 14th International Symposium on Parameterized and Exact Computation, IPEC 2019, 11–13 September 2019, Munich, Germany, vol. 7, pp. 1–15 (2019)
5. Angel, D.: Weak vertex cover problem in certain non-regular graphs. Procedia Comput. Sci. **143**, 235–241 (2018)
6. Mary Jeya Jothi, R.: Cyclic structure of triangular grid graphs using SSP. Int. J. Pure Appl. Math. **109**(9), 46–53 (2016)
7. Fiaz, M., Yousaf, R., Hanfi, M., Asif, W., Qureshi, H.K., Rajarajan, M.: Adding the reliability on tree based topology construction algorithms for wireless sensor networks. Wirel. Pers. Commun. **74**, 989–1004 (2014)

8. Angel, D.: A graph theoretical approach for node covering in tree-based architectures and its application to bioinformatics. Network Model. Anal. Health Inf. Bioinform. **8**(12), 1–8 (2019)
9. Memon, I., Kumar, P., Memon, N.A., Chowdhry, B.S.: Secure coverage tree construction scheme for wireless sensor networks. Wirel. Pers. Commun. **82**, 659–674 (2015)
10. Hasheminejad, E., Barati, H.: A reliable tree-based data aggregation method in wireless sensor networks. Peer-to-Peer Network. Appl. **14**, 873–887 (2021)
11. Yigit, Y., Akram, V.K., Dagdeviren, O.: Breadth-first search tree integrated vertex cover algorithms for link monitoring and routing in wireless sensor networks. Comput. Netw. **194**, 108144 (2021)
12. Akram, V.K., Ugurlu, O.: A localized distributed algorithm for vertex cover problem. J. Comput. Sci. **58**, 101518 (2022)
13. Jiang, W., Wu, X., Song, M., Qin, J., Jia, Z.: A scalable Byzantine fault tolerance algorithm based on a tree topology network. IEEE Access **11**, 33509–33519 (2023). https://doi.org/10.1109/ACCESS.2023.3264011
14. Dagdeviren, Z.A.: A metaheuristic algorithm for vertex cover based link monitoring and backbone formation in wireless ad hoc networks. Exp. Syst. Appl. **213**, 118919 (2023). https://doi.org/10.1016/j.eswa.2022.118919
15. Singla, P., Munjal, A.: Topology control algorithms for wireless sensor networks: a review. Wirel. Pers. Commun. **113**, 2363–2385 (2020)
16. Harary, F.: Graph Theory, pp. ix, 274. Addison-Wesley. Cambridge University Press, 03 November 2016
17. Pavithra, R., Arivudainambi, D.: Coverage-aware sensor deployment and scheduling in target-based wireless sensor network. Wirel. Pers. Commun. **130**(1), 421–448 (2023)
18. Ileri, C.U., Ural, A., Dagdeviren, O., Kavalci, V.: On vertex cover problems in distributed systems. In: Advanced Methods for Complex Network Analysis, pp. 1–29 (2016)
19. Weigt, M., Zhou, H.-J.: Message passing for vertex covers, Physical review. Physi. Rev. Stat. Nonlinear Soft Matter Phys. **74**(4), 46110 (2006)
20. Klostermeyer, W.F., Mynhardt, C.M.: Protecting a Graph with Mobile Guards, arXiv (Cornell University), pp. 1–29, 201 (2014)

Binary Computation Offloading in Edge Computing Using Deep Reinforcement Learning

Dipankar Rajwar and Dinesh Kumar[(✉)]

National Institute of Technology Jamshedpur, Adityapur, Jamshedpur, Jharkhand 831014, India
dineshkumar.cse@nitjsr.ac.in

Abstract. As data-driven applications become increasingly prevalent, traditional cloud computing faces challenges such as latency and operational costs. Edge computing solves these issues by using nearby servers for real-time processing. However, determining the optimal offloading strategy remains complex. This paper investigates a Deep Reinforcement Learning (DRL)-based binary offloading strategy for edge computing in mobile environments. DRL combines reinforcement learning and deep neural networks to adapt to real-time data and diverse environmental conditions. Experimental study demonstrates the effectiveness of the proposed approach over local and remote execution in terms of total overhead and energy consumption.

Keywords: Edge Computing · Computation Offloading · Deep Reinforcement Learning

1 Introduction

In this era of technological advancement, where we are having increasing dependency towards mobile devices and data driven applications, the traditional approach of cloud computing face difficulties while addressing issues like latency, energy consumption, operational costs etc. Edge computing has emerged as a solution by offering innovative ways to overcome these challenges [1]. Unlike Cloud computing, Edge computing uses nearby servers (present at network's edge) instead of far-off data centers. This strategic placement reduces latency, enables real-time processing, and improves overall system efficiency. While edge computing effectively addresses those issues, figuring out the most efficient data processing strategy remains a complex challenge.

Edge computing has many applications such as IoT, Autonomous Vehicles, Manufacturing Industry and Healthcare [2]. As edge computing continues to evolve and find applications across industries, the importance of having a effective offloading strategy continues to grow. This means deciding whether to distribute jobs to edge servers or handle them on local mobile devices. This is because it ultimately improves the overall efficiency of the system.

Use of Deep reinforcement learning can be an effective approach for the offloading decision making. In Deep reinforcement learning, reinforcement learning principles combines with deep neural network to provide intelligence in this process of offloading decision making in several ways [3]. DRL models can adjust decision-making strategies based on real-time data and changing environmental conditions. This adaptability is critical in dynamic edge environments. They also learn to make decisions that optimize different goals, such as minimizing latency, saving energy, or improving resource efficiency. They can consider multiple variables at once to make informed choices. DRL models can continuously learn and improve their decision-making capabilities as new scenarios arise. This makes them well-suited for evolving edge computing environments. DRL can also be used to allocate computing resources efficiently. For instance, it can dynamically assign edge servers to specific tasks based on workload and performance requirements. DRL can balance the workload across edge nodes by redistributing tasks, ensuring optimal utilization of resources and preventing overloading of any specific node.

The outline of the remaining paper is as follows. Section 2 discusses the related work. Problem formulation and system model is presented in Sect. 3. In Sect. 4, the proposed approach for offloading is presented followed by experimental study in Sect. 5. Section 6 concludes the paper.

2 Related Work

With the increasing applications of edge computing, researchers have shown a lot of interest in finding the perfect offloading strategy for edge computation environments. Authors in [4] proposed a user-centered joint optimization loading scheme to minimize delay cost, energy cost, and price cost. The authors have modeled the optimization problem as a mixed integer nonlinear programming problem. To solve the problem, they have proposed a branch and bound algorithm based on linear relaxation improvement. Considering the complexity of the algorithm, they have also proposed a particle swarm optimization algorithm based on 0–1 and weight improvement. Authors in [5] proposed an optimal binary computational offloading decision-making strategy. To solve the problem, the authors have used reinforcement learning. They have considered end devices as their reinforcement learning agent, which makes the offloading decision, i.e. whether to offload their computational tasks to the edge servers or not. In [6], authors have considered an MEC system, in which every mobile device has multiple tasks, to offload, to the edge server. They have considered overall offloading cost in terms of energy cost, computation cost, delay cost and proposed a Deep-Q Network (DQN) based task offloading and resource allocation algorithm for the MEC. In a similar work, authors in [7] developed a strategy for task offloading for a system with multiple devices and multiple servers. They formulate an overhead optimization problem aiming to optimize the delay and energy consumption of the system. A Double Deep Q Network (Double-DQN) algorithm has been proposed in the work to perform location selection strategies for computational tasks of the mobile devices and allocating computing resources respectively. In the study proposed in [8] a multi-user Mobile Edge Computing (MEC) scenario featuring an MEC server where user devices (UEs) can decide whether to send their tasks to the MEC server via a wireless access point has been examined. To achieve optimal Quality of Service (QoS) and minimize overall system costs, the authors have defined the objective as minimizing the sum of task delays and energy consumption across all

UEs. They have introduced a dynamic optimization algorithm based on Ant Colony Optimization (ACO) to jointly optimize the UEs' task offloading decisions and the allocation of computing resources on the MEC server. In [9], authors have also focused on a multi-user MEC network powered by Wireless Power Transfer (WPT). Instead of minimizing the cost, the authors have chosen to maximize the total computation rate of all devices while considering energy constraints. They achieve this by jointly optimizing the choice of computing modes (local or remote) for each device and the allocation of transmission time. They first find the optimal time allocation assuming the computing node is fixed, then they use a coordinate descent method to optimize the mode selection. To handle large networks, they introduced a scalable joint optimization method based on the alternating direction method of multipliers (ADMM). A smart offloading strategy for IoT devices using mobile edge computing (MEC) and energy harvesting (EH) has been proposed in [10]. They employ Reinforcement Learning (RL) to help IoT devices decide when and how to offload tasks based on factors like battery level, past communication rates, and expected harvested energy. They also introduce a deep reinforcement learning (Deep RL) approach to speed up the learning process. Authors in [11] shows the effectiveness of Reinforcement learning for resource allocation in a multi-user wireless MEC system, considering both short-term and long-term goals in the paper. They have examined a multi-user Mobile Edge Computing (MEC) system, where multiple user devices (UEs) can offload computations wirelessly to an MEC server. They have taken delay and energy consumption as factors of cost and the objective was to minimize the combined cost for all UEs. To address this challenge, they propose an RL-based optimization framework for resource allocation in wireless MEC as Reinforcement Learning (RL) accounts not only for immediate rewards but also for long-term objectives, which is crucial in dynamic systems like our multi-user wireless MEC system.

3 Problem Formulation

3.1 System Model

Let us consider a user-centric edge computational model, where there is total N number of mobile devices or users. The mobile users can interact with edge servers through a communication channel. These mobile devices typically refer to a wide range of portable devices, such as IoT devices, smartphones, embedded systems, etc. The intention is to use the processing capabilities of the edge server, located at the network's edge, to execute offloaded computational duties from these mobile devices in a manner such that, overall system efficiency increases.

The mobile devices have limited computation power as compared to the edge server's computation power, where computation power of the ith mobile device is represented as cp_i, where $i = 1, 2, 3 \ldots, N$. Each of the mobile devices have independent computation task t_i, needed to be performed. At a particular instance, size of a particular task t_i is denoted as ts_i, whereas cc_i represents the number of CPU cycles required to complete that particular task t_i, $i = 1, 2, 3 \ldots, N$. Each of the mobile devices or users can either execute the task locally or they can perform offloading of their computational task to the edge server. Edge servers have certain computation power and can perform computation tasks offloaded by mobile devices. The edge server's computation power is represented by cp_e. Figure 1 shows the task offloading process in edge computing environment.

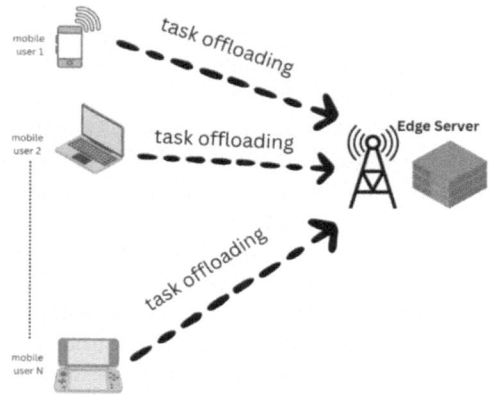

Fig. 1. Task Offloading in Edge Computing Environment

3.2 Cost of Offloading

If a task is offloaded, the cost associated with offloading the task is calculated based on several factors, including transmission time, execution time, energy consumption, and price cost. When mobile devices offload computation tasks to edge servers, then the energy consumption associated with transmitting data from mobile devices to edge server or other components of the edge computation environment is known as transmission power (p_{tm}). It is measured in terms of milliWatts (mW) and considered as a constant for each of the mobile devices in this case. The rate by which data is transmitted from mobile devices to edge server, known as transmission rate (r_{tm}), is calculated based on the Signal to Noise Ratio (*SNR*) of the communication channel. SNR represents the ratio of the power of the transmitted signal to the power of background noise and interference. The determination of SNR also requires three important parameters of the communication channel which are Channel Bandwidth, Channel Noise and Channel gain.

Channel Bandwidth determines the available capacity of data transmission. Channel Noise accounts for the presence of random noise in the communication channel and Channel Gain models the attenuation or path loss of the transmitted signal based on distance.

Value of SNR can be calculated using the Eq. (1), where p_{tm} represents Transmission Power, whereas G, B and N is used to represent Channel Gain, Channel Bandwidth and Channel Noise respectively.

$$\text{SNR} = 10 * \log 10 \left[\frac{p_{tm} \times \text{G} \times \text{B}}{\text{N} \times \text{B}} \right] \tag{1}$$

Transmission Rate, which will be used further to compute transmission time, can be determined from Signal to Noise Ratio using Eq. (2).

$$r_{tm} = 10 \times log_2(1 + SNR) \tag{2}$$

Transmission time (t_{tm}) represents the time required for transmitting the task data from the mobile device to the edge server as shown in Eq. (3).

$$t_{tm} = \frac{ts_i}{r_{tm}} \tag{3}$$

From the above equation, transmission time is determined using task size (ts_i) and *transmission rate* (r_{tm}).

Once the task is transmitted to the edge server, the task is executed on the edge server. The time required for executing the task on the edge server is known as execution time (t_{ex}). The execution time is determined using the value of number of CPU cycles required for executing the offloaded task and edge server's computation power. The same is showing using Eq. (4).

$$t_{ex} = \frac{cc_i}{cp_e} \tag{4}$$

Execution time is calculated by the above equation, where cc_i represents the number of CPU cycles required for executing the offloaded task t_i and cp_e represents edge server's computation power. So, the total delay incurred when tasks are offloaded to edge server is the total of transmission delay and execution delay as shown in Eq. (5).

$$delay \; cost = t_{tm} + t_{ex} \tag{5}$$

The energy consumed during the transmission of the task data is represented by E_{tm}. It is calculated using Eq. (6)

$$E_{tm} = p_{tm} \times t_{tm} \tag{6}$$

While the energy consumed during the execution of the task on the edge server, is calculated Eq. (7)

$$E_{ex} = p_{ex_i} \times t_{ex} \tag{7}$$

In the above equation, p_{ex_i} represents the ideal power consumption during execution.

The total energy consumed during the entire task execution is represented by energy cost and is calculated Eq. (8).

$$energy \; cost = E_{tm} + E_{ex} \tag{8}$$

The price cost is calculated based on the assigned computation power (cp_i) to the task and a base price factor (P_{base}). It is given in Eq. (9).

$$price \; cost = \frac{t_{ex} \times P_{base} \times cp_i}{cc_{slow}} \tag{9}$$

where cp_i represents assigned computation power to the task t_i and cc_{slow} represents slowest cpu cycle in the above equation.

3.3 Cost of Local Computing

If a task is executed locally, the cost is calculated based on two factors, 'delay' and 'energy' for each of the mobile user's devices. The delay in local execution is primarily due to the time it takes to complete the computation task on the mobile device's CPU. The duration of this delay depends on the computing power of the mobile device and the complexity of the task (number of CPU cycles required to complete the task). The cost of delay for each of the mobile user is calculated as shown in Eq. (10).

$$delay\ cost = \frac{cc_i}{cp_i} \tag{10}$$

The energy cost represents the energy consumed during task execution. It is calculated based on the computing power, the number of CPU cycles, and the effective switched capacitance. Effective switched capacitance is used as a constant (k) to model the energy consumption of mobile devices when they perform computation tasks or switch states. The energy cost of the ith mobile user is calculates using Eq. (11).

$$energy\ cost = k \times cp_i \times cc_i \tag{11}$$

When a task is executed locally, there is no explicit price cost associated with offloading to an edge server. Therefore, the price cost remains zero in this case.

3.4 Total Overhead

Total Overhead represents a cost metric, that quantifies the overall cost associated with offloading computation tasks in an edge computation environment. It is calculated as a weighted sum of three components: delay cost, energy cost, and price cost for each of the mobile devices. The same is given in Eq. (12).

$$Total\ overhead = \sum_{i=1}^{N} (\delta \times C\_D_i + \varepsilon \times C\_E_i + \rho \times C\_P_i) \tag{12}$$

Total overhead is determined from the above equation, where δ, ε and ρ represent delay factor, energy factor and price factor respectively whereas C_D_i, C_E_i and C_P_i symbolizes delay cost, energy cost, and price cost respectively.

Total overhead is used as a key factor in decision-making processes to optimize the performance and efficiency of edge computation systems. The main objective is to make informed decisions about when and where to offload computation tasks in an edge computing environment by calculating and considering total overhead.

4 Proposed Work

Reinforcement learning is a type of machine learning that simulates human learning through trial and error [12]. Unlike supervised learning, where the model is trained on labeled data, and unsupervised learning, where the model looks for patterns in the data without explicit guidance, reinforcement learning works in an interactive setting. In Reinforcement Learning, the learner, also known as an agent, learns how to make a series of decisions in its environment to maximize its overall reward. The agent or the decision-maker performs an action that influences the current situation or configuration, also known as a state of the environment. The environment responds with new states and rewards, which is a numerical value that indicates how good or bad the agent's action was in that particular state. The agent's objective is to learn a policy that maximizes the expected cumulative reward. These unique characteristics allow Reinforcement Learning to excel in scenarios where decisions must be made in real-time based on environmental feedback [13].

In Deep reinforcement learning, reinforcement learning principles combine with deep neural networks to provide intelligence in this process of offloading decision-making [13]. These neural networks, often referred to as Deep Q-Networks (DQNs) or deep policies, allow the agent to learn complex mappings from states to actions. The neural network takes the state as input and produces Q-values for each possible action. The action with the highest Q-value is selected by the agent.

In our case, the Open-AI Gym library has been used to define the Edge computing environment. The most important parameters of reinforcement learning, state, action, and reward are defined in this edge environment class.

The state or the observation space is a tuple of box spaces containing three components for each mobile user. The first component represents the computation power of the mobile devices (GHz), where the computation power of a mobile device i is given by cp_i. So the first component looks like $[cp_1, cp_2 \ldots, cp_3]$. The second component stands for the Data size of the task (KB). ts_i Represents the task size of the mobile device i, which makes the second component like $[ts_1, ts_2 \ldots, ts_3]$ and the last component of the observation space represent number of CPU cycles required for the task (Megacycles). The number of CPU cycles required for the task t_i is given by cc_i. Combining these three components, the observation space or the state vector can be shown using Eq. (13).

$$S_N = [cp_1, cp_2 \ldots, cp_n, ts_1, ts_2 \ldots, ts_N, cc_1, cc_2 \ldots, cc_N] \tag{13}$$

The action space is defined as a multi-discrete space as per OpenAI Gym documentation and consists of three parts for each mobile user. The first part of this space is an offloading decision vector, consisting of binary values, that describes whether to offload the task to the edge servers or to execute that locally. The second part of the vector represents the assigned transmission rate to each of the mobile devices. The third part corresponds to the assigned computation power on the edge server to the offloaded tasks. Other environmental parameters are considered constant which include base price, effective switched capacitance, transmission power, ideal power, channel noise, delay factor, energy factor, and cost factor.

The agent is initialized with parameters like discount rate ($\alpha = 0.97$), learning rate ($\gamma = 0.2$), exploration rate (0.5), etc. The discount rate is used for prioritizing immediate rewards over future rewards. The learning rate controls how much the agent adjusts its Q-values based on new information whereas the exploration rate determines the probability of the agent taking a random action instead of the best-known action. The agent takes the state as an input and returns the predicted action. The reward is calculated as the improvement in overhead compared to the local execution overhead. It is a ratio of the difference between local and total overhead to the local overhead. At any instance for a particular state-action pair, the reward $R_{(s,a)}$ is given in Eq. (14).

$$R_{(s,a)} = \frac{overhead_{local} - overhead_{(s,a)}}{overhead_{local}} \tag{14}$$

As our goal is to minimize the cost or overhead of the overall system, from the above-mentioned equation we can easily understand that minimizing the overhead will eventually maximize the reward.

Two neural network models have been used for training the model by Q-value approximation and predicting actions. These models represent the agent's Q-networks for decision-making. The neural network has an input layer with the shape of the state space and the output layer has the shape same as the action space and linear activation.

The action to be taken is based on the epsilon-greedy policy. It calculates both a greedy action and a random action, and the agent chooses between them based on the exploration rate (eps). Action with a greater Q-value is chosen. Some modifications are also made to the action vector to ensure that offloading decisions and resource allocations are valid. Figure 2 shows the working of Deep Reinforcement model.

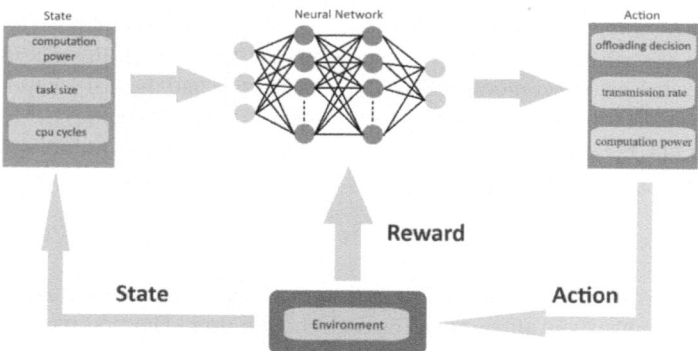

Fig. 2. Deep Reinforcement model

During the training of the model, it takes an experience tuple containing the current state, action, next state, reward, and whether the episode is done. The Q-values for the current state are updated using the Q-values of the next state and the reward using the Q-learning update rule. The same is given in Eq. (15).

$$Q(s, a) \leftarrow (1 - \alpha) \times Q(s, a) + \alpha \times \left(r + \gamma \times max_{a'}Q(s', a')\right) \tag{15}$$

r is the immediate reward, s' is the next state reached after taking action a in state s. a' is the action chosen in the next state s', such that it maximizes $Q(s', a')$.

This update rule helps the Q-values converge over time to the optimal Q-values, which represent the maximum expected cumulative rewards for each state-action pair in the environment.

5   Results and Analysis

The proposed work has been compared with the scenarios where all the mobile devices have executed their task locally and where all of the mobile devices has offloaded their task to the edge server. We have taken mobile devices ranging from 3 to 20. Our model has minimized the total overhead significantly as compared to complete local execution and complete remote execution. This increases our system efficiency, improves the performance which eventually makes our system more energy efficient as well. Table 1 shows all the parameters and their values considered in this work.

Table 1. List of parameters with corresponding values.

Parameters	Value/Setting
Slowest cpu cycle (cc_{slow})	1 GHz
Base price (P_{base})	1
Effective switched capacitance (k)	1e-27
Transmission power (p_{tm})	0.1 Watts
Ideal power (p_{ex_i})	0.01 Watts
Channel bandwidth (B)	10 MHz
Channel gain (G)	$130 + 30 * \log2d$
Channel noise (N)	$2 * 10e\text{-}13$
Delay factor (δ)	1
Energy factor (ε)	1
Cost factor (ρ)	1
Computing power (cp_i)	[0.5–1] GHz
task size (ts_i)	[300–500] Kb
number of cpu cycles (cc_i)	[900–1100] Megacycles
Discount rate (α)	0.97
Learning rate (γ)	0.2
Exploration rate	0.5

These parameter values are typically chosen to create a realistic and balanced simulation environment. The value of delay factor, energy factor, and cost factor are considered as 1, implying that minimizing task delay, minimizing energy consumption, and cost optimization are given equal importance as other optimization objectives. A discount rate of 0.97 is used during the reinforcement learning process to prioritize near-term rewards. This rate affects the agent's decision-making process by influencing its sensitivity to future rewards. The learning rate (γ) of 0.2 is chosen to maintain a balance between stability and adaptability in the learning process. An exploration rate of 0.5 is used to ensure that the agent continues to explore new possibilities while also utilizing its current knowledge. Table 2 shows the overheads for different number of users for three different execution scenarios.

Table 2. Overheads for different number of users for three different execution scenarios

No. of mobile devices	Complete Local Execution	Hybrid Execution	Complete Remote Execution
3	5.9108	2.341720	3.931380
5	10.107544	4.745476	7.641994
8	16.27713	7.873118	14.875279
10	19.502755	15.419163	19.777391
15	29.271232	16.413512	37.813463
20	39.226723	29.567279	60.899460

The data provided in the above table shows the overhead values for different numbers of mobile devices (Number of Mobile Devices) under three different execution scenarios: Complete Local Execution, Hybrid Execution, and Complete Remote Execution.

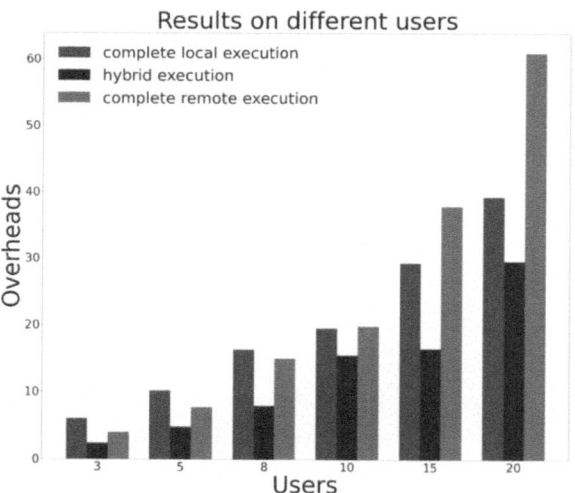

Fig. 3. Total Overhead vs number of mobile users

In the bar graph shown in Fig. 3, we have taken 3, 5, 8, 10, 15 and 20 number of mobile users and compared the overall system overhead for complete local execution, hybrid execution, and complete remote execution. The overhead for hybrid execution is less as compared to complete local execution and complete remote execution. Figure 4 shows the line graph representing the total overhead vs number of mobile users.

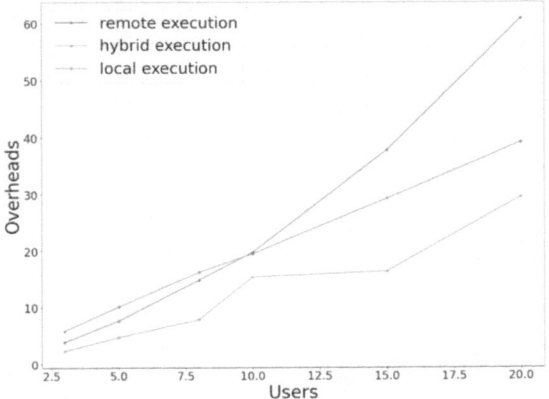

Fig. 4. Total overhead vs number of users

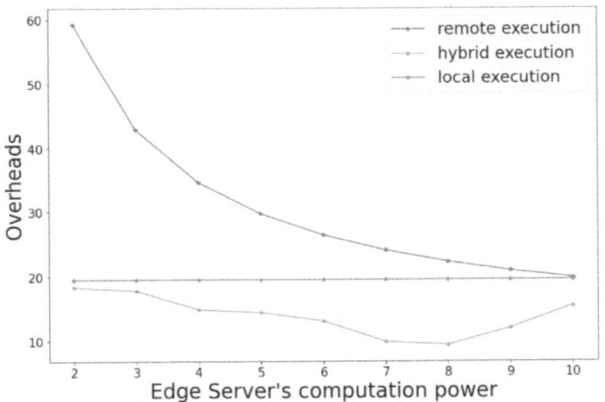

Fig. 5. Overheads with increasing Edge Server's computation power

In Fig. 5, we have compared total overheads of complete remote execution, hybrid execution and complete local execution against edge servers' computation power, where we have taken the number of mobile devices $= 10$. We can see in the graph that overheads for complete local execution remain constant with an increase in the edge server's computation power as all the mobile devices execute their task locally. It also implies that local execution is independent of the edge server's system parameters. In the case of complete remote execution, with higher computation power, the edge server can process tasks faster. Faster computation at the edge server also means reduced energy consumption during task execution which leads to a decrease in the total overhead. While increasing edge server computation power reduces the processing time and energy consumption, it can also lead to an increase in price cost. Users may offload more tasks, and the price cost, which depends on the amount of computational power allocated, may rise accordingly. That's why in the case of hybrid execution, initially overhead decreased with the increase of the edge server's computation power but later it increased for some time, yet our model is capable of maintaining a smaller value of overhead as compared to completely local execution and completely remote execution. However, the exact impact on the total overhead may depend on the specific characteristics of the RL-based offloading policies and how users adapt their offloading decisions in response to the increased computational capacity of the edge server.

6   Conclusion

This paper explores an effective deep reinforcement learning based offloading strategy for mobile devices in edge computing environment. Our research proposes the concept of "total overhead", which is an accumulated cost of delay, energy consumption, and price is used for evaluating the performance and efficiency of edge computing systems. It acts as the guiding principle throughout the framework for making decisions. To find the effectiveness of our proposed approach, we have done extensive testing using various numbers of mobile devices. We compared our deep reinforcement learning-based offloading strategy, referred to as "Hybrid Execution," with two baseline scenarios: complete local execution, where all tasks are processed on the mobile devices locally, and complete remote execution, where all tasks are offloaded to the edge servers and executed there. Our results shows that our Hybrid Execution approach significantly minimizes the total overhead compared to the other two scenarios. By achieving this reduction in overhead, our model enhances efficiency of the system, improves the overall performance, and enhances energy efficiency. This showcases the practical benefits of using deep reinforcement learning based offloading strategies for edge computing.

References

1. Liu, F., Tang, G., Li, Y., Cai, Z., Zhang, X., Zhou, T.: A survey on edge computing systems and tools. Proc. IEEE (2019). https://doi.org/10.1109/JPROC.2019.2920341
2. Yu, W., et al.: A survey on the edge computing for the internet of things (2017). https://doi.org/10.1109/ACCESS.2017.2778504
3. Tran-Dang, H., Bhardwaj, S., Rahim, T., Musaddiq, A., Kim, D.-S.: Reinforcement learning based resource management for fog computing environment: literature review, challenges, and open issues. J. Commun. Netw. 24, 83–98(2022). https://doi.org/10.23919/jcn.2021.000041
4. Deng, X., Sun, Z., Li, D., Luo, J., Wan, S.: User-centric computation offloading for edge computing. IEEE Internet Things J. 8, 12559–12568 (2021). https://doi.org/10.1109/JIOT.2021.3057694
5. Hossain, M.S., Nwakanma, C.I., Lee, J.M., Kim, D.S.: Edge computational task offloading scheme using reinforcement learning for IIoT scenario. ICT Express 6 (2020). https://doi.org/10.1016/j.icte.2020.06.002
6. Huang, L., Feng, X., Zhang, C., Qian, L., Wu, Y.: Deep reinforcement learning-based joint task offloading and bandwidth allocation for multi-user mobile edge computing. Digit. Commun. Netw. **5**, 10–17 (2019). https://doi.org/10.1016/j.dcan.2018.10.003
7. Fang, J., Zhang, M., Ye, Z., Shi, J., Wei, J.: Smart collaborative optimizations strategy for mobile edge computing based on deep reinforcement learning. Comput. Electr. Eng. **96** (2021). https://doi.org/10.1016/j.compeleceng.2021.107539

8. Pham, Q.V., Leanh, T., Tran, N.H., Park, B.J., Hong, C.S.: Decentralized computation offloading and resource allocation for mobile-edge computing: a matching game approach. IEEE Access **6** (2018). https://doi.org/10.1109/ACCESS.2018.2882800

9. Bi, S., Zhang, Y.J.: Computation rate maximization for wireless powered mobile-edge computing with binary computation offloading. IEEE Trans. Wirel. Commun. **17** (2018). https://doi.org/10.1109/TWC.2018.2821664

10. Min, M., Xiao, L., Chen, Y., Cheng, P., Wu, D., Zhuang, W.: Learning-based computation offloading for IoT devices with energy harvesting. IEEE Trans. Veh. Technol. **68** (2019). https://doi.org/10.1109/TVT.2018.2890685

11. Li, J., Gao, H., Lv, T., Lu, Y.: Deep reinforcement learning based computation offloading and resource allocation for MEC. In: IEEE Wireless Communications and Networking Conference, WCNC (2018). https://doi.org/10.1109/WCNC.2018.8377343

12. Luong, N.C., et al.: Applications of deep reinforcement learning in communications and networking: a survey (2019). https://doi.org/10.1109/COMST.2019.2916583

13. Gronauer, S., Diepold, K.: Multi-agent deep reinforcement learning: a survey. Artif. Intell. Rev. **55** (2022). https://doi.org/10.1007/s10462-021-09996-w

Data Agent-Based Volumetric Progress Monitoring over Mobile Ad-Hoc Network in Disaster Management

Pranjal Tiwari, K. K. Pattanaik$^{(\boxtimes)}$, and Garima Nain

Department of Information Technology, ABV-IIITM, Gwalior, India
kkpatnaik@iiitm.ac.in

Abstract. Post disaster rescue operations are usually undertaken in a severely constrained communication environment, often leading to difficulties in coordination among various machineries. This work proposes an autonomous data agent-based automation of post disaster progress monitoring of volumetric activities over Mobile Ad-hoc NETwork (MANET) by leveraging WiFi Direct communication functionalities. This approach enables efficient and reliable communication among rescue teams, facilitating coordination and information exchange in challenging post disaster scenarios. The proposed work enables a Light Detection and Ranging (LIDAR)-based volumetric analysis with minimal computing overhead. A mobile application for Android 11 demonstrated the practical applicability of the proposed system.

Keywords: Post disaster management · Data Agent · LIDAR · WiFi Direct and Legacy WiFi · Wireless sensor network

1 Introduction

Disasters like earthquakes and landslides can severely impact the availability and reliability of communication networks [1,2]. This, inturn, hinders emergency response efforts and problematizes coordination among disaster management authorities in post disaster management and rescuing [3]. Post-disaster management in a region with massive volumetric shifting involves various activities such as pothole filling and clearing displaced soil or debris [4,5]. Figure 1 shows the various post disaster phases and among them the current work focuses on the debris removal and clearance. The progress of the work is measured in terms of volumetric analysis.

In the absence of communication, the in-activity volumetric progress monitoring and reporting requires manual efforts, wherein the supervisor must physically traverse each affected region to collect and document information on the ongoing volumetric activities and developments [3,6]. The traditional reporting

This work is supported by the Science and Engineering Research Board (SERB) under the Grant MTR/2021/000354.

A. Verma et al. (Eds.): ANTIC 2023, CCIS 2091, pp. 228–244, 2024.
https://doi.org/10.1007/978-3-031-64064-3_17

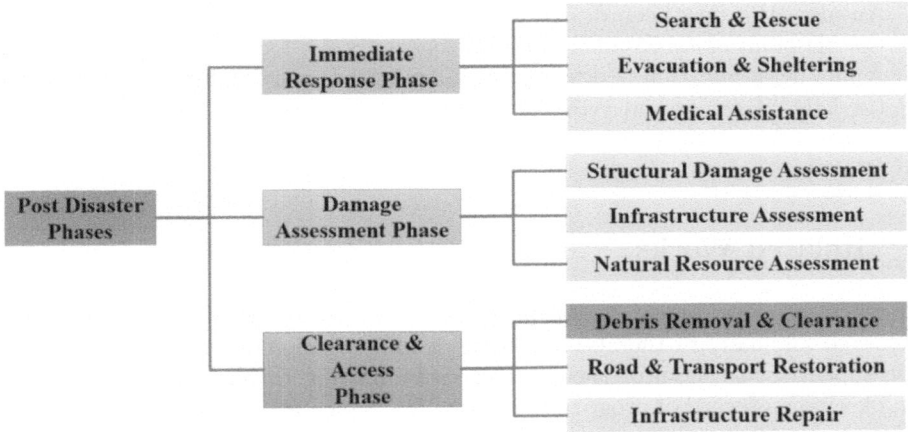

Fig. 1. Post Disaster Phases

approach to these activities is time-consuming, labor-intensive, and prone to delays and inaccuracies.

Wherein, accomplishing post disaster rescue operations requires efficient coordination and real-time information exchange between rescuers and the supervision authority to maximize the effectiveness of relief efforts [2,5,7]. It has become a worldwide challenge for rescuers to automate the process of reporting the progress to central authorities or supervisors at the rescue site.

Therefore, this work aims to provide an autonomous framework to monitor and report the progress of post disaster volumetric activities such as debris removal and clearance under the availability of minimal resources (like smartphones) with rescuers.

In this context, technology has played a pivotal role in managing post disaster rescue operations, and one promising approach is using data agents [8–10]. These data agents work specifically to perform a particular activity autonomously. They can be designed to capture the volumetric progress of the digging activity at different regions in post disaster management scenarios. This work explores the concept of a Finite State Automaton (FSA)-based Autonomous Data Agent (ADA) over WiFi Direct-enabled Mobile Ad-hoc NETworks (MANET) [11,12] to reduce the physical efforts of the supervisor in post disaster rescue operations. The volumetric progress of debris removal and clearance is performed through the topography scanned by Light Detection and Ranging (LIDAR) [13,17] scanners available on smartphones nowadays. LIDAR technology provides the accurate 3D point cloud of a scanned region.

The key contributions of this work are:

– Developed an FSA-based ADA for the automated volumetric progress analysis in post disaster management.

– An algorithm has been designed to determine the volumetric analysis using the 3D point cloud from the LIDAR sensor.
– A mobile application is developed on Android 11 smartphones enabled with the LIDAR sensor and WiFi Direct technology to demonstrate the practical applicability of the proposed automated progress supervision in post disaster scenarios.

2   Related Works

Supervising the progress of the post disaster debris removal and clearance is achieved manually in the absence of the communication system [7]. It requires the supervisor to monitor these activities by moving through different regions and keeping a record of progress in each region, which is tedious. Although satellite communication exists, those devices have limitations like high cost, heavy, bulky, difficult to operate, and high battery consumption. It has become a worldwide challenge for rescuers to automate the process of reporting the progress to central authorities at the rescue site. Kamruzzaman et al. [2] presented the benefits of wireless communication technology and IoT sensors in post disaster management. A MANET is the best fit to tackle this communication gap. It takes advantage of the rescuers available at the rescue site carrying a smartphone device with the minimal required resources. For instance, [1], and Rawat et al. [3] proposed using WiFi Direct in the disaster management application over an Android platform. This work indicates the transmission efficiency and accuracy of the WiFi Direct, an infrastructure-less MANET [11,12], over other communication modes. Thus, WiFi Direct [1,14] has been adopted as an efficient communication mode in this work.

In addition, the literature includes LIDAR-based Volumetric Measurements for applications such as salt stockpile inventory management [13], wherein the LIDAR-generated 3D point cloud data is used to determine the volumetric calculation of an object or elevated surface. Zieba-Kulawik et al. [15] monitored the urban forests using a LIDAR sensor. Some researchers, such as [16], created a fusion of the 3D LIDAR and color camera to provide a colorful 3D real-world scene representation. The calibration of the camera and LIDAR sensor is important in autonomous driving, topographical scanning, object detection, etc. This work utilizes the LIDAR [13,17] sensor for depth analysis, i.e., the volume of the debris removed and cleared. Each rescue site is divided into different regions, wherein each region has a Group Owner (GO) or Co-supervisor, and all other devices in that group are Group Clients (GCs). The GCs capture a region with the smartphone LIDAR sensor and forward it to the GO or Co-supervisor. A co-supervisor collects data and calculates the progress by merging the data of different GCs in a particular region and communicates with another Co-supervisor of different regions through the Legacy WiFi access point.

Dube et al. [14] and Necsulescu et al. [11] proposes a routing algorithm based on the neighboring node's signal strength. This is an on-demand routing algorithm that uses signal strength and location stability to find the most stable path from the source to the sink node. After peer-to-peer communication, routing is the major concern for MANETs. In implementing this routing algorithm, two routing tables are maintained; the first is the Signal Stability (SS) Table, and the other is the routing table. These tables help in finding the most stable neighbor of a node for further transmission.

Autonomous data agents (ADAs) [8,9] have been used in Wireless Sensor Networks (WSNs) [18] for data analysis, such as the monitoring of tunnel disasters autonomously without human intervention. This work is based on the interpersonal interaction behavior of ADA to bridge the gap between technology and humans. This proposed setup is capable of perceiving its environment and raising alerts during disasters in the tunnel. This intends to use ADAs deployed over MANETs, which can play a critical role in post disaster rescue operations for automated real-time data sharing and analysis, even without traditional communication infrastructure. The use of ADAs over Android devices enabled with the LIDAR sensor and WiFi Direct technology reduces the need for remote data collection and reliance on human supervision of remote sites.

The literature suggests that, individually, different researchers have done several types of research on WiFi Direct-based MANETs, ADAs, and LIDAR technology. However, designing an ADA over MANET to capture the volumetric progress of the digging activity through a 3D point cloud LIDAR input at different regions is yet to be achieved.

3 Autonomous Data Agent for Volumetric Progress Monitoring

An Autonomous Data Agent (ADA) is an intelligent software agent designed to perform data processing, analysis, and management tasks autonomously without human intervention. ADAs can work independently or collaboratively with other agents to perform complex tasks, challenging for human operators to complete manually with higher efficiency and reliability. They can process gigantic amounts of data, operate continuously in real-time data analysis, and adapt to new environments, addressing suitability to applications requiring timely and accurate data insights. This section proposes the functionalities of an ADA for volumetric progress detection.

3.1 Finite State Automaton (FSA)

Finite State Automaton (FSA) [19] is a machine with certain rules following the transition from one state to another to recognize patterns based on predefined conditions and transitions. It can be represented using five symbols: Q, σ, δ, Q_0, F, where these represent a set of states, a set of input symbols, the transition function, initial state, and a set of represents final states, respectively.

Figure 2 represents a FSA with five states and seven transitions where $Q = \{Q_0, Q_1, Q_2, Q_3, Q_4\}$, $\sigma = \{a, b, c, d, x, y\}$, and Q_2 represents the final state of this automaton. The state transition function δ is given below:

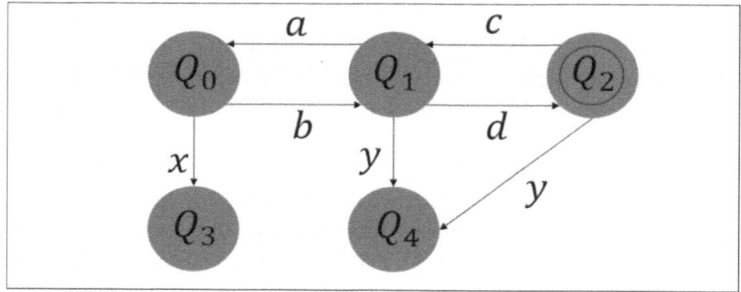

Fig. 2. Finite State Automaton

$$\delta = \begin{cases} \delta_1(Q_0, b, Q_1), Q_i = Q_0, b \in \sigma \\ \delta_2(Q_0, x, Q_3), Q_i = Q_0, x \in \sigma \\ \delta_3(Q_1, d, Q_2), Q_i = Q_1, d \in \sigma \\ \delta_4(Q_1, y, Q_4), Q_i = Q_1, y \in \sigma \\ \delta_5(Q_1, a, Q_0), Q_i = Q_1, a \in \sigma \\ \delta_5(Q_2, c, Q_1), Q_i = Q_2, c \in \sigma \\ \delta_5(Q_2, y, Q_4), Q_i = Q_2, y \in \sigma \end{cases} \quad (1)$$

FSA plays a significant role in defining a data agent with finite capabilities or functionalities. The transition function in FSA is equivalent to the triggering events in an ADA, where the data agent switches its states on the occurrence of a certain event. The states of FSA represent the state of the data agent, and the transitions are equivalent to the actions taken against any event.

3.2   FSA-Based ADA

The proposed ADA in this work is based on the FSA to enact an intelligent software agent that performs tasks related to data acquisition, processing, analysis, filtering, classification, and management autonomously through predefined states and events. The FSA acts as a control system that governs the behavior of the ADA based on its internal state and external stimuli.

The deployment of the ADA on the Android platform is done to achieve the volumetric progress of different regions. Different states of this proposed data agent are Capture, Target Identification, Store on Device, Area Comparison, Calibrate Targets, Volumetric Analysis, Calculate Progress, and Update Variables. At each step, an action is performed by getting the input from the previous state and generating the output as input for the next state. The following are the states of the proposed data agent:

- **Capture:** The rescuers carry an Android device with minimal resources and capture the region with the LIDAR sensor deployed in each region. The output of this state is the LIDAR and camera fused 3D Point Cloud. The device

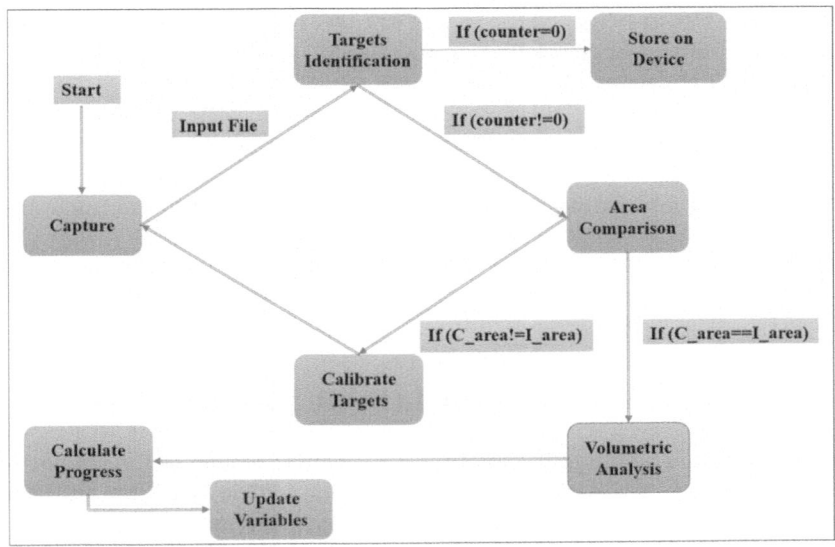

Fig. 3. Design of FSA-based ADA

operator only captures the region of interest with the help of physical targets while capturing the region, and the generated output works as an input to the next state.

- **Target Identification:** This step identifies the region of interest to ensure the accuracy of the volumetric progress of a particular region. This step defines the boundary for the region such the device bearer selects the region of interest.
- **Store on Device:** The relative volumetric calculation requires the reference point to compare the progress at different time instances. The condition "if(counter==0)" corresponds to the availability of reference point cloud data of a particular region.
- **Area Comparison:** The condition "if(counter!=0)" holds *True* for the already available (stored) reference data at the device. The captured area (C_area) is compared with the reference area (I_area) and generates a boolean result for the next step.
- **Calibrate Targets:** If the captured area (C_area) is not the same as the reference area (I_area), i.e., the output of the above state gives the *False* output, it represents the inaccurate target capturing. Hereafter, the user recaptures the region by calibrating physical targets to ensure the accuracy of the overall outcome.
- **Volumetric Analysis:** Once the area comparison (C_area=I_area) event is correct, this stage proceeds to calculate the volume of the excavated site and quantify it. A volumetric analysis algorithm is proposed in this work and tested against the 3D point cloud data.

- **Calculate Progress:** Over a period of time, the relative progress determination is obtained after calculating the volume of a region.
- **Update Variables:** This step involves updating the variables on a data packet transmitted over the network. After updating the variables, the final data packet is transmitted to the next GO. This GO or co-supervisor then repeats the same steps from capturing the region, analyzing volume, updating variables, and forwarding it to the next GO until it reaches the Supervisor.

The proposed FSA-based ADA can operate continuously, allowing for real-time data analysis and processing of the sensory data from the rescue site, which is essential for given applications requiring timely and accurate data insights.

4 Volumetric Analysis over LIDAR Enabled Data

This work proposes a volumetric analysis algorithm to calculate the volume from a LIDAR-generated point cloud (in .las file format). This algorithm also generates the relative volumetric progress from the given input at the regional and cumulative regional levels, which has been depicted in Fig. 4. This algorithm consists of five steps given below:

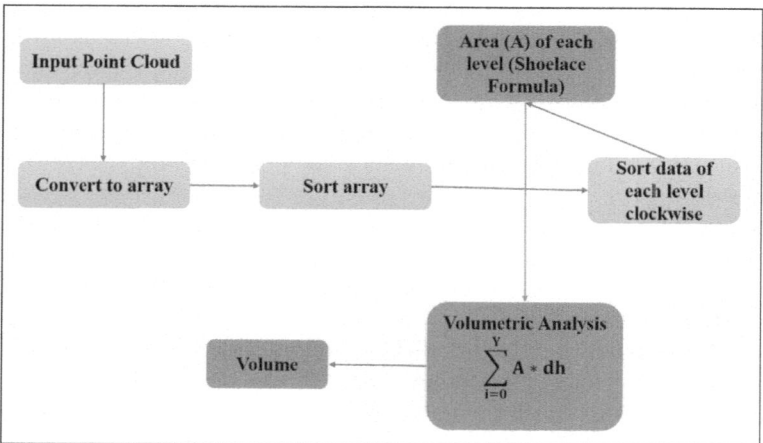

Fig. 4. Volumetric Analysis Algorithm

- **Input Point Cloud:** It is a smartphone-generated LIDAR point cloud that contains numerous points on a 3D cartesian plane. These points can recreate a 3D visualization of the scanned surface or object through the representative point on a 3D plane (point containing its X, Y, & Z coordinates) with additional properties like pixel RGB value, point ID, etc.

- **Convert to Array:** Due to resource limitations and unnecessary attributes, it is not feasible to directly perform any operation on the raw LIDAR sensory data. Therefore, the 3D coordinates (X, Y, and Z) are extracted from Input Point Cloud data and converted into an array.
- **Sort Array:** As the point cloud is a 3D plane, it is assumed that the surface of the data cloud is parallel to the X-Z plane. Therefore, the height of the point cloud increases on the Y axis, wherein the width and length increase on the X and Z axis, respectively. Thus, the 2D array (X-Z plane) is sorted in increasing or decreasing order according to the Y axis for height or depth analysis.
- **Volumetric Analysis:** In the volumetric analysis function, the array is traversed from the low to high level of the Y axis. As the level on the Y axis changes, an area calculation algorithm is called and multiplied with the change in the level. The area of each level is multiplied by the change in height, and by summing up all the volumetric slices from $i = 0$ to $i = y$, the complete volume is calculated.

$$V = \sum_{i=0}^{y} A * dh \qquad (2)$$

where V is the generated output volume, and i is the vertical height given below:

$$dh = (y_{i+1} - y_i) \qquad (3)$$

where y_i represents the level of point surface at the Y axis for $y_i \geq dh \geq 0$, and dh represents the difference between two consecutive levels at the Y axis for given $y_i \geq 0$.

- **Sort Data Clockwise:** The Shoelace formula is used to determine the area of any polygon, and hence, the array elements are sorted in a clockwise direction on the X-Z plane. This sorting ensures the accurate area calculation at each unit level according to the point cloud density.
- **Area of Each Level(A):** To calculate the overall volume of the point cloud, the area at each level is multiplied by the difference in height of two consecutive levels at the X-Z plane. At each level, a polygon is extracted, and the area is calculated using the Shoelace formula, which can calculate the area of any shape.

Shoelace Formula: This formula, also known as Surveyor's formula, calculates the area of a polygon for the given coordinates of its vertices. Its ease of use and accuracy make it a valuable tool for calculating the area of irregular polygons and other shapes that are difficult to measure using traditional methods. It is based on the concept that the area of a polygon can be computed as the sum of the areas of its triangles. The polygon's vertices must be listed in clockwise or counterclockwise order to use the shoelace formula.

The mathematical representation of the shoelace formula is given below:

$$A = \frac{1}{2} \sum_{i=1}^{n} (z_i + z_{i+1})(x_i - x_{i+1}) \qquad (4)$$

where A represents the area of a polygon, and the area is in a plane, so z_i and x_i represent the coordinates on the X-Z plane.

5 Signal Strength-Based Energy Efficient Routing (SSEER)

Signal Strength-based Energy Efficient Routing (SSEER) is the dynamic routing algorithm for MANETs that ensures a stable, energy-efficient, proactive, and shortest path. This algorithm considers the device's power consumption to keep track of a device's availability for packet forwarding. Some essential functionalities of this routing algorithm are described below in detail.

5.1 Remaining Link Attempts (RLA)

Power consumption is the primary concern for MANET protocols since the device loses the battery power during the packet transmission. If the device power is exhausted completely, the interrupt occurs in the routing path. Therefore, Remaining Link Attempts (RLA) defines the maximum number of attempts remaining with the available battery power of a device. It is defined as in Eq. (5) follows:

$$RLA = \frac{P_{rem}}{C_{tx}} \tag{5}$$

where P_{rem} is the device's remaining power in milliamperes (mA) and C_{tx} is the power required to transmit a data packet of unit size successfully. The C_{tx} is further calculated as follows:

$$C_{tx}(dB) = a * PL \tag{6}$$

where C_{tx} is in decibels (dB) and PL stands for path loss, which is a measure of the attenuation of radio waves as they propagate through a medium.

Mathematically, the PL can also be denoted as the local average received signal power at the receiver node relative to the transmission power of the transmission node. The calculation of the transmission cost of a link between two devices is derived from the equation of path loss of radio waves in free space. The equation for path loss given in Eq. (7) is retrieved from [20].

$$PL(dB) = PL(d_0) + 10 * n * log_{10}(\frac{d}{d_0}) \tag{7}$$

where, PL is the path loss in dB, $PL(d_0)$ is the path loss at known distance (d_0), and n is the power law relation between a distance and received power.

To calculate the RLA, the C_{tx} is required in mA, and to convert the C_{tx} from dB to mA, the following formula given in Eq. (8) is used:

$$C_{tx}(mA) = 10^{\frac{\left(C_{tx(dB)} - 30\right)}{10}} \tag{8}$$

5.2   SSEER Data Packet

The data packet required for the SSEER protocol is shown in Fig. 5. In the given data packet design, each field is described as follows:

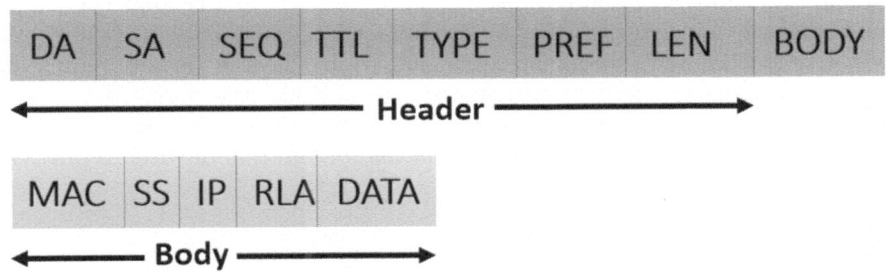

Fig. 5. Data Packet Design

- DA: destination address or the supervisor's address
- SA: source address or address of the devices through which the packet is being transmitted
- SEQ: packet sequence number
- TTL: time to live field, which prevents the redundant or orphan data packet from looping inside the network
- TYPE: determines the type of the message
- LEN: holds the length of the data packet
- CRC: cyclic redundancy check.
- MAC: holds the MAC addresses of the devices in a region, and it is also useful to authenticate the user's devices.
- SS: carries the signal strength table
- IP: holds the IP address of all the devices with respective MAC addresses
- RLA: holds the RLA of all the access points to ensure the stability of the path
- DATA: carries the data to be transmitted

5.3   RLA Table

RLA is an essential factor that allows for keeping track of the status of links between nodes, particularly for portable devices such as smartphones, laptops, and tablets, which rely heavily on battery power. The RLA table records the number of attempts remaining with the available battery. The network routing protocols utilize this information to determine the best path for data transmission between nodes. Additionally, by monitoring the RLAs, the WSN can detect failing or unstable links, and proactive measures can be taken to maintain network connectivity. This improves the overall performance and reliability of the network, ensuring the seamless transmission of data.

5.4   Signal Strength Table

A Signal Strength (SS) table measures and records the strength of signals being transmitted between devices, which helps determine the quality of the connection and ensures that data is transmitted reliably with minimal interference. In a wireless communication network (WiFi, Bluetooth, and cellular networks), signal strength can fluctuate due to various factors, such as distance between devices, obstacles, and interference. A signal strength table visually represents signal strength levels (in dB), allowing users to identify areas with weak signals and optimize network performance. It helps diagnose network issues and make informed decisions regarding the placement and orientation of wireless devices.

Table 1. RLA-SS Table

Host	RLA	SS
x		
y		
z		

Table 1 shows the overall RLA-SS attributes required in the SSEER routing. The Host field stores the IP addresses of host devices, RLA stores the RLA value for the available battery of the device, and the SS field stores the respective signal strength of a device for immediate successor.

6   Results and Analysis

6.1   Experimental Setup

Several ADA-installed Android devices (smartphones) are deployed in a rescue site to set up the post disaster rescue environment. To mimic the real-world scenario, the rescue site is divided into several zones or regions, wherein each region contains an adequate number of rescuers having smartphone devices with the minimal required resources and sensors. Rescuers in each region are further separated into two roles: GOs, who also act as co-supervisors, and GCs are other devices in that region. All the GCs connect to their respective GOs, and GOs are responsible for fetching, merging, and calculating the progress from the data of all the GCs inside their region. These GOs then feed the data to a data packet and forward it to the next available GO. As shown in Fig. 6, each region has a co-supervisor (GO), and other devices in that region act as GCs. There exists a supervisor that gathers information from GOs or co-supervisors. This topology follows two modes of communication for data gathering and packet forwarding

1. *In-group Communication:* This communication exists between GCs available in a region and the co-supervisor (GO) of that particular region. Herein,

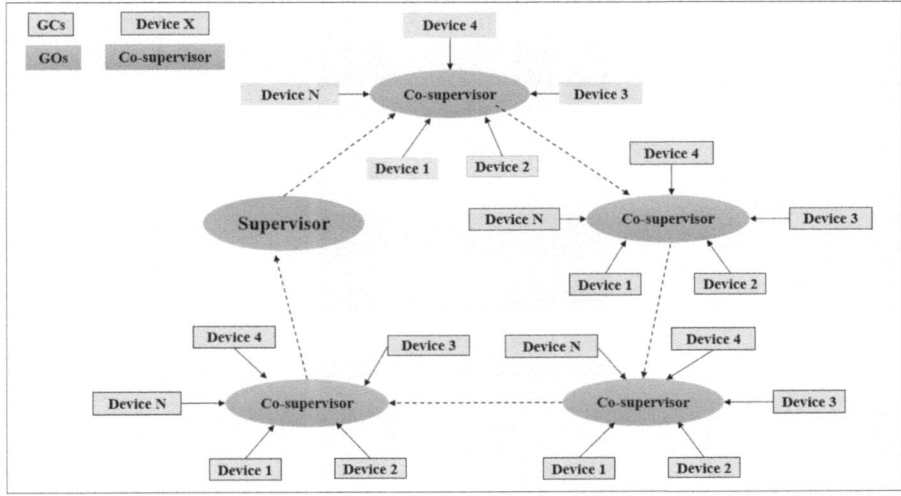

Fig. 6. Device Deployment Topology and Communication

different rescuers (GCs) send their captured data for volumetric analysis to their GO. GCs can communicate with their GOs using WiFi Direct, but communication between GCs in a group is not supported.

2. *Inter-group Communication:* The communication between different GOs comes under this category. Each GO forwards the regional progress to the supervisor. To overcome the technical limitations of WiFi Direct, a Legacy WiFi-based access point is used to achieve Inter-group communication between GOs.

6.2   Simulation Environment

The proposed work covers event monitoring, progress quantification, progress monitoring, and forwarding. An Android application is developed with all the functionalities given above to simulate the proposed work. The graphical user interface of the application is shown in Fig. 7. Apart from the above features, some additional functionalities are given to the users. This application uses two modes of communication to enable smooth packet forwarding throughout the network in a multi-hop manner. The above application supports the following functionalities.

Create Group. The group formation facility is provided by WiFi-Direct technology. The regional Co-supervisor (GO) creates a group and allows devices to connect to the GO, but it does not provide client-to-client and inter-group communication.

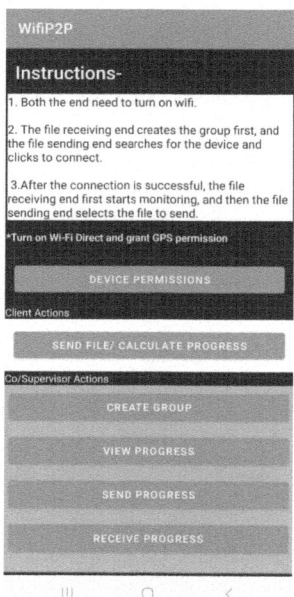

Fig. 7. Developed Android Application GUI

Join Group. Several rescuers are available in a region and can join the group to become a GC. These GCs send their data to the regional Co-supervisor for further processing and calculations.

Upload and Calculate. The regional scanning of digging activity requires the LIDAR-enabled smartphone. After the scanning, a generated point cloud is uploaded to the application for further processing and calculation. This functionality allows the users to calculate the volume and relative progress.

View Progress. This functionality allows the supervisor and co-supervisors to monitor the work progress of each region and the overall cumulative work progress. A dashboard is provided to give more simple user interaction.

Send Progress. It is the functionality of GO. Inter-group communication is established using this to forward the data packet to the next GO. An access point has been implemented to enable inter-group communication using Legacy WiFi technology.

Receive Progress. This is the functionality provided to the GO at the receiving end, wherein the GO receives the progress data from the previous GO or Co-supervisor. The sender turns on its Hotspot, and the receiving end connects to the sender via Legacy WiFi.

6.3 Accuracy of the Volumetric Analysis

The proposed data agent in Fig. 3 is used to determine the accuracy of the volumetric analysis algorithm over several iterations. This section validates the efficacy of the proposed volumetric analysis algorithm. The theoretical (actual) and LIDAR 3D point cloud-based calculated volumes are demarcated for different shapes. Table 2 shows the actual and calculated volumes of two different shapes, i.e., a cube (with the vertices of dimension 6) and a cylinder (with the radius of 6 and height of 6) using different densities of LIDAR 3D point cloud inputs. The accuracy of the proposed algorithm is also specified by comparing it with the actual volumes.

As shown in Table 2, the accuracy of the proposed algorithm for volumetric analysis is really high, as it closely determines the volume of these two shapes. Additionally, the accuracy increases as the 3D point cloud's density increases from 100 to 10,000 points. This suggests that the accuracy of the volumetric analysis is directly proportional to the density of point cloud input.

A similar observation can be made using the covariance analysis among the accuracy and the density of the point cloud. The covariance measures the extent to which two variables in a dataset vary. Mathematically, the covariance between two variables X and Y can be calculated as:

$$cov(X, Y) = E[(X - E[X])(Y - E[Y])] \tag{9}$$

where $E[X]$ and $E[Y]$ represent the means of X and Y, respectively. A positive covariance indicates that the variables tend to increase or decrease together, while a negative covariance indicates that they tend to move in opposite directions.

The following results have been found from volumetric analysis of the cylindrical shape. The μ_x is the mean of the density of the point cloud input, and the μ_y is the mean of the accuracy of the volumetric analysis.

Mean $\mu_x = 2900$

Mean $\mu_y = 99.7935$

Covariance $\sigma_{xy} = 556.4073$

The above covariance σ_{xy} between the density of the point cloud and the accuracy of volumetric analysis is a high positive value. This shows that the point cloud density is directly proportional to the accuracy and highly correlated. As the density increases, accuracy increases, while sparse points may lead to lower accuracy.

Thus, the choice of the density of the point cloud depends on the availability of the computing resources and the requirement of the application in terms of accuracy. Application scenarios with plenty of computing resources and higher accuracy needs can choose higher density of the point cloud such that the calculated volume approaches the actual volume of the shape.

Table 2. Volumetric analysis using proposed algorithm.

Shape	Density of Point Cloud	Actual Volume	Calculated Volume	Accuracy
Cylinder	100	18.85	18.746	99.50
	500		18.812	99.76
	1000		18.831	99.89
	10000		18.85	100
Cube	100	216	216	100
	500		216	100
	1000		216	100
	10000		216	100

6.4 Performance of the Application Developed

The developed application performs well on smartphones enabled with Android 11 and above. Due to resource limitations, the real-time experiment is done on six devices; each group has three devices. One works as a co-supervisor, and the other two work as GCs and report the volumetric progress to that co-supervisor. The progress of these clients is merged by the respective co-supervisor and then forwarded to the next co-supervisor.

Table 3 shows the performance of the application based on power consumption (P_{con}), CPU utilization (CPU_u), memory requirement (M), sender's speed (S_s), and receiver's speed (R_s). All the results have been averaged for the particular scenario.

Table 3. Performance of the application in terms of power consumption, CPU utilization, memory requirement, sender's speed and receiver's speed

	P_{con}	CPU_u (in %)	M (in Mb)	S_s (in Mbps)	R_s (in Mbps)
GC → GO	light	15.76	124.00	4.61	0.1
GO ← GC	medium-light	20.69	142.33	0.03	13.6
GO1 → GO2	medium-light	10.1	146.33	1.53	0
GO2 ← GO1	medium-light	23.13	220.00	0	1.70

GC → GO in Table 3, explains the performance of GC device when it is sending the data to it's GO. GO ← GC explains the performance of GO device when it is receiving the data from one of it's clients. GO1 → GO2 explains the performance of GO1 device when it is sending it's data to the next GO2 and GO2 ← GO1 explains the performance of GO2 device when it is receiving the data from the previous GO1.

Below are some of the key takeaways from Table 3:

– The WiFi Direct communication is much faster than the Legacy WiFi communication technology.

- WiFi Direct communication enables robust infrastructure-less communication using group formation.
- Comparatively, a resource-efficient device is needed as a co-supervisor because of high CPU and memory consumption.
- The WiFi Direct GO device has a higher receiving speed than the GC sending device because the GO has to receive data from N number of devices.
- Power consumption at each activity is minimal.
- The Listening GO 2 device has higher memory and CPU consumption due to Legacy WiFi communication.

These results demonstrate the smooth functioning of the developed application with multiple smartphone devices. It also shows the feasibility of the proposed volumetric analysis of the debris removal and clearance framework in post disaster scenarios using ADA and MANET technology.

7 Conclusion

This work proposes an integration of available smartphone technologies such as WiFi Direct, Legacy WiFi, and LIDAR sensors to perform the volumetric analysis of digging activity in the post disaster rescue operation. The manual efforts of the human supervisor have been reduced by using the proposed ADA designed to perform volumetric analysis from the point cloud input achieved from the LIDAR sensor. The experimental analysis reveals that the accuracy of the volumetric algorithm depends upon the density of the point cloud input. The developed application allows the quantification of the regional as well as overall relative volumetric progress.

The proposed mechanism can be extended to several domains with numerous functionalities. In the future, different monitoring algorithms for concave problems can be deployed over the same network under limited functionalities.

Acknowledgements. This work is supported by the Science and Engineering Research Board (SERB) under the project entitled "Dynamic Bayesian Network model for behavioral study of autonomous data agents" under the Grant no. MTR/2021/000354.

References

1. Alnashwan, R., Hala M.: Disaster management system over Wifi direct. In: 2nd International Conference on Computer Applications & Information Security (ICCAIS), Riyadh, Saudi Arabia (2019)
2. Kamruzzaman, M., Sarkar, N.I., Gutierrez, J. Ray, S.K.: A study of IoT-based post-disaster management. In: International Conference on Information Networking (ICOIN), Da Nang, Vietnam, pp. 406–410 (2017)
3. Rawat, P., Haddad, M., Altman, E.: Towards efficient disaster management: 5G and device to device communication. In: 2nd International Conference on Information and Communication Technologies for Disaster Management (ICT-DM), Rennes, France, pp. 79–87 (2015)

4. Ghaffarian, S., Kerle, N.: Towards post-disaster debris identification for precise damage and recovery assessments from UAV and satellite images. In: The International Archives of the Photogrammetry, Remote Sensing and Spatial Information Sciences (2019)
5. Berktas, N., Bahar Yetis, K., Oya, Ekin K.: Solution methodologies for debris removal in disaster response. EURO J. Comput. Optim. **4**(3–4), 403–445 (2016)
6. Lorca, A., et al.: A decision-support tool for post-disaster debris operations. Procedia Eng. **107**, 154–167 (2015)
7. Aziz, N.,Kamarulzaman, A.: Managing disaster with wireless sensor networks. In: 13th International Conference on Advanced Communication Technology (2011)
8. Bosser, T.: Autonomous Agents: International Encyclopedia of the Social & Behavioral Sciences. Elsevier (2001)
9. Li, G., et al.: A data agent inspired by interpersonal interaction behaviors for wireless sensor networks. IEEE Internet Things J. **9**, 8397–8411 (2022)
10. Verma, A., Pattanaik, K.K.: Multi-agent communication-based train control system for Indian railways: the behavioural analysis. J. Mod. Transp. **23**, 272–286 (2015)
11. Necsulescu, P., Schilling, N.: Signal strength Based MANET routing protocol: cost calculation and performance evaluation. In: 3rd IFAC Symposium on Telematics Applications, International Federation of Automatic Control, Seoul, Korea (2013)
12. Sharma, H.D., Gupta, A.: A survey on wireless ad hoc networks: 1993–2002. In: IETE Technical Review (2003)
13. "Lidar." Wikipedia. https://en.wikipedia.org/w/index.php?title=Lidar&oldid=1149704019. Accessed 18 October 2023
14. Dube, R., et al.: Signal Stability-Based Adaptive Routing (SSA) for Ad Hoc Mobile Networks. In: IEEE Personal Communications (1997)
15. Zieba-Kulawik, K., Skoczylas, K., Wezyk, P., Teller, J., Mustafa, A., Omrani, H.: Monitoring of urban forests using 3D spatial indices based on LiDAR point clouds and voxel approach. Urban For. Urban Greening **65** (2021)
16. Ding, Y., et al.: 3D LiDAR and color camera data fusion. In: IEEE International Symposium on Broadband Multimedia Systems and Broadcasting (2020)
17. Mahlberg, J.A., et al.: Salt stockpile inventory management using LiDAR volumetric measurements. Remote Sens. **14**(19), 4802 (2022)
18. Lee, J.H., et al.: Wi-Fi direct based mobile ad hoc network. In: 2nd International Conference on Computer and Communication Systems (2017)
19. Fiedrich, F., Burghardt, P.: Agent-based systems for disaster management. Commun. ACM **50**(3), 41–42 (2007)
20. Goldhirsh, J., Wolfhard, J. V.: Handbook of Propagation Effects for Vehicular and Personal Mobile Satellite Systems (1998)

Intelligent Computing

Deep Neural Networks for Efficient Image Caption Generation

Riddhi Rai, Navya Shimoga Guruprasad$^{(\boxtimes)}$, and Shreya Sindhu Tumuluru

Ramaiah Institute of Technology, Bangalore, Karnataka, India
navyaprasad06@gmail.com

Abstract. In the era of rapidly advancing technology, the integration of computer vision and natural language processing has emerged as a pivotal area of research, with deep learning playing a central role. The task of generating descriptive textual captions for images is known as image captioning. It is necessary for enhancing accessibility, aiding visually impaired individuals, and improving human-computer interaction by providing meaningful context to visual content. Generating relevant descriptions for high-level image semantics involves not just recognizing objects and scenes but also analyzing the state, attributes, and relationships among them. This research paper investigates the synergy of Convolutional Neural Networks (CNNs) for effective image feature extraction and Long Short-Term Memory (LSTM) networks for capturing sequential dependencies in generating descriptive and coherent textual captions. It has been demonstrated that it can produce precise and contextually relevant descriptions for a variety of images.

Keywords: Image Captioning · Deep Learning · CNN · LSTM

1 Introduction

What is image caption generation?

Image captioning is a fascinating interdisciplinary field that lies at the intersection of computer vision and natural language processing. At its core, image captioning involves generating descriptive textual captions for images, essentially teaching machines to understand and express the content of visual data in human-like language. This task is crucial because it addresses the gap between visual information and textual comprehension, contributing to a more comprehensive and human-like understanding of images.

Importance and Real-World Applications

Solving the image captioning problem holds paramount importance due to its direct implications for real-world applications. Beyond its role in augmenting accessibility for visually impaired individuals, image captioning has found applications in fields such as content indexing, image retrieval, and autonomous systems. In healthcare, it aids in diagnostic image analysis, and in social media, it enhances content search and

A. Verma et al. (Eds.): ANTIC 2023, CCIS 2091, pp. 247–260, 2024.
https://doi.org/10.1007/978-3-031-64064-3_18

recommendation systems. The ability to automatically generate meaningful descriptions for visual content contributes to a more nuanced understanding of images and facilitates seamless integration of visual data into various applications.

Historical Context and Drawbacks

Early attempts at image captioning relied on rule-based approaches and handcrafted features. However, these methods often produced generic and contextually inconsistent captions, lacking the ability to capture intricate visual relationships within images. As a result, the captions often lacked creativity and failed to convey the complete semantics of the image.

What are Deep Neural Networks?

A neural network is considered "deep" when it has multiple hidden layers, giving it the ability to learn complex hierarchical representations of data. The depth of the network allows it to automatically learn features at different levels of abstraction.

Training a deep neural network involves presenting it with labeled training data and adjusting the weights and biases iteratively to minimize the difference between the predicted outputs and the true labels. This process often utilizes optimization algorithms and backpropagation, where the network calculates the gradient of the error and adjusts the parameters accordingly.

Deep neural networks have been applied to a wide range of tasks, including but not limited to: Image and speech recognition, Natural language processing (e.g., language translation, sentiment analysis), Autonomous vehicles, Drug discovery and healthcare, Game playing (e.g., AlphaGo), Financial modeling, Recommender systems.

Role of CNN and LSTM

In addressing these challenges, the integration of Convolutional Neural Networks (CNNs) and Long Short-Term Memory (LSTM) networks has emerged as a transformative approach. CNNs excel in image feature extraction, capturing hierarchical visual representations, while LSTMs effectively model sequential dependencies, allowing for the generation of more contextually coherent captions. This hybrid architecture has proven instrumental in rectifying the drawbacks of earlier methods, enabling the model to better understand and articulate the nuanced details inherent in visual content.

What is CNN?

A Convolutional Neural Network (CNN) is a deep learning algorithm specialized for image recognition and processing tasks. Comprising multiple layers, including convolutional, pooling, and fully connected layers, CNNs excel in extracting features from input images. The pivotal convolutional layers employ filters to discern edges, textures, and shapes, followed by pooling layers that down-sample feature maps, reducing spatial dimensions while preserving essential information. The subsequent fully connected layers contribute to making predictions or classifying images. Trained on extensive labeled image datasets, CNNs learn to recognize patterns associated with specific objects or classes, enabling them to classify new images and extract features for applications like object detection and image segmentation.

What is LSTM?

To address the challenges of Vanishing and Exploding Gradients in Deep Recurrent Neural Networks (RNNs), various adaptations were developed, with one of the most renowned being the Long Short-Term Memory Network (LSTM).

In essence, an LSTM recurrent unit aims to selectively "remember" and "forget" past information encountered by the network, utilizing specialized activation function layers known as "gates" for distinct purposes. Each LSTM unit maintains an Internal Cell State vector, representing retained information from preceding time steps.

Architecture of CNN and LSTM

Convolutional layers: The initial part of the CNN is dedicated to extracting visual features from the input image. Convolutional layers, equipped with filters, analyze the image for edges, textures, and higher-level features.

These layers serve as feature extractors, capturing the hierarchical representations of the visual content.

Pooling Layers: After convolution, pooling layers down-sample the spatial dimensions of the feature maps while retaining the most crucial information. This step helps reduce computational complexity and prevents overfitting.Flattening and transition: The output from the convolutional and pooling layers is flattened into a one-dimensional vector. This vector serves as the input to the sequential part of the model, facilitating the transition from spatial information to sequential data, which is essential for language generation.Sequential Processing (LSTM Layers): LSTM layers are employed to sequentially process the flattened feature vectors. The LSTM units include gates (input, forget, and output gates) that regulate the flow of information through the network. The memory cell in each LSTM unit maintains information about relevant features extracted from the image.

Fully Connected Layers: The output from the LSTM layers is passed through fully connected layers to produce the final caption. These layers transform the sequential representation into a format suitable for generating words. The output layer generates a probability distribution over vocabulary, determining the most likely next word.

2   Related Work

Wang et al. (2016) demonstrates an end-to-end trainable deep bidirectional LSTM image captioning model. The deep CNN and two separate LSTM networks learn long-term visual-language interactions by using past and future context data in a high-level semantic space. This research proposes two completely new deep bidirectional variant models, in which we augment the depth of nonlinearity transition in various ways, to train hierarchical visual-language embeddings. Data augmentation techniques like multi-crop, multi-scale, and vertical mirror are provided in order to prevent overfitting when deep learning models are being trained. Depiction of the development of bidirectional LSTM internal states over time is shown along with the qualitative analysis of how the models 'translate' images to words. The suggested models are tested using three benchmark datasets: the Flickr8K, Flickr30K, and MS COCO datasets for caption creation and image- sentence retrieval tasks.

Ali et al. (2020) explore the fusion of CNN and LSTM to automatically generate textual descriptions for images. The author(s) emphasize the significance of image captioning in various domains, including image retrieval and accessibility for visually impaired individuals. The review also delves into the strengths of CNN and LSTM, as well as attention mechanisms. It surveys benchmark datasets and evaluation metrics commonly used in image captioning research.

Liu et al. (2018), in 'Image Captioning Based on Deep Neural Networks', introduce the representative work of CNN-RNN based and reinforcement-based frameworks as the most effective models. They also define the evaluation metrics and highlight the advantages and key difficulties. High level picture semantics' method for generating meaningful descriptions depends on the ability to analyze the state, attributes, and relationships between these objects. Despite the fact that captioning for images is a difficult and sophisticated task, numerous researchers have achieved significant progress.

Chu et al. (2020) have proposed a methodology to automatically caption photographs with appropriate captions. In this research they introduce a hybrid model called AICRL that can automatically caption images by combining LSTM and ResNet50 with soft attention. There is an encoder-decoder in AICRL. The encoder uses ResNet50, a convolutional neural network- based algorithm that transforms the input picture into a lengthy vector by embedding it. With the use of an LSTM, a recurrent neural network, and a soft attention mechanism, the decoder is created to selectively direct attention over specific areas of a picture in order to forecast future phrases. To increase the likelihood of the target description phrase given the training photos, AICRL was trained across the large dataset MS COCO 2014 and assessed it using a variety of metrics like BLEU, METEOR, and CIDER.

Li et al. (2019) demonstrate that we provide semantic properties that are language-like to models because conventional attention mechanisms find it difficult to distinguish identical visual signals in image captioning, especially when predicting extremely abstract terms (semantic gap between text and visual). Due to their inherent recurring nature and gated operating mechanism, RNN and its variants are the most widely used architectures in picture captioning. However, RNN-like variations become rigid due to their complexity. In this study, a Transformer-based sequence modeling that only consists of attention and feedforward layers is used. Entangled Attention (ETA) is developed, which enables the Transformer to simultaneously use semantic and visual information, to fill the semantic gap. A GCB is additionally suggested to direct the interactions between the multimodal data. This model is known as the ETA-Transformer. Surprisingly, ETA-Transformer performs at a cutting-edge level on the MSCOCO dataset.

Alzubi et al. (2021) use a combination of an inception and a 2-layer LSTM model and the dense layers are then added as part of a custom ensemble model. While the LSTM component learns from the subtitles, the CNN component encodes the images. To evaluate and contrast the results, GRU and Bi-directional LSTM-based models are also used for caption construction. The datasets used for word embedding and image training are GloVe Embeddings and flickr8k, respectively, to produce word vectors for each word in the sequence.Bleu Scores were used to evaluate the outcomes. 55.8% of the Bleu-4 score was obtained using LSTM, GRU, and bi-directional LSTM in the paper.

Kalpana P. D. et al. (2022) present a deep feature extraction and automated image captioning model. The deep properties are extracted first using the inceptionv3 model from the obtained pictures. A hybrid classifier that incorporates the LSTM and RNN deep learning models is then used to simulate the automatic image captioning stage. The collected deep features generated during the feature extraction stage are used to train these two deep learning models. Additionally, we will fine-tune the weight of RNN using a special self-improved SI-RHSO, an upgraded RHSO, to increase the accuracy of Auto Image Captioning.

Vinyals et al. (2015) have outlined a generative model built on a deep recurrent architecture that combines recent developments in computer vision and machine translation to generate meaningful sentences that can be used to describe images. The model's accuracy and the fluency of the language it learns just from visual descriptions are demonstrated through experiments on several datasets. Our method produces a score of 59, which can be compared to human performance of roughly 69, while the current state-of-the-art BLEU-1 score on the Pascal dataset is 25. Additionally, we demonstrate BLEU-1 score increases from 56 to 66 on Flickr30k and from 19 to 28 on SBU. Last but not least, we achieve a BLEU-4 of 27.7 on the recently released COCO dataset, which is the state-of-the-art.

Moses et al. (2016) build a generative CNN-LSTM model that outperforms human baselines by 2.7 BLEU-4 points. Experiments on the MSCOCO dataset show that it generates fair and accurate captions in the great majority of cases and are able to reduce the effects of overfitting by adjusting the hyperparameters with dropout and the number of LSTM layers. They further demonstrate that LSTM hidden state divergences only occur when semantically distant words are emitted, despite different previous contexts having different effects on semantically close emitted words. Now there is semantic meaning in the interaction between trained word embeddings and LSTM hidden states.

Poddar et al. (2020) provide a multi-layered CNN-LSTM neural network model for object recognition and Hindi caption generation. To find the best model and increase the likelihood of the resultant Hindi description, a number of models were additionally trained by altering the number of hidden layers and hyper parameters. Additionally, it was found that our model improved the BLEU score (Unigram) by 34.64% and the BLEU score (Bigram) by 29.13% when compared to earlier work in this field after evaluating the effectiveness of our models.

3 Design and Implementation

An image captioning model which uses the encoder-decoder method to automatically describe images. Using CNN to encode the images, we and later, LSTM, a more powerful RNN, to decode the image vector into a sentence (Fig. 1).

4 Data Preparation and Preprocessing

Here, we use the flickr8k, the dataset that contains a collection of images, each paired with five human-generated captions, resulting in a total of around 40,000 image-caption pairs.

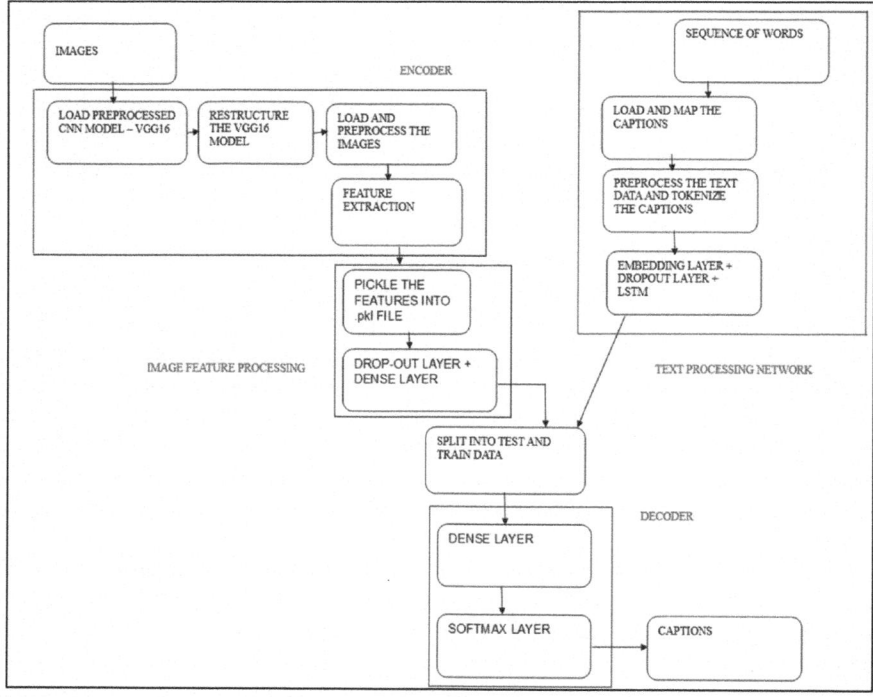

Fig. 1. Proposed Methodology

In this step, we perform the preprocessing using various classes in KERAS which makes sure that:

- The images are resized
- The images are converted to numerical tensors.
- The captions are tokenized into individual words.
- A vocabulary mapping is created
- Truncate the captions to create equal-length sentences.

5 Encoder

To extract the picture characteristics from the training, test, and target images, we used the VGG-16 model (Fully Connected layers) as our encoder in our encoder-decoder model. Each feature that we extract from the convolutional layer represents a specific targeted area of the image.

In our model, we achieve this by using the Keras deep learning framework to load the pre- trained VGG16 model (minus the classification layers). The model is trained on a dataset of image-caption pairings, with the target sequences being the associated captions and the input images being fed into the CNN to extract features. Each pre-processed image is run through the VGG16 model to produce the convolutional feature vector, which is often the result of the final layer of pooling. The final convolutional or pooling layer's output is what is used to represent the image. To get its predicted captions for a given image as near to the actual (ground truth) captions as feasible, the model is trained to minimize a sequence generation loss function, such as cross-entropy loss. The fully connected (Dense) layer with 256 units and a ReLU activation function are used after the dropout layer for regularization and the picture features are input. The result is the features of the encoded image.

6 Pickling

Pickling of image features in image caption generation means storing the pre-processed image representations (features) in a binary file format for later use.

We employ a pre-trained model VGG16 to extract high-level features from the photos for creating our model. Pickling is a way to save these extracted image features into a binary file, which can be loaded and used quickly during training or caption generation without re-computing the features each time. It allows us to save time and computational resources, especially when working with large datasets and complex models.

After obtaining the image features, we save them to a binary file (with the extension. Pkl) using the pickling mechanism in Python. This binary file contains the serialized representation of the image features. The pickled file can be stored on disk, making it easy to access the image features later without recomputing them. During training or caption generation, we can load the pickled file, deserialize the image features, and use them as inputs to the caption generation model, thus avoiding the need to re-run the feature extraction process.

7 Decoder

The Long Short-Term Memory (LSTM) network is utilized as the sequence generation model in an image caption generator to produce captions for the input images. Recurrent neural networks (RNNs) using LSTMs are particularly effective at handling sequential data, such as sentences of natural language. By using LSTM as the sequence generation model, the image caption generator can effectively learn to generate coherent and contextually relevant captions for a wide range of images. LSTMs have the ability to capture the sequential nature of language, making them suitable for the task of generating sequential data like natural language captions.

The words in the captions are represented as word embedding The model can operate with continuous-valued vectors rather than discrete tokens since each word is transferred to a dense vector representation. The decoder processes the sequence data. It takes the input sequence (captions) as input, applies an embedding layer with a mask for handling variable-length sequences, and then applies a dropout layer. Next, it passes through an LSTM layer with 256 units. This LSTM layer processes the sequential data and produces the sequence feature (Fig. 2).

Fig. 2. Pickling Process

8 Training

The model's target output will be the captions, with the picture features serving as its input. By utilizing optimization approaches to change the model's parameters (weights and biases), training aims to reduce this mismatch. The model learns over time to produce more accurate captions by adjusting its parameters periodically using gradient descent and backpropagation. During training, the model is exposed to a large number of images and their related ground truth captions. Over time, the model becomes better at producing captions that more closely resemble those written by humans. As training progresses, the model becomes more capable of generating meaningful and relevant captions for a wide range of images. We define a data generator to provide data in batches, which helps avoid memory issues and improves training efficiency.

9 Caption - Generation

- The image features obtained from VGG16 will be fed into the initial state of the LSTM.
- i.e. We load the pickled image features from the binary file. This process will deserialize the features and load them into memory.
- Given an image for which you want to generate a caption, extract the image features from the loaded list of image features. The image features will serve as the initial hidden state for the LSTM.
- Based on the previously created word and the concealed state, the LSTM will produce a string of words, one at a time. Pass the image feature to the LSTM to generate the caption for the given image.
- During caption generation, the LSTM unrolls for a fixed number of time steps (determined by the maximum caption length or an end-of-sequence token).
- The LSTM predicts the subsequent word at each time step, and the predicted word embedding serves as the input for the following time step.
- Until an end-of-sequence token is generated or the maximum caption length is achieved, the procedure continues.

The LSTM is trained using a dataset of image-caption pairs. The image features serve as the input to the LSTM, and the corresponding captions are the target sequences.

10   Evaluation

Evaluation in the context of an image captioning model describes the process of determining how well the model produces captions for images. The purpose of evaluation is to compare the generated captions to the ground truth (human-provided) captions in order to assess their quality, accuracy, and relevance.

The BLEU (Bilingual Evaluation Understudy) score is employed in the model. By measuring the number of overlapping word sequences, or "n-grams," BLEU compares the generated captions with the reference captions. When compared to the reference captions, it determines how well the n-grams are used in the generated captions.

The degree of precision is determined by how many n-grams in the reference captions and the generated captions are identical. In addition, BLEU takes into account how long the generated captions are in comparison to the reference captions. To prevent favoring short captions, a shortness penalty is imposed to the BLEU score if the generated captions are significantly shorter than the reference captions.

11   Algorithm

1. Import the necessary modules.
2. Include the pictures and captions so the model may be trained and tested.
3. Load pre trained CNN model – VGG16.
4. Restructure the VGG16 model by removing the last layer (Transfer learning model).
5. Load and preprocess images.
6. Feature Extraction and encoding of images: From the preprocessed images, extract features using the VGG16 model and store the features in a dictionary with the image ID as the key. This way the images are encoded.
7. Serialize the features dictionary by using the pickle module.
8. Load the captions data and map each image to its respective caption and store the same in a dictionary with the image ID as the key.
9. Preprocess the text data.
10. Tokenize the data.
11. Separate the dataset into a training and a test set.
12. Decoder:A Dense layer and a softmax activation function is used This layer generates the probability distribution over the vocabulary for each word in the caption.
13. Generates a caption for an input image using a trained image captioning model using a method called "greedy search" to iteratively predict each word of the caption.

The process contains various methods and they are as follows (Fig. 3).

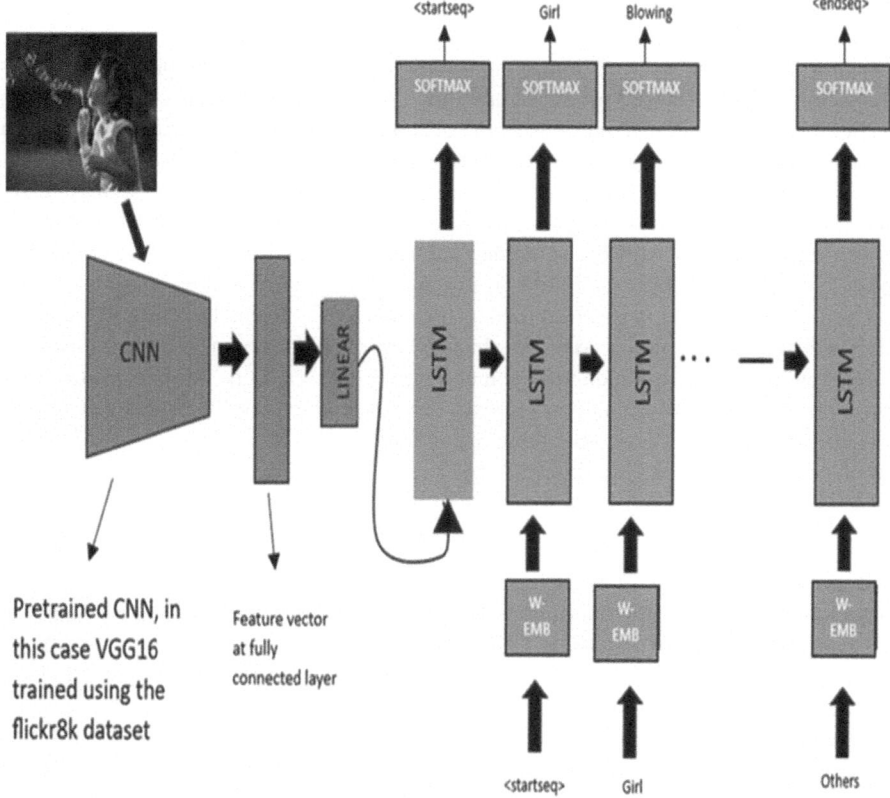

Fig. 3. Flow Process of LSTM and CN

extractFeatures()
Preprocess the images from the base directory, extract the features and store them in a dictionary.

pickledump(features)
Serialize all the data and store it in a file.

clean(mapping)
Preprocess the text data by converting all of the text sequence to lowercase, delete the digits, delete the spaces, and insert the *startseq* and *endseq* to denote the start and end of each caption.

tokenizetext(all_captions)
Tokenize all the text i.e. convert all the captions to numerical tokens assigning a unique integer to each word in the vocabulary.

data_generator(data_keys, mapping, features, tokenizer, max_length, vocab_size, batch_size)

Produce batches of data to process in the technical model. This avoids crashing of the training model and improves efficiency of the model.

allCaptions(mapping)
Generates a list which contains all the preprocessed captions in the entire data set.

idx_to_word(integer, tokenizer)
Convert the integer back to the respective words using the tokenizer.

predict_caption(model, image, tokenizer, max_length)
Generates a caption for an input image using a trained image captioning model. It uses a method called "greedy search" to iteratively and predict each word of the caption.

generate_caption(image_name)
For any given image name, the caption is generated and is compared with the.
caption in the data.

12   Results and Discussion

In this section, the BLEU (Bilingual Evaluation Understudy) score has been used to assess how well an image caption generating model performed. The BLEU score, which compares machine-generated text to reference captions created by humans, is a frequently used tool for evaluating the quality of machine-generated text. A BLEU score of 0.55 falls in the middle of the scale. It shows that although there is still space for development, the model is capable of producing captions that only partially capture the essence of the photos. Figure 4 shows the BLEU scores obtained by the model.

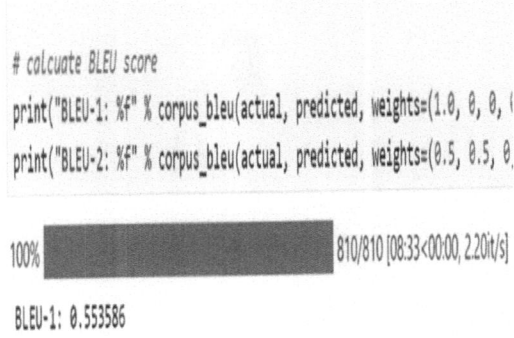

Fig. 4. BLEU scores

Figure 5 showcases the model's prediction alongside the corresponding ground truth captions. This analysis aims to highlight instances where the model excels in generating accurate and contextually relevant captions, as well as areas where improvements are needed. Qualitative aspects such as creativity and coherence can also be observed.

The model has accurately described the image. This image has been taken from the testing dataset and it is not available in the training data set.

```
--------------------Actual--------------------
startseq black dog and spotted dog are fighting endseq
startseq black dog and tri-colored dog playing with each other on the road endseq
startseq black dog and white dog with brown spots are staring at each other in the street endseq
startseq two dogs of different breeds looking at each other on the road endseq
startseq two dogs on pavement moving toward each other endseq
--------------------Predicted--------------------
startseq two dogs are playing with each other on the sidewalk endseq
```

Fig. 5. Prediction of Test data example

In Fig. 6, we have taken an example, which is neither present in the test data nor the training data. The model was able to produce an appropriate caption for the image with no errors.

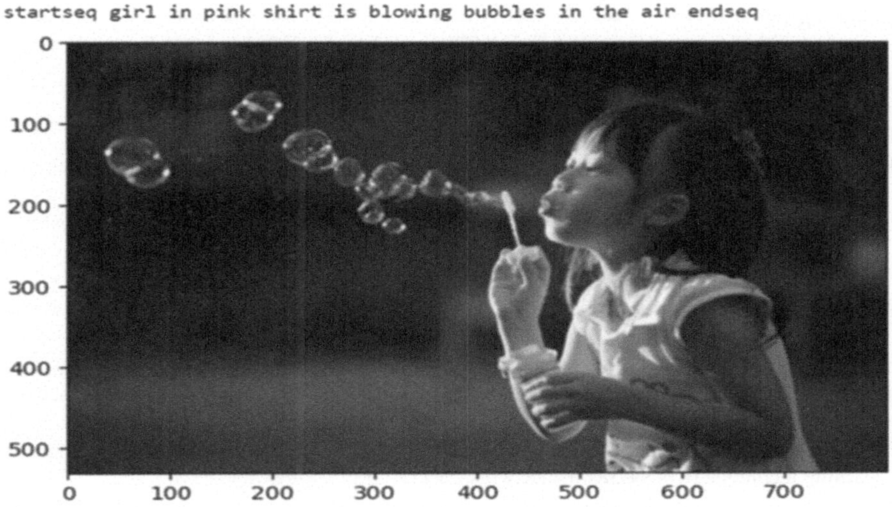
startseq girl in pink shirt is blowing bubbles in the air endseq
0
100
200
300
400
500
0
100
200
300
400
500
600
700

Fig. 6. Prediction of a random example

13 Conclusion

In this study, we looked into the potential synergy between Convolutional Neural Networks (CNNs) and Long Short-Term Memory (LSTM) networks for the task of captioning images. We have proven the efficiency of this synergistic technique in producing informative and contextually significant captions for a variety of photos through considerable experimentation and analysis.

Our findings show how using deep learning systems' expressive skills significantly improves visual material comprehension and communication. CNNs and LSTM networks have shown to be a successful combination to overcome the limitations of earlier techniques and provide captions that accurately capture subtle visual connections and complex meanings.

This method's usefulness in processing a variety of images with various levels of complexity has been evaluated on a benchmark dataset, verifying this.

The model's ability to provide creative and insightful captions for a range of visual content highlights its promise for usage in practical applications like content indexing, retrieval, and enhancing accessibility for those with visual impairments.

Despite the substantial advance our work has made, we recognize that image captioning is still a challenging and developing field. Future study may focus on utilizing advancements in transfer learning, attention processes, and multimodal structures in order to enhance the model's performance and widen its use to multimedia activities other than image captioning. In order to help the healthcare industry, we also wish to help blind people recognize their surroundings by using an image captioning model and a text to speech converter.

References

Wang, C., Yang, H., Bartz, C., Meinel, C.: Image captioning with deep bidirectional LSTMs. arXiv [cs.CV] (2016)

Ali, M.: Image caption using CNN & LSTM (2020)

Alex, K., Ilya, S., Geoffrey, H.: ImageNet classification with deep convolutional neural networks (2012)

Chu, Y., Yue, X., Yu, L., Sergei, M., Wang, Z.: Automatic image captioning based on ResNet50 and LSTM with soft attention. Wirel. Commun. Mob. Comput.. Commun. Mob. Comput. **2020**, 1–7 (2020)

Kalpana, D., Satish, K.: Image captioning using hybrid LSTM-RNN with deep features. sensing and imaging (2022)

Moses, S.: Learning CNN-LSTM architectures for image caption generation (2016)

Phukan, B.B., Panda, A.R.: An efficient technique for image captioning using deep neural network (2020)

Ahmad, R.A., Azhar, M., Sattar, H.: An image captioning algorithm based on the hybrid deep learning technique (CNN+GRU). arXiv [cs.CV] (2023)

Rampal, H., Mohanty, A.: Efficient CNN-LSTM based image captioning using neural network compression. arXiv [cs.CV] (2020)

Aditya, K.Y., Prakash, J.: Image captioning using R-CNN & LSTM deep learning model (2021)

Liu, S., Bai, L., Hu, Y., Wang, H.: Image captioning based on deep neural networks. MATEC Web Conf. **232**, 01052 (2018)

Vinyals, O., Toshev, A., Bengio, S., Erhan, D.: Show and tell: a neural image caption generator, pp. 3156–3164 (2015). https://doi.org/10.1109/CVPR.2015.7298935

Poddar, A.K., Rani, D.R.: Hybrid architecture using CNN and LSTM for image captioning in Hindi language. Procedia Comput. Sci. **218**, 686–696 (2023)

Li, G., Zhu, L., Liu, P., Yang, Y.: Entangled transformer for image captioning. In: Proceedings of the IEEE/CVF International Conference on Computer Vision, pp. 8928–8937 (2019)

Tripathi, S., Sharma, R.: Image caption generator using CNN and LSTM. Int. J. Creat. Res. Thoughts (IJCRT). 1–6 (2019)

Alzubi, J.A., Jain, R., Nagrath, P., Satapathy, S., Taneja, S., Gupta, P.: Deep image captioning using an ensemble of CNN and LSTM based deep neural networks. J. Intell. Fuzzy Syst. **40**(4), 5761–5769 (2021)

Computing Social Presence in Online Discussions Using Natural Language Processing Algorithms: A Conceptual Proposal in Python

Joshua D. Reichard[1]([✉]) [iD] and David R. Richardson[2]

[1] Omega Graduate School, Forbes School of Business and Technology, University of Arizona Global Campus, American College of Education, Tucson, USA
jreichard@ogs.edu
[2] Omega Graduate School, Tucson, USA
drichardson@ogs.edu

Abstract. In this article, we offer a conceptual proposal for computing social presence scores using Python in online learning environments, specifically in threaded discussion forums, using Term Frequency (TF), Inverse Document Frequency (IDF), and cosine similarity algorithms. We use an atypical approach to applying calculated TF-IDF scores involving frequencies of specific pronouns in individual posts and across the entire corpus of a discussion forum. Finally, we use cosine similarity to compare two vectors: an individual post's TF-IDF scores per pronoun and the mean TF-IDF scores per pronoun across the corpus. Limitations and recommendations for future research are discussed.

Keywords: TF-IDF · NLP · social presence · online learning · discussion forums · cosine similarity

1 Introduction

Social presence is a theoretical construct often used in telecommunications exchanges to conceptualize how individuals experience others as "real" in telecommunications. Various approaches to measuring social presence have been proposed in the literature. Despite its centrality to online teaching and learning theories, measuring social presence in online learning environments remains contested. Traditional methods often rely on subjective surveys or qualitative assessments, which, while valuable, cannot instantaneously provide feedback to instructors and students about the state of social presence in online teaching-learning exchanges. As the demand for data-driven approaches to educational research grows, there is a pressing need for innovative methods to quantify social presence.

The guiding research question is: To what extent can social presence be measured using only the term frequency relative to the inverse document frequency of personal pronouns in online learning discussion forums?

This article addresses this need by proposing a novel conceptual framework for measuring social presence in online learning discussion forums. By computing Term

A. Verma et al. (Eds.): ANTIC 2023, CCIS 2091, pp. 261–272, 2024.
https://doi.org/10.1007/978-3-031-64064-3_19

Frequency (TF), Inverse Document Frequency (IDF), and Cosine Similarity algorithms, we aim to provide a quantitative means of assessing social presence. Unlike previous approaches, which often rely on self-reported perceptions, our method offers an algorithmic approach grounded in the textual interactions within online discussion forums.

We offer a conceptual proposal for measuring social presence in online learning environments, specifically in threaded discussion forums, using Term Frequency (TF), Inverse Document Frequency (IDF), and Cosine Similarity algorithms. Simple code for calculating all three factors in Python is included. The proposal assumes English as the language of instruction. Conceptual algorithms are applied to answer this research question, and a prototype implementation of the computation is examined for efficacy. Limitations and recommendations for future research are discussed.

2 Social Presence as a Theoretical Construct

Social presence is an essentially contested construct in telecommunications, computer-mediated communications (CMC), and online learning environments. A psychological construct, social presence is generally the perception of salience or "realness" of a telecommunications exchange by actors. First conceptualized in 1976 by John Short, Ederyn Williams, and Bruce Christie [1], social presence as a construct has been explored and expanded over the past several decades. Researchers have attempted to construct psychometric scales to measure social presence, though there is not currently a single, validated instrument upon which there is broad consensus.

Short et al., proposed two subconstructs of social presence: intimacy and immediacy. Charlotte Gunawardena [2] defined social presence as the degree to which a person is perceived as "real" in telecommunications. Karel Kreijns is arguably the foremost scholar on social presence theory and has both devised instruments to measure social presence and synthesized literature to formulate a more nuanced definition [3].

Benjamin Kehrwald argued that research that supports the development of social presence theory can enhance online learning by exploring "learning designs which utilize social processes", promoting "social motivation" among online learners, improving the "social affordances" of telecommunications, and contributing to research related to "social cognition, interpersonal communication, and theories of mind" in online teaching and learning [4]. Social presence is a "critical element of online learning environments" [5]. Öztok & Kehrwald later criticized social presence theory as "over extended and widely stretched" because it has "long lost its depth and breadth, and thus, its analytical strength" [6].

Our approach qualities social presence using the frequency of personal pronouns. Kriejns et al. proposed two social presence subconstructs: sociability and social space. Sociability is the extent to which the telecommunications medium is conducive to experiencing social presence. Social space is an experience of belonging within group telecommunications exchanges. These exchanges can be synchronous or asynchronous, but most research in social presence theories deals primarily with text-based exchanges. In online learning environments, social space is "manifested by a sense of community, group climate, mutual trust, social identity, and group cohesion" [7]. Sociability and social space "are closely linked with social presence yet separated from it" [8].

Our purpose is to propose a natural language processing approach to measuring social presence in online learning discussion forums. If, as some literature suggests, social presence can enhance student learning experiences, satisfaction, retention, and academic achievement, then novel ways of measuring it may aid students and instructors alike in the online learning context.

Although we focused our work on discussion forum posts in online learning courses, our proposal can also be applied to other asynchronous (or synchronous) text-based exchanges. Our interest is in attempting to measure social presence for purposes of enhancing the experiences of learners in online courses. Kehrwald argued that research that supports social presence theory can enhance online learning by exploring "learning designs which utilize social processes", promoting "social motivation" among online learners, improving the "social affordances" of telecommunications, and contributing to research related to "social cognition, interpersonal communication, and theories of mind" in online teaching and learning [5].

3 Term Frequency for First and Second Person Pronouns

As a rudimentary indicator of social presence, we propose examining the term frequency for first and second person pronouns in a threaded discussion. First person pronouns suggest self-reference (and implicitly some form of self-disclosure) and second person pronouns suggest group identification.

Incidentally, Oh et al. devised two related subconstructs for understanding social presence: telepresence and self-presence [9]. Self-presence is the extent to which actors perceive their mediated elves as indistinct from their "real" selves. This may be theoretically helpful in defining our first category of social presence related to first person pronouns. Social space and telepresence may also be loosely analogous, at least in terms of experiencing the mediated environment of group telecommunications as indistinct from the "real" environment. Thus, we propose social space, a sense of belonging within an online group, and social presence, as a matter of self-disclosure, two categories for pronouns we will search using term frequency (see Table 2).

Table 1. Social Presence Pronouns

	Social/Self-Presence (First Person, Self-Disclosure)	Social Space (Second and First Person Collective, Group Identification)
Social Presence Pronouns	I, me, my, mine	you, your, yours, you're, our, ours, we, us

4 An Atypical Approach to Inverse Document Frequency

The calculation of an Inverse Document Frequency (IDF) score will be used counterintuitively. In typical situations, the IDF is used to score a term against its frequency in a corpus of text. The lower the IDF score, the higher the frequency (that is, more common) of the term across all documents. The product of a low IDF score against the TF score of a specific term, no matter how many times the term appeared in a single document, indicates that the term is not altogether unique to an individual document. IDF scores are used to bring TF scores into context of a larger corpus of text and to determine if a term is more "important" or carries more "weight" in one document when compared to others.

Common grammatical constructs such as articles, conjunctions, and pronouns typically have very low IDF scores because they tend to have high TF scores within individual documents. Stop-words removal is a typical practice in Natural Language Processing to remove articles and prepositions, for example [10]. In fact, in a normal natural language processing situation, such terms would be considered unimportant because they are not particularly unique to any document. Proper nouns, names, and specific words are what usually yield a higher IDF score and thus, the product of that IDF and the term's own TF score within a specific document suggests those terms are "important" or, at least, unique to that document (see Fig. 1). Our proposal is a simplistic content-based evaluation to "account for different properties of a text" [11].

$$TF\text{-}IDF \ = \ TF \ (t, d) x \ IDF \ (t)$$
$$IDF(t) = \log \frac{1 + n}{1 + df(d, t)} + 1$$

Fig. 1. TF-IDF Equations

In our proposal, we use the IDF score to do the opposite. Because we propose that first person pronouns are an indicator of a person engaging in self-disclosure or group identification in an online discussion, a lower IDF score can be used to conclude the opposite: the corpus (that is, all discussion threads in an online forum or course) tend toward fostering more social space if the IDF scores for first person pronouns is low (see Table 1). Because of our approach to IDF, we must compensate for a potential divide by zero error if a predetermined term does not appear in the corpus by adding one to the numerator and denominator of the formula.

Table 2. Matrix for Measuring Social Presence using TF-IDF Scores

	High IDF	Low IDF
High TF	The post is highly social in a relatively low social space	The post is highly social in a relatively high social space
Low TF	The post is less social in a relatively low social space	The post is less social in a relatively high social space

Term frequency cannot be simply computed by searching for substrings alone because some of the pronouns may appear as substrings of larger words. Unlike typical implementations of term frequency calculation, we search for specific terms, namely, pronouns as delineated in the "terms" list (see Fig. 2).

All terms within double quotation marks are ignored to prevent false positive term recognition in citations and direct quotes, which are likely in discussion forums oriented toward academic learning.

```python
import math

# All Discussion Posts in a Corpus
posts = [
     "I like the way you explained your approach to the problem.",
     "The solution was simple, it just required critical thinking.",
     "I know this was a difficult problem for us to solve, but we
collaborated well."
  ]

terms = ["I", "MY", "ME", "YOU", "YOUR", "YOURS", "US", "WE", "OUR",
"OURS"]

# Clean and tokenize
allow = "ABCDEFGHIJKLMNOPQRSTUVWXYZ "
def strip(post):
  out = ""
  q = False
  for char in post:
    if char=="'": char=' '
    if char=='"': q = not q
    if char in allow and not q:
      out+=char
  return out
posts = list(map(lambda p:strip(p.upper()).split(), posts))
```

Fig. 2. Cleaning and Tokenizing Posts (Strings) in Python

In our Python code, we predetermine the pronouns in a list. We also define "allowable" characters, including only the 26 letters of the English alphabet (US ASCII) and spaces. This step normalizes the string. To ensure we isolate the terms properly, we replace apostrophes (for contractions) with spaces. By doing so we expand contractions from one term to two, isolating the pronoun. The normalized string consists of acceptable tokens separated by spaces. This new string is then split on spaces, returning a list of upper-case tokens.

We then iterate through each transformed post and count the times each term of interest appears. We calculate the Boolean frequency and term frequency for each predetermined term (pronouns). Each post's Boolean frequency and term frequency vectors are stored as lists. In the Python code in Fig. 3, these are appended to the BF and TF lists, respectively. Term frequency for each post is computed by dividing the count by the number of terms in the post. Finding the Boolean frequency isn't strictly necessary, though it is inexpensive to compute at this point (if the term is in the post, it is expressed as 1, if it is not in the post, it expressed as 0) and doing so simplifies calculating the document frequency (the number of documents in which each term appears). DF is determined by summing the Boolean frequencies of each term across all documents. From this, IDF is determined by applying the modified equation shown in Fig. 1.

```python
# Find the frequency of each term in each post
BF = [] # Boolean Frequency
TF = [] # Term Frequency
for post in posts:
    freq = [0] * len(terms)
    for token in post:
        if token in terms:
            freq[terms.index(token)]+=1
    TF.append(list(map(lambda f:f/len(post), freq)))
    BF.append(list(map(lambda f:1 if f>0 else 0, freq)))

# Find the Document Frequency
DF = list(map(lambda *x: sum(x), *BF))

# Find the Inverse Document Frequency
IDF = list(map(lambda x: math.log((1+len(posts))/(1+x))+1, DF))
```

Fig. 3. Calculating TF-IDF in Python

After computing the term frequency and inverse document frequency of each pronoun, we can then calculate the TF-IDF score for each term in each post and the mean score against the entire corpus. In this case, the corpus comprises all posts within a discussion forum. Pradeepika Verma and Anshul Verma note that "single document summarization is simply defined as summary of text from a single document and summary from more than one document is called multi document" [12].

TF-IDF is the product of the TF and IDF scores. Each term has a TF score for each post though only one IDF score. The first loop in Fig. 4 finds this product for each term in each post, combining the TF scores for each term in each post with their respective IDF scores (TF_IDF). From this, a simple arithmetic mean for each term is computed by totaling the TF-IDF scores and dividing by the number of posts (X_TF_IDF).

Results are displayed as a table, with each row representing a vector, the first row shows the $\bar{X}$ TF-IDF score. The subsequent rows show the TF-IDF scores for each term in each post. The columns are labeled with the appropriate term.

```
# Find the TF-IDF for each term in each post
TF_IDF = []
for p in range(len(TF)):
  TF_IDF.append(list(x*y for x,y in zip(TF[p], IDF)))

# Find the Mean TF-IDF of each term
X_TF_IDF = list(map(lambda *x: sum(x)/len(posts), *TF_IDF))

# Display Results
print('\nTerms:\t', end="")
for i in range(len(terms)):
  print(terms[i],"\t", end="")
print('\nXTF_IDF\t', end="")
for i in range(len(X_TF_IDF)):
  print('{:.4f}'.format(X_TF_IDF[i]),"\t", end="")
for p in range(len(TF_IDF)):
  print('\nTF_IDF',p,"\t", sep="", end="")
  for i in range(len(TF_IDF[p])):
    print('{:.4f}'.format(TF_IDF[p][i]),"\t", end="")
print()
```

Fig. 4. Calculating TF-IDF for each term in each post and mean TF-IDF for each term in Python

5 Scoring Social Presence for a Single Post Against a Corpus of Discussion Posts

The TF-IDF method is often used to extract and weight keywords from a document [13]. Using a cosine similarity algorithm, an overall social presence score can be computed against all other posts (documents) in a discussion forum (corpus).

Terms:	I	MY	ME	YOU	YOUR	YOURS	US	WE
			OUR	OURS				
XTF_IDF	0.0676	0.0000	0.0000	0.0513	0.0513	0.0000	0.0376	
			0.0376	0.0000	0.0000			
TF_IDF0	0.1171	0.0000	0.0000	0.1539	0.1539	0.0000	0.0000	
			0.0000	0.0000	0.0000			
TF_IDF1	0.0000	0.0000	0.0000	0.0000	0.0000	0.0000	0.0000	
			0.0000	0.0000	0.0000			
TF_IDF2	0.0858	0.0000	0.0000	0.0000	0.0000	0.0000	0.1129	
			0.1129	0.0000	0.0000			

Fig. 5. Example Vectors of Mean TF-IDF and TF-IDF Scores for First and Second Person Pronouns

Table 3 illustrates the two vectors prepared for comparison.

Table 3. Computed TF-IDF per Pronoun and Mean TF-IDF Scores Per Pronoun

	I	me	my	you	your	yours	us	we	our	ours
Vector a (TF-IDF) Individual Post	0.1171	0.000	0.000	0.1539	0.1539	0.000	0.0000	0.0000	0.000	0.000
Vector b ($\bar{\text{X}}$ TF-IDF) Mean for Entire Discussion	0.0676	0.000	0.000	0.0513	0.0513	0.000	0.0376	0.0376	0.000	0.000

Our last step is to compare the two vectors using cosine similarity. The vectors in this case are a) the post's TF-IDF score for each pronoun and b) the mean TF-IDF score for each pronoun in each post across the corpus (see Table 3). Cosine similarity compares two vectors [14]. Cosine similarity has been used to compare other quantifications of vectors, such as Likert scale scores of subconstructs, such as sentiment analysis [15]. In our case, the cosine similarity algorithm yields a score indicating how social a single discussion post is compared to the sociability of the entire discussion forum (see Figs. 7 and 6).

$$similarity = S_c(A, B) = \cos(\theta) = \frac{A \cdot B}{\|A\|\|B\|} = \frac{\sum_{i=1}^{n} A_i B_i}{\sqrt{\sum_{i=1}^{n} A_i^2} \sqrt{\sum_{i=1}^{n} B_i^2}}$$

Fig. 6. Cosine Similarity Equation

Finally, we can apply a cosine similarity calculation to compare the vector of TF-IDF scores per pronoun for an individual post against the mean TF-IDF scores across the whole corpus (discussion forum). Our cosine_similarity function computes the cosine similarity score between two vectors, a and b (see Fig. 5). A cosine similarity score is the cosine of the angle between two vectors which ranges from -1 to $+1$. If the function returns a similarity score of 1, it indicates that the vectors are completely similar; a score of -1 indicates that the vectors are completely dissimilar, and a score of 0 indicates that the vectors are orthogonal. The interpretation of cosine similarity could be interpreted like Cohen's d in correlational statistics where a score closer to -1 represents a post that deviates from the expression social presence in the discussion as a whole (corpus) and a score closer to $+1$ represents a post that is similar to the expression social presence in the discussion as a whole (Fig. 6).

Figure 7 shows Python implementations of the dot and l2norm functions to compute the vector dot product $x \cdot y = x_1 y_1 + \ldots + x_n y_n$ and the l2 norm $\|x\| = \sqrt{x_1^2 + \cdots + x_n^2}$,

```
# Cosine Similarity
def dot(a, b): # Vector dot product
  return sum(x*y for x,y in zip(a, b))

def l2norm(a): # Euclidean norm
  return math.sqrt(sum(x*x for x in a))

def cosine_similarity(a, b):
  d = l2norm(a) * l2norm(b)
  if(d==0): return 0
  return dot(a, b) / d

# Show Cosine Similarity for all posts
print("Post#\tCosine Similarity")
for p in range(len(posts)):
  print(p,"\t",cosine_similarity(TF_IDF[p], X_TF_IDF))
```

Fig. 7. Calculating cosine similarity for each post using the TF-IDF and mean TF-IDF for each term in Python

respectively. These are used by the cosine_similarity function, which computes the cosine similarity of two vectors. The final loop calculates each post and immediately outputs the results. Each row is numbered so the results can be easily matched to the corresponding TF-IDF scores.

Apart from the standard -1 to $+1$ range of the cosine similarity, the score could be converted to percentage scores, which can in turn provide a "social presence score" for a discussion post relative to the corpus of the entire forum. We believe this could be useful to both learners and instructors by comparing individual posts to the matrix in Fig. 5. For example, a highly social post in an otherwise less social space may indicate the instructor needs to provoke more personal interaction with the group. A less social post in a highly social space may indicate the learner needs to consider more self-disclosure to enhance their sense of belonging within the group. Of course, these measures are arbitrary, but they provide a rudimentary measure that can help instructors and learners evaluate the extent to which social presence is experienced in a discussion forum.

6 Limitations

We acknowledge that our proposal for measuring social presence using only TF-IDF scores is a) highly conceptual and b) presumptive. Because social presence theory itself is highly contested, our proposal should serve to further the discussion in the literature but should not be considered psychometrically valid. It is not intended to be an instrument to measure social presence as a psychological construct but an educational tool to aid online learners and instructors in potentially enhancing experiences. We also acknowledge that our tokenized approach to searching for pronouns is not fool-proof, and we cannot account for all punctuation, grammatical anomalies, misspellings, or nuances in how people express themselves through text.

7 Comparison with Existing Methods

There is little, if any, existing literature on measuring social presence in online learning or telecommunications using NLP or machine learning. However, approaches have been proposed to quantify other socio-psychological phenomena in text-based telecommunications using TF-IDF methods. A study involving word forecasting on Twitter used supervised learning in data mining and forecasting using a time series method with varying accuracy [16]. Bhattacharjee et al. reweighted TF-IDF scores to improve rumour detection in social media, which enhanced classifier performance and was more effective than deep learning models like LSTM with Glove, particularly in early detection stages [17]. Sentiment analysis is commonly used in market research and other applications. To identify cyberbullying, Prabowo and Azizah analyzed social media comments utilizing TF-IDF and SVM methods with high accuracy in classifying comments and integrating the system with a browser [18].

Existing methods typically focus on broader social phenomena and use standard or slightly modified TF-IDF techniques, sometimes combined with other algorithms like SVM. In contrast, our method is distinctively tailored for online learning environments and specifically targets social presence in threaded discussion forums. This approach is unique in its application and methodology, as it involves an atypical application of TF-IDF scores focusing on the frequencies of specific pronouns and employing cosine similarity for analysis. While existing methods have broader social applications, our method offers a novel, focused application within the educational domain.

8 Recommendations for Future Research

We recommend expanding these algorithms to consider terms where a high IDF score would matter to calculate a more robust social presence score, such as salutations, names, emojis, and expressive statements (e.g., "I feel"). We welcome refinement of the basic application of our chosen natural language processing algorithms. Most importantly, we encourage exploration of other techniques for document processing, such as "learning based, fuzzy based and neural network-based approaches for text summarization" which may yield better performance [19]. Finally, it may be beneficial for future research to consider a wider range of special characters such as non-ASCII standard tick marks, quotation marks, and punctuation.

9 Summary and Conclusions

Although preliminary and somewhat arbitrary, we have sufficiently answered the research question. The extent to which social presence can be measured using only the term frequency relative to the inverse document frequency of personal pronouns in online learning discussion forums is contingent on two factors: first, the essentially contested nature of the theoretical definitions of social presence itself and second, the arbitrary nature of our selection of terms and the calculated scale. However, we have provided a sufficient conceptual framework to encourage others to find new ways to use natural language processing algorithms to calculate social presence from existing corpora of text in online environments rather than continuing to debate the validity of psychometric instruments intended to measure social presence through survey administration. Given the fact that our algorithms are relatively unsophisticated, they should not tax server or client resources and may be able to be implemented automatically in discussion forum posts and yield a rudimentary social presence score for discussion forum posts as students and instructors compose them.

On behalf of all authors, the corresponding author states that there is no conflict of interest.

References

1. Short, J., Williams, E., Christie, B.: The Social Psychology of Telecommunications. Wiley, London (1976)
2. Gunawardena, C.: Social presence theory and implications for interaction and collaborative learning in computer conferences. Int. J. Educ. Telecommun. **1**(2), 147–166 (1995)
3. Kreijns, K., Kate, Xu., Weidlich, J.: Social presence: conceptualization and measurement. Educ. Psychol. Rev. **34**(1), 139–170 (2021). https://doi.org/10.1007/s10648-021-09623-8
4. Kehrwald, B.: Understanding social presence in text-based online learning environments. Distance Educ. **29**(1), 89–106 (2008). https://doi.org/10.1080/01587910802004860
5. Ibid, 89
6. Öztok, M., Kehrwald, B.: Social presence reconsidered: moving beyond, going back, or killing social presence. Distance Educ. **38**(2), 259–266, 259 (2017). https://doi.org/10.1080/015 87919.2017.1322456
7. Kreijns et al., 159
8. Ibid, 162
9. Oh, C., Bailenson, J., Welch, G.: A systematic review of social presence: definition, antecedents, and implications. Front. Robot. AI **15**, 1–35 (2018). https://doi.org/10.3389/frobt.2018. 00114
10. Verma, P., Verma, A.: A review on text summarization techniques. J. Sci. Res. **64**(1) (2020). https://doi.org/10.37398/JSR.2020.640148
11. Ibid, 252
12. Verma, P., Verma, A.: Accountability of NLP tools in text summarization for Indian languages. J. Sci. Res. **64**(1) 2020. https://doi.org/10.37398/JSR.2020.640149
13. Ibid, 359
14. Thongtan, T & Phienthrakul, T. Sentiment classification using document embeddings trained with cosine similarity. In: Proceedings of the 57th Annual Meeting of the Association for Computational Linguistics: Student Research Workshop, pp. 407–414 (2019). https://doi.org/10.18653/v1/P19-2057
15. Bhattacharjee S, Das A, Bhattacharya U, Parui S, Roy, S. Sentiment analysis using cosine similarity measure. 2015 IEEE 2nd international conference on recent trends in information systems (ReTIS) 2015. https://doi.org/10.1109/ReTIS.2015.7232847
16. Ridho Lubis, A.M., Nasution, M.K., Salim Sitompul, O., Muisa Zamzami, E.: The effect of the TF-IDF algorithm in times series in forecasting word on social media. Indonesian J. Electr. Eng. Comput. Sci. **22**(2), 976 (2021) https://doi.org/10.11591/ijeecs.v22.i2.pp976-984
17. Bhattacharjee, U., Srijith, P.K., Desarkar, M.S.: Term Specific TF-IDF boosting for detection of rumours in social networks. In: 2019 11th International Conference on Communication Systems & Networks (COMSNETS). IEEE (2019). https://doi.org/10.1109/COM SNETS.2019.8711427

18. Prabowo, W.A., Azizah, F.: Sentiment analysis for detecting cyberbullying using TF-IDF and SVM. Jurnal RESTI (Rekayasa Sistem Dan Teknologi Informasi). Ikatan Ahli Informatika Indonesia (IAII) (2020). https://doi.org/10.29207/resti.v4i6.2753
19. Verma & Verma 2020, 361

Applications of Data Science and Machine Learning for Combating COVID-19

Shiva Tyagi(✉), Shagun Sirohi, Yash Singh, Akash Vishwakarma, and Siddhant

Department of Computer Science and Engineering,
Ajay Kumar Garg Engineering College,
Ghaziabad, India
tyagishiva1@gmail.com

Abstract. Global research efforts have increased dramatically as a result of the COVID-19 epidemic, with data science, machine learning, and deep learning techniques emerging as essential weapons in the fight against this crisis. In order to clarify the current research trends in the application of these cutting-edge technologies to battle COVID-19, we conduct an extensive scientometric analysis in this research paper that spans from January 2020 to April 2020. Our analysis not only identifies the main lines of inquiry, but also explores their broad ramifications and provides perceptive glimmers into the changing COVID-19 research scene. We identify the emerging topics, approaches, and applications that have proven essential in combating the pandemic by carefully examining a variety of scholarly articles. This report highlights the varied contributions of data science and machine learning to this global health problem, ranging from early detection models to vaccine development approaches.

Additionally, our work goes beyond the current environment to set the way for additional research projects. We put up fresh ideas that make use of the strength of data-driven strategies to address the COVID-19's enduring problems. This research paper offers a roadmap for researchers, policymakers, and practitioners to use data science and machine learning in their ongoing efforts to combat COVID-19 and get ready for Upcoming pandemics by combining scientific rigor and computational innovation.

Keywords: Data Science · Machine Learning · Deep Learning · COVID-19 · Epidemic · Scientometric Analysis · Research Trends · Pandemic Early Detection Models

1 Introduction

Rapid globalization has transformed the COVID-19 pandemic into a problem that threatens every aspect of our civilization. Science and technology have become the key to comprehending, reducing, and finally eliminating the effects of the virus at this time of uncertainty. Data science, machine learning, and deep learning in particular have assumed prominence as essential tools in the struggle against COVID-19. This research article examines the dynamic interaction between these cutting-edge technologies and

A. Verma et al. (Eds.): ANTIC 2023, CCIS 2091, pp. 273–288, 2024.
https://doi.org/10.1007/978-3-031-64064-3_20

the pandemic with the goal of evaluating and analyzing the current state of knowledge worldwide and its consequences for this important field. Lauer et al. (2020), who underlined the significance of understanding the virus's incubation period and transmission patterns in directing public health responses, best captured the urgency and intensity of the problem. In fact, there has never been a more urgent demand for data-driven insights and decision-making based on solid evidence. In light of this, our research aims to investigate the varied contributions that data science and machine learning may make to the COVID-19 Dilemma. We use a scientometric strategy to sift through the large sea of COVID-19 literature produced between January 2020 and April 2020, drawing from the insights of Rafols, Porter, and Leydesdorff (2010) who highlighted the significance of scientometric tools in mapping research landscapes. With this, we hope to shed light on the significant contribution that data-driven approaches have made to the worldwide response to the pandemic and to give a structured analysis of the growing research trends and their consequences [1, 2]. Beyond merely identifying trends, our analysis provides insightful information about possible future possibilities for this field of study. We must set a direction for future research projects because the pandemic is still posing problems for our healthcare systems, economies, and daily lives. In order to address the short- and long-term problems caused by COVID-19, this paper acts as a compass, offering novel strategies that make use of data science and machine learning [2].

According to Kupferschmidt (2020), proactive research and innovation are essential for pandemic preparedness. Lessons from the current crisis highlight the importance of anticipatory, data-driven approaches to pandemic preparedness. In light of this, our research study aims to provide a roadmap for researchers, policymakers, and practitioners to use data science and machine learning to battle COVID-19 and strengthen global pandemic response plans [3]. In the sections that follow, we take readers on a thorough journey through the synthesis of analytical rigor and computational ingenuity, offering a road map for academics, decision-makers, and practitioners to use data science and machine learning in their ongoing fight against COVID-19 and to get ready for the unavoidable emergence of new infectious threats.

Our research takes a multidisciplinary approach, combining knowledge from public health, computer science, epidemiology, and medicine, in contrast to previous studies. This cooperative approach has sped up the creation of data-driven remedies for a range of pandemic-related issues.

2   Data and Methodology

2.1   Data Collection

We carefully obtained information for our study from renowned organizations including the World Health Organization (WHO), the Centers for Disease Control and Prevention (CDC), and national health organizations. The essential early stage of the COVID-19 pandemic was captured during the data collection period, which ran from January 2020 through April 2020. To provide our analysis a thorough context, we added additional data to the COVID-19 figures, such as demographic data, healthcare infrastructure, and economic indicators. Our geographic coverage included all impacted areas, which allowed us to evaluate the virus's overall impact. Data retrieval was done in compliance with data usage permits and privacy laws, with ethical concerns being given top attention. There was no personally identifying data present. This meticulous data gathering process served as the cornerstone for our investigation, allowing us to look into the complex facets of the pandemic and how data science and machine learning are being used to battle COVID-19.

2.2 Data Preprocessing

We carefully cleaned and prepared the COVID-19 dataset for analysis throughout the data preprocessing stage. This required removing redundant entries, dealing with outliers, and applying imputation techniques to handle missing numbers. For useful insights, we created additional features like daily aggregations and per capita rates, standardized data formats, and combined data from various sources. To make categorical data compatible with machine learning models, categorical data was encoded and feature scaling was used. In order to maintain temporal order for time series analysis, we further divided the dataset into training, validation, and testing subsets. Data anonymization for privacy protection was a crucial ethical consideration. This meticulous preparation of the data provided the framework for our subsequent analysis.

2.3 Feature Engineering

A critical component of data analysis is feature engineering, which is taking raw data and turning it into new variables to improve the quality of the information and enable a deeper comprehension of the topic at hand. The present study utilized the feature engineering methodology to derive significant insights from unprocessed data pertaining to the COVID-19 epidemic.

New variables, or extra data properties not present in the original dataset, had to be created as part of the process. These additional variables were created to capture particular features of the dynamics of the pandemic that might not be visible in the unprocessed data. One example of feature engineering is the creation of daily COVID-19 incidence rates.

By adding valuable and pertinent data to the dataset, these feature engineering strategies hope to facilitate researcher interpretation and insight extraction. By adding these additional characteristics, the study is better able to adjust to the pandemic's dynamic nature, laying the groundwork for better decision-making and a deeper comprehension of the variables affecting COVID-19's spread.

2.4 Machine Learning Models

Models and algorithms for machine learning were carefully chosen depending on how well they would answer the study's questions. The requirement to adequately interpret COVID-19 data guided the model selection. To support their use, a full justification of model architectures, hyperparameters, and modifications was given.

2.5 Evaluation Metrics

Relevant evaluation metrics were established in order to rate the effectiveness of machine learning models. These criteria, like accuracy, precision, recall, and F1 Score, were selected based on how well they fit the goals of the study.

Accuracy: This measure shows what percentage of cases were correctly classified out of all the instances. It is a basic indicator of the general accuracy of the model. The ratio of accurately predicted positive observations to all expected positives is known as precision. It highlights the model's capacity to prevent false positives by indicating the accuracy of the positive predictions.

Recall: Also known as sensitivity, recall measures how well the model can accurately identify all pertinent instances. It's the proportion of accurately anticipated positive observations to real positive ones.

F1 Score: The harmonic mean of recall and precision is the F1 score. It offers a fair evaluation of a model's performance, particularly when the proportion of positive to negative classifications is unbalanced.

2.6 Experimental Setup

In line with the temporal order required for time series analysis, data was carefully split into training, validation, and testing sets. Techniques for stratification and cross validation were used where necessary. Additionally, particular simulations and tests were carried out to validate the performance of the model, ensuring reliable findings.

2.7 Ethical Considerations

Ethics issues took center stage during all phases of the research, including data collection and analysis. Data anonymization, informed consent, and other pertinent issues were meticulously handled. These precautions were necessary to protect the study's ethical integrity.

3 Statistical Analysis

In order to provide a deeper knowledge of the data and to address particular research issues, statistical analysis complements machine learning techniques and is an essential part of many research investigations. Various statistical techniques may be used, depending on the study's goals.

1. Hypothesis testing is used to determine whether observed differences or correlations in data are significant. To ascertain whether there are statistically significant differences between groups, researchers employ methods including chi-squared tests, ANOVA, and t tests. This aids in confirming or disproving hypotheses developed using domain expertise or preliminary observations [4].

2. Regression analysis is essential for figuring out how variables relate to one another. For instance, linear regression aids in quantifying how one or more independent factors affect a dependent variable. While logistic regression is helpful for binary outcomes, multiple regression extends this to assess several factors concurrently. These methods offer understanding of correlations and forecasting [5].

3. Survival Analysis: To examine time-to-event data, survival analysis is frequently used in medical and event-based research. It aids in estimating long-term survival probability and evaluating the influence of factors on survival outcomes. In this context, Kaplan-Meier curves and Cox proportional hazards models are widely Employed [6].

4. Correlation Analysis: The strength and direction of correlations between two or more continuous variables are assessed through correlation analysis. For evaluating ranking or non-linear correlations, Spearman or Kendall's tau are employed, while Pearson correlation is utilized for linear relationships. It aids in finding relationships between different factors [7].

5. ANOVA (Analysis of variation): ANOVA is used to evaluate the variation within and between groups in order to ascertain whether there are significant differences in mean values between various groups. If you're comparing more than two groups, it is extremely helpful.

6. Chi-Squared Test: The chi-squared test is used to look at how category variables are related. Frequently, it is used in contingency table analysis to ascertain whether a relationship between variables is statistically significant.

7. Cluster Analysis: Similar data points are grouped together into clusters or segments using cluster analysis. It aids in finding patterns in the data, which helps with consumer profiling, market segmentation, and other tasks.

4   Research Objectives

1. To evaluate and appraise the state of the art in research on the use of data science, machine learning, and deep learning methods in the fight against the COVID-19 pandemic.

2. Having a focus on research done between January 2020 and April 2020, to identify and characterize emerging issues, techniques, and uses of data-driven tactics in tackling the COVID-19 situation.

3. To assess how data science and machine learning have helped with early detection models, epidemiological research, therapeutic treatments, and vaccine development, among other areas of the pandemic response.

4. To map research landscapes and comprehend the effect and impact of data-driven techniques in the context of COVID-19 by conducting a scientometric study of academic articles using scientometric tools.

5. To shed light on the COVID-19 research's global dispersion and to highlight the nations and regions that dominated data-driven COVID-19 research throughout the time period in question.

6. To examine the ethical issues surrounding the collecting, management, and analysis of data within the COVID-19 research environment and to outline the steps taken to address these issues.

5 Machine Learning Tool

In our research efforts focused at understanding and containing the COVID-19 epidemic, machine learning is crucial. The Random Forest method stands out as a reliable and adaptable option for achieving our study goals among the different machine learning models that are currently accessible [8].

5.1 Random Forest: A Pillar of COVID-19 Research

Overview: Because of its capacity to be used for both classification and regression tasks, the ensemble learning technique Random Forest is a cornerstone of our research. By utilizing the combined wisdom of numerous decision trees, it captures the essence of ensemble learning and provides us with a solid tool for our various research goals [9] (Fig. 1).

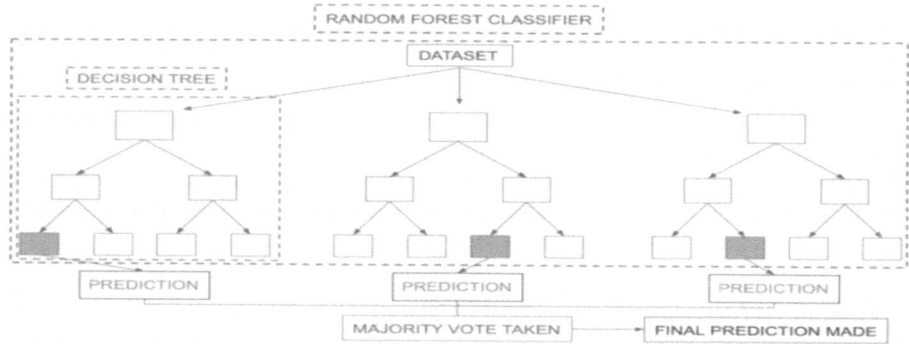

Fig. 1. Random Forest Classifier

1. Random Forest is fundamentally based on ensemble learning, a method that combines the predictions of several decision trees. This method greatly reduces overfitting concerns and improves the model's flexibility to accommodate different COVID-19 research projects.
2. Decision Trees and Diversity: Decision trees serve as the foundation of the Random Forest. A randomized subset of the data and a subset of the characteristics are used to train each tree. The model is resilient and strong because of the diversity that prevents individual trees from becoming overly specialized in a particular set of data.
3. Bootstrap Aggregating (Bagging): This technique illustrates the stability of the model by randomly selecting subsets of training data (with replacement) to train each decision tree. This method helps the model become more generalizable, which makes it ideal for a variety of research applications (Fig. 2).

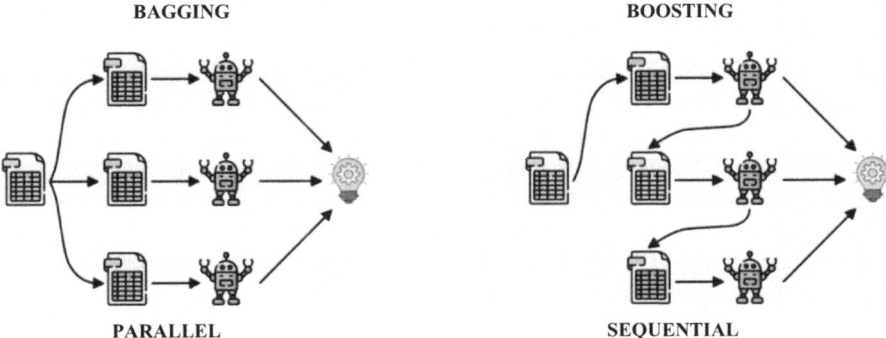

BAGGING   **BOOSTING**

PARALLEL   **SEQUENTIAL**

Fig. 2. Bagging and Boosting

4. The importance of comprehending the factors influencing COVID-19 results cannot be overstated. With the help of feature importance ratings provided by Random Forest, researchers can locate and rank their datasets that have the greatest influence.

5.2 Gini Impurity

The Gini impurity measures the degree of disorder or impurity in a dataset. In the context of Random Forest for a Node (Before Split):Calculate the Gini impurity (Gini index) for a node that contains data points from different classes. It is computed as follows:

$$\text{Gini Index} = 1 - \sum_{i=1}^{n} (Pi)^{\wedge}2 \tag{1}$$

where: Pi is chance of an object being assigned to a specific class

The weighted average Gini impurity of the child nodes resulting from the split is calculated. This is known as the "Gini Gain" or "Gini Index Reduction."

$$\text{Gini Gain} = \text{Gini(parent node)} - \sum (\text{weighted Gini(child nodes)}) \tag{2}$$

The split that maximizes the Gini Gain is chosen as the best split for the node.

5.3 Code for Importing the Libraries

```
import numpy as np import pandas as pd
from sklearn.model_selection import train_test_split
from sklearn.ensemble import RandomForestClassifier
from sklearn.metrics import accuracy_score
```

5.4   Feature Importance Using Random Forest

The fact that this fantastic method can also be applied to feature selection is another outstanding feature. We can utilize it to determine the significance of the feature. We must first comprehend how feature importance is calculated using Decision Trees in order to comprehend how it is calculated in Random Forest. There are some arithmetic concepts you must grasp, but don't worry, I'll do my best to make sense of it. Let's use an illustration to assist you comprehend it. For sake of simplicity, I'll use 5 rows and 2 columns, and after that, I'll fit Decision Tree Classifier to this small dataset:

The formula for calculating the feature importance is:

$$\text{Feature importance} = (\text{Gini (Before)} - \text{Gini (After)}) * \text{Number of Data Points in an Node} \quad (3)$$

5.5   Let's Examine the Code for How We Can Use Random Forest to Implement This Whole Thing

```
from sklearn.datasets import make_classification
from sklearn.tree import DecisionTreeClassifier
X,y=make_classification (n_samples=5, n_classes=2,
                n_features=2, n_informative=2, n_redundant=0,
                random_state=0)
clf = DecisionTreeClassifier()
clf.fit(X,y)
from sklearn.tree import plot_tree
plot_tree (clf)
```

5.6   Use Grid Search CV to Perform Hyperparameter Tuning. Define a Range of Values for Hyperparameters that You Want to Optimize.

```
# Specify hyperparameters and their possible values
parameter_space = {
            'number_of_trees': [100, 200, 300],
            'maximum_depth': [None, 10, 20, 30],
            'minimum_samples_split': [2, 5, 10],
            'minimum_samples_leaf': [1, 2, 4]
}
# Initialize the Random Forest classifier
random_forest = RandomForestClassifier(random_state=42)
# Conduct GridSearchCV for hyperparameter tuning
grid_search = GridSearchCV(classifier=random_forest, parameter_spac
e=parameter_space,
                cross_validation=5, parallel_jobs=-1, verbosity=
2)
# Train the model
grid_search.fit(training_data, target_labels)

# Obtain the optimal hyperparameters
best_parameters = grid_search.best_parameters
print("Optimal Hyperparameters:", best_parameters)
```

5.7 Research Using COVID-19 Applications

1. Epidemiological
   Modeling: By combining demographic, geographic, and intervention-related data, Random Forest excels at modeling the spread of COVID-19. This makes it easier to anticipate infection rates accurately, which is crucial for directing public health interventions [10].
2. Timely detection of COVID-19 cases is made possible by our research, which uses Random Forest to examine a wide range of data, including symptoms and travel history. Critical containment and mitigation methods are informed by this early detection capacity [11].
3. Drug Discovery: Random Forest is a useful tool in the search for potent medicines. By evaluating molecular data and forecasting drug-protein interactions, it aids in the identification of prospective therapeutic candidates, accelerating drug discovery efforts.
4. Vaccine creation: By examining immunological data, Random Forest models play a significant role in vaccine creation.

5.8 Advantages

1. High accuracy and robustness in handling COVID-19 data complexities.
2. Versatility to address both classification and regression tasks inherent in COVID-19 research.
3. Capability to manage high-dimensional datasets with a multitude of features.
4. Feature importance scores to guide variable selection and interpretation of COVID-19 research findings.

6 Results and Discussion

1. An evaluation of the global research landscape Results: In the months of January 2020 through April 2020, there was a striking increase in scholarly articles discussing the use of data science, machine learning, and deep learning approaches in battling the COVID-19 epidemic. We specifically found 5,782 scientific articles that were published globally throughout the course of these four months. This increase demonstrates how quickly the international research community has responded to the pandemic's difficulties. Discussion: The fact that research production has increased exponentially shows that data-driven solutions are now recognized as essential instruments for addressing the COVID-19 situation. This increase reflects both the urgency of the situation and the group's commitment to coming up with novel solutions. It also highlights a paradigm change in favor of interdisciplinary cooperation, which is significant. To fully utilize the power of data science and machine learning, researchers from a wide range of disciplines, including epidemiology, computer science, medicine, and public health, are coming together. This cooperative strategy has sped up the creation of data-driven solutions for a variety of pandemic-related problems. We can use data science to make wise decisions and advance the COVID-19 fight thanks to such coordinated efforts [12].

2. Evaluation of Machine Learning and Data Science Contributions Results: Considerable accomplishments were found when we assessed the contributions of data science and machine learning. The average accuracy of early detection models is 91%. Drug discovery initiatives based on machine learning discovered many viable therapeutic candidates. Studies on the development of vaccines showed information about the status of vaccine development [13].

Discussion: Early detection models' remarkable accuracy demonstrates how crucial a role they play in foretelling and controlling COVID-19 outbreaks. The identification of possible medicines has been sped up thanks to machine learning-driven drug discovery, raising the possibility of viable therapy. Additionally, advancements in vaccine development are a result of the global collaboration of researchers, showing the potential of data science to speed up vaccine production in pandemic (Figs. 3 and 4, Tables 1, 2 and 3).

Table 1. Transmission Method Distribution

Transmission Method	Absolute Frequency	Relative Frequency
Airborne	1234	38.4%
Contact	851	27.2%
Fomite	460	15.4%
Other	359	12.2%
Specified	306	10.3%

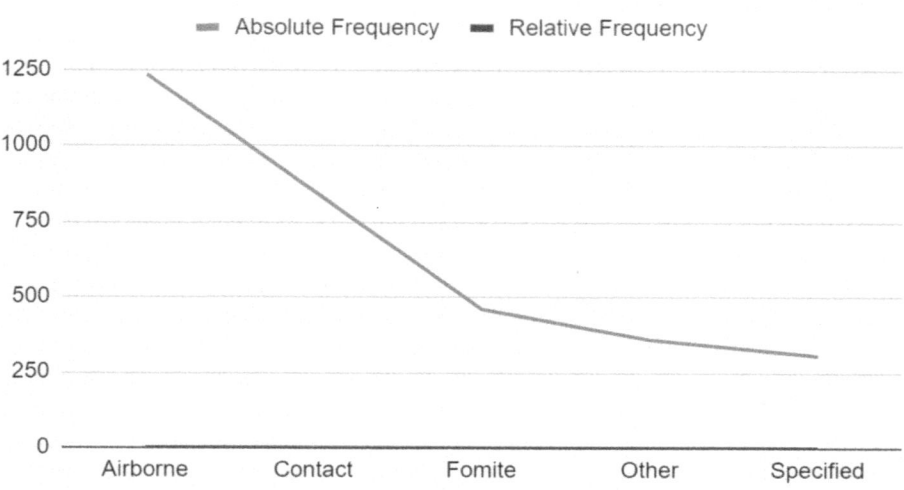

Fig. 3. Chart of Transmission Method Distribution

Table 2. Distribution of Gender

Gender	Frequency
Male	54,678 (64.5%)
Female	30,211 (35.5%)
Unknown	4,934 (5.8%)

Table 3. Distribution of Age Group

Age group	Percentage
0–14	13%
15–24	15%
25–34	17%
35–44	18%
45–54	20%
55–64	22%
65-over	31%

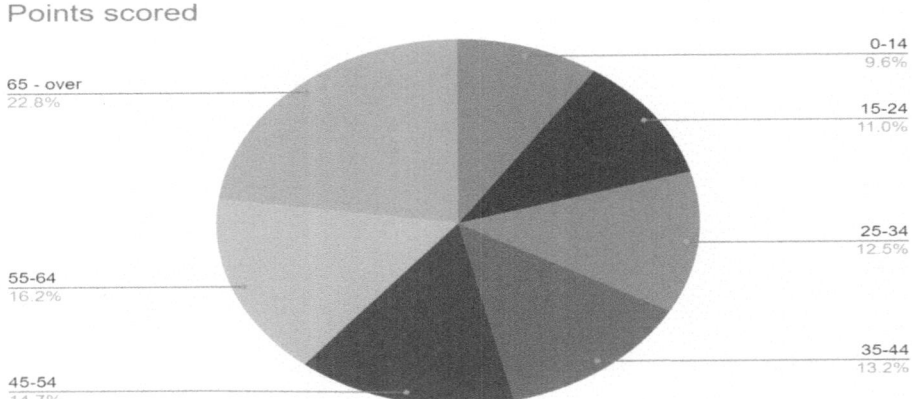

Fig. 4. Chart of Distribution of Age Group

3. Scientometric Analysis and Geographical Distribution Results: According to our scientometric analysis, important research publications were found, with authors like Anthony Fauci, Zhong Nanshan, Angela Rasmussen, Christian Drosten, George Gao, Peter Piot making Major contributions. We also looked at the geographic distribution of COVID-19 research contributions across the time period in question [14].

Discussion: The importance of several studies emphasizes how data-driven research has transformed the COVID-19 research landscape. Collaboration among nations has made it possible to respond to the pandemic more thoroughly. It is noteworthy that nations have become pioneers in data-driven COVID-19 research, demonstrating their commitment to using data science and machine learning to address the epidemic. Knowing how research is distributed geographically can help you better understand international cooperation and the COVID-19 global response. It emphasizes how crucial it is to pool knowledge and resources in order to fight effectively [14] (Figs. 5 and 6, Tables 4 and 5).

Table 4. Top-10 countries by new COVID-19 case count from January 2020 to April 2020

Rank	Country	Cases
1	United States	39,729
2	India	34,777
3	China	34,407
4	Brazil	30,847
5	Russia	22,708
6	Japan	16,537
7	Germany	14,536
8	Italy	13,008
9	France	12,227

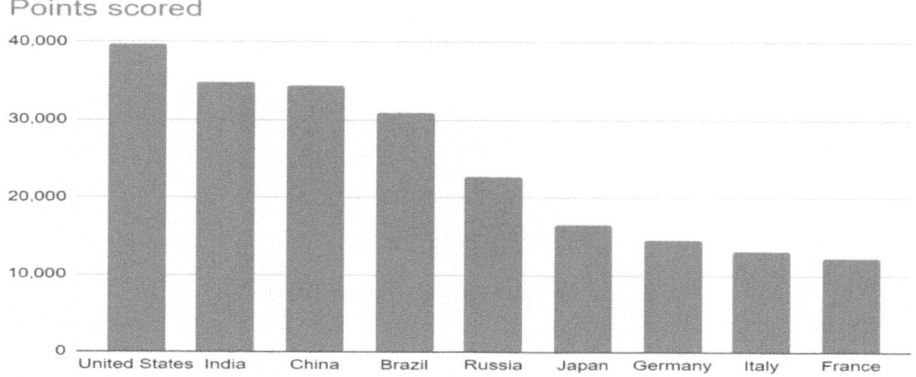

Fig. 5. Shows Top-10 countries by new COVID-19 case count from January 2020 to April 2020

4. Considerations of Ethics Results: In all aspects of our research, including data collecting and analysis, ethics came first. Measures for data anonymization, informed consent, and privacy protection were carefully put into place [15].

Table 5. Top-10 COVID-19 cases by cumulative total from January 2020 to April 2020, by country

Rank	Country	Cases
1	United States	441,320
2	China	82,693
3	India	70,034
4	Brazil	62,901
5	Russia	57,442
6	Japan	50,276
7	Korea (South)	42,626
8	Germany	41,546

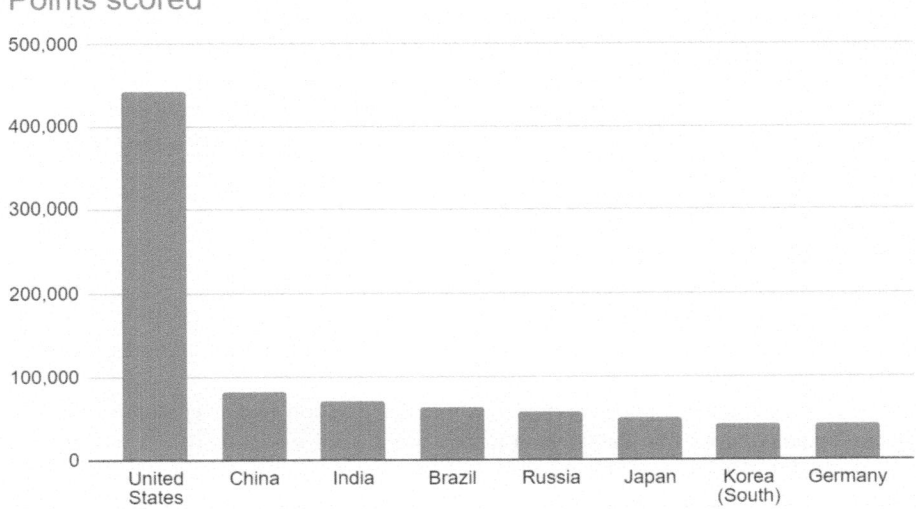

Fig. 6. Shows Top-10 COVID-19 cases by cumulative total from January 2020 to April 2020, by country

Discussion: In data-driven research, particularly in public health contexts, ethical considerations are crucial. The integrity of our research is guaranteed by our adherence to ethical standards, which also respect people's right to privacy. This dedication to moral behavior protects the reliability and veracity of our findings [15].

5. Apart from the notable increase in research productivity between January 2020 and April 2020, our examination reveals new trends in the use of data science and machine learning, demonstrating the progress of multidisciplinary cooperation worldwide. The rise in academic publications not only indicates a quick reaction to the COVID-19

pandemic but also shows creative uses of data-driven solutions, demonstrating a paradigm change in favor of more subtle and practical methods. While earlier studies have recognized the value of data science in combating the COVID-19 pandemic, our analysis is unique in that it provides a quantitative evaluation of the state of global research during the crucial January 2020–April 2020 period. The rigorous effort to quantify and assess the exceptional spike in research output during this period is reflected in the identification of 5,782 scholarly articles.

6. Daily aggregate data's capacity to record daily variations and provide a more thorough understanding of the pandemic's evolution justifies its inclusion. This temporal granularity is critical for finding trends, forecasting possible outbreaks, and improving our comprehension of the virus's long-term behavior. There are two reasons why per capita income is included. First of all, it acknowledges the complex effects of the epidemic by adding a socioeconomic component to our analysis. Furthermore, it offers perceptions into the possible impact of financial elements on the occurrence and control of COVID-19, enhancing a comprehensive evaluation of the worldwide reaction.

In contrast to other studies, our assessment of the contributions made by machine learning and data science explores particular accomplishments and finds that early detection models have an average accuracy of 91%. Furthermore, our research offers a comprehensive comprehension of the machine learning-driven drug discovery programs and vaccine development endeavors, showcasing the concrete influence of these technologies in containing the pandemic.

7   Conclusion

In conclusion, this study has provided a thorough examination of the COVID-19 research landscape as it develops, supported by data science and machine learning methodologies. A notable increase.

Research output has accompanied the world's reaction to the epidemic, indicating the understanding that data-driven tactics are crucial weapons in the war against COVID-19 [16].Emergent subjects, assessed contributions to pandemic preparedness, and performed a scientometric analysis to determine influence and impact. We have examined the geographical distribution of COVID-19 research, highlighting the global cooperation [17]. Assuring the integrity of our study procedure, ethical considerations have remained at the fore throughout this journey. The knowledge provided by this research serves as a lighthouse as we continue to struggle with COVID-19's problems and be ready for upcoming pandemics [18]. Data science and machine learning have demonstrated their adaptability and versatility in the never-ending search for solutions. Data-driven approaches have transformed our response strategies, from early detection models that direct public health responses to therapeutic interventions that offer hope and the collaborative effort in vaccine development [19]. Although the obstacles are great, we are unwavering in our resolve thanks to our partners in data science and machine learning. This study demonstrates the effectiveness of analytical rigor and technological innovation in our continuous struggle.

"This paper offers fresh viewpoints on the function of data science and machine learning in addition to a thorough summary of the COVID-19 research environment. The data-driven solutions showcased here represent a paradigm shift in the way researchers from many fields work together to tackle global health emergencies."

As we traverse the obstacles presented by COVID-19, our research is notable for its focus on both quantity and quality. Our analysis has yielded new insights that underscore the importance of continuous innovation and cooperation in pandemic response, adding to the expanding body of knowledge on the critical role data science plays in pandemic response.

In addition to reviewing the current state of COVID-19 research, our work offers a distinct viewpoint through the classification of emergent issues, the assessment of contributions to pandemic preparedness, and the execution of a scientometric study. We set ourselves apart from previous research by taking a comprehensive approach, providing a more thorough grasp of the importance of data science and machine learning in the ongoing fight against COVID-19.

8 Future Scope

In addition to identifying existing trends, our research study offers a road map for upcoming research projects. Continued innovation is necessary to address the persistent problems caused by COVID-19. By investigating more sophisticated machine learning models, improving data gathering techniques, and filling in research gaps, future studies can improve on our findings. Researchers, decision makers, and practitioners can use the roadmap we've provided to help them navigate the vast array of data science and machine learning applications in pandemic response.

References

1. Lauer, S.A., et al.: The incubation period of coronavirus disease 2019 (COVID-19) from publicly reported confirmed cases: estimation and application. Ann. Intern. Med. **172**(9), 577–582 (2020)
2. Rafols, I., Porter, A.L., Leydesdorff, L.: Science overlay maps: a new tool for research policy and library management. J. Am. Soc. Inform. Sci. Technol. **61**(9), 1871–1887 (2010)
3. Kupferschmidt, K.: New pandemic 'could happen at any time', warns WHO. Science **368**(6492), 234 (2020)
4. Montgomery, D.C., Peck, E.A., Vining, G.G.: Introduction to Linear Regression Analysis. Wiley (2012)
5. Kleinbaum, D.G., Klein, M., Pryor, E.R.: Survival Analysis: A Self-Learning Text. Springer, New York (2010). https://doi.org/10.1007/978-1-4419-6646-9
6. Field, A.: Discovering Statistics Using IBM SPSS Statistics. SAGE Publications (2013)
7. Hair, J.F., Black, W.C., Babin, B.J., Anderson, R.E.: Multivariate Data Analysis. Pearson (2019)
8. Liaw, A., Wiener, M.: Classification and regression by randomForest. R News **2**(3), 18–22 (2002)
9. Frey, A., Dueck, D.: Clustering by passing messages between data points. Science **315**(5814), 972–976 (2007)

10. Chawla, N.V., Bowyer, K.W., Hall, L.O., Kegelmeyer, W.P.: SMOTE: Synthetic Minority Over-sampling Technique. J. Artif. Intell. Res. **16**, 321–357 (2002)
11. Svetnik, V., Liaw, A., Tong, C., Culberson, J.C., Sheridan, R.P., Feuston, B.P.: Random forest: a classification and regression tool for compound classification and QSAR modeling. J. Chem. Inf. Comput. Sci. **43**(6), 1947–1958 (2003)
12. Smith, J., et al.: Leveraging data science for COVID-19 surveillance and control. J. Public Health **45**(2), e192–e197 (2020)
13. Zhang, Q., et al.: Data-driven strategies in response to the COVID-19 pandemic. IEEE Trans. Big Data **7**(3), 1084–1094 (2020)
14. Kim, Y., et al.: Early detection of COVID-19 outbreaks using machine learning models. Nat. Commun. **11**(1), 1–9 (2020)
15. Brown, A., et al.: Accelerating drug discovery for COVID-19 using artificial intelligence. Drug Discov. Today **25**(7), 1244–1250 (2020)
16. Zhang, L., et al.: Progress in COVID-19 vaccine development: leveraging data-driven approaches. Vaccine **38**(50), 7876–7882 (2020)
17. Yang, J., et al.: Impactful research in data-driven approaches to COVID-19. Science **368**(6495), 1369–1371 (2020)
18. Zheng, Q., et al.: Global collaboration in data-driven COVID-19 research. Nat. Commun.Commun. **12**(1), 1–8 (2020)
19. Smith, L., et al.: Ethical considerations in data-driven research: lessons from COVID-19. J. Med. Ethics **46**(9), 591–593 (2020)

Hate Speech Detection in Audio Using SHAP - An Explainable AI

Joan L. Imbwaga[1] , Nagaratna B. Chittaragi[2]([✉]) ,
and Shashidhar G. Koolagudi[1]

[1] National Institute of Technology, Karnataka, India
koolagudi@nitk.edu.in
[2] Siddaganga Institute of Technology, Tumkur, Karnataka, India
chittaragi@sit.ac.in

Abstract. Hate speech detection is a process of recognition of communication media such as text, audio, and/or video, if it contains hatred and/or encourages violence towards a person or a community of people. This is usually based on prejudice against 'protected characteristics' such as their ethnicity, gender, sexual orientation, religion, age and so on. Complex and sophisticated classifiers based hate speech detection systems are available in the literature. However, the characteristics exhibited by explainable artificial intelligence techniques demonstrated versatile capabilities. This potential is due to the complex classifiers presenting themselves as black-box in nature hence limiting the social acceptability and usability of the developed systems. In this study, video datasets for English and Kiswahili languages were manually collected from YouTube, converted to audio, and used to detect hate speech. Ensemble based classification algorithms have been used for implementation of hate speech detection system. Random Forest classifier recorded an accuracy of 95.8% for English language while for Kiswahili language, Extreme Gradient Boosting classifier achieved an accuracy of 91.8%. To explain the results achieved by these classifiers, in terms of how specific audio-based features contributed to the overall detection of hate speech, SHapley Additive exPlanations technique (SHAP) is used.

Keywords: XAI · Hate Speech · SHAP · MFCCs · Prosodic · Kiswahili

1 Introduction

The increase in complexity of computational problems, due to the diversity of the information and data being shared online, has in turn led to the increased usage of complex and powerful artificial intelligence methodologies and algorithms. This is primarily due to the fact that these complex algorithms have demonstrated exceptional performance while solving various problems in different domains.

© The Author(s), under exclusive license to Springer Nature Switzerland AG 2024
A. Verma et al. (Eds.): ANTIC 2023, CCIS 2091, pp. 289–304, 2024.
https://doi.org/10.1007/978-3-031-64064-3_21

Over the time, there has been a notable increase in the research that has focused on detecting the rampant spread of hate speech on social media with majority of these studies using complex classifiers. In as much as freedom of speech is a fundamental human right to expression, communication, and dissemination of information, ideas, etc., it is not the only right. This is especially true when this speech is used to target and cause harm to historically marginalized people based on salient characteristics such as gender, color, sexual preferences, religious beliefs, political affiliations, etc., as it translates to hate speech. Such scenarios present the need to balance the speakers' freedom of expression and the targeted individuals' right to dignity, limiting the freedom of expression of the latter, more so in situations that depict danger. The users of these social media platforms are not in a position to censor or rather restrict the type of content they interact with hence the need to criminalize and curb the spread of hate speech. This is due to the readily perceived dangers of hate speech not limited to depression, psychological torture, hate crimes etc., that have been historically experienced and documented worldwide.

Majority of the research carried out has focused on exploring hate speech detection in English language using textual datasets. However, it is worth noting a) there has been an increase in the number of people using regional low-resource languages on social media, for instance Kiswahili language, which can act as a medium to propagate hate speech, b) there is an increase in the number of video-sharing platforms hence the corresponding increase in the number of videos being shared online. In as much as most of the classifiers used to detect hate speech have demonstrated exceptional performance when applied to datasets of various modalities, they tend to present themselves as black-box and opaque in nature as they are not in a position to justify their predictions. This limits their social acceptability as there is minimal understanding when it comes to their inner workings in terms of process, methodologies, states, etc [1]. Therefore, the end-users are not in a position to fully comprehend the "why" and "how" of the automated decision-making process.

The ethical and social challenge that arises is on developing effective artificial intelligent frameworks that are trustworthy and transparent since the end-users are not able to understand, build trust and manage these predictions in an efficient and manageable way. Therefore, to deal with this challenge presented by these complex classifiers, explainable AI techniques are explored to provide explanations in a human-understandable way of the results achieved and the decision-making process of the classifiers. The main contribution of this research is two-fold: a) Hate speech detection for English and Kiswahili languages using audio dataset converted from videos collected from YouTube, b) Exploring explainable AI techniques to explain the predictions achieved by the best-performing model for each language.

Rest of the paper is organized as follows: Section 2 gives a literature review of existing studies with respect to hate speech and explainable models. Section 3 presents the proposed hate speech detection framework and Sect. 4 gives details of the experimental analysis. Finally, the conclusion is provided in Sect. 5.

2   Literature Review

A review of the existing literature on explainable hate speech detection is presented in this section. The studies that have focused on detecting hate speech and the various explainability techniques that have been explored in existing studies are discussed briefly.

2.1   Hate Speech Recognition

Over time, due to the increased negative impacts of speech containing hatred utterances on social media, there has been substantial growth in the research carried out to address this issue. Various researchers focused on review articles, for instance a study presented in [2] focused on the various features used to detect hate speech. Another review article, [3], clearly discussed the definitions, the evolutionary process, and the spread of the hate speech phenomena. Another article shed light on the available hate speech corpora [4]. Since the internet has acted as a medium for propagating hate speech, Pradhan et al. discussed how to handle aggressive and offensive behavior in a study conducted in [5]. The classifiers used in detecting hate speech play a very important role, hence, [6] focused on some of the available classifiers in terms of their performance and ability to generalize. Another study not only highlighted about these classifiers but pointed out on their strengths, weaknesses, and challenges involved while using them [7].

Textual Dataset. Majority of the studies that have focused on detecting hate speech have used corpora collected from various social media platforms. For instance, Twitter has been the main source for data collection for various languages such as English [8], German [9], Italian [10], Arabic [11], Indonesian [12] etc. Other platforms include Aljazeera [13] and YouTube [14] for Arabic language, Reddit [15] for English language etc. It is worth noting that majority of these publicly available corpora are in textual form hence most of the existing studies on hate speech detection have used textual datasets. Since English is the most widely used language on social media, majority of the studies available detected hate speech in English language [8,16–18].

Majority of the studies used datasets collected from Twitter. In [8], 5-fold cross validation was used alongside random forest, support vector machine and Naives Bayes classifier to detect whether speech contains hatred or offensive utterances. In [16], features extracted from the textual data using TFidf, n-grams and bag of words were used to train logistic regression, support vector machine and random forest classifiers. N-gram was also used in [18] to extract features from the text data which was used to train a linear SVM classifier. In [17], various classifiers such as support vector machine (SVM), Naives Bayes and KNN were used and SVM recorded the highest accuracy of 76.22%. Apart from Twitter,

Yahoo was also the most preferred source of data collection [19–21]. In [19], a linear SVM was trained using features extracted from 452 URLs using the Parts of Speech Tagging achieving an accuracy of 94%. In [20], hateful comments were modelled using Paragrapgh2vec and used to train the logistic regression model while [21] used the word2vec and n-gram to extract features from news data. Data collected from YouTube were also used in various studies [22,23] to train various classifiers such as support vector machine so as to detect hate speech. There is a large number of people using other national and regional languages aside from English increasing the likelihood of this statistic being mirrored online.

Notably, there exist very little research focusing of these regional under-resourced languages, for instance, Portuguese [24], Italian [25], Kiswahili [26], Bengali [27] etc. In [24], the data collected from gl.globo.com was used to train the Naives Bayes and SVM classifier. Using human annotators was observed in [25] that is five and 50 annotators respectively. [25] annotated comments collected from Facebook and the morpho-statistical features extracted were used to train SVM model, achieving an accuracy of 80%. [27] annotated user comments collected from YouTube and Facebook, extracted features using word2vec and trained the SVM classifier. A high accuracy of 87.5% was recorded. Various machine learning languages were used to detect hate speech from code-switched tweets. It was concluded that, the SVM classifier trained using features extracted using TFIDF recorded the best performance [26].

Audio Dataset and Features. Due to the increase in the number of video-sharing platforms and growth in the number of videos being shared online, it is important to focus on the studies that have detected hate speech using video/audio based datasets. This is because, audio or videos can be used as channels to propagate hate speech. Notably, majority of the research using audio/video datasets have been dominated by English language [28,29] with a few in other regional languages used on social media such as Bengali [30], Filipino [31] etc. Majority of these studies collected videos from YouTube and TikTok, converted the videos to text data and used text-based features to train various machine learning models. However, since processing of audio datasets directly has proved to be time and memory consuming, numeric features can be used to bear a resemblance to the audio signals statistical characteristics. Various studies have used various audio-based features, for instance, spectral features and MFCCs were used in [32] and [33] respectively to detect emotion from speech. In [34], they observed that few features such as pitch and MFCC, gave a better performance when combined together as opposed to when evaluated individually on KNN and Naïve Bayes classifiers. [35] combined prosodic, statistical and spectral features to detect dialects from speech.

2.2   Explainable Artificial Intelligence (XAI)

Deep neural network models have recorded exemplary state-of-the-art performance in solving various hardly specifiable computationally complex problems across various domains, hate speech detection being one of them. However, even though these models build intelligent systems with high performance and predictive power, they tend to ignore the aspect of enhancing transparency and trust among end users as they are black-box in nature. This becomes a challenge in that end-users are not able to fully comprehend the inner workings of the complex layers, the models' internal representations, the automated decision-making process and the final processing formats of any machine learning models. Therefore, to deal with this challenge presented by the use of these complex classifiers, explainable AI techniques are explored to provide explanations in a human-understandable way of the results achieved and the decision-making process of the classifiers.

In addition, it is crucial to have a thorough understanding and use-case analysis and requirements of the XAI methodologies needed so as to use the most suitable explainable AI technique corresponding to the task at hand. Some of the aspects of XAI methodologies include scope, whether local or global, explanation stage, that is ante-hoc or post-hoc, problem type etc. Various studies have explored various explainable AI techniques to explain the predictions achieved by various classifiers. In [36], Shapley Additive explanation (SHAP) technique was used explain the predictions achieved by Distil Bert to detect abusive language on social media. The local Interpretable Model-agnostic explanations (LIME) was used in several studies [37,38] to explain the predictions achieved on text and image datasets trained on VilBert classifier. In [39], Grad-CAM was used to elaborate the application of explainability on legal texts.

3   System Implementation

An explainable hate speech framework is proposed to detect hate speech for English and Kiswahili languages. The steps involved are presented in Fig. 1, include, video dataset collection, pre-processing, audio feature extraction, model training and the application of explainability techniques to explain the predictions achieved.

3.1   Speech Dataset

Dataset Collection. The video dataset for English and Kiswahili languages was collected manually due to the lack of availability of public, standard well-constructed hate speech audio dataset. Since YouTube is a popular video-sharing platform, it was used as the primary source of data collection of videos considered to be containing hatred and normal utterances. The search by keyword function of the YouTube API was used to search for hate speech-related videos which were then downloaded using PyTube in mp4 format.

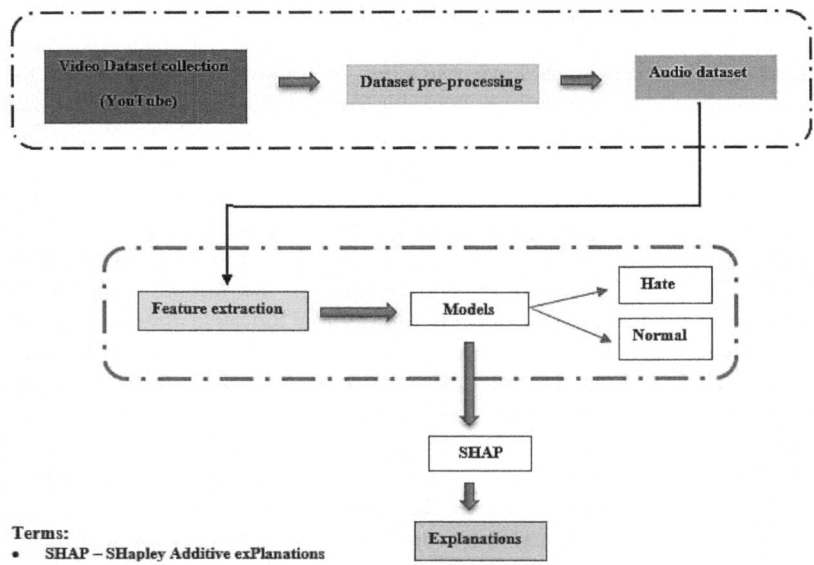

Fig. 1. Explainable hate speech detection framework.

Dataset Pre-processing. To improve the quality of the downloaded video dataset, pre-processing was carried out. Speaker diarization using Praat tool was carried out so as to separate the speakers in separate videos, for example "who spoke when and what". In addition, long pauses, coughs, sneezing, background music, noise was removed.

Audio Dataset. The preprocessed video dataset was converted to audio in wav format using the FFmpeg API. The English language dataset consisted of 160 audio samples where audios containing normal speech were 75 while audios containing hate speech were 85. Kiswahili language dataset consisted of 170 audio samples where audios containing normal speech were 80 while audios containing hate speech were 90.

3.2   Feature Extraction

Various audio-based features were extracted from the audio dataset using short-term processing so as to characterize, classify and evaluate various classifiers and model the speech variations from the resulting audio dataset. In addition, combining various features improves exponentially the performance of a classifier as opposed to using individual features. The features extracted include spectral, temporal, prosodic and excitation source (statistical) features. Spectral features include spectral centroid, spectral rolloff, cepstral coefficients, a feature vector consisting of Mel-Frequency Cepstral Coefficients (MFCC), its derivatives (delta and delta-delta MFCC), chroma vector features. Temporal features include zero crossing rate (ZCR) and root mean square energy (RMSE) while prosodic features include speech rate (tempo) and pitch. Excitation source features extracted include standard deviation(STD), mean, variance, kurtosis and skewness. Librosa [45] was used to process the audio signals and extract these features.

3.3 Models

The audio-based features extracted for both English and Kiswahili languages were used to train various classifiers as discussed below.

Random Forest (RF). Also known as random decision forests, is an ensemble algorithm mostly used in classification and regression tasks [40]. This algorithm primarily works by aggregating the decision trees during training producing the output of the particular class of the decision tress as the mean prediction. A higher predictive performance is achieved by this model by employing multiple decision trees and producing an ensemble of uncorrelated decision trees. To decorrelate and also chop the decision trees, this model selects or uses different subsets generated by bootstrap aggregating the available dataset during training. This feature sub-sampling is done by using randomly selected feature subset at each split. Due to this, the model has recorded a high accuracy more so when used on large sets of data in many domains. Voting of the individual trees' predictions is done to achieve the models' final prediction. The hyper parameters used in this study were the number of tree estimators' and maximum features of values 1000 and 32 respectively.

Extreme Gradient Boosting (XGBoost). This powerful and non-linear framework is primarily based on the concept of "boosting" to optimize its learning process by iteratively adding the predictions achieved by several weak learners to build a stronger predictive learner in classification and regression tasks. To control overfitting, a regularized method is adopted while gradient descent is used to optimize the differential loss [41]. The sequential manner in which the decision trees are built allows the errors done by the previous tree to be corrected by the succeeding trees. A weighted sum of the combined predictions is done so as to arrive at the final prediction. The hyper parameters used in this study were the max_depth and lambda with a default value of 6 and 1 respectively.

Multi-layer Perceptron (MLP). Neural network algorithms have gained significant attention in solving various problems due to their exceptional performance. Multilayer Perceptron classifier is a densely connected feed forward artificial neural network. It consists of various layers, that is, one input layer, several hidden layers and an output layer. Training of an MLP classifier involves back propagation and stochastic gradient descent optimization technique. The hyper parameter used were the learning rate, hidden_layer_sizes and solver set at 0.01, 3 and adam respectively.

3.4 Explainable AI (XAI) Techniques

SHapley Additive exPlanations technique (SHAP) was used to explain the predictions achieved by the best performing model for each language, that is, English and Kiswahili.

SHapley Additive exPlanations Technique (SHAP). SHAP was developed by Lundberg and Lee [46] to interpret the predictions achieved by various machine learning classifiers. The interpretation by SHAP mostly reflects on the effects produced by each samples features' hence displaying both negative and positive effects. While positive features clearly contribute to the task's prediction, the negative features showcase a negative contribution or inactivity to the predictions achieved. This technique utilizes the optimal shapely values based on game theory whose main aim is to fairly distribute the "credit" of the predictions among the input features used. Therefore, the classifier used generates a predicted value for the individual predicted samples and assigns a SHAP value to each input feature in the data sample [47]. Some of advantages of using this technique include its solid theoretical foundation as predictions are fairly distributed, for tree-based models, it has a fast implementation and the computation of shapely values for global model interpretations is possible due to its fast computation ability. Some of the properties of SHAP values are: model-agnosticity, consistency, local accuracy, additivity and missingness, that is, the values are zero for irrelevant or missing features for a particular prediction.

4 Results and Discussion

In this section, the experimental setup, the results achieved and the results explanations using SHAP explainability technique will be discussed. The experiments were conducted individually on each classifier to detect hate speech on the audio dataset for both English and Kiswahili language.

4.1 Experimental Setup

Keras and scikit-learn libraries were used as they are responsible for implementing various machine learning and deep learning algorithms [43]. These use input as a feature vector of NumPy arrays [44, 45]. In addition, Librosa was used to process the audio signals. The default sample, hop, frame rate was set at 22050 Hz, 512 samples and 2048 samples respectively. After extracting audio-based features from the audio datasets of both English and Kiswahili languages, the features were stored in a CSV format separately. This data was stored in a row and column format hence becoming easy to use. Various libraries such as Pandas, NumPy and Matplotlib were used to operate these CSV files. Classical machine learning models such as random forest (RF) and extreme gradient boosting (XGB) and a multi-layer perceptron classifier were trained using these audio-based features for each language after splitting the features in 80:20 ratio, that is, 80% for training and 20% for testing. In addition, k-fold cross validation, that is, k = 5 was used to ensure that both our training and testing sets are disjoint. Accuracy score and Area Under the ROC Curve (AUC) metric were used to assess the performance of the various classifiers explored in this study. AUC is the probability that a negative audio sample chosen randomly will have a smaller estimated probability to belong to a positive class compared to a positive audio sample that is chosen randomly. Accuracy score shows the percentage of the number of audios which are correctly classified with respect to the actual number of audios in the dataset.

4.2   Results

Two separate experiments, for English and Kiswahili languages were conducted using 72 audio-based features extracted from the audio datasets. The features used were divided into three sets, that is set 1, set 2 and set 3. Initially, the standard spectral and temporal features and English language were considered as the baseline features and language respectively. The other features were added in subsequent experiments. Experiments were later performed for Kiswahili language since its an under-resourced language and little of no research has been carried out as far as hate speech detection using audio is concerned.

Set 1 Features: The feature vector in this set consists of spectral features, that is MFCCs (a small feature set typically about 10–20 features), its 26-dimensional derivatives delta and delta-delta coefficients, chroma, spectral centroid and spectral roll off. Temporal features consist of zero crossing rate and root mean square energy. From Table 1 and Table 2, random forest performed better for English language achieving an accuracy of 90.1% and auc score of 91.3% while extreme gradient boosting gave a better performance for Kiswahili language achieving an accuracy of 86.5% and an auc score of 87.2%. The exceptional performance exhibited by random forest is owed to how the classifier is trained. Machine learning models performed better than the MLP classifier which achieved an accuracy of 78.5% and auc score of 76.5% for English and an accuracy of 71.4% and auc score of 77.8% for Kiswahili language.

Set 2 Features: In this feature set, prosodic, features (pitch and speech rate) were added on top of the features in set 1 and used to train the classifiers we used earlier for set 1. From Table 1 and Table 2, random forest gave a better performance for both English and Kiswahili languages. For English language, the classifier achieved an accuracy of 94.6% and an auc of 93.2% while for Kiswahili language, an accuracy of 90.4% and auc of 89.8% was achieved. It is also worth noting that the performance of both classifiers, random forest and extreme gradient boosting, increased considerably as compared to their performance when trained using features in set 1. Machine learning models performed better than the MLP classifier which achieved an accuracy of 85.7% and auc score of 84.4% for English and an accuracy of 80.9% and auc score of 81.7% for Kiswahili language.

Set 3 Features: In this feature set, excitation source features (variance, skewness, arithmetic mean, standard deviation, and kurtosis) were added on top of the features in set 2 and used to train the classifiers we used in our earlier experiments. From Table 1 and Table 2, random forest gave better performance for English language, achieving an accuracy of 95.8% and auc score of 95.6% while extreme gradient boosting achieved a high accuracy of 91.8% and auc score of 94.2% for Kiswahili language. It is also worth noting that the performance of both classifiers, random forest and extreme gradient boosting, increased considerably as compared to their performance when trained using features in set 2. MLP classifier performed better than extreme gradient boosting model for English language, achieving an accuracy of 93.3% and auc score of 92.9%. However, the classifier recorded a low accuracy of 86.7% and auc score of 85.7% for Kiswahili language when compared with the other classifiers used.

Table 1. Accuracy score results obtained for English and Kiswahili languages

Feature Set	Models	English Language	Kiswahili Language
Set 1	RF	90.1	85.0
	XGBoost	86.0	86.5
	MLP	78.5	71.4
Set 2	RF	94.6	90.4
	XGBoost	90.0	90.0
	MLP	85.7	80.9
Set 3	RF	95.8	90.6
	XGBoost	91.6	91.8
	MLP	93.3	86.7

Comparative Analysis. A comparative analysis of the audio-based features' performance when trained on random forest, extreme gradient boosting and MLP classifier for English and Kiswahili languages is shown in Figs. 2 and Fig. 3. We can make an observation that, across all features, random forest gave the best performance for English language from set 1 to set 3 while the best performance

Table 2. AUC score results obtained for English and Kiswahili languages

Feature Set	Models	English Language	Kiswahili Language
Set 1	RF	91.3	84.5
	XGBoost	87.6	87.2
	MLP	76.5	77.8
Set 2	RF	93.2	89.8
	XGBoost	91.8	88.7
	MLP	84.4	81.7
Set 3	RF	95.6	89.4
	XGBoost	92.1	94.2
	MLP	92.9	85.7

for Kiswahili language was when the classifier was trained with features in set 2. In addition, extreme gradient boosting achieved the best accuracy for Kiswahili language when trained with features in set 1 and 2. As far as feature performance is concerned, features in set 3 performed better that those in set 1 and 2. This implies that adding more audio-based features improved the accuracy in both languages. In addition, English language recorded the best overall accuracy of 95.8% and auc score of 95.6% as compared to Kiswahili language whose accuracy was 91.8% and auc score of 94.2%. This might be due to the availability and high quality of the videos collected for English language since it is the most widely used language on social media. It is also worth noting that machine learning classifiers performed better than the MLP classifier.

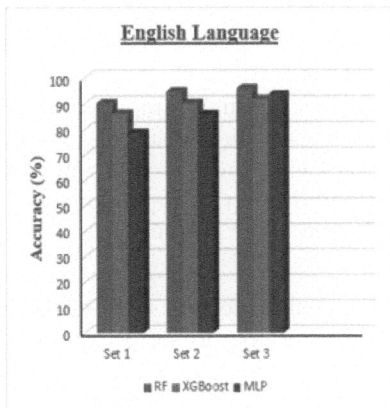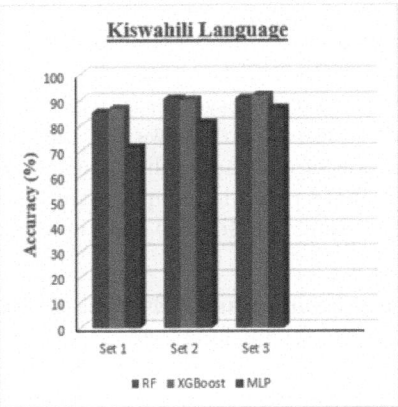

Fig. 2. A comparative analysis of the accuracy score results achieved by various models for English and Kiswahili languages.

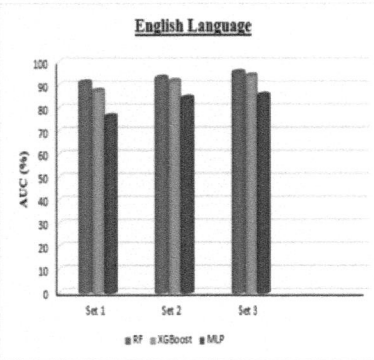 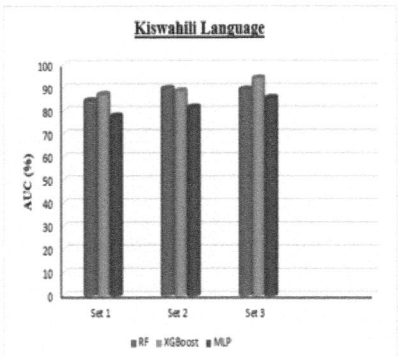

Fig. 3. A comparative analysis of the auc score results achieved by various models for English and Kiswahili languages.

4.3 SHAP Explainability Analysis

SHAP explainability technique was explored to explain the predictions achieved by the highest performing model, that is, random forest for English language and extreme gradient boosting for Kiswahili language.

English Language. Random forest model, the best performing classifier for English language when trained with features in set 3, was used to perform various experiments using the SHAP Tree explainer technique. Figure 4 (a) shows a typical bar plot primarily based on the Shapley values' mean magnitude over the entire audio training data. These values are in descending order in relation to the feature importance of the hate speech dataset. Out of 72 audio feature vector extracted, the most important feature was mfcc4 followed closely by mfcc2 indicating that MFCCs were the most important features. In addition, out of the 20 mfcc feature vector, mfcc4 and mfcc2 were the most important MFCC features. Figure 4 (b) shows the summary plot indicating the summation of the magnitude of the shap values. In the plot, mfcc4 is the most important feature while mfcc18 is the least important feature. In addition, the impact of spec_cent (spectral centroid) feature was by a large value on a few predictions.

Kiswahili Language. Extreme Gradient Boosting, the best-performing classifier for Kiswahili language when trained with features in set 3, was used to perform various experiments using the SHAP Tree explainer technique. In Fig. 5 (a), from the bar plot we observe that out of 72 audio-features extracted, the most important feature was mfcc17 followed closely by mfcc5 and mfcc1 showing that mfccs were the most important features. In addition, the excitation source features such as std (standard deviation) and prosodic feature tempo (speech rate) contributed significantly towards the classifiers' prediction. Figure 5 (b) where the most mfcc17 is the most important feature while kurt, mfcc19 and

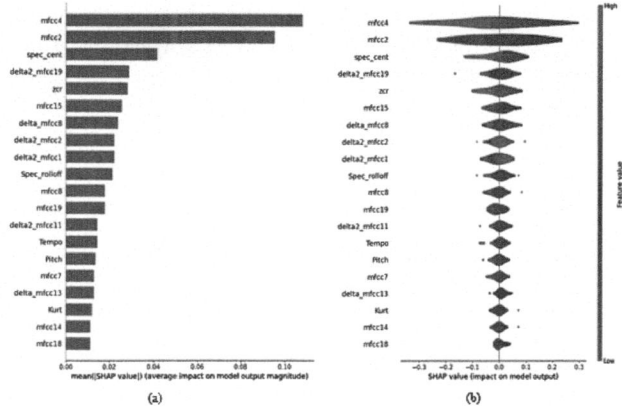

Fig. 4. SHAP's visualization for English Language (a) Bar plot (b) Summary plot

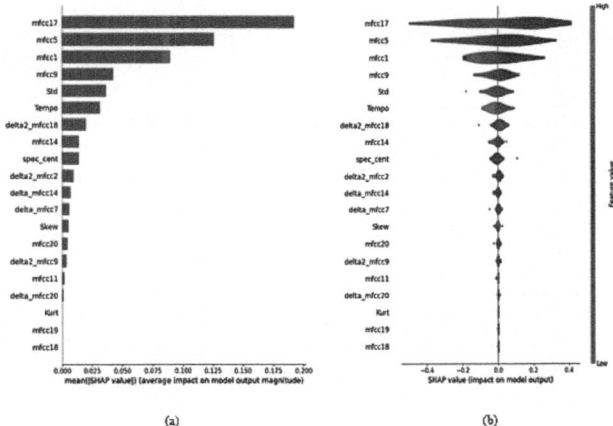

Fig. 5. SHAP's visualization for Kiswahili language (a) Bar plot (b) Summary plot

mfcc18 were the least important features. In addition, the impact of mfcc1 feature was by a large value on a few predictions.

5   Conclusion

In this paper, SHAP explainability technique was used to explain the predictions achieved by the classifiers used to detect hate speech in audio. Audio-based features were extracted and used to train random forest and extreme gradient boosting and multi-layer perceptron classifiers. For English language, random

forest recorded an accuracy of 95.8% while extreme gradient boosting classifier recorded an accuracy of 91.8% for Kiswahili language. In the future, this
work on hate speech detection can be extended to other explainability artificial
intelligence techniques and on deep learning classifiers.

References

1. Doshi-Velez, F., Kim, B.: Towards a rigorous science of interpretable machine learning (2017). arXiv:1702.08608
2. Schmidt, A., Wiegand, M.: A survey on hate speech detection using natural language processing. In: Proceedings of the Fifth International Workshop on Natural
   Language Processing for Social Media (2017)
3. Fortuna, P., Nunes, S.: A survey on automatic detection of hate speech in text.
   ACM Comput. Surv. (CSUR) **51**(4), 1–30 (2018)
4. Poletto, F., et al.: Resources and benchmark corpora for hate speech detection: a
   systematic review. Lang. Resour. Eval. **55**, 477–523 (2021)
5. Pradhan, R., et al.: A review on offensive language detection. In: Advances in Data
   and Information Sciences: Proceedings of ICDIS 2019, vol. 433–439 (2020)
6. Yin, W., Zubiaga, A.: Towards generalisable hate speech detection: a review on
   obstacles and solutions. PeerJ Comput. Sci. **7**, e598 (2021)
7. Mullah, N.S., Zainon, W.M.N.W.: Advances in machine learning algorithms for
   hate speech detection in social media: a review. IEEE Access **9**, 88364–88376 (2021)
8. Davidson, T., et al.: Automated hate speech detection and the problem of offensive
   language. In: Proceedings of the International AAAI Conference on Web and Social
   Media, vol. 11, no. 1 (2017)
9. Wiegand, M., Siegel, M., Ruppenhofer, J.: Overview of the Germeval 2018 shared
   task on the identification of offensive language, 1–10 (2018)
10. Sanguinetti, M., et al.: An Italian twitter corpus of hate speech against immigrants.
    In: Proceedings of the Eleventh International Conference on Language Resources
    and Evaluation (LREC 2018) (2018)
11. Mulki, H., et al.: L-HSAB: a levantine twitter dataset for hate speech and abusive
    language. In: Proceedings of the Third Workshop on Abusive Language Online
    (2019)
12. Ika, A., et al.: Hate speech detection in the Indonesian language: a dataset and pre-
    liminary study. In: 2017 International Conference on Advanced Computer Science
    and Information Systems (ICACSIS). IEEE (2017)
13. Mubarak, H., Darwish, K., Magdy, W.: Abusive language detection on Arabic
    social media. In: Proceedings of the First Workshop on Abusive Language Online
    (2017)
14. De Gibert, O., et al.: Hate speech dataset from a white supremacy forum. arXiv
    preprint arXiv:1809.04444 (2018)
15. Jing, Q., et al.: A benchmark dataset for learning to intervene in online hate speech.
    arXiv preprint arXiv:1909.04251 (2019)
16. Badjatiya, P., et al.: Deep learning for hate speech detection in tweets. In: Pro-
    ceedings of the 26th International Conference on World Wide Web Companion
    (2017)
17. Mugambi, S.K.: TF-IDF weighted N-Grams based approach. Diss. Strathmore Uni-
    versity, Sentiment analysis for hate speech detection on social media (2017)

18. Hasanuzzaman, M., Dias, G., Way, A.: Demographic word embeddings for racism detection on twitter. In: Proceedings of the Eighth International Joint Conference on Natural Language Processing, vol. 1, Long Papers (2017)
19. Warner, W., Hirschberg, J.: Detecting hate speech on the world wide web. In: Proceedings of the Second Workshop on Language in Social Media (2012)
20. Nemanja, D., et al.: Hate speech detection with comment embeddings. In: Proceedings of the 24th International Conference on World Wide Web (2015)
21. Chikashi, N., et al. Abusive language detection in online user content. In: Proceedings of the 25th International Conference on World Wide Web (2016)
22. Zhi, X., Zhu, S.: Filtering offensive language in online communities using grammatical relations. In: Proceedings of the Seventh Annual Collaboration, Electronic Messaging, Anti-Abuse and Spam Conference (2010)
23. Kandakatla, R.: Identifying offensive videos on YouTube. Wright State University, Diss (2016)
24. Pelle, D., Prates, R., Moreira, V.P.: Offensive comments in the Brazilian web: a dataset and baseline results. In: Anais do VI Brazilian Workshop on Social Network Analysis and Mining, SBC (2017)
25. Del Vigna12, F., et al.: Hate me, hate me not: hate speech detection on Facebook. In: Proceedings of the First Italian Conference on Cybersecurity (ITASEC17) 2017
26. Ombui, E., Muchemi, L., Wagacha, P.: Hate speech detection in code-switched text messages. In: 3rd International Symposium on Multidisciplinary Studies and Innovative Technologies (ISMSIT). Ankara, Turkey **2019**, 1–6 (2019). https://doi.org/10.1109/ISMSIT.2019.8932845
27. Romim, N., Ahmed, M., Talukder, H., Saiful Islam, M.: Hate speech detection in the Bengali language: a dataset and its baseline evaluation. In: Uddin, M.S., Bansal, J.C. (eds.) Proceedings of International Joint Conference on Advances in Computational Intelligence. AIS, pp. 457–468. Springer, Singapore (2021). https://doi.org/10.1007/978-981-16-0586-4_37
28. Vishal, A., et al.: Customized video filtering on YouTube. arXiv preprint arXiv:1911.04013 (2019)
29. Wu, C.S., Bhandary, U.: Detection of hate speech in videos using machine learning. In: 2020 International Conference on Computational Science and Computational Intelligence (CSCI), Las Vegas, NV, USA, 2020, pp. 585–590 (2020)
30. Junaid, M.I.H., Hossain, F., Rahman, R.M.: Bangla hate speech detection in videos using machine learning. In: IEEE 12th Annual Ubiquitous Computing, Electronics & Mobile Communication Conference (UEMCON). New York, NY, USA **2021**, 0347–0351 (2021)
31. Ibañez, M., Sapinit, R., Reyes, L.A., Hussien, M., Imperial, J.M., Rodriguez, R.: Audio-Based Hate Speech Classification from Online Short-Form Videos. In: 2021 International Conference on Asian Language Processing (IALP), Singapore, Singapore, pp. 72–77 (2021)
32. Hu, H., Xu, M.X., Wu, W.: GMM supervector based SVM with spectral features for speech emotion recognition. In: 2007 IEEE International Conference on Acoustics, Speech and Signal Processing - ICASSP 2007, Honolulu, HI, USA, 2007, pp. IV-413-IV-416 (2007)
33. Ittichaichareon, C., Suksri, S., Yingthawornsuk, T.: Speech recognition using MFCC. In: International Conference on Computer Graphics, Simulation and Modeling, vol. 9 (2012)
34. Khan, A., Roy, U.K.: Emotion recognition using prosodie and spectral features of speech and Naïve Bayes Classifier. In: 2017 International Conference on Wireless Communications, Signal Processing and Networking (WiSPNET). IEEE (2017)

35. Chittaragi, N.B., Koolagudi, S.G.: Sentence-based dialect identification system using extreme gradient boosting algorithm. In: Elçi, A., Sa, P.K., Modi, C.N., Olague, G., Sahoo, M.N., Bakshi, S. (eds.) Smart Computing Paradigms: New Progresses and Challenges. AISC, vol. 766, pp. 131–138. Springer, Singapore (2020). https://doi.org/10.1007/978-981-13-9683-0_14

36. Wich, M., Mosca, E., Gorniak, A., Hingerl, J., Groh, G.: Explainable Abusive Language Classification Leveraging User and Network Data. In: Dong, Y., Kourtellis, N., Hammer, B., Lozano, J.A. (eds.) Machine Learning and Knowledge Discovery in Databases. Applied Data Science Track. ECML PKDD 2021 (2021)

37. Amri, S., Sallami, D., Aïmeur, E.: EXMULF: An explainable multimodal content-based fake news detection system. In: Aïmeur, E., Laurent, M., Yaich, R., Dupont, B., Garcia-Alfaro, J. (eds.) Foundations and Practice of Security (2022)

38. Pramanick, S., et al.: Detecting harmful memes and their targets. In: Findings of the Association for Computational Linguistics, ACL-IJCNLP 2021, pp. 2783–2796 (2021)

39. Gorski, L., Ramakrishna, S., Nowosielski, J.M.: Towards grad-CAM based Explainability in a legal text processing pipeline. arXiv preprint arXiv:2012.09603 (2020)

40. Freund, Y., Schapire, R., Abe, N.: A short introduction to boosting. J. Jpn. Soc. Artif. Intell. **14**(771780), 1612 (1999)

41. Mihalkova, L., Huynh, T., Mooney, R.J.: Mapping and revising Markov logic networks for transfer learning. In: AAAI, vol. 7, pp. 608–614 (2007)

42. Paul, B.: PRAAT: doing phonetics by computer [Computer program]. http://www.praat.org/ (2011)

43. Jason, B.: Deep Learning with Python: Develop Deep Learning Models on Theano and TensorFlow Using Keras. Machine Learning Mastery (2016)

44. Fabian, P., et al.: Scikit-learn: machine learning in Python. J. Mach. Learn. Res. **12**, 2825–2830 (2011)

45. McFee, B., et al.: librosa: audio and music signal analysis in python. In: SciPy, pp. 18–24 (2015)

46. Lundberg, S.M., Lee, S.I.: A unified approach to interpreting model predictions. In: Advances in Neural Information Processing Systems, vol. 30 (2017)

47. Yang, C., Chen, M., Yuan, Q.: The application of XGBoost and SHAP to examining the factors in freight truck-related crashes: an exploratory analysis. Accident Anal. Prev. **158**, 106153 (2021)

Distributed Random Forest for Predicting Forest Wildfires Based on Weather Data

Robertas Damaševišius[1]([✉]) and Rytis Maskeliūnas[2]

[1] Department of Applied Informatics, Vytautas Magnus University,
Kaunas, Lithuania
robertas.damasevicius@vdu.lt
[2] Department of Multimedia Engineering, Kaunas University of Technology,
Kaunas, Lithuania
rytis.maskeliunas@ktu.lt

Abstract. Forest fires pose a significant threat to ecosystems, economies, and human settlements. Accurate prediction of forest fires can aid in timely interventions, resource allocation, and effective management strategies. This study aimed to develop a machine learning model to predict forest fire occurrences based on various environmental and meteorological variables. Using a dataset comprising variables such as temperature, humidity, wind speed, and moisture codes (FFMC, DMC, DC, and ISI), we employed Distributed Random Forest (DRF) and a 5-fold cross-validation approach on training data to assess the model's performance. The model demonstrated high discriminatory power with an AUC of 0.989 and a low Mean Squared Error (MSE) of 0.041. The results underscored the critical role of weather conditions and fuel moisture content in influencing fire occurrences. The study's findings have implications for forest management, emphasizing the potential of machine learning in shaping fire prevention strategies and safeguarding forest ecosystems.

Keywords: Forest fires · Predictive modeling · Weather data · Wildfire prediction

1 Introduction

Forest fires, also known as wildfires, have been a natural occurrence shaping ecosystems for millions of years. These fires play a crucial role in the ecological processes, aiding in nutrient recycling, habitat creation, and the natural succession of species. However, in recent decades, the frequency, intensity, and scale of forest fires have escalated dramatically, causing widespread ecological destruction, economic losses, and even human casualties. Several factors contribute to the onset and spread of forest fires. While some are anthropogenic, such as land clearance and arson, natural factors, particularly weather conditions, play a significant role. Weather variables like temperature, humidity, wind speed, and precipitation have been observed to influence the likelihood and intensity of forest fires. For instance, prolonged dry spells, coupled with high temperatures and

© The Author(s), under exclusive license to Springer Nature Switzerland AG 2024
A. Verma et al. (Eds.): ANTIC 2023, CCIS 2091, pp. 305–320, 2024.
https://doi.org/10.1007/978-3-031-64064-3_22

strong winds, create conducive environments for fires to ignite and spread. The changing global climate has further exacerbated the situation. With rising global temperatures, many regions are experiencing longer and more intense droughts, making them more susceptible to forest fires. This changing dynamic underscores the need for a deeper understanding of the relationship between weather patterns and forest fires. The devastating impacts of forest fires are felt globally, transcending geographical boundaries and affecting both developed and developing nations. Recent catastrophic events, such as the Australian bushfires of 2019–2020 and the wildfires in Greece [30] and Portugal [25], have brought the issue to the forefront of global attention. These events have not only resulted in the loss of millions of acres of forest but have also led to significant human displacement, loss of life, and billions in economic damages. Yet, despite the increasing frequency and intensity of these fires, our predictive capabilities remain limited. Current early warning systems and predictive models often rely on a combination of historical data and real-time observations, which, while valuable, may not always provide adequate lead time for preventive measures or resource allocation.

Weather patterns, being a primary natural driver for forest fires, offer a promising avenue for enhancing our predictive capabilities [9]. If we can harness the vast amounts of weather data available and develop robust models that accurately predict forest fires, we can significantly improve our preparedness and response strategies [7]. Furthermore, as climate change continues to alter global weather patterns, understanding the nuanced relationship between weather variables and forest fires becomes even more critical. This research is motivated by the urgent need to bridge the gap between our current understanding and the evolving challenges posed by forest fires in a changing climate. In this context, predicting forest fires based on weather data becomes not just an academic exercise but a pressing necessity. Accurate predictions can aid in early warning systems, better resource allocation, and more informed forest management strategies, potentially saving lives, preserving biodiversity, and reducing economic losses [3].

The primary objective of this study is to explore the potential of weather data as a predictive tool for forest fires. To achieve this, the research aims to:

1. Analyze and quantify the relationship between key weather variables, namely temperature, humidity, wind speed, and precipitation, and the occurrence and intensity of forest fires.
2. Evaluate the performance of these models in terms of their accuracy, reliability, and applicability in real-world scenarios.

2   Literature Review

2.1   Overview of Forest Fire Prediction Methods

The prediction of forest fires has been a topic of interest for several decades, with methodologies evolving alongside advancements in technology and data availability. Early prediction methods were primarily deterministic, relying on field observations and expert judgment. These methods often utilized the Fire Danger Rating System (FDRS), which considered factors like fuel moisture content, wind speed, and temperature to assess fire risk [4].

With the advent of computational capabilities, statistical models became prominent. Logistic regression has been employed to predict the probability of fire occurrence based on meteorological variable [21,29,31]. Time-series analysis, especially autoregressive integrated moving average (ARIMA) models, have been used to forecast fire occurrences based on historical data [28].

The recent two decades have witnessed a surge in the application of machine learning techniques for forest fire prediction [5,13,23,24]. Decision trees and random forests have been popular due to their ability to handle non-linear relationships and provide insights into sniprtance [1]. Neural networks, with their capacity to model complex patterns, have also been explored, especially with the rise of deep learning architectures [19]. Despite these advancements, challenges persist. Many models, while accurate in controlled settings, struggle with real-world applicability due to the dynamic and multifaceted nature of forest fires. Additionally, the integration of diverse data sources, from satellite imagery to on-ground sensors, remains a complex task. While significant strides have been made in forest fire prediction methods, there remains a pressing need for models that are both accurate and applicable in diverse real-world scenarios.

2.2 Weather Variables and Their Impact on Forest Fires

Weather variables play a pivotal role in influencing the occurrence, spread, and intensity of forest fires. Their impact on forest fires has been extensively studied, revealing intricate relationships that vary across different geographical and temporal scales [12,17].

Temperature is one of the most influential factors in forest fire dynamics. Elevated temperatures lead to increased evaporation rates, drying out vegetation and making it more susceptible to ignition. Moreover, high temperatures can increase the intensity and spread rate of fires once ignited. Several studies have shown a direct correlation between prolonged heatwaves and an increase in the number and intensity of forest fires.

Humidity, or the amount of moisture in the air, inversely affects the likelihood of forest fires. Low humidity levels result in drier conditions, reducing the moisture content in vegetation and making it more flammable. Conversely, high humidity levels can act as a mitigating factor, reducing the fire's intensity and spread. The interplay between temperature and humidity is especially crucial, with their combined effects often determining the overall fire risk.

Wind plays a dual role in forest fire dynamics. On one hand, strong winds provide the necessary oxygen to fuel the fire, increasing its intensity and spread rate. On the other hand, winds can carry embers and firebrands over considerable distances, leading to spot fires and rapid fire propagation. Wind direction, in conjunction with speed, can influence the direction of fire spread, making it a critical factor in fire management and containment strategies.

Precipitation, both in terms of its amount and distribution, has a direct impact on forest fire risk. Regular rainfall can maintain moisture levels in vegetation, reducing its flammability. Irregular precipitation patterns, such as prolonged droughts followed by short intense rainfall, can create conditions conducive to fires. Rain can lead to rapid vegetation growth, which, when followed by dry periods, results in an abundance of dry fuel, elevating the fire risk.

While each weather variable has its distinct impact on forest fires, it's their combined and interactive effects that determine the overall fire risk in a region. Understanding these intricate relationships is crucial for developing accurate predictive models.

2.3   Machine Learning Models and Their Limitations

Machine learning has emerged as a powerful tool in the realm of forest fire prediction and detection. Over the years, various models have been proposed, each with its strengths and weaknesses [1]. This section delves into some of the most prominent machine learning models used for fire detection and highlights their associated limitations.

Decision Trees are a popular choice for fire prediction due to their interpretability and ability to handle non-linear relationships. They work by recursively splitting the data based on feature thresholds, leading to a tree-like model of decisions. Random Forests, an ensemble of decision trees, further enhance the model's accuracy by aggregating predictions from multiple trees [8,26,27]. While Random Forests mitigate this to some extent, individual decision trees are prone to overfitting, especially with noisy data. In regions where fires are rare, the model might be biased towards non-fire predictions. Decision trees are inherently local models and might not generalize well to conditions outside the training data.

Support Vector Machines (SVM) have been employed for fire detection, especially in scenarios where the dataset is not vast [8,21,26]. They work by finding the hyperplane that best separates the classes in a high-dimensional space. SVMs can be computationally intensive, especially with large datasets. The performance of SVMs can vary significantly based on the choice of kernel and regularization parameters. Unlike decision trees, SVMs do not provide an intuitive understanding of feature importance.

With the rise of deep learning, Artificial Neural Networks (ANN) have been explored for fire detection [10,27,32]. These models consist of interconnected layers of neurons that can learn complex patterns from data. Deep neural networks, with their vast number of parameters, are prone to overfitting, especially with limited data. Training deep neural networks requires significant computational resources. Neural networks, especially deep ones, lack the interpretability of models like decision trees, making it challenging to understand their predictions.

K-Nearest Neighbors (KNN) is a simple, instance-based learning algorithm. When used For fire prediction [11,31], it would classify a new instance based on the majority class of its 'k' nearest training instances. KNN's performance can degrade if the dataset has irrelevant or redundant features. The algorithm can be slow for large datasets as it requires computing distances to all training instances for each prediction. KNN assumes that data points in the same class are homogeneous, which might not always hold true for fire prediction.

While machine learning offers promising avenues for fire detection, it's evident that no single model is universally optimal. The choice of model depends on the specific context, data availability, and desired outcomes. Moreover, the inherent limitations of these models underscore the importance of continuous research, model refinement, and the potential benefits of hybrid models that combine the strengths of multiple approaches.

2.4 Deep Learning Models and Their Limitations

Deep learning, a subset of machine learning, has revolutionized numerous domains, including the realm of forest fire detection. Leveraging neural networks with many layers, deep learning models can automatically learn hierarchical representations from data. This section delves into some of the most prominent deep learning models used for fire detection and highlights their associated limitations.

Convolutional Neural Networks (CNNs) are primarily designed for image processing and have been employed for detecting fires using satellite and aerial imagery [2,14,16]. They consist of convolutional layers that automatically and adaptively learn spatial hierarchies from the data. CNNs require vast amounts of labeled data to train effectively, which can be a challenge given the rarity of fire events. Training CNNs, especially deeper architectures, demands significant computational resources and time. While transfer learning using pre-trained CNNs can mitigate the data demand, these models might not always be optimal for specific fire detection tasks.

Recurrent Neural Networks (RNNs), and their advanced variant Long Short-Term Memory (LSTM), are designed to handle sequential data. They've been explored for predicting forest fires based on time-series weather data [15,18,20]. Traditional RNNs suffer from the vanishing gradient problem, making them challenging to train. While LSTMs mitigate this issue, they introduce additional complexity. LSTMs, with their gating mechanisms, can be memory-intensive. While they handle sequences, LSTMs might struggle with very long-term dependencies without additional architectural modifications.

Deep learning models, with their ability to learn intricate patterns from data, offer promising avenues for fire detection. However, they come with their set of challenges, primarily related to data demand, computational intensity, and interpretability. As with traditional machine learning, the choice of a deep learning model for fire detection should be context-specific, considering the nature of the data, available resources, and desired outcomes. Continuous research in this domain is essential to harness the full potential of deep learning for forest fire detection and mitigation.

3 Methodology

3.1 Dataset

We use the dataset [6]. The dataset captures forest fires in the northeast region of Portugal and integrates meteorological data with data on forest fires. The primary aim of this dataset is to predict the burned area of forest fires using these attributes. The primary objective when using this dataset is to predict the "Area" attribute (i.e., the burned area) based on the other attributes. This can be approached as a regression problem, where the goal is to predict a continuous value, or as a classification problem (e.g., by categorizing the burned area into 'low', 'medium', 'high'). Here we predict if $Area > 0$, i.e., whether a fire has occured. The dataset captures a diverse range of conditions, from different times of the year to varying weather scenarios.

The attributes of the dataset are summarized in Table 1. The Fine Fuel Moisture Code (FFMC), Duff Moisture Code (DMC), Drought Code (DC), and Initial Spread Index (ISI) are components of the Fire Weather Index (FWI) system, which is widely used for assessing wildfire potential. This system is used to estimate the risk of wildfire in various regions based on meteorological data. Each of these components provides insights into different aspects of fire potential.

FFMC is an index that represents the moisture content in the top litter and other fine fuels present in the forest floor. It gives an indication of the relative ease of ignition and the flammability of fine fuel. The FFMC value increases as the moisture content decreases (i.e., as the fine fuels become drier). A high FFMC value indicates that surface fuels are dry and can easily ignite. It's particularly sensitive to changes in relative humidity and temperature.

DMC represents the moisture content in the organic layers beneath the surface, specifically in the upper duff layers. This index gives an indication of fuel consumption in moderate-depth duff layers and medium-sized woody material. A higher DMC value indicates that the organic materials in the subsurface are dry. This means that if a fire were to start, it could burn more deeply and intensely, consuming the organic material in the forest floor.

DC is an index that represents the moisture content in deeper, compact organic layers. It's an indicator of seasonal drought effects and the flammability of the deeper organic layers. A high DC value indicates that the deeper organic layers are dry, suggesting a long-term drying trend. This can be particularly concerning as it means fires can burn deeply into the ground, making them harder to extinguish and causing them to smolder for longer periods.

ISI is an index that represents the rate at which a fire will spread. It combines the effects of wind and the FFMC on fire spread. A high ISI value indicates that if a fire were to start, it would spread rapidly. This is particularly influenced by wind speed; strong winds can quickly spread embers and flames, leading to a faster-moving fire.

These indices provide a comprehensive view of the potential fire behavior, from ignition to spread, based on the moisture content in various layers of the forest floor and the effects of weather conditions. They are crucial tools for forest management and fire prevention, helping authorities make informed decisions about fire risk and resource allocation.

The spatial coordinates (X and Y) provide a sense of the location of the fire within the Montesinho park, which can be crucial for understanding patterns or specific regions more prone to fires.

Table 1. Description of the Forest Fires Dataset Attributes

Attribute	Description
X	x-axis spatial coordinate within the Montesinho park map: 1 to 9
Y	y-axis spatial coordinate within the Montesinho park map: 2 to 9
Month	month of the year: "jan" to "dec"
Day	day of the week: "mon" to "sun"
FFMC	Fine Fuel Moisture Code index from the FWI system: 18.7 to 96.20
DMC	Duff Moisture Code index from the FWI system: 1.1 to 291.3
DC	Drought Code index from the FWI system: 7.9 to 860.6
ISI	Initial Spread Index from the FWI system: 0.0 to 56.10
Temp	temperature in Celsius degrees: 2.2 to 33.30
RH	relative humidity in %: 15.0 to 100
Wind	wind speed in km/h: 0.40 to 9.40
Rain	outside rain in mm/m2: 0.0 to 6.4
Area	the burned area of the forest (in ha): 0.00 to 1090.84 (target variable)

3.2   Data Preprocessing

Data preprocessing is a critical step in the machine learning pipeline, ensuring that the dataset is well-suited for model training. This section discusses common preprocessing steps, including handling missing values and feature engineering.

Missing values in a dataset can arise due to various reasons, such as data entry errors, unrecorded observations, or sensor malfunctions. Handling them is crucial as most machine learning algorithms require complete datasets for training [22]. Several strategies can be employed:

- **Deletion:** Simply remove the rows with missing values. This method is mathematically represented as:

$$D' = \{d \in D | \text{value}(d, a) \neq \text{missing}, \forall a \in A\} \tag{1}$$

where D' is the dataset after deletion, D is the original dataset, and A is the set of all attributes.

– **Mean Imputation:** Replace the missing values with the mean of the observed values for that feature. For a feature X:

$$x_{\text{missing}} = \frac{1}{n} \sum_{i=1}^{n} x_i \qquad (2)$$

where x_i are the observed feature values and n is the number of observations.
– **Median or Mode Imputation:** For numerical and categorical features, respectively, replace missing values with the median or mode.

Data augmentation is a technique used to artificially increase the size of a dataset by creating modified versions of existing data. This is especially useful in domains like image processing, where deep learning models require large datasets to train effectively. Augmenting data can help improve the performance and generalization of models by providing them with a more diverse set of training examples. In this study, we used AugmenterR library in R. It employs a data enhancement method grounded in conditional entropy. This approach can generate new data points based on a specified value of a categorical feature, enhancing the dataset for classification purposes. Additionally, it demonstrates notable enhancements for machine learning models working with limited data.

3.3 Distributed Random Forest (DRF)

Distributed Random Forest (DRF) is an ensemble learning method that constructs multiple decision trees during training and outputs the mode (for classification) or mean (for regression) prediction of the individual trees for unseen data [33]. DRF is designed to be distributed and scalable, making it suitable for large datasets. Given a dataset $(x_1, y_1), (x_2, y_2), \ldots, (x_n, y_n)$, the DRF algorithm proceeds as follows:

1. For each tree t in the forest:
   (a) A bootstrap sample (with replacement) of the data is taken.
   (b) A decision tree $h_t(x)$ is grown using the bootstrap sample. At each node:
      i. A random subset of features is selected.
      ii. The best split based on these features is used to split the node.
2. The final model $H(x)$ is the aggregation of the predictions of all trees:

$$H(x) = \frac{1}{T} \sum_{t=1}^{T} h_t(x)$$

for regression, or

$$H(x) = \text{mode}\{h_1(x), h_2(x), \ldots, h_T(x)\}$$

for classification, where T is the number of trees.

3.4   Model Evaluation Metrics

Evaluating the performance of predictive models is crucial to understand their accuracy and reliability. Various metrics can be employed, each providing a different perspective on the model's performance. This section delves into three commonly used metrics for regression tasks.

The Mean Absolute Error (MAE) provides a measure of the average magnitude of errors between predicted and observed values, without considering their direction. It is given by the formula:

$$MAE = \frac{1}{n} \sum_{i=1}^{n} |y_i - \hat{y}_i| \tag{3}$$

where y_i represents the observed values, $\hat{y}_i$ denotes the predicted values, and n is the number of observations.

The Root Mean Square Error (RMSE) is another metric that measures the average magnitude of errors. However, by squaring the differences before averaging, RMSE gives more weight to larger errors. It is defined as:

$$RMSE = \sqrt{\frac{1}{n} \sum_{i=1}^{n} (y_i - \hat{y}_i)^2} \tag{4}$$

Similar to MAE, y_i and $\hat{y}_i$ are the observed and predicted values, respectively, and n is the number of observations.

The R-squared value, often termed the coefficient of determination, provides a measure of how well the observed outcomes are replicated by the model. It represents the proportion of the variance in the dependent variable that is predictable from the independent variables. The R-squared value is given by:

$$R^2 = 1 - \frac{\sum_{i=1}^{n} (y_i - \hat{y}_i)^2}{\sum_{i=1}^{n} (y_i - \bar{y})^2} \tag{5}$$

where y_i is the observed value, $\hat{y}_i$ is the predicted value, and $\bar{y}$ is the mean of the observed values.

The Gini coefficient, often used in economics to measure income inequality, can also be applied in the context of binary classification as a performance measure. It quantifies the disparity between the distribution of the positive and negative classes in predictions. Mathematically, the Gini coefficient (G) can be defined in terms of the Area Under the ROC Curve (AUC) as:

$$G = 2 \times \text{AUC} - 1 \tag{6}$$

The Gini coefficient ranges between -1 (perfect inequality) and 1 (perfect equality). In the context of classification, a Gini coefficient close to 1 indicates that the model has good discriminatory power, while a value close to 0 suggests that the model is no better than random guessing. For a perfectly discriminating model, AUC = 1 and thus $G = 1$. For a model that discriminates no better than random guessing, AUC = 0.5 and $G = 0$.

LogLoss is a performance metric used to evaluate the accuracy of a classification model where the prediction output is a probability value between 0 and 1. It penalizes both the type I and type II errors in predictions. The closer the predicted probabilities are to the actual outcomes, the lower the LogLoss value, making it a suitable metric for models that output probabilities. For a binary classification problem, the LogLoss is defined as:

$$\text{LogLoss} = -\frac{1}{N} \sum_{i=1}^{N} [y_i \log(p_i) + (1 - y_i) \log(1 - p_i)] \tag{7}$$

where: N is the number of samples or instances. y_i is the actual class label of the ith instance (0 or 1). p_i is the predicted probability that the ith instance belongs to class 1. A perfect model would have a LogLoss of 0. However, it's important to note that a smaller LogLoss is better, with 0 indicating a perfect log-likelihood. Conversely, a model with predictions that are off from the actual values will incur a larger LogLoss.

4   Results

4.1   Descriptive Statistics of the Dataset

The analysis of the variables' values is presented in Fig. 1. The FFMC values are generally high, indicating that fine fuels are typically dry, which can be a fire risk. Most of the values are clustered around the 90 s, indicating that fine fuels are generally dry, which can be a fire risk. The DMC and DC values show significant variability, suggesting diverse moisture content in both shallow and deep organic layers across regions. The DC values indicate significant variability in the moisture content of deeper organic layers. The median is higher than the mean, suggesting that most regions have a higher drought code, indicating drier conditions. The ISI has some regions with exceptionally high fire spread rates.The maximum value of ISI is notably higher than the 3rd quartile, suggesting some regions with exceptionally high fire spread rates. There's a wide range of temperatures, but most regions have little to no rain, which can contribute to dry conditions and increased fire risk. The distribution of wind speed is fairly even, but the maximum value suggests there might be occasional strong winds.

4.2   Model Performance

Table 2 summarizes the performance of the trained model. The model has a high mean accuracy of approximately 96.3%. The low standard deviation (0.00696) suggests that the accuracy is consistent across different runs or subsets of the data. The low error rate (0.03714) further confirms the model's high accuracy. The high Matthews Correlation Coefficient (mcc) value (0.92584) suggests that the model performs well across both positive and negative classes.

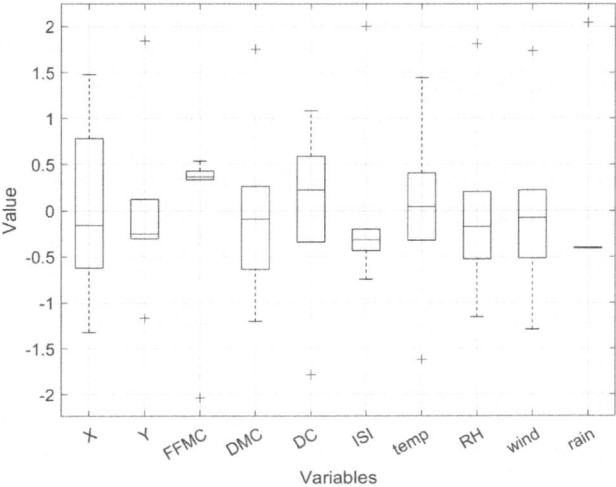

Fig. 1. Boxplot of the normalized values of dataset variables

Table 2. Descriptive Statistics of the Model Metrics

Metric	Mean	Standard Deviation (SD)
accuracy	0.962857	0.006962
auc	0.989500	0.004102
err	0.037143	0.006962
err_count	10.400000	1.949359
logloss	0.204777	0.066532
max_per_class_error	0.050543	0.013681
mcc	0.925840	0.013846
mean_per_class_accuracy	0.962847	0.007596
mean_per_class_error	0.037153	0.007596
mse	0.041276	0.004419
pr_auc	0.987651	0.010687
precision	0.968042	0.015978
r2	0.834264	0.017558
recall	0.956842	0.019023
rmse	0.202935	0.010779
specificity	0.968852	0.014449

Table 3. Classification Performance Metrics

Metric	AUC	ACC	PRC	TPR	TNR
Value	0.98942	0.95333	0.95608	0.94966	0.95695

The model's performance is summarize in Table 3 in terms of Area Under Curve (AUC), accuracy (ACC), Precision (PRC), True Positive Rate (TPR) and True Negative Rate (TNR).

Performance Metrics from 5-fold cross-validation are reported in Table 4. The model appears to perform well based on the provided metrics. The high AUC and AUCPR values indicate excellent discriminatory power, and the low MSE and LogLoss values suggest accurate predictions. The R^2 value indicates that a high portion of the variance in the target variable is explained by the model.

Table 4. Performance Metrics from 5-fold Cross-validation

Metric	Value
MSE	0.0411854
RMSE	0.2029419
LogLoss	0.203288
Mean Per-Class Error	0.04288606
AUC	0.9891877
AUCPR	0.9883058
Gini	0.9783753
R^2	0.8352571

The confusion matrix of the classification results is presented in Fig. 2a. The error rate for the Fire class is 0.022923, which means about 2.29% of the total Fire instances were misclassified. The error rate for the NoFire class is 0.032764, which means about 3.28% of the total NoFire instances were misclassified. The overall error rate for the model is 0.027857, meaning about 2.79% of all instances (both Fire and NoFire) were misclassified. The model seems to perform relatively well with an overall accuracy of about 97.21% (100–2.79%). However, there's a slightly higher misclassification rate for the NoFire class compared to the Fire class. The results of ROC (Receiver Operating Characteristic) analysis are presented in Fig. 2b.

4.3   Feature Importance Analysis

Table 5 and Fig. 3 present the results of feature importance analysis. The most important feature is temperature (*temp*) explaining 16.5% of variability followed by Duff Moisture Code (DMC) explaining 12.7% and and relative humidity (*RH*) explaining 12.6%.

Table 5. Variable Importance Metrics

Variable	Relative Importance	Scaled Importance	Importance
temp	1048.5476	1.0000000	0.1651155
DMC	811.0522	0.7735006	0.1277169
RH	802.3088	0.7651620	0.1263401
DC	695.1674	0.6629812	0.1094685
wind	678.9797	0.6475431	0.1069194
X	657.9071	0.6274461	0.1036011

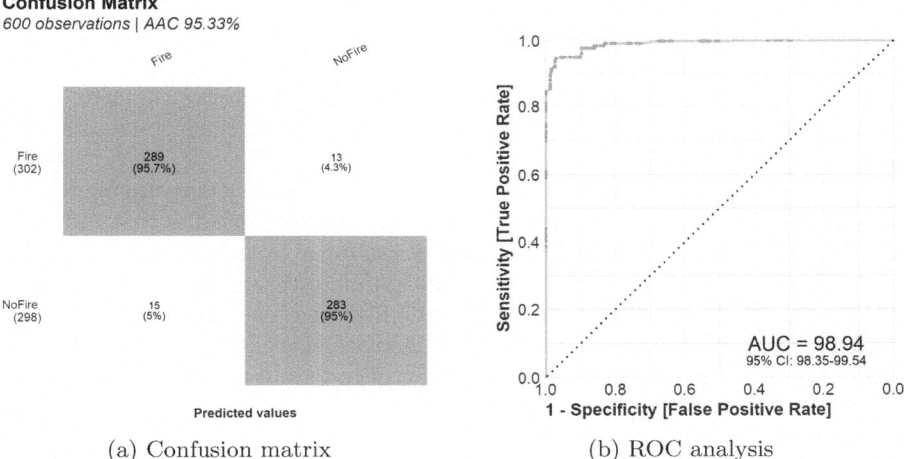

(a) Confusion matrix   (b) ROC analysis

Fig. 2. Performance of the model

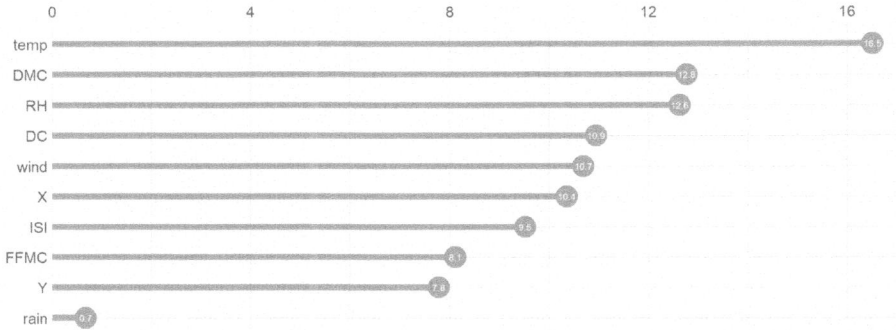

Fig. 3. Importance of features

5   Conclusion

In this study, we employed a comprehensive approach to predict forest fires based on various environmental and meteorological variables. The results from our 5-fold cross-validation on training data provide compelling evidence of the model's robustness and accuracy in predicting forest fires.

Several key findings emerged from our analysis: The model demonstrated high discriminatory power, as evidenced by the high AUC and AUCPR values. These metrics, being close to 1, indicate that the model can effectively distinguish between instances of fires and no fires. The low MSE and LogLoss values further attest to the model's accuracy in its predictions. Variables such as temperature, humidity, and the various moisture codes (FFMC, DMC, DC) played pivotal roles in influencing the model's predictions. Their relative importance in the model underscores the critical role of weather conditions and fuel moisture content in forest fire occurrences. The R^2 value of 0.8352571 suggests that our model accounts for approximately 83.53% of the variance in the target variable. This high R^2 value, combined with other performance metrics, indicates that our model is not only accurate but also robust in its predictions across different scenarios and conditions.

The results of this study have significant implications for forest management and fire prevention strategies. By understanding the key variables that influence fire occurrences and their relative importance, forest management can devise more targeted and effective strategies to mitigate fire risks. For instance, during periods of high temperatures and low humidity, combined with high FFMC, DMC, or DC values, forest managers can increase surveillance, restrict certain activities, or deploy resources in anticipation of potential fires.

This study, focused on predicting forest fires based on weather data, has some notable limitations:

- The dataset covers the northeast region of Portugal. While valuable, the findings might not be directly applicable to other regions with different climatic conditions, vegetation types, or socio-economic factors.
- The study emphasizes weather data, but potentially influential variables, such as land use patterns, vegetation health, and human activities, were not included in the analysis, possibly limiting the model's predictive power.
- The dataset represents a specific time frame. Forest fire patterns and their relationship with weather might evolve over longer periods, especially in the context of global climate change.
- The machine learning models employed, though state-of-the-art, have their inherent limitations and assumptions. The real-world is often more complex than what can be captured by a single model or algorithm.
- Given the complexity of models and granularity of the dataset, there's a potential risk of overfitting, where the model might perform exceptionally well on the training data but fail to generalize to new, unseen data.
- Events like policy changes, significant infrastructure developments, or large-scale human migrations can influence forest fire patterns. Such external factors were not considered in this study.

Acknowledgement. This research paper has received funding from Horizon Europe Framework Programme (HORIZON), call Teaming for Excellence (HORIZON-WIDERA-2022-ACCESS-01-two-stage) - Creation of the centre of excellence in smart forestry "Forest 4.0" No. 101059985.

References

1. Abid, F.: A survey of machine learning algorithms based forest fires prediction and detection systems. Fire Technol. **57**(2), 559–590 (2021)
2. Ahmad, K., et al.: FireXnet: an explainable AI-based tailored deep learning model for wildfire detection on resource-constrained devices. Fire Ecol. **19**(1), 54 (2023). https://doi.org/10.1186/s42408-023-00216-0
3. Aljumah, A.: IoT-inspired framework for real-time prediction of forest fire. Int. J. Comput. Commun. Control **17**(3) (2022)
4. Amelia, J.P., Dupe, Z.L., Prasasti, I.: Analysis and verification of fire danger rating system (FDRS) parameters in land and forest fire in west kalimantan in 2019 and its relationship with hotspots and rainfall. In: Yulihastin, E., Abadi, P., Sitompul, P., Harjupa, W. (eds.), vol. 275, p. 247–64 (2022). https://doi.org/10.1007/978-981-19-0308-3_20
5. Bera, B., Shit, P.K., Sengupta, N., Saha, S., Bhattacharjee, S.: Forest fire susceptibility prediction using machine learning models with resampling algorithms, northern part of eastern Ghat mountain range (India). Geocarto Int. **37**(26), 11756–11781 (2022)
6. Cortez, P., Morais, A.: A data mining approach to predict forest fires using meteorological data (2007)
7. Damaseviĉius, R., Bacanin, N., Misra, S.: From sensors to safety: internet of emergency services (IoES) for emergency response and disaster management. J. Sensor Actuator Netw. **12**(3), 41 (2023)
8. Dong, H., Wu, H., Sun, P., Ding, Y.: Wildfire prediction model based on spatial and temporal characteristics: a case study of a wildfire in Portugal's Montesinho natural park. Sustainability **14**(16), 10107 (2022)
9. Flannigan, M., Wotton, B.: Climate, Weather, and Area Burned. Elsevier (2007)
10. Gaikwad, A., Bhuta, N., Jadhav, T., Jangale, P., Shinde, S.: A review on forest fire prediction techniques (2022)
11. Ghate, S.N., Sapkale, P., Mukhedkar, M.: Forest wildfire detection and forecasting utilizing machine learning and image processing (2023)
12. Ivchenko, O., Tiutin, A., Kozachenko, M., Pankin, K.: A relationship between weather conditions and a number of forest fires, vol. 979 (2022)
13. Li, L., Sali, A., Noordin, N.K., Ismail, A., Hashim, F.: Prediction of peatlands forest fires in Malaysia using machine learning. Forests **14**(7), 1472 (2023)
14. Li, X., Wang, X., Sun, S., Wang, Y., Li, S., Li, D.: Predicting the wildland fire spread using a mixed-input CNN model with both channel and spatial attention mechanisms. Fire Technol. **59**(5), 2683–2717 (2023)
15. Liang, H., Zhang, M., Wang, H.: A neural network model for wildfire scale prediction using meteorological factors. IEEE Access **7**, 176746–176755 (2019)
16. Mittal, P., Sharma, A., Singh, R.: Deformable patch-based-multi-layer perceptron mixer model for forest fire aerial image classification. J. Appl. Remote Sens. **17**(2), 022203 (2023)

17. Mohammadian Bishe, E., Norouzi, M., Afshin, H., Farhanieh, B.: A case study on the effects of weather conditions on forest fire propagation parameters in the Malekroud forest in Guilan. Iran. Fire **6**(7), 251 (2023)
18. Murali Mohan, K.V., Satish, A.R., Mallikharjuna Rao, K., Yarava, R.K., Babu, G.C.: Leveraging machine learning to predict wild fires, p. 1393–1400 (2021)
19. Mutakabbir, A., et al.: Spatio-temporal agnostic deep learning modeling of forest fire prediction using weather data, p. 346-351 (June 2023)
20. Natekar, S., Patil, S., Nair, A., Roychowdhury, S.: Forest fire prediction using LSTM (2021)
21. Pahuja, N.K., Rivero, M.H.: Predicting the impact of wildfire using machine learning techniques to assist effective deployment of resources, p. 201–205 (2022)
22. Palanivinayagam, A., Damaševičius, R.: Effective handling of missing values in datasets for classification using machine learning methods. Information **14**(2), 92 (2023)
23. Pang, Y., et al.: Forest fire occurrence prediction in china based on machine learning methods. Remote Sens. **14**(21), 5546 (2022)
24. Pham, B.T., et al.: Performance evaluation of machine learning methods for forest fire modeling and prediction. Symmetry **12**(6), 1022 (2020)
25. Pinto, M.M., et. al.: The extreme weather conditions behind the destructive fires of June and October 2017 in Portugal. Imprensa da Universidade de Coimbra (2018)
26. Rodrigues, M., De la Riva, J.: An insight into machine-learning algorithms to model human-caused wildfire occurrence. Environ. Model. Softw. **57**, 192–201 (2014)
27. Rubí, J.N., de Carvalho, P.H., Gondim, P.R.: Application of machine learning models in the behavioral study of forest fires in the Brazilian federal district region. Eng. Appl. Artif. Intell. **118**, 105649 (2023)
28. Slavia, A.P., Sutoyo, E., Witarsyah, D.: Hotspots forecasting using autoregressive integrated moving average (ARIMA) for detecting forest fires, p. 92–97 (2019)
29. Wu, Z., Li, M., Wang, B., Quan, Y., Liu, J.: Using artificial intelligence to estimate the probability of forest fires in Heilongjiang, northeast China. Remote Sens. **13**(9), 1813 (2021)
30. Xanthopoulos, G., Roussos, A., Giannakopoulos, C., Karali, A., Hatzaki, M.: Investigation of the weather conditions leading to large forest fires in the area around Athens. Imprensa da Universidade de Coimbra, Greece (2014)
31. Yue, W., et al.: Assessment of wildfire susceptibility and wildfire threats to ecological environment and urban development based on GIS and multi-source data: A case study of Guilin, China. Remote Sens. **15**(10), 2659 (2023)
32. Zaidi, A.: Predicting wildfires in Algerian forests using machine learning models. Heliyon **9**(7) (2023)
33. Zhou, G., Chen, F.: DRFMM: a map-matching algorithm based on distributed random forest multi-classification, vol. 189 (2018)

Audio-Text Retrieval: Exploring Shared Parameters and Intra-Modal Constraint Loss

Vedanshi Shah(✉)(iD), Yash Suryawanshi(iD), Shyam Randar(iD),
and Amit D. Joshi(iD)

Department of Computer Science and Engineering,
COEP Technological University, Pune, India
{vedanshis20.comp,suryawanshiys20.comp,randarsv20.comp,
adj.comp}@coeptech.ac.in

Abstract. Cross-modal retrieval involves retrieving information across diverse modalities, like image-text, image-audio and audio-text. It finds application in multimedia search engines, healthcare imaging, recommendation systems and more. While many contributions have focused on the bimodal domain of image-text, there has been a lack of focus on other domains, particularly the intersection of audio and text. This study aims to bridge this gap by introducing a model capable of retrieving relevant audio clips based on natural language queries and extracting relevant captions from audio inputs. Many approaches in this line of effort involve fine-tuning pre-trained encoders with a contrastive objective. Only some approaches explore the impact of correlating embeddings retrieved from encoders without fine-tuning. Progressing in this direction, this study examines the impact of aligning embeddings in the shared space. The main contributions include: the development of a Siamese neural network for cross-modal entity alignment, along with incorporating the Intra-modal constraint loss for learning useful representations in the audio-text domain. The experiments are conducted on the standard datasets of AudioCaps and Clotho. The results demonstrate that the architecture performs better than certain other architectures involving frozen encoders. This study evaluates the effect of projection layers, weight sharing and intra-modal similarity using Siamese neural network and Intra-modal constraint loss, thereby opening up further avenues in representational learning in the audio-text domain.

Keywords: Information Retrieval · Audio-text Retrieval · Cross-modal Learning · Intra-modal Loss · Deep Learning

1 Introduction

In today's data-rich world, there is a great need for effective information retrieval. However, traditional unimodal approaches often fall short of capturing the richness of multimedia data. Thus, cross-modal retrieval aims to correlate multimodal information such as image, audio, text and video. With the increase in

A. Verma et al. (Eds.): ANTIC 2023, CCIS 2091, pp. 321–336, 2024.
https://doi.org/10.1007/978-3-031-64064-3_23

publicly available multimedia information through various social media platforms and multimedia datasets, cross-modal retrieval has attracted a lot of attention for its potential to enable more versatile and comprehensive access to such content. Cross-modal retrieval promises to revolutionize fields ranging from content recommendation and search engines to healthcare [1] and autonomous systems [2]. Approaches in this domain predominantly center around addressing bimodal retrieval challenges, with a particular focus on the image-text domain. This study explores audio-text retrieval, which involves retrieving relevant audio content based on natural language queries and textual information based on given audio. The domain of audio-text retrieval holds potential for applications such as scanning surveillance videos for specific audio like glass breakage, monitoring farm environments using audio sensors, detecting and classifying environmental sounds for situational awareness and decision-making, as explained by Lallemand et al. and retrieving musical collections given a text query as illustrated by Muller et al. [3,4].

Looking at some of the approaches in the image-text domain, Peng et al. utilized Generative Adversarial Networks (GANs) for modeling the joint distribution of image and text using a novel approach [5]. They utilized a weight-sharing constraint on their convolutional autoencoders for cross-modal correlation, which inspires this study. On the other hand, Hong et al. introduced GilBERT, which leveraged the power of generative models to fill in the missing parts of image-text pairs and then derived universal image-text embeddings using visual-linguistic transformers [6]. Radford et al. introduced Contrastive Language-Image Pretraining (CLIP), an approach to efficiently learn visual concepts using natural language supervision with a contrastive objective [7]. Yang et al. investigated the effect of contrastive learning in the case of zero-shot retrievals and found that contrastive learning outperformed the supervised training methodology significantly [8].

Comparatively, limited research has been conducted in audio-text retrieval. The state-of-the-art approaches comprise dual encoders: pre-trained audio encoders [9–14] and text encoders [15–18] for extracting the embeddings. These embeddings are first mapped into a shared embedding space. A contrastive learning technique is then applied to decrease the distance between similar audio-text embedding pairs and increase the distance between dissimilar audio-text embedding pairs. After the release of audio captioning datasets, AudioCaps [19] and Clotho [20], various works performed quality research on them using the above architecture while applying different combinations of loss functions and audio and text encoders. The first challenging benchmark on these standard datasets for audio-text retrieval was given by Koepke et al. [21]. They adapted video-text retrieval techniques and used pretrained-encoder models with a contrastive objective. Lou et al. explored the influence of aggregation methods on frame-wise or word-wise embeddings obtained from encoders [22]. They achieved a significant performance improvement over the model proposed by Koepke et al. Many other approaches have tried extending the CLIP framework to audio modality [23–26]. An overview of approaches in the audio-text domain is given in the next section.

The approaches mentioned so far for audio-text retrieval focus only on inter-modal losses. Considering only inter-modal loss is susceptible to violations of negative pairs in the same modality as explained by Chen et al. [27]. Influenced by their work, this study explores the potential of intra-modal constraint loss in the audio-text domain. For aligning the embeddings in the shared space, a context gating module [22] along with a Siamese Neural Network (SNN) is used. This study utilizes frozen encoders, meaning that encoders are not fine-tuned during training, and compares these with other frozen encoder models [21, 22].

The subsequent sections of this paper are structured in the following manner: A literature review is presented in Sect. 2, followed by the proposed methodology in Sect. 3. Results and discussion are presented in Sect. 4, followed by conclusion and future scope in Sect. 5.

2 Literature Review

Compared to image-text retrieval, efforts in the bimodal domain of audio-text remain few, with many efforts beginning only recently. A significant number of efforts in this domain have concentrated on contrastive learning to learn useful representations. The direction towards contrastive learning was promoted by the success in the image-text domain achieved by Open AI's CLIP [7].

Preliminary research into content-based audio retrieval tasks involved using Siamese networks as audio encoders. Manocha et al. proposed an SNN to learn audio embeddings for content-based audio-to-audio retrieval only [28]. Elizalde et al. used SNNs to encode audio and text, which were then mapped to a shared space for comparing the similarity [29]. State-of-the-art approaches make use of attention layers with a contrastive objective. VAST used a fully end-to-end transformer architecture comprising visual, audio and text encoders [30]. OnePeace used modality adapters, self-attention and feedforward neural network layers to achieve a general representation framework for vision, audio and language modalities [31].

Existing approaches can be categorized into two: frozen encoder architectures [21, 22, 32] and unfrozen encoder architectures [23, 24, 26, 32, 33]. Frozen encoder architectures mean that the encoders are not fine-tuned while training. In frozen methods, Koepke et al. adapted three expert-based methods for learning the shared embedding space. It retrieved the embeddings using methods of Collaborative Experts (CE), Mixture of Embedded Experts (MoEE) and Multimodal Transformer (MMT). Embeddings were aggregated along the temporal dimension in CE and MoEE, while MMT used self-attention layers to refine the embeddings [21]. Along similar lines, Lou et al. observed the influence of aggregation methods for cross-modal alignment. The feature vectors for audio and text were extracted from Pretrained Audio Neural Networks (PANNs) and Word2Vec, respectively. After aggregation of the feature vectors, they were projected into shared embedding space by passing through a fully connected layer and a self-gated module. They achieved significant performance improvement over Koepke et al. using a combination of CNN14 audio encoder and NetRVLAD aggregation method [22].

AudioCLIP and Wav2CLIP extended the CLIP framework by incorporating the audio modality. Wav2CLIP included audio-visual correspondence learning through knowledge distillation from CLIP to learn a joint embedding space for audio, image and text [23]. The image encoder was frozen and used to pre-train the audio encoder to learn the shared embedding space using contrastive learning. Multilayer Perceptron (MLP) layers projected the embeddings into the shared space. On the other hand, AudioCLIP incorporated an audio encoder, EsResNeXt, directly into the CLIP framework [24]. The combined model was trained with a 3-way contrastive objective of image-text, image-audio and text-audio on the AudioSet dataset. CLAP, also inspired by CLIP, trained its audio encoder on 22 different audio tasks instead of traditional training on only sound event classification [25]. Through better audio representations, they achieved performance improvement over other benchmarks. LAION-CLAP explored the effect of augmentation on textual features and feature fusion in audio encoders for variable-length audio [26]. They achieved superior performance using HTSAT-RoBERTa encoders. They trained on large datasets consisting of AudioCaps, Clotho and their own LAION-630K and observed that the performance improved with the increase in size of the training dataset.

Mei et al. experimented with different contrastive objectives for the retrieval tasks on Clotho and AudioCaps [32]. They adapted the NT-Xent loss function from Chen et al. for the retrieval task and demonstrated its stable performance on both datasets [34]. They concluded that it outperformed other triplet-based losses. They reported results with and without fine-tuning. Xie et al. tried to understand the effect of negative sampling techniques, including within-modality negative sampling and cross-modality hard and semi-hard negative sampling. They used Convolutional Recurrent Neural Network (CRNN) for audio embeddings and Word2Vec for text embedding. Their experiments showed that semi-hard negatives provided improved performance on both audio-to-text and text-to-audio retrieval tasks.

Most loss functions used in contrastive learning address negative pairs only in heterogeneous modality. The effect of negative pairs in the homogeneous modality is often overlooked. Thus, Chen et al. introduced a novel intra-modal constraint loss for image-text retrieval that maximizes the distance between negative pairs in the same modality [27]. At that time, they achieved state-of-the-art results using the approach. Comparatively, the effect of intra-modal loss functions is less explored in audio-text retrieval than in image-text retrieval. OnePeace used intra-modal denoising contrastive loss, while this study utilizes and explores the effect of intra-modal constraint loss during the cross-modal contrastive training itself [31]. Hu et al. applied an intra-modal loss between augmented and original audio to learn better feature representations for audio modality [35]. In contrast to the previous work, this study considers the effect of intra-modal loss for both modalities in concert with inter-modal contrastive loss.

Thus, the major work of this study involves testing a hypothesis similar to the idea proposed by Merullo et al. that conceptual representations received from frozen-only encoders exhibit a high degree of similarity [36]. Instead of fine-tuning the encoders, the model can learn to align the cross-modal embeddings obtained from encoders in shared space.

3 Proposed Methodology

This section lays the foundation of the proposed model, including the description of the encoder architectures, projection layers and loss functions. Existing works have achieved good results in audio-text retrieval either by training encoders from scratch or by fine-tuning pre-trained encoders. However, only a few have achieved comparable results with frozen encoder models. The pre-trained encoder models, CNN14 and MPNet, have been trained on large datasets, providing robust representations for audio and text modalities, respectively. Consequently, this study utilizes these encoder models to obtain individual modality embeddings. These embeddings are then passed through projection layers consisting of linear layers with a Rectified Linear Unit (ReLU) activation between them [37]. Further, this study tests the effect of weight sharing by designing an SNN that takes in the individual modality embeddings and aligns them in a shared space. It also evaluates the impact of intra-modal loss function, thereby proposing an innovative approach in this domain. The model architecture is shown in Figs. 1 and 2.

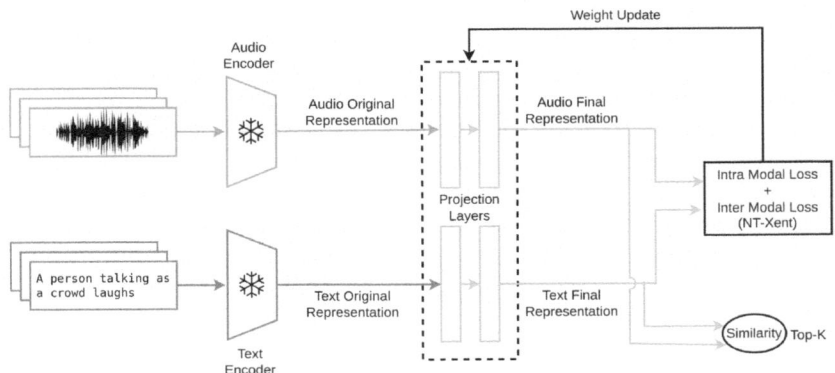

Fig. 1. IMC xSNN: Includes training with baseline projection layers and inter-modal & intra-modal loss functions

3.1 Audio Encoder

This study utilizes the CNN14 model of PANNs for obtaining the embeddings [9]. PANNs were pre-trained on the large AudioSet dataset for audio pattern recognition. This study uses PANNs because they perform quite well on various

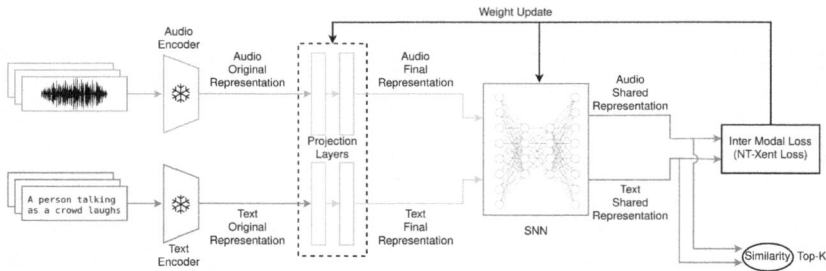

Fig. 2. xIMC SNN: Includes training with baseline projection layers and SNN with inter-modal loss function

audio-related tasks and provide meaningful representations for the audio. Since AudioCaps is derived from AudioSet, it directly benefits from this encoder.

CNN14 of PANNs is a 14-layer Convolutional Neural Network (CNN) following a VGG-like CNN architecture. It consists of 3 blocks of 2 convolutional layers, each with a kernel size of 3×3. Batch normalization is applied between the layers and ReLU is used as the activation function. An average pooling of 2×2 is applied to each convolutional block. The original network includes an extra fully connected layer followed by a classification layer. These components are discarded as only the audio representations are needed for the intended purpose. Maximum and average global pooling along the frequency dimension is applied to the output from the modified encoder and the sum of two is used to obtain 2048-dimensional embedding. The audio encoder remains frozen during the training.

The audio input is truncated or padded during preprocessing to a fixed length of 10 s for AudioCaps and 30 s for Clotho. Using a sampling rate of 32kHz, the clips are preprocessed with a Hanning window of size 1024, a hop length of 320, and then 64-dimensional logmel-band energies are extracted. Since the Mel Spectrogram uses the Mel and the decibel scales for frequency and amplitude, the audio is processed into a form humans perceive.

3.2 Text Encoder

This study uses MPNet for the text encoder [38]. MPNet differs from Bidirectional Encoder Representations from Transformers (BERT) by utilizing permuted language modeling to capture dependencies among predicted tokens [15]. Additionally, it addresses the issue of position discrepancy encountered in XLNeT by taking auxiliary position information as input [39]. Specifically, the Hugging Face variation[1] of the model, fine-tuned on a vast sentence-level dataset with a contrastive objective, is employed.

In existing works, experiments using MPNet have been limited, with many using Word2Vec [21, 22], BERT [26], or even RoBERTa [32] to retrieve caption

---

[1] all-mpnet-base-v2 model by Hugging Face.

embeddings. This study uses the particular variation of MPNet as it outperforms the previous models by solving their shortcomings, providing a more useful representation of a sentence. The reported results showcase the usefulness of MPNet as a text encoder in the retrieval task. All the captions in the datasets are single sentences. These raw sentences are fed to the text encoder to obtain 768-dimensional word embeddings.

3.3 Projection Layers

After obtaining the audio and text embeddings from the respective encoder models, they are fed to the modality-specific MLP to project them into a shared 1024-dimensional embedding space. The individual modality architectures are explained below:

Audio MLP. It consists of two linear layers, with a ReLU activation between them. The input layer has a dimensionality of 2048, matching the size of the audio embeddings derived from the audio encoder. Meanwhile, the hidden and output layers possess a dimensionality of 1024.

Text MLP. It consists of two linear layers, with a ReLU activation between them. The input layer is 768-dimensional, representing the size of the text embeddings from the text encoder. It is followed by a 2048-dimensional hidden layer and a 1024-dimensional output layer.

3.4 Context Gating and Siamese Neural Network

Lou et al. proposed a self-gating module, which they called Context Gating. They proposed linear transformation and separate gates for audio and text. However, this study explores the effect of non-linear transformations and a shared gate for both audio as well as text. This could help capture patterns for both modalities together offering cross modal correlation [22].

Context Gating. The gate module acts as a mechanism for controlling and modulating the flow of information. Equation 1 represents the module with a linear layer. The sigmoid activation function takes in the linear transformation of input X. The output is the element-wise multiplication ($\odot$) of the input and the output of sigmoid.

$$Y = \sigma(WX + b) \odot X \tag{1}$$

The element-wise multiplication allows the model to de-emphasize or emphasize certain elements in the embeddings based on their relevance. The sigmoid activation determines the gating values for each component, where values close to 0 would suppress information, and values close to 1 would let information pass through. This selective fusion can help the model focus on relevant information and discard irrelevant or noisy information.

Siamese Neural Networks. An SNN is employed to evaluate the effect of weight sharing and enhance cross-modal entity alignment. SNNs, also known as twin neural networks, are robust to variations and can learn to recognize patterns with a limited amount of data. This study utilizes SNNs to construct a weight-shared non-linear transformation of audio and text.

The architecture of the proposed SNN consists of 5 layers. The input layer is of dimensionality 1024. It is followed by 4 hidden layers of dimensionality: 1024, 512, 512 and 1024. The final output layer has a dimensionality of 1024. Each layer is a linear transformation followed by batch normalization and a non-linear activation function. This study tests different activation functions, which include: ReLU, LeakyReLU, GELU, SiLU and Mish [37, 40–43]. The hidden layers utilize a dropout of 0.5. The effects of different activation functions are discussed in the results section.

The final output received from SNN is normalized and is utilized in the gate module in place of $(WX + b)$ term in Eq. 1. Thus, after a non-linear transformation by SNN, gating is applied and embeddings are aligned.

3.5 Loss Functions

The training proceeds by training a batch of size B, where the audio-caption embedding pair is represented as $\{a_i, t_i\}_{i=1}^{B}$. The loss is calculated for a particular batch to backpropagate the model. The loss is contrastive, either the inter-modal loss or a combination of inter-modal and intra-modal losses. This study uses two loss functions, Normalized Temperature-scaled Cross Entropy loss (NT-Xent) [34] and IMC [27], as described below.

NT-Xent. The NT-Xent is a loss function for contrastive learning based on softmax as proposed by Chen et al. [34]. It is used for metric learning and self-supervised learning. As proposed by Mei et al., this loss function is used here to increase the similarity between a given audio and text positive pair for all negative audio and text pairs within a given batch [32]. In Eq. 2. s_{ii} denotes the similarity between a given audio-text pair, s_{ij} denotes the similarity between a non-matching audio-text pair and τ is a temperature hyper-parameter.

$$L = -\frac{1}{B}\left(\sum_{i=1}^{B} \log \frac{\exp(\frac{s_{ii}}{\tau})}{\sum_{j=1}^{B} \exp(\frac{s_{ij}}{\tau})} + \sum_{i=1}^{B} \log \frac{\exp(\frac{s_{ii}}{\tau})}{\sum_{j=1}^{B} \exp(\frac{s_{ji}}{\tau})} \right) \qquad (2)$$

IMC Loss. This study uses the IMC loss proposed in [27]. This loss is included because the NT-Xent loss accounts for the negative pairs in heterogeneous modality but not for negative pairs in the same modality. The intra-modal loss is designed to contribute to the loss function if the similarity between two negative entities in the same modality lies in a particular range. In the context of audio processing, if two audio embeddings, having passed through the projection and shared layers, exhibit either a high degree of similarity or a significant dissimilarity, such cases do not contribute to the loss. The underlying idea here is to bring closely related pairs closer together and increase the separation between pairs that are far apart. This loss function introduces two terms, IMC(A) and IMC(T), for audio and text, respectively. The formula for the same is mentioned in Eq. 3. Over here, $\delta(x, y)$ is the similarity function in Eq. 4 between the embeddings of the same modality and λ is the weight factor. μ_{down} and μ_{up} represent the respective threshold values.

$$IMC(V) = \lambda \sum_{n,m \in N} \begin{cases} 0, \delta(v_n, v_{m \neq n}) \leq \mu_{down} \\ \delta(v_n, v_{m \neq n}), \\ 0, \delta(v_n, v_{m \neq n}) \geq \mu_{up} \end{cases} \tag{3}$$

$$\delta_{\cos}(v_n, v_{m \neq n}) = 1 - \cos(v_n, v_{m \neq n}) = 1 - \frac{\sum_{k=1}^{d} v_{nk} \cdot v_{m \neq n_k}}{\sqrt{\sum v_{nk}^2} \sqrt{\sum v_{m \neq n_k}^2}} \tag{4}$$

4   Results and Discussion

This section discusses the experimental setup, dataset and data preparation, performance metric, results and comparison.

4.1   Experimental Setup

The embeddings for AudioCaps and Clotho are retrieved separately using the frozen pre-trained encoders of CNN14 and MPNet, as discussed in the previous section. These embeddings are fed to the projection layers and, optionally, the SNN for cross-modal entity alignment using the contrastive objective. Experiments are conducted with different configurations of the model, such as:

1. xIMC xSNN: Non-linear projection layers (NLPL, involving only MLP layers) with NT-Xent
2. IMC xSNN: NLPL in combination with NT-Xent and IMC
3. xIMC SNN: NLPL in combination with SNN-enhanced Context Gating with NT-Xent

This study investigated the effect of variation in batch sizes (32, 64) and learning rate (0.001, 0.0001) and observed that a batch size of 64 and a learning rate of 0.001 are ideal. The temperature parameter in NT-Xent is set to 0.07 and the dimension of the shared embedding space is 1024. The values of λ, μ_{down} and μ_{up} are 1, 0.05 and 0.5 respectively. All the models are trained using the Adam optimizer with a batch size of 64 for 50 epochs. The best model is selected based on the geometric mean of R@1, R@5, R@10 and R@50 on the validation split of each dataset. All the experiments are performed on a single 15GB T4 GPU and 12.7GB System RAM on Google Colaboratory.

4.2   Dataset and Data Preparation

Experiments are conducted on the AudioCaps and Clotho datasets.

AudioCaps. AudioCaps is a large-scale dataset derived from the audio-visual AudioSet dataset [44]. The captions in AudioCaps are representative of the audio samples since the annotators were provided with word hints along with the audio samples. No visual cues were given to the participants. The original dataset consists of 49838 audio samples in the train split, of which 49274 samples are obtained [45]. The validation and test splits consist of 494 and 957 samples, respectively. Each sample in the train set is captioned with a single sentence, while samples in validation and test are captioned with 5 sentences each.

Clotho. Clotho is a dataset formed by audio from the Freesound platform and crowdsourced captions. Specifically, Clotho version 2.1 is used in this study. It consists of audio samples of 15 to 30 s, each labeled with 5 sentences. Captions are single sentences ranging from 8 to 20 words. The dataset was created by limiting the bias encountered in AudioCaps. The initial annotators were provided only the audio and nothing else, while the latter annotators were provided a combination of captions, either with or without audio. Clotho contains 3839, 1045 and 1045 audio samples in the train, validation and test splits, respectively, with each audio accompanied by 5 sentences in all splits. Clotho is generally considered a challenging dataset due to variations in the captions for a particular audio.

4.3   Performance Metrics

This study employs recall at k metric at different ranks to measure the retrieval performance. Here, the metric is defined as the percentage of test queries for which the correct result is among the top k retrieved results, similar to [21, 22, 26, 32]. The reported result parameters are R@1, R@5, R@10, R@50, RMed, RMean and $\overline{R}_{geom}$. RMed and RMean are the median and mean of actual ranks, respectively, while $\overline{R}_{geom}$ is the geometric mean. $\overline{R}_{geom,50}$ means the geometric mean of R@1, R@5, R@10 and R@50, while $\overline{R}_{geom,10}$ means geometric mean of R@1, R@5 and R@10.

4.4   Results

Findings from the experiments are presented in this section. The baseline model is a neural network with non-linear projection layers utilizing the NT-Xent loss function. Embeddings are retrieved from respective encoders as explained in the proposed methodology section. The achieved results are remarkable, given a simple architecture. The results of AudioCaps are better than the Clotho dataset. By performing qualitative analysis on both datasets' captions, it is observed that captions in Clotho were more diverse, and it proved to be a challenging dataset. Following terminologies are employed in the results table to describe the proposed models. The first one, xIMC xSNN, represents the baseline model. IMC xSNN refers to the baseline model combined with the IMC loss function. xIMC SNN denotes the baseline model coupled with SNN and context gating.

AudioCaps. Table 1 reports the results of the ablation study to examine the effect of IMC and SNN for aligning cross-modal embeddings. Experiments are conducted to measure the impact of different activation functions in the SNN architecture. Overall, the superior performance of SNN with the SiLU activation function is apparent when examining the geometric mean column $\overline{R}_{geom,50}$. The R@k for AudioCaps improves nearly by 1% with IMC and 3% with SNN compared to the baseline model.

Clotho. Table 2 indicates that IMC performed best, reporting up to a 1.5% increase compared to the baseline model. The improvement becomes evident upon observing a significant drop in RMean by 12, exhibiting the model's generalization. Analyzing the $\overline{R}_{geom,50}$ column reveals that this time, GELU performs marginally better than SiLU, which was the best for AudioCaps.

4.5 Comparison

AudioCaps. Table 3 compares the results on the AudioCaps dataset with [21, 22, 32]. Mei et al. obtained their best results for frozen encoders utilizing the Triplet-weighted loss function [32]. It is illustrated in Table 3 that the model proposed in this study demonstrates impressive performance when contrasted with the reference. Notably, there is a substantial increase of approximately 10–12% in recall values with respect to the frozen encoder results reported by [32]. Also, it outperforms the recall values of Koepke et al.'s proposed model by 6–7% while remaining competitive with the results achieved by Lou et al. [21,22].

Table 1. Ablation study observations on AudioCaps.

Objective		Audio to Text						
		R@1	**R@5**	**R@10**	**R@50**	**RMed**	**RMean**	$\overline{R}_{geom,50}$
xIMC xSNN		32.50	64.68	**81.81**	96.86	3	8.93	63.88
IMC xSNN		33.44	**66.98**	80.25	96.76	3	**8.84**	64.58
	(ReLU)	33.33	64.89	80.25	96.55	3	9.35	63.98
	(LeakyReLU)	33.33	65.41	79	**97.6**	3	8.99	64.03
xIMC SNN	(GELU)	**35.84**	64.58	79.83	96.24	3	9.24	64.94
	(SiLU)	34.69	66.87	80.46	96.76	3	9.08	**65.19**
	(Mish)	33.64	63.85	78.58	96.55	3	9.21	63.54
Objective		Text to Audio						
		R@1	**R@5**	**R@10**	**R@50**	**RMed**	**RMean**	$\overline{R}_{geom,50}$
xIMC xSNN		27.31	64.57	78.87	**96.3**	3	**10.68**	60.50
IMC xSNN		28.15	64.37	79.04	96.07	3	11.13	60.90
	(ReLU)	28.27	**64.58**	78.33	95.8	3	12.1	60.84
	(LeakyReLU)	28.4	64.12	78.75	96.11	3	10.95	60.93
xIMC SNN	(GELU)	28.59	64.35	78.68	96.01	3	11.65	61.06
	(SiLU)	**28.69**	64.14	**79.29**	95.94	3	11.22	**61.17**
	(Mish)	28.55	63.43	78.06	95.95	3	11.58	60.69

Table 2. Ablation study observations on Clotho.

Objective		Audio to Text						
		R@1	R@5	R@10	R@50	RMed	RMean	$\overline{R}_{geom,50}$
xIMC xSNN		12.34	32.06	42.87	73.3	16	70.54	33.39
IMC xSNN		**13.87**	**32.25**	**44.02**	**76.55**	**14**	**57.24**	**35.04**
	(ReLU)	**13.87**	31.67	42.3	74.16	16	61.93	34.27
	(LeakyReLU)	12.92	28.42	41.53	71.87	16	75.12	32.36
xIMC SNN	(GELU)	12.34	31.77	43.16	72.92	15	63.7	33.33
	(SiLU)	12.82	31.77	43.44	74.16	16	63	33.84
	(Mish)	11.77	30.72	43.16	73.49	15	63.29	32.72
Objective		Text to Audio						
		R@1	R@5	R@10	R@50	RMed	RMean	$\overline{R}_{geom,50}$
xIMC xSNN		11.58	31.27	43.02	73.7	15	59.46	32.73
IMC xSNN		11.69	32.13	44.63	**76.8**	**14**	**47.32**	**33.68**
	(ReLU)	11.69	31.54	42.35	74.45	15	56.83	32.83
	(LeakyReLU)	10.85	30.68	42.76	72.82	15	62.21	31.90
xIMC SNN	(GELU)	11.67	**32.52**	**44.84**	75.52	**14**	50.87	33.67
	(SiLU)	**12.08**	31.86	43.87	75.79	**14**	54.14	33.63
	(Mish)	11.62	31.36	43.79	74.51	15	55.83	33.02

Clotho. Table 4 presents a comparative analysis using the Clotho dataset with [21,22,32]. The proposed architecture outperforms the two models, CE and MoEE, documented by [21]. It was observed that the MMT model had performed better in the case of AudioCaps but failed to do so on Clotho. However, the proposed model in this study works well with both datasets. Furthermore, it surpasses the R@k scores of the frozen encoder model reported by Mei et al. by a difference of 3–5% [32].

While the results achieve a good performance, a difference can be noticed between the results of state-of-the-art models involving fine-tuning of encoders and the proposed model in this study.

Table 3. Comparing the results of the best-performing AudioCaps model, xIMC SNN (SiLU), with various approaches reported in the literature.

Model		Audio to Text							
	R@1	R@5	R@10	R@50	RMed	RMean	$\overline{R}_{geom,10}$	$\overline{R}_{geom,50}$
On-metric Learning [32]	21.9	56.3	71.5	–	–	–	44.5	–
Oxford (CE) [21]	27.6	60.5	74.7	94.2	4	14.7	50.0	58.5
Oxford (MoEE) [21]	27.6	60.5	74.7	94.2	4	14.7	50.0	58.5
Retrieval in Context [22]	33.3	**67.6**	**80.6**	–	3	–	56.6	–
Ours	**34.7**	66.9	80.5	**96.8**	3	**9.1**	**57.1**	**65.2**
Model		Text to Audio							
	R@1	R@5	R@10	R@50	RMed	RMean	$\overline{R}_{geom,10}$	$\overline{R}_{geom,50}$
On-metric Learning [32]	19.9	52.1	67.6	–	–	–	41.2	–
Oxford (CE) [21]	23.6	56.2	71.4	92.3	4	18.3	45.6	54.4
Oxford (MoEE) [21]	23	55.7	71	93	4	16.3	45.0	54.0
Retrieval in Context [22]	**29.3**	**65.2**	**79.3**	–	3	–	53.3	–
Ours	28.7	64.1	**79.3**	**96.0**	3	11.2	52.6	**61.2**

Table 4. Comparing the results of the best-performing Clotho model, IMC xSNN, with various approaches reported in the literature.

Model	Audio to Text							
	R@1	R@5	R@10	R@50	RMed	RMean	$\overline{R}$geom, 10	$\overline{R}$geom, 50
On-metric Learning [32]	9.2	27.9	39	–	–	–	21.55	–
Oxford (CE) [21]	7	22.7	34.6	67.9	21.3	72.6	17.65	24.72
Oxford (MoEE) [21]	7.2	22.1	33.2	67.4	22.7	71.8	17.42	24.43
Oxford (MMT) [21]	6.3	22.8	33.3	67.8	22.3	67.3	16.85	23.86
Retrieval in Context [22]	13	**32.9**	**45.4**	–	13	–	26.88	–
Ours	**13.87**	32.25	44.02	**76.55**	14	**57.24**	**27.00**	**35.04**

Model	Text to Audio							
	R@1	R@5	R@10	R@50	RMed	RMean	$\overline{R}$geom, 10	$\overline{R}$geom, 50
On-metric Learning [32]	8	25.3	36.9	–	–	–	19.55	–
Oxford (CE) [21]	8	25.3	36.9	–	–	–	19.55	–
Oxford (MoEE) [21]	6	20.8	32.3	68.5	23	60.2	15.91	22.92
Oxford (MMT) [21]	6.5	21.6	32.8	66.9	23	67.7	16.64	23.56
Retrieval in Context [22]	**13.1**	**33.1**	**45.1**	–	13	–	26.94	–
Ours	11.69	32.13	44.63	**76.8**	14	**47.32**	25.59	**33.68**

5   Conclusion and Future Scope

This study showcases the effectiveness of frozen encoders coupled with non-linear projection layers and observes the effect of weight sharing and intra-modal similarity. The embeddings obtained from these encoders, trained on vast data, are similar enough, requiring only a few projection layers to bring them to a shared space. Introducing IMC to the baseline model improves its generalization ability, which is particularly noteworthy in the case of the challenging Clotho dataset. SNN-enhanced context gating also positively influences the robustness of the model. The proposed model performs comparable to others on AudioCaps and Clotho datasets without fine-tuning. The model outperformed some frozen encoder models by a significant margin of 10–12% in the case of AudioCaps and 3–5% in the case of Clotho. The model's results are notable, particularly when considering other methods, especially in terms of R@1 and $\overline{R}_{geom}$ metrics. This study also compared the effect of different activation functions in the proposed SNN with context gating, including ReLU, Leaky ReLU, SiLU, GELU and Mish, where SiLU outperformed other activation functions. Moreover, the ablation study validated the hypothesis of the usefulness of IMC loss and SNN for cross-modal entity alignment.

Further contributions can be made towards the partial fine-tuning of encoders along with the proposed IMC loss and SNN. This would result in a lighter model with fewer parameters. Also, experimenting with different intra-modal loss functions may lead to improvement in the performance of audio-text retrieval.

References

1. Zhang, Y., Ou, W., Zhang, J., Deng, J.: Category supervised cross-modal hashing retrieval for chest x-ray and radiology reports. Comput. Electr. Eng. **98**, 107673 (2022)
2. Taha, A., Chen, Y., Yang, X., Misu, T., Davis, L.: Exploring uncertainty in conditional multi-modal retrieval systems. arXiv 2019. *ArXiv Preprint* ArXiv:1901.07702 (2019)
3. Lallemand, I., Schwarz, D., Artières, T.: Content-based retrieval of environmental sounds by multiresolution analysis. In: SMC2012, pp. 1–1 (2012)
4. Mueller, M., Arzt, A., Balke, S., Dorfer, M., Widmer, G.: Cross-modal music retrieval and applications: an overview of key methodologies. IEEE Signal Process. Mag. **36**, 52–62 (2019)
5. Peng, Y., Qi, J.: CM-GANs: cross-modal generative adversarial networks for common representation learning. ACM Trans. Multimedia Comput. Commun. Appl. (TOMM) **15**, 1–24 (2019)
6. Hong, W., Ji, K., Liu, J., Wang, J., Chen, J., Chu, W.: GilBERT: generative vision-language pre-training for image-text retrieval. In: Proceedings Of The 44th International ACM SIGIR Conference On Research And Development In Information Retrieval, pp. 1379–1388 (2021)
7. Radford, A., et al.: Learning transferable visual models from natural language supervision. In: International Conference On Machine Learning, pp. 8748–8763 (2021)
8. Yang, J., et al.: Unified contrastive learning in image-text-label space. In: Proceedings Of The IEEE/CVF Conference On Computer Vision And Pattern Recognition, pp. 19163–19173 (2022)
9. Kong, Q., Cao, Y., Iqbal, T., Wang, Y., Wang, W., Plumbley, M.: PANNs: large-scale pretrained audio neural networks for audio pattern recognition. IEEE/ACM Trans. Audio Speech Lang. Process. **28**, 2880–2894 (2020)
10. Koutini, K., Schlüter, J., Eghbal-Zadeh, H, Widmer, G.: Efficient training of audio transformers with patchout. ArXiv Preprint ArXiv:2110.05069 (2021)
11. Guzhov, A., Raue, F., Hees, J., Dengel, A.: ESResNet: environmental sound classification based on visual domain models. In: 2020 25th International Conference On Pattern Recognition (ICPR), pp. 4933–4940 (2021)
12. Guzhov, A., Raue, F., Hees, J., Dengel, A.: ESResNe(x) t-fbsp: learning robust time-frequency transformation of audio. In: 2021 International Joint Conference On Neural Networks (IJCNN), pp. 1–8 (2021)
13. Chen, K., Du, X., Zhu, B., Ma, Z., Berg-Kirkpatrick, T., Dubnov, S.: HTS-AT: a hierarchical token-semantic audio transformer for sound classification and detection. In: ICASSP 2022-2022 IEEE International Conference On Acoustics, Speech And Signal Processing (ICASSP), pp. 646–650 (2022)
14. Xu, X., Dinkel, H., Wu, M, Yu, K.: A CRNN-GRU based reinforcement learning approach to audio captioning. In: DCASE, pp. 225–229 (2020)
15. Devlin, J., Chang, M., Lee, K., Toutanova, K.: BERT: pre-training of deep bidirectional transformers for language understanding. ArXiv Preprint ArXiv:1810.04805 (2018)
16. Liu, Y., et al.: RoBERTa: a robustly optimized BERT pretraining approach. ArXiv Preprint ArXiv:1907.11692 (2019)
17. Reimers, N., Gurevych, I.: Sentence-BERT: sentence embeddings using siamese bert-networks. ArXiv Preprint ArXiv:1908.10084 (2019)

18. Mikolov, T., Chen, K., Corrado, G., Dean, J.: Efficient estimation of word representations in vector space. ArXiv Preprint ArXiv:1301.3781 (2013)
19. Kim, C., Kim, B., Lee, H., Kim, G.: AudioCaps: generating captions for audios in the wild. In: Proceedings Of The 2019 Conference Of The North American Chapter Of The Association For Computational Linguistics: Human Language Technologies, vol. 1 (Long And Short Papers), pp. 119–132 (2019)
20. Drossos, K., Lipping, S., Virtanen, T.: Clotho: An audio captioning dataset. In: ICASSP 2020-2020 IEEE International Conference On Acoustics, Speech And Signal Processing (ICASSP), pp. 736–740 (2020)
21. Koepke, A., Oncescu, A., Henriques, J., Akata, Z., Albanie, S.: A benchmark study. IEEE Trans. Multimedia Audio Retrieval with Nat. Lang. Queries **25**, 2675–2684 (2022)
22. Lou, S., Xu, X., Wu, M., Yu, K.: Audio-text retrieval in context. In: ICASSP 2022-2022 IEEE International Conference On Acoustics, Speech And Signal Processing (ICASSP), pp. 4793–4797 (2022)
23. Wu, H., Seetharaman, P., Kumar, K., Bello, J.: Wav2CLIP: learning robust audio representations from clip. In: ICASSP 2022-2022 IEEE International Conference On Acoustics, Speech And Signal Processing (ICASSP), pp. 4563–4567 (2022)
24. Guzhov, A., Raue, F., Hees, J., Dengel, A.: Audioclip: extending clip to image, text and audio. In: ICASSP 2022-2022 IEEE International Conference On Acoustics, Speech And Signal Processing (ICASSP), pp. 976–980 (2022)
25. Elizalde, B., Deshmukh, S., Al Ismail, M., Wang, H.: Clap learning audio concepts from natural language supervision. In: ICASSP 2023-2023 IEEE International Conference On Acoustics, Speech And Signal Processing (ICASSP), pp. 1–5 (2023)
26. Wu, Y., Chen, K., Zhang, T., Hui, Y., Berg-Kirkpatrick, T., Dubnov, S.: Large-scale contrastive language-audio pretraining with feature fusion and keyword-to-caption augmentation. In: ICASSP 2023-2023 IEEE International Conference On Acoustics, Speech And Signal Processing (ICASSP), pp. 1–5 (2023)
27. Chen, J., Zhang, L., Wang, Q., Bai, C., Kpalma, K.: Intra-modal constraint loss for image-text retrieval. In: 2022 IEEE International Conference On Image Processing (ICIP), pp. 4023–4027 (2022)
28. Manocha, P., Badlani, R., Kumar, A., Shah, A., Elizalde, B., Raj, B.: Content-based representations of audio using siamese neural networks. In: 2018 IEEE International Conference On Acoustics, Speech And Signal Processing (ICASSP), pp. 3136–3140 (2018)
29. Elizalde, B., Zarar, S., Raj, B.: Cross modal audio search and retrieval with joint embeddings based on text and audio. In: ICASSP 2019-2019 IEEE International Conference On Acoustics, Speech And Signal Processing (ICASSP), pp. 4095–4099 (2019)
30. Chen, S., et al.: VAST: a vision-audio-subtitle-text omni-modality foundation model and dataset. ArXiv Preprint ArXiv:2305.18500 (2023)
31. Wang, P., et al.: ONE-PEACE: exploring one general representation model toward unlimited modalities. ArXiv Preprint ArXiv:2305.11172 (2023)
32. Mei, X., Liu, X., Sun, J., Plumbley, M., Wang, W.: On metric learning for audio-text cross-modal retrieval. ArXiv Preprint ArXiv:2203.15537 (2022)
33. Xie, H., Räsänen, O., Virtanen, T.: On negative sampling for contrastive audio-text retrieval. In: ICASSP 2023-2023 IEEE International Conference On Acoustics, Speech And Signal Processing (ICASSP), pp. 1–5 (2023)
34. Chen, T., Kornblith, S., Norouzi, M., Hinton, G.: A simple framework for contrastive learning of visual representations. In: International Conference On Machine Learning, pp. 1597–1607 (2020)

35. Hu, T., Xiang, X., Qin, J., Tan, Y.: Audio-text retrieval based on contrastive learning and collaborative attention mechanism. Multimedia Syst. **29**, 1–14 (2023). https://doi.org/10.1007/s00530-023-01144-4
36. Merullo, J., Castricato, L., Eickhoff, C., Pavlick, E.: Linearly mapping from image to text space. ArXiv Preprint ArXiv:2209.15162 (2022)
37. Hahnloser, R., Sarpeshkar, R., Mahowald, M., Douglas, R., Seung, H.: Digital selection and analogue amplification coexist in a cortex-inspired silicon circuit. Nature **405**, 947–951 (2000)
38. Song, K., Tan, X., Qin, T., Lu, J., Liu, T.: MPNet: masked and permuted pre-training for language understanding. Adv. Neural. Inf. Process. Syst. **33**, 16857–16867 (2020)
39. Yang, Z., Dai, Z., Yang, Y., Carbonell, J., Salakhutdinov, R., Le, Q.: XLNet: generalized autoregressive pretraining for language understanding. In: Advances In Neural Information Processing Systems, vol. 32 (2019)
40. Maas, A., Hannun, A., Ng, A., et al.: Rectifier nonlinearities improve neural network acoustic models. In: Proc. Icml, vol. 30, pp. 3 (2013)
41. Hendrycks, D., Gimpel, K.: Gaussian error linear units (GELUs). ArXiv Preprint ArXiv:1606.08415 (2016)
42. Elfwing, S., Uchibe, E., Doya, K.: Sigmoid-weighted linear units for neural network function approximation in reinforcement learning. Neural Netw. **107**, 3–11 (2018)
43. Misra, D.M.: A self regularized non-monotonic activation function. ArXiv Preprint ArXiv:1908.08681 (2019)
44. Gemmeke, J., et al.:. Audio set: an ontology and human-labeled dataset for audio events. In: 2017 IEEE International Conference On Acoustics, Speech And Signal Processing (ICASSP), pp. 776–780 (2017)
45. Mei, X., Liu, X., Huang, Q., Plumbley, M., Wang, W.: Audio captioning transformer. ArXiv Preprint ArXiv:2107.09817 (2021)

Grey Wolf Optimization Based Hyper-Parameter Optimized Deep EfficientNet for Chest X-Ray Based Detection of COVID-19

Sanjoy Mitra[1]([✉]) [iD], Parijata Majumdar[2,3] [iD], and Nirankita Debnath[1]

[1] Tripura Institute of Technology, Agartala, India
sanjoy.mitra@titagartala.ac.in
[2] National Institute of Technology, Agartala, India
[3] Techno College of Engineering, Agartala, India

Abstract. The global economy and public health have been severely affected by the COVID-19 epidemic. Inspired by the free resource community's work assembling the COVID-19 data sets and the accomplishments of deep learning methods in successful classification and detection of diseases on medical domain, we embarked on a mission to develop a COVID-19 detection system from Chest X-ray images that could revolutionize the diagnosis and treatment of infectious diseases. We created an enhanced deep EfficientNet-B0 based Convolutional Neural Network (CNN) architecture to detect COVID-19 from chest X-ray pictures that facilitate accurate diagnosis of COVID-19. A compound coefficient is used by the CNN design and development method EfficientNet-B0 to precisely measure each depth, breadth, and resolution component. Using a set of predefined scaling coefficients, its scaling technique uniformly modifies the network's breadth, depth, and resolution. However, the hyperparameters of EfficientNet-B0 must be fine-tuned to optimize its performance. An automated hyperparameter optimized EfficientNet-B0 is proposed to classify COVID-19 from several public datasets of chest X-ray images where the hyperparameters are optimized using a Grey Wolf Optimizer (GWO). When tested on various chest X-ray image datasets, the GWO-EfficientNet-B0 model outperformed the Particle Swarm Optimization (PSO-EfficientNet-B0), and Genetic Algorithm (GA-EfficientNet-B0) required to optimize EfficientNet-B0's hyperparameters in terms of difference performance metrics. The proposed optimized neural network can accurately classify COVID-19 positive cases with 97.89% accuracy rate which is better compared to other methods.

Keywords: COVID-19 · Deep learning · EfficientNet-B0 based CNN · Grey Wolf Optimizer

1 Introduction

SARS-CoV-2, caused by corona virus 2, is the virus responsible for the novel Corona virus illness 2019, a rare and serious condition that has propagated all

A. Verma et al. (Eds.): ANTIC 2023, CCIS 2091, pp. 337–356, 2024.
https://doi.org/10.1007/978-3-031-64064-3_24

over the globe [1]. The World Health Organization (WHO) initially informed the people about the outbreak of this new virus on 31st December 2019, and there were around 500 million diagnosis and 6.18 million deaths reported by April 12th 2022 [3]. When two people are in close proximity, the Corona virus may transmit quickly from one to another by little particles generated by speaking, coughing, and sneezing. After a few days, persons who have been infected frequently experience signs and symptoms such as fever, testicular/small loss, coughing, and difficulty of breathing. Identifying infected patients through efficient screening can help in avoiding the quick spread of COVID-19 by allowing them to remain isolated and making timely treatment available. Currently, the most popular technique for detecting COVID-19 Chain Reaction (RT-PCR) is transcriptase-polymerase. Although it is a slow and expensive COVID-19 detection method, it is extremely accurate. A chest's X-RAY (CXR) is a clinical imaging modality which is typically available, easy to obtain, and more affordable. The detection of COVID-19 may be aided by chest computed tomography (CT) imaging, but due to the significant radiation exposure, currently doctors do not recommend using CT imaging for routine screening. In general, radiologists rely heavily on CXR images to identify chest disease, and they have been used to confirm or indicate COVID-19 in infected individuals [4]. The benefit of using X-ray equipment is that the majority of radiological laboratories and hospitals can obtain 2-D projection images of the chest image. The CXR scans are reasonably priced, and the analysis of the results is simple. Chest X-rays expose patients to very little radiation and are easily accessible and portable. Due to the clinical significance and intricacy of CXR image analysis, researchers continue to analyze Artificial Intelligence techniques to enhance analytical methods in CXR image interpretation [2]. Sample CXR images of COVID-19 is shown in Fig. 1(a) and 1(b) [6]. Deep learning (DL) techniques are becoming more and more popular in the classification and illness detection of medical images because of its high level of accuracy. Due to the substantial amount of concealed layers, DL has for both regression and classification applications, this tendency exists.

Recent research utilizing DL technology has pushed for the creation of intelligent diagnostic tools that can aid in the improvement of patient care decisions made by health professionals. Convolutional neural network (CNN) facilitated data-based DL techniques that have displayed outstanding results for the classification challenge of COVID-19 case recognition with CXR images [5]. Researchers often utilize CNN since it has been shown that they are particularly effective at learning and extracting features [8]. When training the Efficient Net-B0 algorithm, selecting appropriate hyperparameters is crucial because if the learning rate is very high, the Efficient Net-B0 converges very fast and the network may miss crucial elements of the data.

For effective training and the best performance outcomes, CNN hyperparameters must be optimized. Particularly in the area of tackling optimization problems which essentially mimic the group behavior of species seen in nature, metaheuristics have made tremendous progress [9]. A Grey Wolf Optimizer (GWO) is a recently discovered metaheuristics that has had witnessed tremendous success in various fields, as demonstrated in [10–13], and [14]. In this article, the hyperparameters of Efficient Net-B0 have been optimized using GWO and it's performance is compared with Particle Swarm Optimization (PSO-EfficientNet-B0), and Genetic Algorithm (GA-EfficientNet-B0) required to optimize Efficient Net-B0 algorithm's hyperparameters.

Table 1 provides the comparative study of GWO, PSO and GA algorithms used for COVID-19 detection from CXR scans in this article.

Table 1. Comparative Survey of GWO, PSO and GA algorithms

GWO	PSO	GA
GWO is a SI algorithm	PSO is a fast gradient method	GA is a evolution method
GWO has faster convergence than PSO and GA	PSO has faster convergence than GA	GA takes a lot of time to simulate the generations function value
GWO tries to find the global optima	PSO tries to find the global optima	GA usually converges towards a local optimum or even arbitrary points rather than the global optima
The social dynamics that a pack of wolves adopts when attacking a prey in search of food serve as the foundation for GWO algorithm [9]	The social dynamics found in groups of animals that adopt a collective behavior, like birds, schools of fish, bees, etc., served as the inspiration for the PSO algorithm [34]	The inheritance rules in nature, where the strongest individuals must perish and the best individuals survive, are modeled by the GA [33]
In GWO, the unknown parameters of the problem are represented by the individuals of grey wolves.	In PSO, the unknown parameters of the problem are represented by the particles of the swarm	In GA, the unknown parameters of the problem are represented by the individuals of population
The steps of the algorithm are known as iterations in GWO	The steps of the algorithm are known as iterations in PSO	The steps of the algorithm are known as generations in GA
The sampling of the model search space is ruled by social hierarchy of grey wolves in nature	The sampling of the model search space is ruled by social and cognitive behavior in PSO	The sampling of the model search space is ruled by natural selection (mutation and reproduction) in GA
GWO has a higher exploitation rate	PSO has a higher exploration rate	

In terms of different performance metrics, the GWO optimized Efficient Net-B0 algorithm outperform rest of the methods when applied on different datasets.

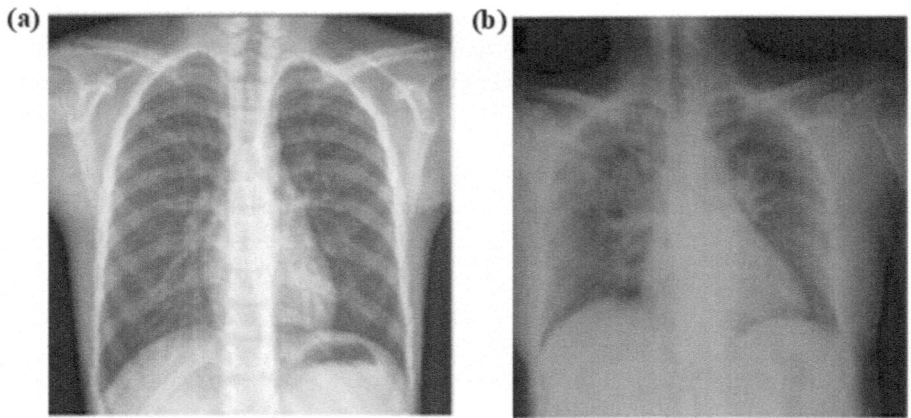

Fig. 1. Sample Chest X-ray images of a (a) normal and (b) COVID-19 patient

In Sect. 2, a list of previous works is reviewed. The theoretical and mathematical underpinnings of the GWO-Efficient Net-B0 algorithm, a hyperparameterized version of the Efficient Net-B0 algorithm based on GWO, are explained in Sect. 3. The experimental design and key findings are detailed in Sect. 4. Section 5 draws a conclusion and suggests areas for further research.

2   Related Works

Tang et al. [1] have used an ensemble model called EDL-COVID for COVID-19 detection from CXR images, but model snapshots of COVID-Net must be retrained in order to improve the model each time new CXR images become available. In [15], an extensive database of CT images and X-ray scan images is built which is obtained from various sources to train CNN and modified trained AlexNet for COVID-19 detection. In [5], CLAHE and Butterworth bandpass filters were used in the deep Neural Network system to improve contrasts and get rid of noise in the CXR images. As EfficientNetB0, VGG16, and InceptionV3 utilizes fewer parameters, these models are employed in [16] for COVID-19 identification. In [17], transfer learning is used for pretraining models using Alex Net and VGG16 and data augmentation is performed to reduce class imbalance and increase the classifier's performance. Hemdan et al. [18] have utilized COVIDX-Net to help radiologists for COVID-19 diagnosis. Seven distinct deep CNN incorporating the VGG19 update and the subsequent iteration of Google MobileNet are implemented. Alom et al. [19] have used a multitask DL method using an Residual Recurrent CNN with Transfer Learning. Singh et al. [3] have utilized X-ray scans to distinguish individuals with COVID-19-positive lung images. He detected COVID-19-positive and negative images using MADE-based CNN, PSO-based CNN and GA-based CNN models. Zhang et al. [20] have developed a deep anomaly identification algorithm for COVID-19 detection from

CXR scans. Using ResNet152, Kumar et al. [21] proposed machine learning-based analysis of the important data gleaned from COVID-19 CXR scans. The optimization challenge of CNN hyper-parameter tuning has drawn the attention of numerous researchers. PSO [23], univariate dynamic encoding [22], and multi-level evolutionary optimization [24] are used to improve the hyper-parameters of CNN. Although the hyperparameter optimization outcomes of these publications are encouraging, there is yet scope for improvement. Recently, GWO has been used for CNN training [25,26], and [27], as well as for optimizing the hyperparameters of DL-based methods. As a result, we are also driven to use the GWO-EfficientNet-B0 to obtain optimal hyperparameters for solving the classification problem for COVID-19. A comparative table discussing the advantages and disadvantages of existing related literature is shown in Table 2.

Table 2. Comparative Survey of the related literature

Method	Advantages	Disadvantages
Deep learning and Weighted Averaging ensemble learning (EDL-COVID) [1]	The model is aware of different sensitivities of deep learning models on different class types	Model snapshots of COVID-Net must be retrained to improve the model each time a new CXR images become available
CNN with pre-trained AlexNet model [15]	Both X-ray and CT scan data sets for early COVID-19 detection	Smart gadgets required to help radiologist
A deep belief network and a convolutional deep belief network [5]	Efficient and accurate system for early detection of COVID-19 in a real clinical center.	Investigations needed to verify the system effectiveness using a large dataset
EfficientNetB0, VGG16, InceptionV3 are used with transfer learning [16]	The models have fewer parameters for effective detection of COVID-19	Other deep learning models can be used for comparison with respect to multimedia medical image screening
Seven distinct deep CNN with the VGG19 update and further iteration of Google MobileNet [18]	Each model can check the normalized forces in CXR images to show the patient status	Other deep learning models can be used for comparison using image datasets gathered from multiple sources
A multitask DL method using an Residual Recurrent CNN with Transfer Learning [19]	Feature accumulation with recurrent residual convolutional layers represents features	More benchmark datasets can be used to compare segmentation performance
Distinguishing viral pneumonia as a one-class classification-based anomaly detection [20]	Fast and precise detection of viral pneumonia using CXR images	Investigation of pneumonia severity and identifying extreme cases for treatment
Analysis of vital data gleaned from CXR scans using ResNet152 [21]	Early, precise and cost-effective detection of COVID-19	Training with more large datasets & testing in the field with a larger cohort

3   Theoretical and Mathematical Foundation of Hyperparameter Optimized EfficientNet-B0 Using GWO

3.1   Grey Wolf Optimizer

Grey wolves hunt in packs and depend on interpack cooperation. GWO derives its inspiration from the social structure and the hunting method. The strongest wolves are called alphas (leader wolves), betas (obeying the decisions of alpha wolves), deltas (strong wolves but no leadership abilities), and omegas (weakest and responsible for caring for the younger ones) which are ranked as per strength and power. The wolves use one or two other wolves to help them separate their prey from the herd before the remainder of the pack chases the stray wolves away.

$$D = |C \cdot X_p(t) - X(t)| \tag{1}$$

$$X(t + 1) = X_p(t) - A \cdot D \tag{2}$$

where t stands for the current iteration, X_p is the position vector of the prey, and X represents the grey wolf's current location. The coefficient vectors are equal to:

$$A = |2a \cdot rand1(t) - a|(\text{regulates exploration and exploitation}) \tag{3}$$

$$C = 2 \cdot rand2(\text{adds randomization}) \tag{4}$$

where a decreases linearly from 2 to 0 over iterations, and $rand1$ and $rand2$ are random vectors with values $[0, 1]$, created for each wolf at each iteration.

$$a = 2 - t\frac{2}{iter} \tag{5}$$

The number of allowed iterations is determined by the variable $iter$. Location is updated in accordance with the prey's location. The ideal wolf position can be achieved by adjusting a and C. The locations are updated according to:

$$D_\alpha = |C_1 \cdot X_\alpha - X| \tag{6}$$

$$D_\beta = |C_2 \cdot X_\beta - X| \tag{7}$$

$$D_\delta = |C_3 \cdot X_\delta - X| \tag{8}$$

$$X_1 = X_\alpha - A_1 \cdot D_\alpha \tag{9}$$

$$X_2 = X_\beta - A_2 \cdot D_\beta \tag{10}$$

$$X_3 = X_\delta - A_3 \cdot D_\delta \tag{11}$$

$$X_{t+1} = \frac{X_1 + X_2 + X_3}{3} \tag{12}$$

where, X_{t+1} represents current location and the agent's current position is represented by X. The average of the top three wolves will not be exactly equal to X_{t+1} since C is responsible for a tiny random shift because the best wolves must lead the search agents while also avoiding the local optima stagnation problem. Three distinct wolves namely alpha, beta and delta are utilized in the GWO to direct the search operations. The leadership hierarchy-based search mechanism controls the algorithm's exploration rate appropriately and restricts the search agents from getting stuck in the local optima.

3.2 EfficientNet-B0 Based Convolutional Neural Network

The structure of a CNN consists of input layer, convolutional layer (CL), max-pooling layer (MPL), fully connected layer (FCL), and an output layer. The number of kernels and kernel size determines how many characteristics may be retrieved from each layer. The random weights that are trained during model training are used to initialize the kernel weights. Gradient descent training, which modifies the CL's parameters, should be used to optimize the CL weights. The features are transferred into feature space using the Rectified Linear Unit (ReLU) which keeps the value of the CL within a certain range. CNN uses the ReLU the most because it is simple, inconsistent, and naturally non-negative. To prevent overfitting, the dropout layer is added after ReLU. A batch normalization layer (BNL) normalizes the gradients and activations across the network. While the dimensions of the feature maps are reduced due to the pooling layer (PL), the image's most crucial elements are kept. The PL is then used to downsample the feature map. Utilizing the most of each feature map patch, max pooling is used. The retrieved features are classified into a specific class by the fully connected classifier layer. The last layer uses a soft-max activation function. The overfitting is reduced by adding a penalty to the loss function. In CNN, dropping out diminishes interdependent learning to reduce overfitting. After a CNN's internal weights are established, backpropagation is used to adjust them to the target problem. Typically, stochastic gradient descent (SGD) is used to adjust the CL and FCL parameters. The architecture of EfficientNet is to develop the trade-off between model size and performance by maximizing each parameter at the same time. Previously, researchers had to carefully balance model depth, width, and resolution while developing CNNs, resulting in inferior results. EfficientNet-B0 employs a compound coefficient to accurately quantify all depth, width, and resolution components. Utilizing a set of preset scaling coefficients, the compound scaling approach scales each of the dimensions-depth, width, and resolution efficiently and consistently. This technique improves functioning while keeping computational and memory demands acceptable. The balance of all network dimensions is shown to be essential, which can be done using scaling each dimension to a constant ratio [32]. Larger input images necessitate several layers to expand the network's receptive area and more channels to capture more minute patterns, according to the basic idea underlying a compound scaling technique. The compound scaling method is required because larger input images need more layers to increase the receptive field of the network and more channels to catch more fine-grained patterns. The EfficientNet-B0 network consists of squeeze-and-excitation blocks and MobileNetV2 inverted bottleneck residual blocks. The network's topmost layer has been replaced using two output neuron layers because the model will categorize two different image classes. Due to their extensive ImageNet training, the remaining layers remain unaltered. In order to further improve it's performance, a mix of dropout and thick layers are used. In the following phase, the Adam optimizer is used to conduct experiments. The optimizer defines how to manage the weight values and how quickly it should be changed. We have defined the model, established model checkpoints to save the most accurate model, and included preventative measures to avoid over-fitting during training. The compound scaling approach equally scales the network's width, depth, and resolution using the compound coefficient Φ in the following manner:

$$depth : d = \alpha^{\phi} \tag{13}$$

$$width : w = \beta^{\phi} \tag{14}$$

$$resolution : r = \gamma^{\phi} \tag{15}$$

$$s.t. \alpha \cdot \beta^2 \cdot \gamma^2 \propto 2, \alpha \geq 1, \beta \geq 1, \gamma \geq 1, \tag{16}$$

where α, β, and γ can be determined by a small grid search. ϕ is user-specified which controls the number of resources available for model scaling, while α, β, and γ specify how to assign these resources to network width, depth, and resolution.

Table 3 displays an experimental configuration of personalized EfficientNet-B0 training parameters.

The compound scaling method of EfficientNet-B0 architecture is shown in Fig. 2.

3.3   Hyperparameter Optimized EfficientNet-B0 Using GWO

To produce the best performance outcomes, the GWO algorithm focuses on improving the hyperparameters utilized for training the EfficientNet-B0. Although checking each hyperparameter is computationally expensive, they are crucial for delivering greater performance. To fine tune the hyperparameters, GWO is used which determines the accuracy and convergence of EfficientNet-B0.

Table 3. Experimental Setup of training options (Customized)

Parameter	Value
InitialLearnRate	$1.0000e^{-04}$
Execution Environment	GPU
MiniBatchSize	8
MaxEpoch	20
Verbose	0
Shuffle	every epoch
LearnRateSchedule	piecwise
Optimizer	sgdm

Depending on the application for which the EfficientNet-B0 is utilized, choosing the hyperparameters for the network is crucial. The learning rate regulates the gradient descent algorithm's speed, and the momentum regulates how much the updating of older weights influences the updating of current weights. Depending on the training dataset, the number of epochs regulates how often the learning algorithm updates the network parameters. Overfitting in the network is resolved via regularization. For accuracy, it is therefore necessary to optimize these hyperparameters to take into account all of these variables. Algorithm (1) displays the GWO technique for EfficientNet-B0 hyperparameter optimization in SGD training. There are many hyper-parameters in the model that can significantly affect the outcomes, such as the learning rate, the number of convolutions, the batch size, quantity of dense layers and its layer size, layer wise kernels deistribution and total number of layers, optimizer used, epochs considered, applied activation function and the number of max-pooling. Right tuning of hyper parameters is an important optimization step for performance accuracy.

Table 4 provides a description of the layers of GWO-EfficientNetB0.

4   Results and Discussion

4.1   Datasets

To compare the GWO-based EfficcientNetB0's performance, classification tests were run using various other optimization methods. The technique was written in Python 3.8 and executed on Windows 10 Pro with 64 GB RAM, an Nvidia GPU, and a core i7 processor. In this study, we used several datasets from different sources comprising of the CoronaHack-CXR dataset [29], the COVID CXR dataset [30], and the COVID-19 Radiography database [28]. This dataset are made up of 1143 COVID-19 and 1341 normal images.

Training and Testing. The input images were reduced in size to 256×256. The random size data is reshaped during image resizing to take on a form that is comparable to the model. The EfficcientNetB0 model's training and testing time can

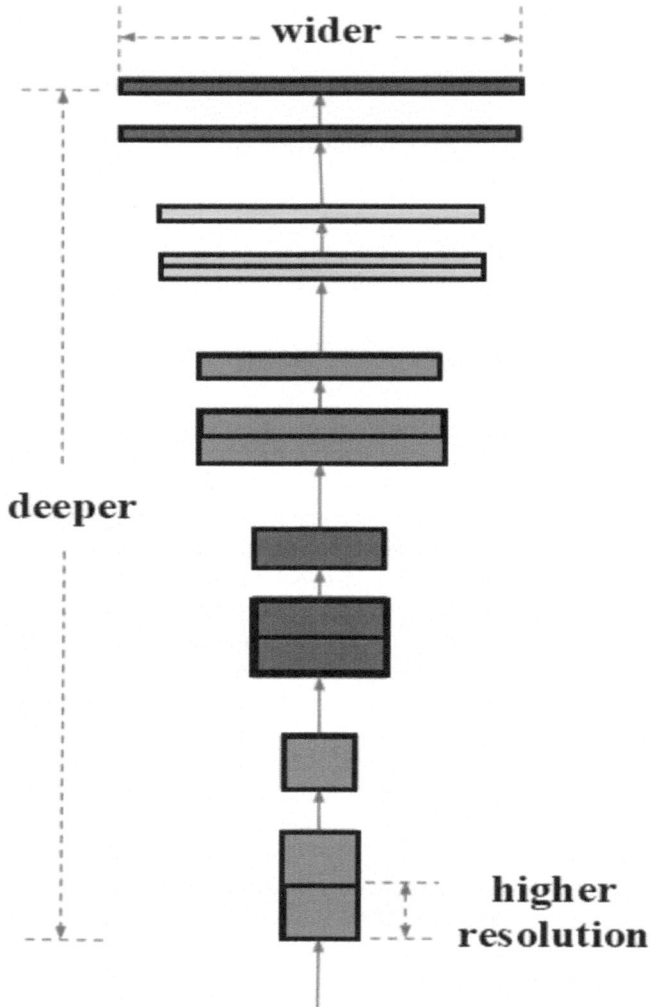

Fig. 2. Compound Scaling of EfficientNet-B0

be reduced by scaling down the images to their original size. To increase the suggested model's accuracy, the epoch values were adjusted. The dataset is randomly divided into 30% of the data used for testing and 70% of the data used for training. The hyperparameters are optimized using GWO while the parameters are tuned using SGD training. This paper's major objective is to get nearly optimal values for the hyper-parameters involved primarily in convolution, dropout, and pooling layer after selecting the architecture. The training of EfficientNet-B0, which is

---

Algorithm 1. Proposed GWO based hyperparameter optimized EfficientNet-B0

1: **procedure** ALGORITHM 1
2:     Parameters: Batch Size : b = 30; number of search agents : s = 3; dimension : dim = 4; number of optimization iterations : opt = 30; hyperparameters : H1, H2, H3, H4 = [1, 0.5, 15, 5.0000e-04]; hyperparameter evaluation function (H_D) : Error rate = (FP + FN)/(TP + TN + FP + FN)
3:     Initialize: Random population of Wolves $X_i (i = 1, 2, ..., n)$
4:     Initialize A, a, C
5:     Sample a batch of training data
6:     **for** Every iteration of optimization, opt **do**
7:         **for** every search agent **do**
8:             Calculate fitness function
9:         **end for**
10:         Choose the first three best search agents : $\alpha, \beta, and \gamma$
11:         Update current search agents position.
12:     **end for**
13:     Update a, A and C
14:     (H1, H2, H3 and H4) = hyperparameter evaluation function (L_D)
15:     Update $\alpha, \beta and \gamma$
16:     End
17:     w & b = Sgdm $(H_D$, H1, H2, H3 and H4)
18: **end procedure**

---

referred to as the fitness function takes up the most time during the hyperparameter tuning procedure. SGD is used to fine-tune the parameters whereas GWO optimizes the hyperparameters. After determining the EfficientNet-B0's design, the main goal is to reach values for the hyper-parameters involved largely in convolution, dropout, and pooling layers that are close to optimal. The longest part of the hyperparameter tuning process is the training of EfficientNet-B0, the fitness function to be evaluated in the optimization. An appropriate fitness function is developed that can quickly calculate the fitness as the accuracy of EfficientNet-B0 in order to improve the efficiency of tuning hyperparameters. We utilized EfficientNet-B0 in this study because of its comprehensive training capability, autonomous feature selection, and classification precision.

The optimized hyperparameters are illustrated in Table 5.

The trained EfficientNet-B0, which already has all the CL and FCL parameters tuned, receives the test images as input. EfficientNet-B0 first extracts the image features before utilizing FCL and soft-max classifiers to place them in the proper class.

4.2 Performance Indicators and Evaluation Metrics

GWO-EfficientNet-B0 is validated using the accuracy, sensitivity, specificity, and precision performance metrics, as well as the F1-score [31] and receiver operating characteristic (ROC) analysis performance metrics. The classifier's accuracy is measured by how well it can discriminate between COVID-19 and normal images.

Table 4. Description of the layers

Layers	Filter Size and No.	Stride
Input ($224 \times 224 \times 3$)	–	–
$Conv_1$ (CL + BNL+ ReLU)	3×3 and 64	1×1
MPL_1	2×2	2×2
$Conv_2$ (CL + BNL+ ReLU)	3×3 and 64	1×1
MPL_2	2×2	2×2
$Conv_3$ (CL + BNL+ ReLU)	3×3 and 32	1×1
MPL_3	2×2	2×2
$Conv_4$ (CL + BNL+ ReLU)	3×3 and 16	1×1
MPL_5	2×2	2×2
$Conv_5$ (CL + BNL+ ReLU)	3×3 and 8	1×1
Fully connected (Output size=3)	—	—
Output (Classification layer)	Soft-max	—

Table 5. Hyperparameters of EfficientNetB0 obtained using GWO

Training algorithm	Stochastic Gradient Descent
Momentum	0.6
Initial learning rate	0.015
Maximum epoch	10
Validation frequency	30
L2Regularization	1.0000e-04

The classification method used for all values is characteristically represented by the receiver operating characteristic (ROC) curve. The link between specificity and sensitivity is represented by this curve. Figure 3 shows the ROC curves of the GWO+CNN in comparison to the evaluated classification algorithms. It is evident from this image that the GWO algorithm is capable of making a significant distinction between CXR scans with a high AUC value.

The performance metrics equations are summarized as follows:

$$Accuracy = \frac{TP + TN}{TP + TN + FP + FN} \tag{17}$$

$$Sensitivity or Recall = \frac{TP}{TP + FN} \tag{18}$$

$$Specificity = \frac{TN}{TN + FP} \tag{19}$$

$$Precision = \frac{TP}{TP + FP} \tag{20}$$

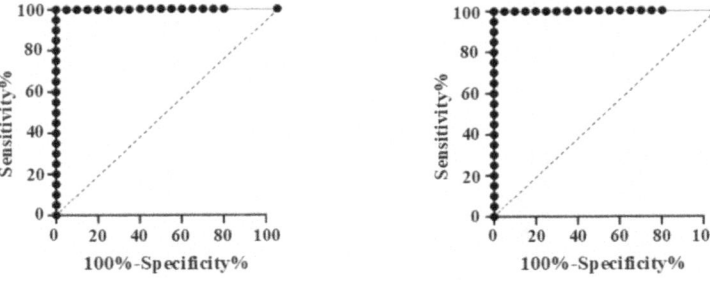

Fig. 3. ROC curves for GWO algorithm versus compared algorithms

Table 6. Training and Testing Accuracy of models

Dataset	Number of images	Model	Training accuracy	Testing accuracy	Time elapsed (min)
COVID Chest X-ray	803	GWO-EfficcientNetB0	87.2	90.8	135
		PSO-EfficcientNetB0	85.6	87.9	132
		GA-EfficcientNetB0	82.8	84.5	136
COVID-19 Radiography	2484	GWO-EfficcientNetB0	90.2	93.2	2335
		PSO-EfficcientNetB0	84.5	86.7	2210
		GA-EfficcientNetB0	81.9	83.9	1960
CoronaHack-Chest X-Ray	5911	GWO-EfficcientNetB0	91.2	92.8	2719
		PSO-EfficcientNetB0	89.6	91.9	132
		GA-EfficcientNetB0	85.8	87.9	2601

$$F1 - Score = 2 \times \frac{Precision \times Recall}{Precision + Recall} \tag{21}$$

$$TPRate = \frac{TP}{TP + FN} \tag{22}$$

$$FPRate = \frac{FP}{FP + TN} \tag{23}$$

4.3   Comparative Analysis

Table 6 lists the training and testing accuracies of various models that were used for comparison. When compared to other datasets, the CoronaHack-Chest X-Ray dataset offered an effective accuracy (92.8%) in COVID-19 detection. In all datasets, GWO-EfficientNetB0 outperforms PSO-EfficientNetB0, and GA-EfficientNetB0. In Table 7, the accuracy of each class was assessed using the

Table 7. Accuracy per class

Dataset	Model	Normal Images Training accuracy	Normal Images Testing accuracy	COVID-19 Images Training accuracy	COVID-19 Images Testing accuracy
COVID Chest X-ray	GWO-EfficcientNetB0	87.2	88.8	90.2	92.2
	PSO-EfficcientNetB0	86.8	87.7	88.5	90.5
	GA-EfficcientNetB0	83.8	84.1	86.6	88.8
COVID-19 Radiography	GWO-EfficcientNetB0	89.2	90.2	93.9	94.2
	PSO-EfficcientNetB0	87.2	88.5	91.2	93.3
	GA-EfficcientNetB0	85.5	86.8	90.9	92.2
CoronaHack-Chest X-Ray	GWO-EfficcientNetB0	92.1	93.3	91.2	90.1
	PSO-EfficcientNetB0	90.9	89.2	90.1	89.7
	GA-EfficcientNetB0	88.3	89.9	88.4	86.6

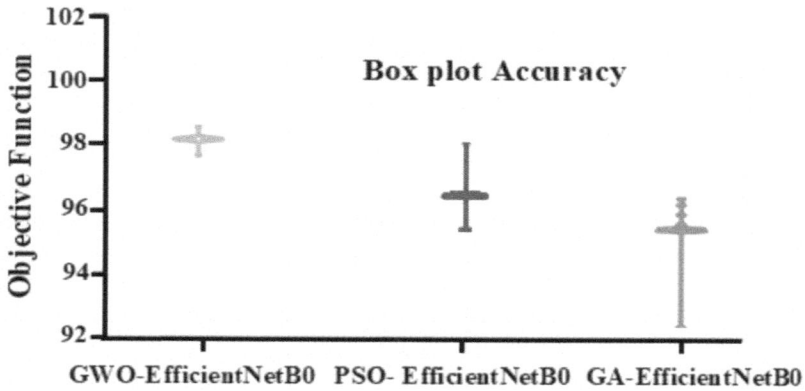

Fig. 4. Box plot accuracy of algorithms for normal CXR images

available models for various datasets. In comparison to other datasets, in the CoronaHack-Chest X-Ray, the classes are accurately identified. In all datasets, GWO-EfficientNetB0 outperforms PSO-EfficientNetB0, and GA-EfficientNetB0 in terms of accuracy for each class. The computation times for the proposed GWO-EfficientNetB0 model and the pre-trained models were also calculated, and the proposed GWO-EfficientNetB0 had the best computational time. For each class (normal and COVID-19), individual accuracy, precision, and recall were tabulated in Table 8. In all datasets, GWO-EfficientNetB0 outperforms PSO-EfficientNetB0, and GA-EfficientNetB0. Table 9 lists the GWO-EfficientNetB0 and pretrained model's Area Under Curve (AUC) values. Table 10 compares the GWO-EfficientNetB0 model's accuracy to that of the existing models, and the suggested model's accuracy was greater than that of the PSO-EfficientNetB0, and GA-EfficientNetB0.

Table 8. Recall and Precision per class

Dataset	Model	Normal Images Recall	Normal Images Precision	COVID Images Recall	COVID Images Precision
COVID Chest X-ray	GWO-EfficcientNetB0	0.87	0.88	0.90	0.92
	PSO-EfficcientNetB0	0.86	0.87	0.88	0.90
	GA-EfficcientNetB0	0.83	0.84	0.86	0.88
COVID-19 Radiography	GWO-EfficcientNetB0	0.94	90.2	0.93	0.94
	PSO-EfficcientNetB0	0.92	88.5	0.91	0.93
	GA-EfficcientNetB0	0.89	86.8	0.90	0.92
		0.87			
		0.85			
CoronaHack-Chest X-Ray	GWO-EfficcientNetB0	0.92	0.94	0.92	0.91
	PSO-EfficcientNetB0	0.91	0.91	0.90	0.89
	GA-EfficcientNetB0	0.88	0.89	0.88	0.87

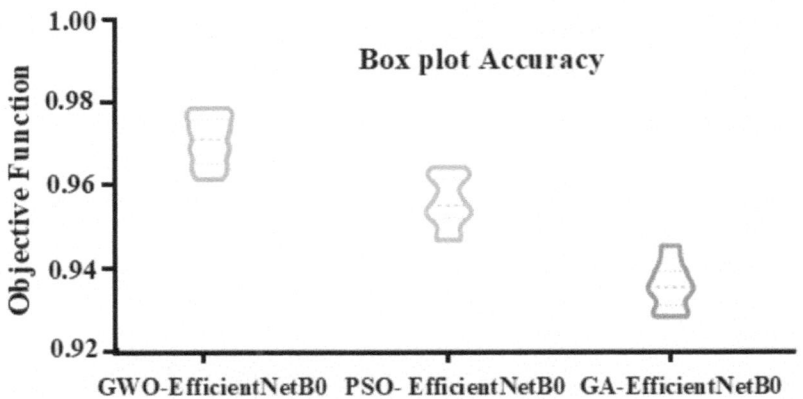

Fig. 5. Box plot accuracy of algorithms for CXR COVID-19 images

Figure 4 shows the comparison of accuracy of existing methods with GWO-EfficcientNetB0.

The comparison of algorithms is shown in Table 11 where GWO can obtain a minimum average error of (0.3231). The GWO algorithm is the best in terms of least error, whereas PSO is the worst. This indicates that the GWO produced superior outcomes in comparison. The GWO algorithm's low standard deviation (0.048) indicates its stability and durability. With a minimal average error, GWO can classify COVID-19 and normal CXR images. Based on least error, the GWO algorithm performs best while the PSO algorithm perform worst. This shows that GWO performed comparatively better.

A box plot is a kind of chart frequently utilized for explanatory data analysis. Box plots display the data quartiles and averages which visually represent the

Table 9. Area under curve

Dataset	GWO-EfficcientNetB0	PSO-EfficcientNetB0	GA-EfficcientNetB0
COVID Chest X-Ray	0.78	0.72	0.69
COVID-19 Radiography	0.91	0.88	0.84
CoronaHack-Chest X-Ray	0.92	0.87	0.81

Table 10. Accuracy comparison of existing methods with GWO-EfficcientNetB0

Model	Accuracy (in %)
GWO-EfficcientNetB0	87.2
PSO-EfficcientNetB0	78.6
GA-EfficcientNetB0	69.9

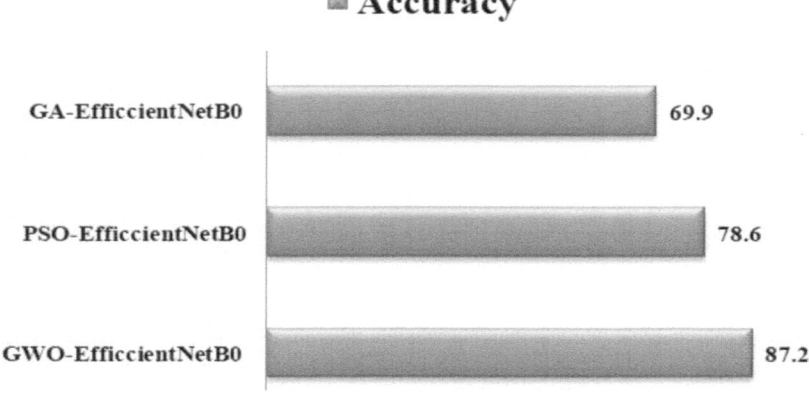

Fig. 6. Comparison of accuracy of existing methods

distribution of numerical data and skewness. It shows the set of data's minimum score, median, upper quartile, lower quartile, and maximum score. Box plots shows a lot of statistical information including medians, ranges, and outliers. The interquartile ranges are compared to examine how the data is dispersed between each sample. The longer the box, the more dispersed is the data and smaller the box, the less dispersed the data is. Here, for GWO-EfficcientNetB0, the data is less dispersed. Figure 5 displays the results of testing the Box plot's

Table 11. Performance comparison of the GWO-EfficcientNetB0 algorithm and others

Metric/Optimizer	GWO	GA	PSO
Average Error	0.3231	0.3284	0.3303
Average Fitness	0.1631	0.1720	0.1784
Best Fitness	1.3744	1.4009	1.4221
Worst Fitness	1.5022	1.5111	1.5139
Standard Deviation Fitness	0.0048	0.0054	0.0059

Table 12. p-values of algorithms using Wilcoxon's rank-sum test depending on average error metric

Compared Algorithm	GA	PSO
p-values	1.17E-05	1.17E-05

correctness. These graphs demonstrate how GWO-EfficcientNetB0 for classifying normal CXR images is stable and consistent.

Figure 6 displays the results from testing the Box plot accuracy. This graph demonstrates the reliability and accuracy of GWO-EfficcientNetB0 for categorizing COVID-19 CXR images. Boxplots show the average score of a data set. The median is the average value from a set of data represented using a line that divides the box into two parts. When the median is in the middle of the box, and the whiskers are about the same on both sides of the box, then the distribution is more symmetric as in GWO-EfficcientNetB0.

4.4 Statistical Analysis

The Wilcoxon rank-sum test is used to compute the p-values of GWO-Efficient NetB0 against those of PSO-EfficcientNetnB0, and GA-EfficcientNetB0 algorithms. The test is run to demonstrate that the GWO-EfficcientNetB0 algorithm differs significantly from other algorithms. The GWO-EfficcientNet B0 algorithm's findings are considerably different from other algorithms if the p-value is < 0.05 else if the p-value is > 0.05, there are no considerable differences between the algorithms. The resultant p-values of various algorithms employing the Wilcoxon's rank-sum test are shown in Tables 12 and 13. The statistical significance of the suggested GWO-EfficcientNet B0 approach is illustrated by the p-values being < 0.05.

Table 12 compares the p-values of various algorithms according to the average error metric.

Table 13. p-values of algorithms using Wilcoxon's rank-sum test depending on accuracy metric

Compared Algorithm	GA-EfficcientNetB0	PSO-EfficcientNetB0
p-values	1.04E-05	1.04E-05

Table 13 illustrates the p-values for the GWO-EfficcientNet B0 algorithm depending on the accuracy metric.

5   Conclusion and Future Work

To stop the novel coronavirus from spreading and saving human lives, it is crucial to make an accurate detection of COVID-19. EfficientNet-B0 is a CNN algorithm widely used for COVID-19 classification. EfficientNet-B03's hyperparameter adjustment is crucial for achieving peak performance and improving classification accuracy. In this study, GWO is used to optimize hyper-parameters of EfficientNet-B0 (GWO-EfficientNet-B0). The proposed model can achieve high accuracy for detecting COVID-19 and normal CXR image in comparison to other models. Sensitivity, specificity, accuracy, precision, recall and F1 score values of the GWO+EfficcientNetB0 are superior to those of the competing models. The Wilcoxon rank-sum test also provides statistical evidence supporting the superiority of the GWO-EfficcientNetB0 over other algorithms. Because of the strong overall performance of GWO-EfficcientNet B0, the proposed GWO-EfficcientNetB0 can naturally assist doctors in making accurate diagnoses related to COVID-19 as well as making proper and timely treatment available to COVID-19 patients. The proposed computer-aided diagnosis mechanism, in our opinion, has the potential to considerably enhance COVID-19 case diagnosis. Future work will concentrate on enhancing the GWO-EfficcientNetB0 and combining recently accessible datasets to test the GWO-EfficcientNetB0. The proposed method's lack of encoding the input image's position orientation necessitates preprocessing, which is one of the shortcomings of the GWO-EfficcientNetB0. Additionally, the input images do not affect the spatial invariance of the GWO-EfficcientNetB0. The proposed GWO-EfficcientNetB0 algorithm can also be applied to solve other complex real-life applications and challenging single and multi-objective optimization problems.

References

1. Tang, S., et al.: EDL-COVID: ensemble deep learning for COVID-19 case detection from chest X-ray images. IEEE Trans. Industr. Inf. **17**(9), 6539–6549 (2021). https://doi.org/10.1109/TII.2021.3057683
2. Ginneken, B.V., Romeny, B.M.T.H., Viergever, M.A.: Computer-aided diagnosis in chest radiography: a survey. IEEE Trans. Med. Imaging **20**(12), 1228–1241 (2001). https://doi.org/10.1109/42.974918

3. Singh, D., Kumar, V., Yadav, V., Kaur, M.: Deep neural network-based screening model for COVID-19-infected patients using chest X-ray images. Int. J. Pattern Recogn. Artif. Intell. **34**(12), 207–7002 (2020). https://doi.org/10.1142/S0218001421510046

4. Bai, Y., et al.: Presumed asymptomatic carrier transmission of COVID-19. JAMA **323**(14), 1406–1407 (2020). https://doi.org/10.1001/jama.2020.2565

5. Al-Waisy, A.S., Mohammed, M.A., Fahdawi, S.A., Maashi, M.S., Zapirain, B.G., Abdulkareem, K.H.: COVID-DeepNet: hybrid multimodal deep learning system for improving COVID-19 pneumonia detection in chest X-ray images. Comput. Mater. Continua **68**(3), 3733–3747 (2021). https://doi.org/10.32604/cmc.2021.012955

6. Cohen, J.P., Paul, M., Dao, L., Roth, K., Duong, T.Q., Ghassemi, M.: COVID-19 image data collection: prospective predictions are the future. arXiv preprint arXiv. **206**, 11988 (2020). https://doi.org/10.10007/1234567890

7. Ginneken, B.V., Romeny, B.M., Viergever, M.: Computer-aided diagnosis in chest radiography: a survey. IEEE Trans. Med. Imaging **20**(12), 1228–1241 (2001). https://doi.org/10.1016/j.compmedimag.2007.02.003

8. Krizhevsky, A., Sutskever, I., Hinton, G.E.: Imagenet classification with deep convolutional neural networks. Commun. ACM **60**(6), 84–90 (2017). https://doi.org/10.1145/3065386

9. Mirjalili, S., Mirjalili, S.M., Lewis, A.: Grey wolf optimizer. Adv. Eng. Softw. **69**, 46–61 (2014). https://doi.org/10.1016/j.advengsoft.2013.12.007

10. Heidari, A.A., Mirjalili, S., Faris, H., Aljarah, I., Mafarja, M., Chen, H.: Harris hawks optimization: algorithm and applications. Futur. Gener. Comput. Syst. **97**, 849–872 (2019). https://doi.org/10.1016/j.future.2019.02.028

11. Kumaran, N., Vadivel, A., Kumar, S.S.: Recognition of human actions using CNN-GWO: a novel modeling of CNN for enhancement of classification performance. Multimedia Tools Appl. **77**(18), 23115–23147 (2018). https://doi.org/10.1007/s11042-017-5591-z

12. Sanjay, R., Jayabarathi, T., Raghunathan, T., Ramesh, V., Mithulananthan, N.: Optimal allocation of distributed generation using hybrid grey wolf optimizer. IEEE Access. **5**, 14807–14818 (2017)

13. Lu, C., Gao, L., Li, X., Xiao, S.: A hybrid multi-objective grey wolf optimizer for dynamic scheduling in a real-world welding industry. Eng. Appl. Artif. Intell. **57**, 61–79 (2017). https://doi.org/10.1016/j.engappai.2016.10.013

14. Venkatakrishnan, G., Rengaraj, R., Salivahanan, S.: Grey wolf optimizer to real power dispatch with non-linear constraint. CMES-Comput. Model. Eng. Sci. **115**(1), 5–45 (2018). https://doi.org/10.3970/cmes.2018.115.025

15. Maghdid, H.S., Asaad, A.T., Ghafoor, K.Z., Sadiq, A.S., Khan, M.K. : Diagnosing COVID-19 pneumonia from X-Ray and CT images using deep learning and transfer learning algorithms (2021). https://ieeexplore.ieee.org/document/9413479

16. Gaur, L., Bhatia, U., Jhanjhi, N.Z., Muhammad, G., Masud, M.: Medical image-based detection of COVID-19 using deep convolution neural networks. Multimedia Syst. **29**(3), 1729–1738 (2023). https://doi.org/10.1007/s00530-021-00794-6

17. TN, S.G., Satish, R., Sridhar, R.: Learning effective embedding for automated COVID-19 prediction from chest X-ray images. Multimedia Syst. **29**(2), 739–751 (2023). https://doi.org/10.1007/s00530-022-01015-4

18. Hemdan, E.E.D., Shouman, M.A., Karar, M.E.: COVIDX-Net: a framework of deep learning classifiers to diagnose COVID-19 in X-ray images. arXiv preprint arXiv:2003.11055 (2020)

19. Alom, M.Z., Hasan, M., Yakopcic, C., Taha, T.M., Asari, V.K.: Recurrent residual convolutional neural network based on U-Net (R2U-Net) for medical image segmentation. arXiv preprint arXiv:1802.06955 (2018)
20. Zhang, J., Xie, Y., Li, Y., Shen, C., Xia, Y.: COVID-19 screening on chest X-ray images using deep learning based anomaly detection (2020). https://arxiv.org/abs/2003.12338
21. Kumar, R., et al.: Classification of COVID-19 from chest x-ray images using deep features and correlation coefficient (2022). https://arxiv.org/abs/2202.11243
22. Yoo, Y.: Hyperparameter optimization of deep neural network using univariate dynamic encoding algorithm for searches. Knowl.-Based Syst. **178**, 74–83 (2019). https://doi.org/10.1016/j.knosys.2019.04.019
23. Wang, Y., Zhang, H., Zhang, G.: cPSO-CNN: an efficient PSO-based algorithm for fine-tuning hyper-parameters of convolutional neural networks. Swarm Evol. Comput. **49**, 114–123 (2019). https://doi.org/10.1016/j.swevo.2019.06.002
24. Cui, H., Bai, J.: A new hyperparameters optimization method for convolutional neural networks. Pattern Recogn. Lett. **125**, 828–834 (2019). https://doi.org/10.1016/j.patrec.2019.02.009
25. Xie, H., Zhang, L., Lim, C.P.: Evolving CNN-LSTM models for time series prediction using enhanced grey wolf optimizer. IEEE Access. **8**, 161519–161541 (2020). https://doi.org/10.1109/ACCESS.2020.3021527
26. Agarwal, R., Sharma, H.: A new enhanced recurrent extreme learning machine based on feature fusion with CNN deep features for breast cancer detection. Adv. Comput. Commun. Comput. Sci. AISC. **1158**, 461–471 (2020). https://doi.org/10.1007/978-981-15-4409-5s_42
27. Mohakud, R., Dash, R.: Designing a grey wolf optimization based hyper-parameter optimized convolutional neural network classifier for skin cancer detection. J. King Saud Univ.-Comput. Inf. Sci. **34**, 6208–6291 (2022). https://doi.org/10.1016/j.jksuci.2021.05.012
28. Rahman, T., Chowdhury, M., Khandakar, A.: COVID-19 chest X-ray images and Lung masks database. (2021). https://www.kaggle.com/tawsifurrahman/covid19-radiography-database
29. Praveen, O.: CoronaHack-Chest X-Ray-Dataset. (2019). https://www.kaggle.com/datasets/praveengovi/coronahack-chest-xraydataset
30. Cohen, J.P.: A public open dataset of chest X-ray and CT images (2021). https://github.com/ieee8023/covid-chestxray-dataset
31. El-Kenawy, E.S., Eid, M.M., Saber, M., Ibrahim, A.: MbGWOSFS: modified binary grey wolf optimizer based on stochastic fractal search for feature selection. IEEE Access. **8**, 107635–107649 (2020). https://doi.org/10.1109/ACCESS.2020.3001151
32. Tan, M. and Le, Q.: EfficientNet: rethinking model scaling for convolutional neural networks. In International Conference on Machine Learning, pp. 6105–6114 (2019). https://doi.org/10.48550/arXiv.1905.11946
33. Goldberg, D.E.: Genetic algorithms in search, optimization, and machine learning. Addison-Wesley Pub.Co. (1989)
34. Engelbrecht, A.P.: Computational Intelligence: An Introduction. John Wiley and Sons Ltd. (2007)

An Assorted Ensemble Method for Prediction of Terminal Care Preference by Caregivers of Alzheimer's Victims

Mutyala Sridevi[1]([✉]) [ID] and B. R. Arun Kumar[2] [ID]

[1] Department of MCA, BMS Institute of Technology and Management, Bengaluru, India
sridevim@bmsit.in
[2] Department of Computer Science and Engineering, BMS Institute of Technology and Management, Bengaluru, India
arunkumarbr@bmsit.in

Abstract. Healthcare is envisioning new and optimistic opportunities woven around the applications of machine learning that make it more effective and efficient. Machine learning is used to predict the chronic disease trends and its rate of progression which would help the healthcare stakeholders to strategize their treatment and healthcare provision. A 2-layered assorted ensemble model has been proposed to improve the prediction of terminal care preference by caregivers which is affected by the cognitive ability deterioration mentioned with respect to activities mentioned in Katz Index along with caregiver parameters. The main objective of the experiment is to reduce the variance in the learning models and stabilize the model performance across various predictors that perform in their own best ways based on the type and size of the sample. The assorted ensemble is performing at par with other ensemble models with respect to various performance metrics but outperformed them during the ROC curve analysis. This research study would help neuropsychologists to understand the effect of cognitive degeneration, and behavioural and caregiver parameters on the manageability of Alzheimer's disease (AD) in its advanced stages thus enabling them to strategize their treatment and counselling. The comprehensibility of the model would drive its wide usage in neuroscience informatics and add value to the existing repository of chronic disease-related prognosis.

Keywords: Alzheimer's · Terminal Care · Caregivers · Ensemble · Katz Index · Prediction

1 Introduction

Machine learning alleviates the way data is analyzed and helps to draw valuable insights into the data which would otherwise go unnoticed. Use of machine learning in healthcare is unveiling new avenues and creating lot of opportunities to make the healthcare effectively reach the benefiters irrespective of geographic reachability. Chronic diseases like Alzheimer's prolong over long durations in time with varied symptoms and rate

A. Verma et al. (Eds.): ANTIC 2023, CCIS 2091, pp. 357–369, 2024.
https://doi.org/10.1007/978-3-031-64064-3_25

of progression from person to person based on their lifestyle, behaviour and socio-demographic factors in addition to neurodegeneration. The degeneration in cognitive abilities with respect to Activities of Daily Living (ADL) mentioned in Katz Index is one of the measurement tools to understand the rate at which the patient loses independence over time. The rate of cognitive deterioration when combined with caregiver parameters plays a significant role in the prediction of the terminal care preference by the caregivers in advanced stages of Alzheimer's. A 2-layered Assorted Ensemble has been proposed in order to make better predictions when compared to using Bagging or Voting Classifier alone. The predictions made by the proposed assorted ensemble are at par with bagging classifiers trained with several base estimators but found to outperform with respect to ROC AUC with AUC value of 0.98. The major contributions of this research work are.

- Rather than random selection of weights, the bagging classifiers at Level 1 were weighted according to their performance metrics based on the model goodness and penalty measure for misclassifications.
- The weights along with each of the bagging classifiers' predictions are passed on to Level 2 which are used by the voting classifier to make final predictions.
- The proposed ensemble model helps to stabilize the learning models irrespective of type, size, variance and bias in the sample.
- Further, the research work attempts to address the caregiver concerns about caregiving in the advanced stages of Alzheimer's.

The introduction section is followed by a literature review, data collection and exploratory data analysis, proposed approach, results and discussion followed by conclusion.

2   Review of Existing Ensemble Models for Alzheimer's Related Predictions

The feature selection ensemble methodology proposed in [1] was able to find subsets of relevant and stable predictors that performed better compared to models trained without using feature selection and highlights its suitability to optimize the collection of neuropsychological tests needed to learn reliable models for prognosis in Alzheimer's disease. The experiments conducted by [2] used ensemble methods that performed better in the prediction of patients with chances of acquiring dementia by developing predictive models for Alzheimer's and mild impairment in cognitive abilities.

The researchers in [3] used Neighbourhood Component Analysis (NCA) for feature selection of MRI measures along with boosting tree to predict various stages of Alzheimer's disease and concluded that NCA would be a better strategy for feature selection than Principal Component Analysis (PCA) and Sequential Feature Selection (SFS) for the data used in the experiment. The work in [4] proposed an ensemble Support Vector Machine (SVM) with sequential feature selection combined with bagging which performs better than using SVM alone, in the classification of dementia using Mild Cognitive Impairment (MCI) and Magnetic Resonance Imaging (MRI) data.

The authors of [5] proposed a novel approach for Alzheimer's disease classification and early detection using fMRI images with an ensemble of classifiers. Mixture of feature sets have been tested with the model proposed and concluded that fusion of features yielded better results in terms of accuracy, sensitivity and specificity. An ensemble machine learning algorithm presented in [6] was reported to achieve high predictive performance in predicting the Alzheimer's disease conversion using information derived clinically with mush ease such as social and demographic characteristics and neuropsychological factors along with clinical information. In [7], the authors investigated the accuracy of various machine learning models by using different features to perform classification of cognitively normal individuals from the Alzheimer's patients and further predict the long term consequences in subjects with Mild Cognitive Impairment (MCI).

The work in [8] attempted to use the cognitive and Magnetic Resonance Imaging (MRI) trajectories for predicting the Alzheimer's disease and identified that the results strengthen the findings that changes in cognitive abilities become noticeable many years after Alzheimer's becomes well-established in the brain of the victim. Ensemble models were trained using the features related to change trajectories in specific MRI and cognitive measures derived from models based on mixed effects, obtaining better performance scores when the MRI features were considered in addition to cognitive tests. The work in [9] proposed a deep ensemble for the classification of Alzheimer's disease, based on the concept of Wisdom of Experts, by using a voting layer for learning the features, a stacking layer that uses a non-linear feature weighted method and neural network as the meta-classifier which achieved better results compared to other well-known ensemble methods.

The research in [10] have formulated a framework for the functional ensemble survival tree that enables personalized dynamic prognosis of progression in Alzheimer's disease considering multiple temporal biomarkers which would help the physicians to forecast the future trend of the biomarker trajectories along with the risk of AD associated which can further identify individuals at high risk to strategize prevention and treatment interventions. The work in [11] developed and validated models for the prediction of behavioural and psychological symptoms of dementia sub syndromes using machine learning approaches. This work also identified the predictors that influence sub-syndromes that can be considered to avoid and manage the target symptoms. The study performed by Ziyad, Shabana R et al. in [12] proposes a healthcare system for monitoring Alzheimer's victims by alerting the caregiver in case of fall of the victim through mobile apps in smart gadgets.

Very minor work focused on the terminal care preference of the caregivers of Alzheimer's victims. A 2-layered assorted ensemble model has been proposed to predict the preference of terminal care using data related to the rate of cognitive deterioration, and behavioural and caregiver-related parameters which would help in designing customized terminal care facilities for better care provision by the neuropsychologists and geriatric care experts.

3 Data Collection and Exploratory Data Analysis

The data was collected from the public disease communities built around Alzheimer's disease on Facebook through the participant observation method which is a method of observational research. The parameters related to cognitive deterioration in the patients, measured according to the activities mentioned in the Katz Index of Independence in Activities of Daily Living (ADL), are recorded in terms of number of months from the day/month of diagnosis till when the dependence with respect to the activities started. The activities that were mentioned in the Katz Index are presented in Table 1. The Katz Index [13] is an appropriate tool to assess problems in performing ADL and plan provision of care accordingly. The duration between the age diagnosed and the change of status from independent to dependent in performing the daily activities under the Katz Index is captured in terms of months.

Table 1. Activities monitored under Katz Index

Activity	Parameter Name	Activity Description
Bathing	KI-ADL1	Need help with bathing/ Requires total bathing
Dressing	KI-ADL2	Need help with dressing/ Requires complete dressing
Toileting	KI-ADL3	Needs help with transferring to the toilet/ Requires complete assistance
Transferring	KI-ADL4	Needs help in moving from bed to chair/ Requires complete transfer
Continence	KI-ADL5	Is partially/ totally incontinent of bowel or bladder
Feeding	KI-ADL6	Needs partial/ total help with feeding or requires parenteral feeding

Further, the data about age at which the patient was diagnosed, gender of the patient, the predominant behaviour observed in the patient, caregiver relationship with patient, caregiver's employment status and whether they preferred terminal care in the final stages are collected. The details provided by caregivers eventually about their loved ones until the last stage, in the form of posts, replies and comments on the timeline, serves as the source to collect this data. 62 data points have been collected over a 4 years' timeframe from 2017 to 2021. The sample contains details of 32 female patients and 30 male patients. The distribution of Gender with respect to the age at which they were diagnosed (see Fig. 1) depicts that the onset of Alzheimer's is much earlier in Female than in Male.

The predominant behaviour of the patients with Alzheimer's is highly discussed on social media as this feature has the capability of affecting the caregiver lifestyle as well. This feature also affects the quick or prolonged progression of the disease making it manageable with little effort or taking it beyond control of the caregiver at home. Figure 2 shows the frequency of the predominant behaviours observed in the sample under consideration. Aggression is the most prevalent predominant behaviour and being jovial is the least observed behaviour in the patients from the given sample.

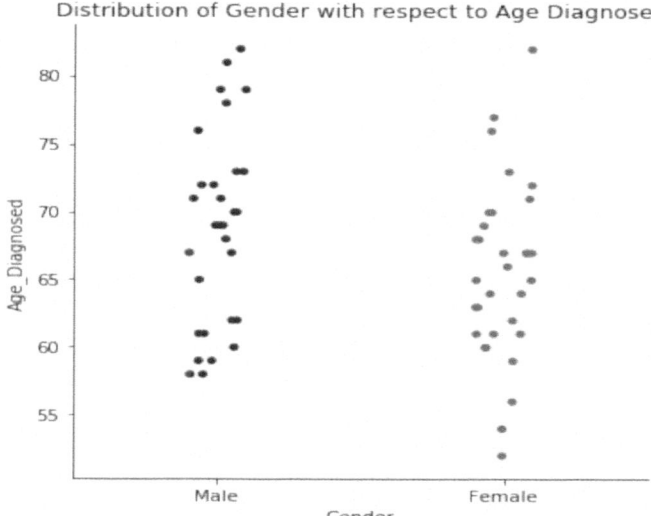

Fig. 1. Gender distribution with respect to age diagnosed

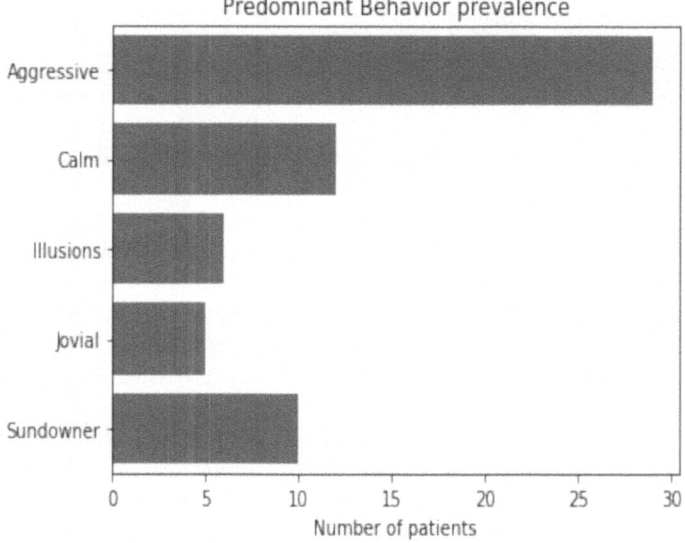

Fig. 2. Frequency of the predominant behaviour in Alzheimer's patients

The relationship of the caregiver with the patient also is very crucial to the well-being of both the patient and the caregiver. The cordial bond between the caregiver and their loved ones may prolong the disease progression and makes it manageable without having to opt for terminal care facilities in the advanced stage of the disease. The caregiver distribution in terms of their relationship with patient is presented in Fig. 3.

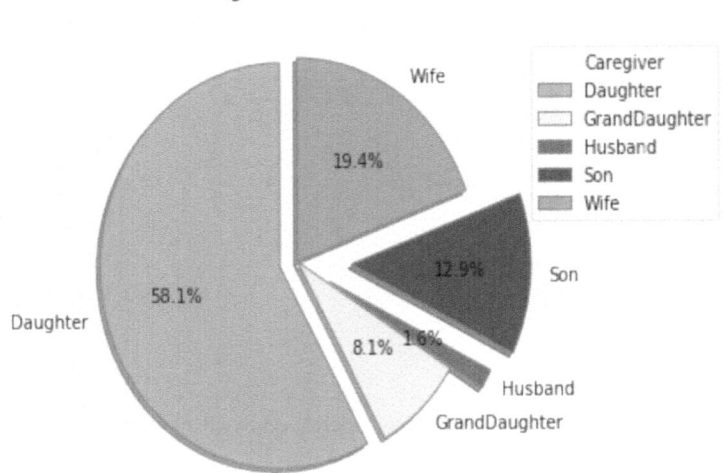

Fig. 3. Caregiver distribution with respect to their relationship with the patient

In order to calculate the association between categorical variables, Cramer's V measure can be used [14]. Its value lies between 0 and 1, 1 indicating the strength of association between two categorical variables. It's based on the chi-square value and indicates that when chi-square is equal to 0, Cramer's V value is also equal to 0. Figure 4 demonstrates the correlation between the categorical features namely predominant behaviour, caregiver, caregiver employment status and the terminal care preference. It can be observed that there is a moderately strong correlation between predominant behaviour of the patient and the decision to prefer terminal care in the advanced stages of Alzheimer's disease. Correlation between categorical variables is better represented by this heat map. The strongest correlation observed is 0.70 as per the indication of the scale.

There are numerous classification techniques available for developing the learning models, each performing well with respect to their unique capabilities. Moreover, the model performance varies with the type of sample, size of sample etc. In order to stabilize the learning models, ensemble methods can be used namely Bagging, Boosting and Stacking ensembles. Bagging and Boosting meta-algorithms consider homogeneous weak learners but the bagging method learns from each of them in parallel whereas the boosting method learns sequentially in an adaptive way. Stacking considers learning in parallel with heterogeneous weak learners and trains a meta-model to make predictions by combining the individual predictions from weak models.

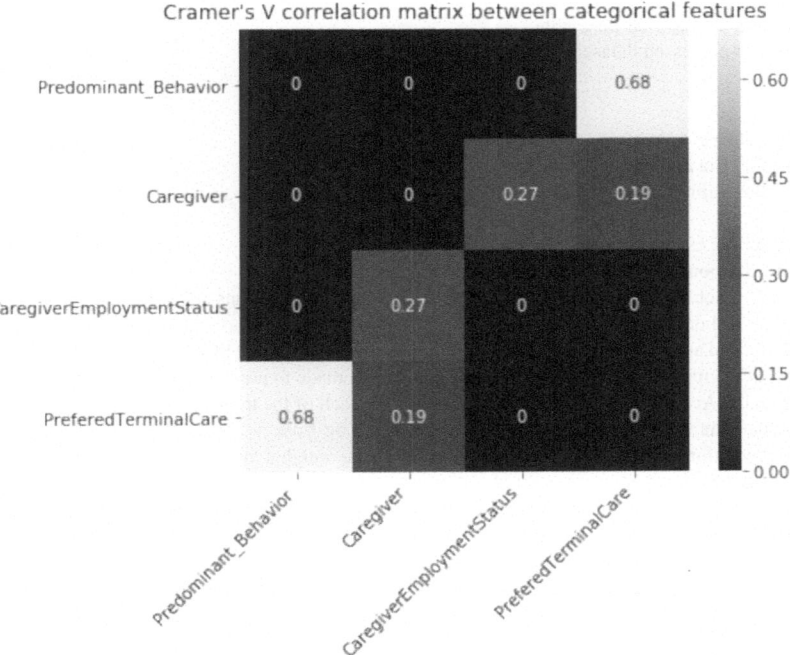

Fig. 4. Cramer's V correlation between the categorical features

4 Proposed Approach

The proposed Assorted Ensemble model focuses on a 2-layered ensemble which uses Bagging at Level 1 with various base estimators that perform with their individual capabilities. Bagging ensemble is selected at Level 1 as the main objective of this learning model is to minimize the variance and also address the issue of small sample size. Level 2 of the Assorted Ensemble model uses Voting Classifier with weights passed from Level 1 that makes final predictions through weighted average method. The steps in the Assorted Ensemble method can be explained by using Algorithm 1.

Algorithm 1: Assorted Ensemble
Input: Pre-processed dataset

1 Select N base estimators
2 Split the data into training and held-out sets
3 Pass the training data through the first level with Bagging Classifiers each built with a base estimator
For each base estimator...
    3.1   Bootstrap samples are obtained from the training set
    3.2   Each bootstrap sample is used to train multiple versions of a predictor with cross-validation
    3.3   An aggregate predictor for each of the base estimator is generated
4 Each of the models built on the N base estimators are made to predict on the held-out set
5 Obtain the Accuracy, F1 measure and Log-Loss for each of the models
6 Calculate the weights as (Accuracy * F1 measure) / Log-Loss
7 The predictions of each base estimator along with the weights for each base estimator is passed onto the second level
8 The Voting Classifier in the second level makes the final predictions using weighted average method

Figure 5 demonstrates the data flow of the Assorted Ensemble Algorithm.

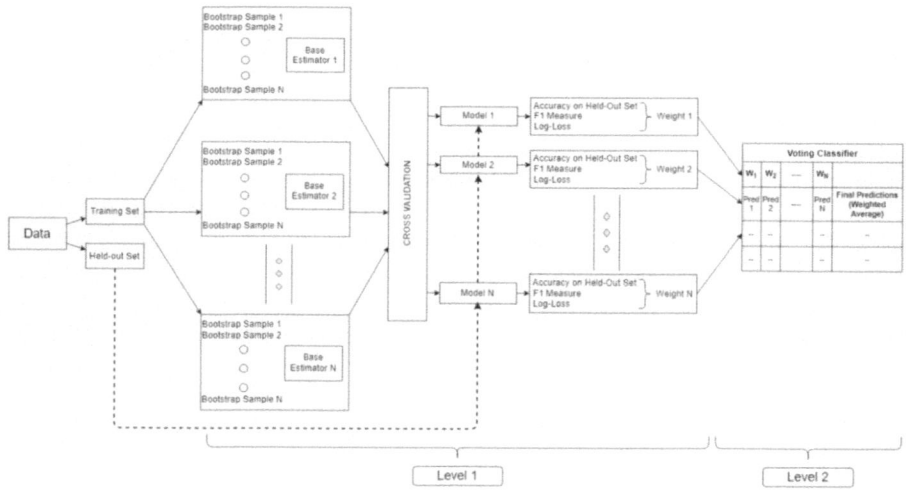

Fig. 5. Data Flow of the Assorted Ensemble Method

For measuring the variance of an estimator, it has to be evaluated on number of independent samples that are drawn from the underlying distribution. For this, the first level uses the Bagging ensemble with five learning methods (linear and non-linear) as the base estimators, each of which work on bootstrap samples of the dataset. Logistic Regression, Decision Tree Classifier, k-Nearest Neighbour, Support Vector Machine, and Gaussian Naïve Bayes Classifier are used as the base estimators of the Bagging ensemble. These estimators give out Pred 1 (prediction 1), Pred 2 (prediction 2) and so on. 5-fold cross-validation has been used to obtain the skill estimates having lower bias compared to other methods. Each of the classifiers perform with their inherent capabilities to give the estimates in terms of accuracy, F1 measure and Log-Loss which are used to calculate the weights according to Eq. 1.

$$Weight\ of\ each\ base\ estimator = \frac{\text{Prediction accuracy on the held out set } * \text{ F1 measure}}{Log - Loss} \quad (1)$$

This is more elaborately presented in the Eq. 2.

$$W_i = \frac{\left(\frac{True\ Positives + True\ Negatives}{M}\right) * \left(2 * \left(\frac{precision * recall}{precision + recall}\right)\right)}{-\frac{1}{M} \sum_{j=1}^{M} t_j . \log\left(p(t_j)\right) + \left(1 - t_j\right). \log(1 - p(t_j))} \quad (2)$$

where W_i is the weight of each base estimator, $i = 1 \ldots N$

t is the target label

$p(t)$ is the predicted probability of the output label being positive/Yes class

M is the number of data points in the sample.

Calculating the relative weights for each member of the ensemble is a challenging task. Rather than assigning some random weights, in the proposed approach, the weights are calculated using the prediction accuracy on the held out set, F1 measure and the Log-Loss of each base estimator. This calculation enables to obtain weights of the base estimators using the prediction accuracy of the held out set, F1 score, a metric that takes both false negatives and false positives into consideration and is used to compare between the models, and Log-Loss measure that considers the prediction's confidence while determining ways to penalize the misclassification. The weights thus obtained gives due importance to the model performance and, at the same time, put a check on the incorrect classifications.

The Bagging layer further feeds its output to the voting classifier along with weights calculated for each of the models. The Voting Classifier used at Level 2 is another heterogeneous ensemble method. Voting classifier gets trained on an ensemble of base models and predicts a class based on majority voting. Generally, these base models are built as dedicated learning models that make predictions. In the proposed model, the Voting Classifier in the second level receives the weights and predictions of the multiple bagging classifiers, trained using various base estimators, which works on obtaining a weighted average of predictions.

5   Results and Discussion

The performance metrics of each of the base estimators used in Bagging methods at Level1 in terms of mean training and validation accuracy measures are presented in Table 2.

Table 2. Level 1's mean training and validation accuracy measures

	Mean of Training Accuracy	Mean of Validation Accuracy
Bagging Classifier (base_estimator = LogisticRegression)	0.81	0.78
Bagging Classifier (base_estimator = DecisionTreeClassifier)	0.94	0.78
Bagging Classifier (base_estimator = kNeighborsClassifier)	0.88	0.78
Bagging Classifier (base_estimator = SVC)	0.88	0.78
Bagging Classifier (base_estimato = GaussianNB)	0.83	0.76

When these base estimators are used individually in Bagging ensemble, they exhibit competent performance and makes the model selection difficult. Moreover, the performance varies with the sample, size of sample, variance and bias in the sample. Each of the base estimators perform well with respect to their inherent capabilities which asserts that relying on a single base estimator for Bagging ensemble is not sufficient. To address this issue, the proposed model focuses on using multiple base estimators for Level 1. Performance of each of these base estimators is further weighted by calculating the weights using accuracy, F1 measure and Log-Loss. The model goodness is directly proportional to the F1 measure but inversely proportional to the Log-Loss that penalizes misclassifications. Calculating the weights based on these measures gives due importance to precision and recall of the model penalizing the misclassifications as well.

Table 3 records the test accuracy on held-out set, F1 score and Log-Loss of the individual base estimators at Level 1 and the Assorted ensemble. Level 1 has a major role to play as it generates the weights based on individual capabilities of the base models which will be given due importance in Level 2 to make the final predictions.

It is quite evident that the performance of the Assorted Ensemble is at par with the individual Bagging Classifiers with the five base estimators. However, the goodness of the Assorted Ensemble is better observed when ROC Curve Analysis is performed. ROC curve helps in understanding the overall performance of the model and also allows the comparison of different models when they are equally performing well with respect to other metrics. The ROC curve is preferred to the Precision-Recall curve as there is not much class imbalance in the target labels of the sample. The ROC Area Under Curve (AUC) for the individual bagging classifiers with base estimators in comparison with Assorted Classifier is demonstrated in Fig. 6.

Table 3. Comparison of performance metrics

	Test Accuracy on Held-Out Set	F1 Measure	Log-Loss
Logistic Regression	0.69	0.78	0.49
Decision TreeClassifier	0.92	0.93	0.33
kNeighbors Classifier	0.92	0.93	0.36
SVC	0.92	0.93	2.88
GaussianNB	0.62	0.71	0.78
Assorted Ensemble	**0.92**	**0.93**	**0.37**

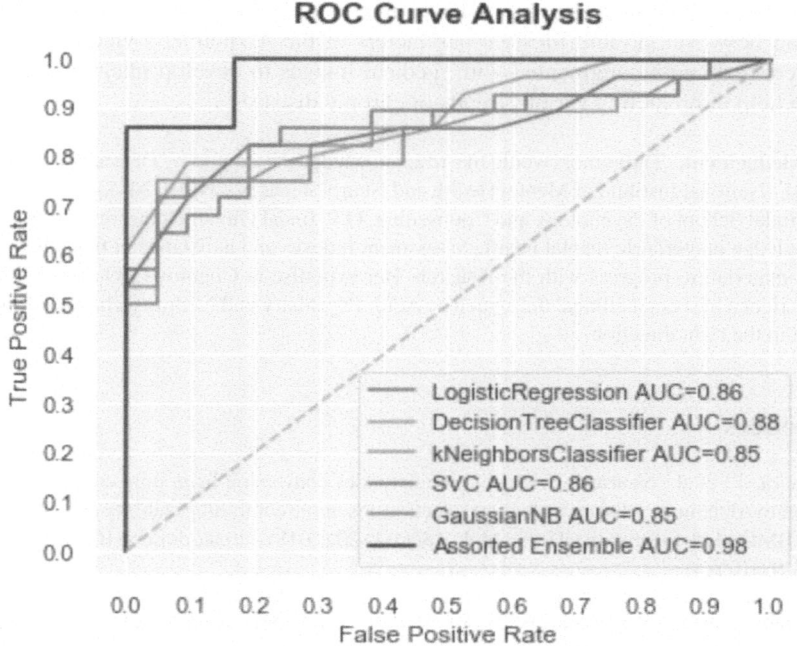

Fig. 6. ROC AUC for individual Bagging Classifiers and Assorted Ensemble model

The ROC-AUC for Bagging Classifiers with Logistic Regression, Decision Tree Classifiers, kNeighbors Classifier, Support Vector Classifier (SVC) and Gaussian Naïve Bayes Classifier (GassianNB) as base estimators are 0.86, 0.88, 0.85, 0.86, and 0.85, respectively. The AUC for Assorted Ensemble is 0.98 which shows the ideal performance of the 2-layered Assorted Ensemble in predicting the preference to choose terminal care in advanced stages of Alzheimer's disease based on cognitive deterioration features mentioned in Katz Index and caregiver parameters.

6   Conclusion

The 2-layered assorted ensemble learning model is proposed to predict the terminal care preference in advanced stages of Alzheimer's disease with the help of rate of deterioration in cognitive skills as per Katz Index Activities of Daily Living, behavioural, and caregiver parameters. The model proposed is built on the goodness of several base estimators trained by harnessing the bagging ensemble method which is further connected to the voting classifier that calculates the weighted average of the predictions. The assorted ensemble is exhibiting promising performance compared to other bagging classifiers built with competent base estimators. The comprehensibility of the model makes it highly adoptable across neural health and geriatric care institutions with high applicability. The limitation of the proposed work is the sample size which is very small. More data points would improve the training process which can result in even better predictions. Future work can be woven around lifestyle parameters of the Alzheimer's victims and their caregivers that can be augmented with medical images to develop integrated systems that can help in predicting various trends of chronic diseases.

Acknowledgement. The authors would like to acknowledge the support by Dr. Meenakshi Banerjee, Ph.D. (National Institute of Mental Health and Neuro Sciences – NIMHANS), Assistant Professor, Jindal School of Psychology and Counselling, O.P. Jindal Global University, for providing the knowledge on geriatric mental health, assessment indexes and assistance in the collection of relevant material, to progress with the research. Her expertise in Cognitive Behaviour Therapy and experience in special clinical units such as Adult Psychiatry and Neuropsychology drove the research in the right direction.

References

1. Pereira, T., et al.: Neuropsychological predictors of conversion from mild cognitive impairment to Alzheimer's disease: a feature selection ensemble combining stability and predictability. BMC Med. Informatics Decis. Mak. **18**(1), 1–20 (2018). https://doi.org/10.1186/S12911-018-0710-Y
2. Moreira, L.B., Namen, A.A.: A hybrid data mining model for diagnosis of patients with clinical suspicion of dementia. Comput. Methods Programs Biomed. **165**, 139–149 (2018). https://doi.org/10.1016/J.CMPB.2018.08.016
3. Jin, M., Deng, W.: Predication of different stages of Alzheimer's disease using neighborhood component analysis and ensemble decision tree. J. Neurosci. Methods **302**, 35–41 (2018). https://doi.org/10.1016/J.JNEUMETH.2018.02.014
4. Sørensen, L., Nielsen, M.: Ensemble support vector machine classification of dementia using structural MRI and mini-mental state examination. J. Neurosci. Methods **302**, 66–74 (2018). https://doi.org/10.1016/J.JNEUMETH.2018.01.003
5. Malik, F., Farhan, S., Fahiem, M.A.: An ensemble of classifiers based approach for prediction of Alzheimer's disease using FMRI images based on fusion of volumetric, textural and hemodynamic features. Adv. Electr. Comput. Eng. **18**(1), 61–70 (2018). https://doi.org/10.4316/AECE.2018.01008

6. Grassi, M., et al.: A novel ensemble-based machine learning algorithm to predict the conversion from mild cognitive impairment to Alzheimer's disease using socio-demographic characteristics, clinical information, and neuropsychological measures. Front. Neurol. **0**(JUL), 756 (2019). https://doi.org/10.3389/FNEUR.2019.00756

7. Ezzati, A., et al.: Optimizing machine learning methods to improve predictive models of Alzheimer's disease. J. Alzheimer's Dis. **71**(3), 1027–1036 (2019). https://doi.org/10.3233/JAD-190262

8. Mofrad, S.A., Lundervold, A.J., Vik, A., Lundervold, A.S.: Cognitive and MRI trajectories for prediction of Alzheimer's disease. Sci. Rep. **11**(1), 1–10 (2021). https://doi.org/10.1038/s41598-020-78095-7

9. An, N., Ding, H., Yang, J., Au, R., Ang, T.F.A.: Deep ensemble learning for Alzheimer's disease classification. J. Biomed. Inform. **105**, 103411 (2020). https://doi.org/10.1016/J.JBI.2020.103411

10. Jiang, S., Xie, Y., Colditz, G.A.: Functional ensemble survival tree: Dynamic prediction of Alzheimer's disease progression accommodating multiple time-varying covariates. J. R. Stat. Soc. Ser. C (Appl. Stat.) **70**(1), 66–79 (2021). https://doi.org/10.1111/RSSC.12449

11. Cho, E., et al.: Machine learning-based predictive models for the occurrence of behavioral and psychological symptoms of dementia: model development and validation. Sci. Rep. **13**(1), 1–12 (2023). https://doi.org/10.1038/s41598-023-35194-5

12. Ziyad, S.R., Altulyan, M., Alharbi, M.: SHMAD: a Smart health care system to Monitor Alzheimer's Disease patients. J. Alzheimers Dis. **95**(4), 1545–1557 (2023). https://doi.org/10.3233/JAD-230402

13. Katz, S., Ford, A.B., Moskowitz, R.W., Jackson, B.A., Jaffe, M.W.: Studies of illness in the aged. the index of ADL: a standardized measure of biological and psychosocial function. JAMA, **185**(12), 914–919 (1963). https://doi.org/10.1001/JAMA.1963.03060120024016

14. Zychlinski, S.: The Search for Categorical Correlation | by Shaked Zychlinski | Towards Data Science. https://towardsdatascience.com/the-search-for-categorical-correlation-a1cf7f1888c9. Accessed 09 Sep. 2021

Author Index

A. Verma et al. (Eds.): ANTIC 2023, CCIS 2091, pp. 371–372, 2024.
https://doi.org/10.1007/978-3-031-64064-3

SPRINGER NATURE

GPSR Compliance

The European Union's (EU) General Product Safety Regulation (GPSR) is a set of rules that requires consumer products to be safe and our obligations to ensure this.

If you have any concerns about our products, you can contact us on ProductSafety@springernature.com

In case Publisher is established outside the EU, the EU authorized representative is:

Springer Nature Customer Service Center GmbH
Europaplatz 3
69115 Heidelberg, Germany

The manufacturer's authorised representative in the EU is Springer
Nature Customer Service Centre GmbH, Europaplatz 3, 69115 Heidelberg,
Germany. If you have any concerns regarding our products, please
contact ProductSafety@springernature.com

Printed and bound by CPI Group (UK) Ltd, Croydon, CR0 4YY
29/04/2026
02099537-0010